Fodor's 2000

South Florida

The complete guide, thoroughly up-to-date

Packed with details that will make your trip

The must-see sights, off and on the beaten path

What to see, what to skip

Mix-and-match vacation itineraries

City strolls, countryside adventures

Smart lodging and dining options

Essential local do's and taboos

Transportation tips, distances and directions

Key contacts, savvy travel tips

When to go, what to pack

Clear, accurate, easy-to-use maps

Excerpted from Fodor's Florida 2000

Previously published as *Fodor's Miami & the Keys*

Fodor's Travel Publications, Inc. • New York, Toronto, London, Sydney, Auckland
www.fodors.com/florida

Fodor's South Florida

EDITOR: Andrea E. Lehman

Editorial Contributors: Pamela Acheson, Catherine Fredman, Kendall Hamersly, Herb Hiller, Alan Macher, Diane Marshall, Gary McKechnie, Helayne Schiff, Geoffrey Tomb

Editorial Production: Tom Holton

Maps: David Lindroth, *cartographer*; Robert Blake, *map editor*

Design: Fabrizio La Rocca, *creative director*; Guido Caroti, *art director*; Jolie Novak, *photo editor*

Cover Design: Pentagram

Production/Manufacturing: Robert B. Shields

Cover Photograph: Jack Hollingsworth

Copyright

Special Sales

Fodor's Travel Publications are available at special discounts for bulk purchases for sales promotions or premiums. Special editions, including personalized covers, excerpts of existing guides, and corporate imprints, can be created in large quantities for special needs. For more information, contact your local bookseller or write to Special Markets, Fodor's Travel Publications, 201 East 50th Street, New York, NY 10022. Inquiries from Canada should be directed to your local Canadian bookseller or sent to Random House of Canada, Ltd., Marketing Department, 2775 Matheson Boulevard East, Mississauga, Ontario L4W 4P7. Inquiries from the United Kingdom should be sent to Fodor's Travel Publications, 20 Vauxhall Bridge Road, London SW1V 2SA, England.

PRINTED IN THE UNITED STATES OF AMERICA

10 9 8 7 6 5 4 3 2 1

Important Tip

Although all prices, opening times, and other details in this book are based on information supplied to us at press time, changes occur all the time in the travel world, and Fodor's cannot accept responsibility for facts that become outdated or for inadvertent errors or omissions. So **always confirm information when it matters,** especially if you're making a detour to visit a specific place.

CONTENTS

ON THE ROAD WITH FODOR'S

EVERY Y2K TRIP is a significant trip. So if there was ever a time you needed excellent travel information, it's now. Acutely aware of that fact, we've pulled out all stops in preparing *Fodor's South Florida*. To guide you in putting together your South Florida experience, we've created multiday itineraries and neighborhood walks. And to direct you to the places that are truly worth your time and money in this important year, we've rallied the team of endearingly picky know-it-alls we're pleased to call our writers. Having seen all corners of South Florida, they're real experts. If you knew them, you'd poll them for tips yourself.

On her way to the Caribbean, former New York publishing exec **Pamela Acheson** stopped in the Sunshine State and fell in love, after discovering that there's much more to it than theme parks. She likes nothing better than to drive around to neat little towns, undiscovered beaches, and other less-traveled places as she writes about her new home.

Starting behind an old manual typewriter at his hometown newspaper, **Alan Macher** has written everything from human-interest stories to speeches. He makes his home in Boca Raton, where he can play tennis and bike along Route A1A year-round.

Intrepid traveler and intrepid shopper **Diane Marshall** was formerly editor and publisher of the newsletter "The Savvy Shopper: The Traveler's Guide to Shopping Around the World." From her home in the Keys, she has written for numerous travel guides, newspapers, magazines, and on-line services.

Florida native and Elvis fan **Gary McKechnie** has written humor and travel articles for newspapers and magazines nationwide and has produced award-winning training films and resort videos.

Don't Forget to Write

Keeping a travel guide fresh and up-to-date is a big job. So we love your feedback—positive and negative—and follow up on all suggestions. Contact the South Florida editor at editors@fodors.com or c/o Fodor's, 201 East 50th Street, New York, New York 10022. And have a wonderful trip!

Karen Cure

Karen Cure
Editorial Director

The Florida Peninsula

ESSENTIAL INFORMATION

*Basic Information on Traveling in South Florida,
Savvy Tips to Make Your Trip a Breeze, and
Companies and Organizations to Contact*

AIR TRAVEL

BOOKING YOUR FLIGHT

When you book **look for nonstop
flights** and **remember that "direct"
flights stop at least once.** Try to avoid
connecting flights, which require a
change of plane.

CARRIERS

➤ MAJOR AIRLINES: **American** (☎
800/523–3223). **Continental** (☎ 800/
525–0280). **Delta** (☎ 800/221–
1212). **Midway** (☎ 800/446–4392).
Northwest (☎ 800/225–2525).
Southwest (☎ 800/435–9792). **TWA**
(☎ 800/221–2000). **United** (☎ 800/
241–6522). **US Airways** (☎ 800/428–
4322).

➤ REGIONAL AIRLINES: **AirTran** (☎
800/247–8726) to Fort Lauderdale
and West Palm Beach.

Midwest Express (☎ 800/452–2022)
to Fort Lauderdale.

➤ FROM THE U.K.: **American** (☎
0345/789–789). **British Airways** (☎
0345/222–111). **Continental** (☎
0800/776–464) via Newark. **Delta**
(☎ 0800/414–767). **Northwest** (☎
0990/561–000) via Detroit or Minneapolis. **TWA** (☎ 0800/222–222)
via St. Louis. **United** (☎ 0800/888–
555). **Virgin Atlantic** (☎ 01293/747–
747).

CHECK-IN & BOARDING

Assuming that not everyone with a
ticket will show up, airlines routinely
overbook planes. When that happens,
airlines ask for volunteers to give up
their seats. In return these volunteers
usually get a certificate for a free
flight and are rebooked on the next
flight out. If there are not enough
volunteers, the airline must choose
who will be denied boarding. The
first to get bumped are passengers
who checked in late and those flying
on discounted tickets, so **get to the
gate and check in as early as possi-**
ble, especially during peak periods.
Heightened security at Miami International Airport has meant that it's
suggested you check in 90 minutes
before departure for a domestic flight,
two hours for an international flight.

Always **bring a government-issued
photo ID to the airport.** You may be
asked to show it before you are
allowed to check in.

CUTTING COSTS

The least-expensive airfares to Florida
must usually be purchased in advance
and are non-refundable. It's smart to
**call a number of airlines, and when
you are quoted a good price, book it
on the spot**—the same fare may not
be available the next day. Always
check different routings and look into
using different airports. Travel agents,
especially low-fare specialists (☞
Discounts & Deals, *below*), are
helpful.

Consolidators are another good
source. They buy tickets for scheduled
international flights at reduced rates
from the airlines, then sell them at
prices that beat the best fare available
directly from the airlines, usually
without restrictions. Sometimes you
can even get your money back if you
need to return the ticket. Carefully
read the fine print detailing penalties
for changes and cancellations, and
**confirm your consolidator reservation
with the airline.**

When you **fly as a courier** you trade
your checked-luggage space for a
ticket deeply subsidized by a courier
service. There are restrictions on
when you can book and how long
you can stay.

➤ CONSOLIDATORS: **Cheap Tickets** (☎
800/377–1000). **Up & Away Travel**
(☎ 212/889–2345). **Discount Airline
Ticket Service** (☎ 800/576–1600).
Unitravel (☎ 800/325–2222). **World
Travel Network** (☎ 800/409–6753).

➤ CHEAP RATES FROM THE U.K.: **Flight Express Travel** (77 New Bond St., London W1Y 9DB, ☎ 0171/409–3311). **Trailfinders** (42–50 Earls Court Rd., London W8 6FT, ☎ 0171/937–5400). **Travel Cuts** (295A Regent St., London W1R 7YA, ☎ 0171/637–3161).

ENJOYING THE FLIGHT

For more legroom **request an emergency-aisle seat.** Don't sit in the row in front of the emergency aisle or in front of a bulkhead, where seats may not recline. If you have dietary concerns, **ask for special meals when booking.** These can be vegetarian, low-cholesterol, or kosher, for example. On long flights, try to maintain a normal routine, to help fight jetlag. At night **get some sleep.** By day **eat lightly, drink water** (not alcohol), and **move around the cabin** to stretch your legs.

FLYING TIMES

Typical flying times are 3 hours from New York, 4 hours from Chicago, and 5–5½ hours from Los Angeles.

HOW TO COMPLAIN

If your baggage goes astray or your flight goes awry, complain right away. Most carriers require that you **file a claim immediately.**

➤ AIRLINE COMPLAINTS: U.S. Department of Transportation **Aviation Consumer Protection Division** (✉ C-75, Room 4107, Washington, DC 20590, ☎ 202/366–2220). Federal Aviation Administration Consumer Hotline (☎ 800/322–7873).

AIRPORTS

Because South Florida is dotted with both major and regional airports, you can usually pick one quite close to your destination and often choose from a couple of nearby options. If you're destined for the north side of Miami-Dade County (metro Miami), **consider flying into Fort Lauderdale–Hollywood International**; it's much easier to use than Miami International.

➤ AIRPORT INFORMATION: **Fort Lauderdale–Hollywood International** (☎ 954/359–1200). **Miami International** (☎ 305/876–7000). **Palm Beach International** (☎ 561/471–7420).

BIKE TRAVEL

BIKES IN FLIGHT

Most airlines accommodate bikes as luggage, provided they are dismantled and boxed. For bike boxes, often free at bike shops, you'll pay about $5 (at least $100 for bike bags) from airlines. International travelers can sometimes substitute a bike for a piece of checked luggage at no charge; otherwise, the cost is about $100. Domestic and Canadian airlines charge $25–$50.

BUS TRAVEL

FARES & SCHEDULES

Greyhound passes through practically every major city in Florida. For schedules and fares, **contact your local Greyhound Information Center.**

➤ BUS INFORMATION: **Greyhound** (☎ 800/231–2222).

CAMERAS & PHOTOGRAPHY

➤ PHOTO HELP: **Kodak Information Center** (☎ 800/242–2424). *Kodak Guide to Shooting Great Travel Pictures,* available in bookstores or from Fodor's Travel Publications (☎ 800/533–6478; $16.50 plus $4 shipping).

EQUIPMENT PRECAUTIONS

Always **keep your film and tape out of the sun or a parked car on a hot day.** Carry an extra supply of batteries, and **be prepared to turn on your camera or camcorder** to prove to security personnel that the device is real. Always **ask for hand inspection of film,** which becomes clouded after successive exposures to airport X-ray machines, and **keep videotapes away from metal detectors.**

CAR RENTAL

On-season rates in Miami begin at $36 a day and $170 a week for an economy car with air-conditioning, an automatic transmission, and unlimited mileage. Rates in Fort Lauderdale begin at $36 a day and $159 a week. This does not include tax on car rentals, which is 6%. Bear in mind that rates fluctuate tremendously—both above and below these quoted figures—depending on demand and the season. Rental cars are more expensive (and harder to find) during peak holidays and in season.

It used to be that major rental agencies were located at the airport whereas cheaper firms weren't. Now, however, all over Florida even the majors might be off airport property. It varies firm to firm and airport to airport. Speedy check-in and frequent shuttle buses make off-airport rentals almost as convenient as on-site service. However, it's wise to allow a little extra time for bus travel between the rental agency and the airport.

CUTTING COSTS

To get the best deal **book through a travel agent who will shop around.** Also **price local car-rental companies,** although the service and maintenance may not be as good as those of a major player. Remember to ask about required deposits, cancellation penalties, and drop-off charges if you're planning to pick up the car in one city and leave it in another. If you're traveling during a holiday period, also make sure that a confirmed reservation guarantees you a car.

Do **look into wholesalers,** companies that do not own fleets but rent in bulk from those that do and often offer better rates than traditional car-rental operations.

➤ MAJOR AGENCIES: **Alamo** (☎ 800/327–9633; 0181/759–6200 in the U.K.). **Avis** (☎ 800/331–1212; 800/879–2847 in Canada; 02/9353–9000 in Australia; 09/525–1982 in New Zealand). **Budget** (☎ 800/527–0700; 0144/227–6266 in the U.K.). **Dollar** (☎ 800/800–4000; 0181/897–0811 in the U.K., where it is known as Eurodollar; 02/9223–1444 in Australia). **Hertz** (☎ 800/654–3131; 800/263–0600 in Canada; 0181/897–2072 in the U.K.; 02/9669–2444 in Australia; 03/358–6777 in New Zealand). **National InterRent** (☎ 800/227–7368; 0345/222525 in the U.K., where it is known as Europcar InterRent).

➤ LOCAL AGENCIES: **Apex Rent A Car** (☎ 954/782–3400) in Fort Lauderdale. **Florida Auto Rental** (☎ 954/764–1008 or 800/327–3791) in Fort Lauderdale. **InterAmerican Car Rental** (☎ 305/871–3030) in Fort

Lauderdale and Miami Beach. **Tropical Rent-a-Car** ☎ 305/294–8136) in Key West.

➤ WHOLESALERS: **Auto Europe** (☎ 207/842–2000 or 800/223–5555, FAX 800/235–6321).

INSURANCE

When driving a rented car you are generally responsible for any damage to or loss of the vehicle as well as for any property damage or personal injury that you may cause. Before you rent see what coverage your personal auto-insurance policy and credit cards already provide.

For about $15 to $20 per day, rental companies sell protection, known as a collision- or loss-damage waiver (CDW or LDW), that eliminates your liability for damage to the car.

In most states you don't need a CDW if you have personal auto insurance or other liability insurance. However, **make sure you have enough coverage to pay for the car.** If you do not have auto insurance or an umbrella policy that covers damage to third parties, purchasing liability insurance and a CDW or LDW is highly recommended.

REQUIREMENTS & RESTRICTIONS

In Florida you must be 21 to rent a car, and rates may be higher if you're under 25. You'll pay extra for child seats (about $3 per day), which are compulsory for children under five, and for additional drivers (about $2 per day). Non-U.S. residents will need a reservation voucher, a passport, a driver's license, and a travel policy that covers each driver, in order to pick up a car.

SURCHARGES

Before you pick up a car in one city and leave it in another **ask about drop-off charges or one-way service fees,** which can be substantial. Note, too, that some rental agencies charge extra if you return the car before the time specified in your contract. To avoid a hefty refueling fee **fill the tank just before you turn in the car,** but be aware that gas stations near the rental outlet may overcharge.

CAR TRAVEL

Three major interstates lead to Florida. I–95 begins in Maine, runs south through the Mid-Atlantic states, and enters Florida just north of Jacksonville. It continues south past Daytona Beach, the Space Coast, Vero Beach, Palm Beach, and Fort Lauderdale, eventually ending in Miami.

I–75 begins in Michigan at the Canadian border and runs south through Ohio, Kentucky, Tennessee, and Georgia, then moves south through the center of the state before veering west into Tampa. It follows the west coast south to Naples, then crosses the state through the northern section of the Everglades, and ends in Fort Lauderdale.

ROAD CONDITIONS

Florida has its share of traffic problems. Downtown areas of such major cities as Miami can be extremely congested during rush hours, usually 7 to 9 AM and 4 to 6 PM on weekdays. When you drive the interstate system in Florida, try to **plan your trip so that you are not entering, leaving, or passing through a large city during rush hour,** when traffic can slow to 10 mph for 10 mi or more. In addition, snowbirds usually rent in Florida for a month at a time, which means they all arrive on the first of the month and leave on the 31st. Believe it or not, from November to March, when the end and beginning of a month occur on a weekend, north–south routes like I–75 and I–95 almost come to a standstill during daylight hours. It's best to avoid traveling on these days if possible.

RULES OF THE ROAD

Speed limits are 55 mph on state highways, 30 mph within city limits and residential areas, and 55–70 mph on interstates and Florida's Turnpike. Be alert for signs announcing exceptions.

SAFETY

Before setting off on any drive, **make sure you know where you're going** and carry a map. At the car-rental agency or at your hotel **ask if there are any areas that you should avoid.** Always **keep your doors locked,** and ask questions only at toll booths, gas stations, or other obviously safe locations. Also, **don't stop if your car is bumped from behind** or if you're asked for directions. One hesitates to foster rude behavior, but at least for now the roads are too risky to stop any place you're not familiar with (other than as traffic laws require). If you'll be renting a car, **ask the car-rental agency for a cellular phone.** Alamo, Avis, and Hertz are among the companies with in-car phones.

CHILDREN IN FLORIDA

If you are renting a car don't forget to **arrange for a car seat** when you reserve.

FLYING

If your children are two or older **ask about children's airfares.** As a general rule, infants under two not occupying a seat fly at greatly reduced fares or even for free.

Experts agree that it's a good idea to use safety seats aloft for children weighing less than 40 pounds. Airlines set their own policies: U.S. carriers usually require that the child be ticketed, even if he or she is young enough to ride free, since the seats must be strapped into regular seats. Do **check your airline's policy about using safety seats during takeoff and landing.** And since safety seats are not allowed just everywhere in the plane, get your seat assignments early.

When reserving, **request children's meals or a freestanding bassinet** if you need them. But note that bulkhead seats, where you must sit to use the bassinet may lack an overhead bin or storage space on the floor.

LODGING

Florida may have the highest concentration of hotels with organized children's programs in the United States. Activities range from simple fun and recreation to learning about the Keys' environment from marine-science counselors at Cheeca Lodge. Sometimes kids' programs are complimentary; sometimes there's a charge. Not all accept children in diapers, and some offer programs when their central reservations services say they

SMART TRAVEL TIPS

don't. Some programs are only of-fered during peak seasons or restrict hours in less-busy times. It always pays to **confirm details with the hotel in advance.** And **reserve space as soon as possible;** programs are often full by the morning or evening you need them.

Most hotels in Florida allow children under a certain age to stay in their parents' room at no extra charge, but others charge for them as extra adults; be sure to **find out the cutoff age for children's discounts.**

➤ FORT LAUDERDALE: **Marriott's Harbor Beach Resort's Beachside Buddies** (3030 Holiday Dr., Fort Lauderdale, FL 33316, ☎ 954/525–4000 or 800/228–9290), ages 5–12.

➤ THE KEYS: **Cheeca Lodge's Camp Cheeca** (MM 82, OS, Box 527, Islam-orada, FL 33036, ☎ 800/327–2888), ages 6–12. **Westin Beach Resort's Westin Kids Club** (MM 96.9, BS, 97000 Overseas Hwy., Key Largo, FL 33037, ☎ 305/852–5553 or 800/325–3535), ages 5–12.

➤ MIAMI AREA: **Sonesta Beach Re-sort's Just Us Kids** (350 Ocean Dr., Key Biscayne, FL 33149, ☎ 800/766–3782), ages 5–13.

➤ PALM BEACH AND THE TREASURE COAST: **Club Med's Sandpiper** (Port St. Lucie [mailing address: 40 W. 57th St., New York, NY 10019], ☎ 800/258–2633), Baby Club ages 4–24 months, Mini Club ages 2–11. **Indian River Plantation Marriott Beach Resort's Pineapple Bunch Children's Camp** (555 N.E. Ocean Blvd., Hutchinson Island, Stuart, FL 34996, ☎ 561/225–3700), ages 4–12, plus a teen program.

SIGHTS & ATTRACTIONS

Places that are especially good for children are indicated by a rubber duckie icon in the margin.

CONSUMER PROTECTION

Whenever shopping or buying travel services in Florida, **pay with a major credit card** so you can cancel payment or get reimbursed if there's a prob-lem. If you're doing business with a particular company for the first time, **contact your local Better Business Bureau and the attorney general's**

offices in your state and the com-pany's home state, as well. Have any complaints been filed? Finally, if you're buying a package or tour, always **consider travel insurance** that includes default coverage (☞ Insur-ance, *below*).

➤ LOCAL BBBs: **Council of Better Business Bureaus** (⊠ 4200 Wilson Blvd., Suite 800, Arlington, VA 22203, ☎ 703/276–0100, FAX 703/525–8277).

CUSTOMS & DUTIES

When shopping, **keep receipts** for all purchases. Upon reentering the coun-try, **be ready to show customs officials what you've bought.** If you feel a duty is incorrect or object to the way your clearance was handled, note the inspector's badge number and ask to see a supervisor. If the problem isn't resolved, write to the appropriate authorities, beginning with the port director at your point of entry.

IN AUSTRALIA

Australia residents who are 18 or older may bring home A$400 worth of souvenirs and gifts (including jewelry), 250 cigarettes or 250 grams of tobacco, and 1,125 ml of alcohol (including wine, beer, and spirits). Residents under 18 may bring back A$200 worth of goods. Prohibited items include meat products. Seeds, plants, and fruits need to be declared upon arrival.

➤ INFORMATION: **Australian Customs Service** (Regional Director, ⊠ Box 8, Sydney, NSW 2001, ☎ 02/9213–2000, FAX 02/9213–4000).

IN CANADA

Canadian residents who have been out of Canada for at least 7 days may bring home C$500 worth of goods duty-free. If you've been away less than 7 days but more than 48 hours, the duty-free allowance drops to C$200; if your trip lasts 24–48 hours, the allowance is C$50. You may not pool allowances with family mem-bers. Goods claimed under the C$500 exemption may follow you by mail; those claimed under the lesser exemp-tions must accompany you. Alcohol and tobacco products may be in-cluded in the 7-day and 48-hour exemptions but not in the 24-hour exemption. If you meet the age requirements of the province or territory through which you reenter Canada, you may bring in, duty-free, 1.14 liters (40 imperial ounces) of wine or liquor *or* 24 12-ounce cans or bottles of beer or ale. If you are 16 or older you may bring in, duty-free, 200 cigarettes and 50 cigars. Check ahead of time with Revenue Canada or the Department of Agriculture for policies regarding meat products, seeds, plants, and fruits.

You may send an unlimited number of gifts worth up to C$60 each duty-free to Canada. Label the package UNSOLICITED GIFT—VALUE UNDER $60. Alcohol and tobacco are excluded.

➤ INFORMATION: **Revenue Canada** (✉ 2265 St. Laurent Blvd. S, Ottawa, Ontario K1G 4K3, ☎ 613/993–0534; 800/461–9999 in Canada).

IN NEW ZEALAND

Homeward-bound residents 17 or older may bring back $700 worth of souvenirs and gifts. Your duty-free allowance also includes 4.5 liters of wine or beer; one 1,125-ml bottle of spirits; and either 200 cigarettes, 250 grams of tobacco, 50 cigars, or a combination of the three up to 250 grams. Prohibited items include meat products, seeds, plants, and fruits.

➤ INFORMATION: **New Zealand Customs** (Custom House, ✉ 50 Anzac Ave., Box 29, Auckland, New Zealand, ☎ 09/359–6655, FAX 09/359–6732).

IN THE U.K.

From countries outside the EU, including the United States, you may bring home, duty-free, 200 cigarettes or 50 cigars; 1 liter of spirits or 2 liters of fortified or sparkling wine or liqueurs; 2 liters of still table wine; 60 milliliters of perfume; 250 milliliters of toilet water; plus £136 worth of other goods, including gifts and souvenirs. If returning from outside the EU, prohibited items include meat products, seeds, plants, and fruits.

➤ INFORMATION: **HM Customs and Excise** (✉ Dorset House, Stamford St., Bromley Kent BR1 1XX, ☎ 0171/202–4227).

IN THE U.S.

Non-U.S. residents ages 21 and older may import into the United States 200 cigarettes or 50 cigars or 2 kilograms of tobacco, 1 liter of alcohol, and gifts worth $100. Meat products, seeds, plants, and fruits are prohibited.

➤ INFORMATION: **U.S. Customs Service** (inquiries, ✉ 1300 Pennsylvania Ave. NW, Washington, DC 20229, ☎ 202/927–6724; complaints, ✉ Office of Regulations and Rulings, 1300 Pennsylvania Ave. NW, Washington, DC 20229; registration of equipment, ✉ Resource Management, 1300 Pennsylvania Ave. NW, Washington, DC 20229, ☎ 202/927–0540).

DINING

The restaurants we list are the cream of the crop in each price category.

CATEGORY	COST*
$$$$	over $50
$$$	$35–$50
$$	$20–$35
$	under $20

per person for a three-course meal, excluding drinks, service, and 6% sales tax (more in some counties)

One cautionary word: Raw oysters have been identified as a problem for people with chronic illness of the liver, stomach, or blood, or who have immune disorders. Since 1993, all Florida restaurants serving raw oysters are required to post a notice in plain view of all patrons warning of the risks associated with consuming them.

RESERVATIONS & DRESS

Reservations are always a good idea: we mention them only when they're essential or are not accepted. Book as far ahead as you can, and reconfirm as soon as you arrive. We mention dress only when men are required to wear a jacket or a jacket and tie.

DISABILITIES & ACCESSIBILITY

➤ COMPLAINTS: **Disability Rights Section** (✉ U.S. Department of Justice, Civil Rights Division, Box 66738, Washington, DC 20035-6738, ☎ 202/514–0301; 800/514–0301; 202/514–0301 TTY; 800/514–0301 TTY, FAX 202/307–1198) for general complaints. **Aviation Consumer Protection Division** (☞ Air Travel, *above*) for airline-related problems. **Civil Rights Office** (✉ U.S. Department of Transportation, Departmental Office of Civil Rights, S-30, 400 7th St. SW, Room 10215, Washington, DC 20590, ☎ 202/366–4648, FAX 202/366–9371) for problems with surface transportation.

LODGING

When discussing accessibility with an operator or reservations agent **ask hard questions.** Are there any stairs, inside *or* out? Are there grab bars next to the toilet *and* in the shower/tub? How wide is the doorway to the room? To the bathroom? For the most extensive facilities meeting the latest legal specifications **opt for newer accommodations.**

TRAVEL AGENCIES

In the United States, although the Americans with Disabilities Act requires that travel firms serve the needs of all travelers, some agencies specialize in working with people with disabilities.

➤ TRAVELERS WITH MOBILITY PROBLEMS: **Access Adventures** (✉ 206 Chestnut Ridge Rd., Rochester, NY 14624, ☎ 716/889–9096), run by a former physical-rehabilitation counselor. **Accessible Vans of the Rockies, Activity and Travel Agency** (✉ 2040 W. Hamilton Pl., Sheridan, CO 80110, ☎ 303/806–5047 or 888/837–0065, FAX 303/781–2329). **CareVacations** (✉ 5-5110 50th Ave., Leduc, Alberta T9E 6V4, ☎ 780/986–6404 or 780/986–8332) has group tours and is especially helpful with cruise vacations. **Flying Wheels Travel** (✉ 143 W. Bridge St., Box 382, Owatonna, MN 55060, ☎ 507/451–5005 or 800/535–6790, FAX 507/451–1685). **Hinsdale Travel Service** (✉ 201 E. Ogden Ave., Suite 100, Hinsdale, IL 60521, ☎ 630/325–1335).

➤ TRAVELERS WITH DEVELOPMENTAL DISABILITIES: **New Directions** (✉ 5276 Hollister Ave., Suite 207, Santa Barbara, CA 93111, ☎ 805/967–2841 or 888/967–2841, FAX 805/964–7344). **Sprout** (✉ 893 Amsterdam Ave., New York, NY 10025, ☎ 212/222–9575 or 888/222–9575, FAX 212/222–9768).

DISCOUNTS & DEALS

Be a smart shopper and **compare all your options** before making decisions. A plane ticket bought with a promotional coupon from travel clubs, coupon books, and direct-mail offers may not be cheaper than the least expensive fare from a discount ticket agency. And always keep in mind that what you get is just as important as what you save.

DISCOUNT RESERVATIONS

To save money **look into discount-reservations services** with toll-free numbers, which use their buying power to get a better price on hotels, airline tickets, even car rentals. When booking a room, always **call the hotel's local toll-free number** (if one is available) rather than the central reservations number—you'll often get a better price. Always ask about special packages or corporate rates.

➤ AIRLINE TICKETS: ☎ **800/FLY–4–LESS.** ☎ **800/FLY–ASAP.**

➤ HOTEL ROOMS: **Accommodations Express** (☎ 800/444–7666). **Central Reservation Service (CRS)** (☎ 800/548–3311). **Hotel Reservations Network** (☎ 800/964–6835). **Players Express Vacations** (☎ 800/458–6161). **Room Finders USA** (☎ 800/473–7829). **RMC Travel** (☎ 800/245–5738). **Steigenberger Reservation Service** (☎ 800/223–5652).

PACKAGE DEALS

Don't confuse packages and guided tours. When you buy a package, you travel on your own, just as though you had planned the trip yourself. Fly/drive packages, which combine airfare and car rental, are often a good deal.

ECOTOURISM

Florida's varied environment is one of its chief draws; it's also very fragile. If you're out in nature, follow the basic rules of environmental responsibility: Take nothing but pictures; leave nothing but footprints. Most important, **be extremely careful around the tenuous dunes.** Picking the sea grasses that hold the dunes in place can carry stiff fines, as can walking or playing or digging in the dunes. So stay on the beach, gaze at the beautiful dunes, but don't go on them. An afternoon of roughhousing can completely destroy a dune. Ecotours (listed under Guided Tours in each chapter's A to Z section) operate throughout the state and can help you see some of what makes Florida so distinct, usually in a way that makes the least impact possible.

GAY & LESBIAN TRAVEL

Destinations within Florida that have a reputation for being especially gay and lesbian friendly include South Beach and Key West.

➤ GAY- AND LESBIAN-FRIENDLY TRAVEL AGENCIES: **Different Roads Travel** (✉ 8383 Wilshire Blvd., Suite 902, Beverly Hills, CA 90211, ☎ 323/651–5557 or 800/429–8747, FAX 323/651–3678). **Kennedy Travel** (✉ 314 Jericho Turnpike, Floral Park, NY 11001, ☎ 516/352–4888 or 800/237–7433, FAX 516/354–8849). **Now Voyager** (✉ 4406 18th St., San Francisco, CA 94114, ☎ 415/626–1169 or 800/255–6951, FAX 415/626–8626). **Yellowbrick Road** (✉ 1500 W. Balmoral Ave., Chicago, IL 60640, ☎ 773/561–1800 or 800/642–2488, FAX 773/561–4497). **Skylink Travel and Tour** (✉ 1006 Mendocino Ave., Santa Rosa, CA 95401, ☎ 707/546–9888 or 800/225–5759, FAX 707/546–9891), serving lesbian travelers.

HEALTH

BEACH AND SUN SAFETY

If you are unaccustomed to strong subtropical sun, you run a risk of sunburn and heat prostration, even in winter. So **hit the beach or play tennis, golf, or another outdoor sport before 10 or after 3.** If you must be out at midday, **limit strenuous exercise, drink plenty of liquids, and wear a hat.** If you begin to feel faint, get out of the sun immediately and sip water slowly. Even on overcast days, ultraviolet rays shine through the haze, so **use a sunscreen with an SPF of at least 15,** and have children wear a waterproof SPF 30 or better.

While you're frolicking on the beach, **steer clear of what looks like blue bubbles on the sand.** These are Por-

tuguese man-of-wars, and their tentacles can cause an allergic reaction. Also be careful of other large jellyfish, some of which can sting.

Before swimming, **make sure there's no undertow.** (Since you can't necessarily see if there is one, check with a lifeguard.) Rip currents, caused when the tide rushes out through a narrow break in a sandbar, can overpower even the strongest swimmer. If you're caught in one, resist the urge to swim straight back to shore—you'll never make it. Instead, stay calm, swim parallel to the shore until you are outside the current's pull, and then work your way in. And always **exercise extra caution when the surf is up.**

If you walk across a grassy area on the way to the beach, you'll probably encounter sand spurs. They are quite tiny, light brown, and remarkably prickly. You'll feel them before you see them; if you get stuck with one, just pull it out.

DIVERS' ALERT

Do not fly within 24 hours of scuba diving.

HOLIDAYS

Major national holidays include New Year's Day (Jan. 1); Martin Luther King, Jr., Day (3rd Mon. in Jan.); President's Day (3rd Mon. in Feb.); Memorial Day (last Mon. in May); Independence Day (July 4); Labor Day (1st Mon. in Sept.); Thanksgiving Day (4th Thurs. in Nov.); Christmas Eve and Christmas Day (Dec. 24 and 25); and New Year's Eve (Dec. 31).

INSURANCE

The most useful travel insurance plan is a comprehensive policy that includes coverage for trip cancellation and interruption, default, trip delay, and medical expenses (with a waiver for preexisting conditions).

Without insurance you will lose all or most of your money if you cancel your trip, regardless of the reason. Default insurance covers you if your tour operator, airline, or cruise line goes out of business. Trip-delay covers expenses that arise because of bad weather or mechanical delays.

SMART TRAVEL TIPS

Study the fine print when comparing policies.

British and Australian citizens need extra medical coverage when traveling overseas.

Always **buy travel policies directly from the insurance company**; if you buy it from a cruise line, airline, or tour operator that goes out of business you probably will not be covered for the agency or operator's default, a major risk. Before you make any purchase **review your existing health and home-owner's policies** to find what they cover away from home.

➤ TRAVEL INSURERS: In the U.S., **Access America** (⊠ 6600 W. Broad St., Richmond, VA 23230, ☎ 804/285–3300 or 800/284–8300), **Travel Guard International** (⊠ 1145 Clark St., Stevens Point, WI 54481, ☎ 715/345–0505 or 800/826–1300). In Canada, **Voyager Insurance** (⊠ 44 Peel Center Dr., Brampton, Ontario L6T 4M8, ☎ 905/791–8700; 800/668–4342 in Canada).

➤ INSURANCE INFORMATION: In the U.K., the **Association of British Insurers** (⊠ 51–55 Gresham St., London EC2V 7HQ, ☎ 0171/600–3333, FAX 0171/696–8999). In Australia, the **Insurance Council of Australia** (☎ 03/9614–1077, FAX 03/9614–7924).

LODGING

South Florida has every conceivable type of lodging—from tree houses to penthouses, mansions for hire to hostels. Even with occupancy rates inching above 70%, there are almost always rooms available, except maybe at Christmas and other holidays. Affordable lodgings can be found in even the most glittery resort towns, typically motel rooms that may cost as little as $50–$60 a night; they may not be in the best part of town, mind you, but they won't be in the worst, either (perhaps along busy highways where you'll need the roar of the air-conditioning to drown out the traffic). Since beachfront properties tend to be more expensive, **look for properties a little off the beach.**

Children are welcome generally everywhere in South Florida. Pets are another matter, so **inquire ahead of time if you're bringing an animal with you.**

In the busy seasons—over Christmas and from late January through Easter—always **reserve ahead for the top properties.** Fall is the slowest season: Rates are low and availability is high. Key West is jam-packed for Fantasy Fest at Halloween. If you're not booking through a travel agent, call the visitors bureau or the chamber of commerce in the area where you're going to check whether any special event is scheduled for when you plan to arrive. If demand isn't especially high for the time you have in mind, you can often **save by showing up at a lodging in mid- to late afternoon**—desk clerks are typically willing to negotiate with travelers in order to fill those rooms late in the day. In addition, **check with chambers of commerce for discount coupons for selected properties.**

The lodgings we list are the cream of the crop in each price category. We always list the facilities that are available—but we don't specify whether they cost extra: When pricing accommodations, always ask what's included and what costs extra.

CATEGORY	COST*
$$$$	over $220
$$$	$140–$220
$$	$80–$140
$	under $80

All prices are for a standard double room, excluding 6% sales tax (more in some counties) and 1%–4% tourist tax.

APARTMENT & VILLA RENTALS

If you want a home base that's roomy enough for a family and comes with cooking facilities **consider a furnished rental.** These can save you money, especially if you're traveling with a group. Home-exchange directories sometimes list rentals as well as exchanges.

➤ INTERNATIONAL AGENTS: **Europa-Let/Tropical Inn-Let** (⊠ 92 N. Main St., Ashland, OR 97520, ☎ 541/482–5806 or 800/462–4486, FAX 541/482–0660). **Hometours International** (⊠ Box 11503, Knoxville, TN 37939, ☎ 423/690–8484 or 800/367–4668). **Interhome** (⊠ 1990 N.E. 163rd St., Suite 110, Miami Beach, FL 33162,

☎ 305/940–2299 or 800/882–6864, FAX 305/940–2911). **Rent-a-Home International** (✉ 7200 34th Ave. NW, Seattle, WA 98117, ☎ 206/789–9377, FAX 206/789–9379). **Vacation Home Rentals Worldwide** (✉ 235 Kensington Ave., Norwood, NJ 07648, ☎ 201/767–9393 or 800/633–3284, FAX 201/767–5510). **Hideaways International** (✉ 767 Islington St., Portsmouth, NH 03801, ☎ 603/430–4433 or 800/843–4433, FAX 603/430–4444; membership $99).

B&BS

Small inns and guest houses are increasingly numerous in South Florida, but they vary tremendously, ranging from economical places that are plain but serve a good home-style breakfast to elegantly furnished Victorian houses with four-course gourmet morning meals and rates to match. Many offer a homelike setting. In fact, many are in private homes with owners who treat you almost like family, while others are more businesslike. It's a good idea to **make specific inquiries of B&Bs you're interested in.**

➤ HISTORIC INN ASSOCIATION: **Inn Route, Inc.** (Box 6187, Palm Harbor, FL 34684, ☎ FAX 281/499–1374 or 800/524–1880).

➤ RESERVATION SERVICE: **Bed & Breakfast Co., Tropical Florida** (Box 262, Miami, FL 33243, ☎ FAX 305/661–3270).

CAMPING

For information on camping facilities, **contact the national and state parks and forests you plan to visit and the Florida Department of Environmental Protection** (☞ Parks & Preserves, *below*).

To find a commercial campground, **pick up a copy of the free annual "Florida Camping Directory,"** which lists 220 campgrounds, with 66,000 sites. It's available at Florida welcome centers, from the Florida Tourism Industry Marketing Corporation (☞ Visitor Information, *below*), and from the Florida Association of RV Parks & Campgrounds.

➤ CAMPING ASSOCIATION: **Florida Association of RV Parks & Camp-** grounds (1340 Vickers Dr., Tallahassee, FL 32303-3041, ☎ 850/562–7151, FAX 850/562–7179).

CONDOS

➤ CONDO GUIDE: *The Condo Lux Vacationer's Guide to Condominium Rentals in the Southeast* (Vintage Books/Random House, New York; $9.95), by Jill Little.

HOME EXCHANGES

If you would like to exchange your home for someone else's **join a home-exchange organization,** which will send you its updated listings of available exchanges for a year and will include your own listing in at least one of them. It's up to you to make specific arrangements.

➤ EXCHANGE CLUBS: **HomeLink International** (✉ Box 650, Key West, FL 33041, ☎ 305/294–7766 or 800/638–3841, FAX 305/294–1448; $88 per year). **Intervac U.S.** (✉ Box 590504, San Francisco, CA 94159, ☎ 800/756–4663, FAX 415/435–7440; $83 per year).

HOSTELS

No matter what your age you can **save on lodging costs by staying at hostels.** In some 5,000 locations in more than 70 countries around the world, Hostelling International (HI), the umbrella group for a number of national youth-hostel associations, offers single-sex, dorm-style beds and, at many hostels, couples rooms and family accommodations. Membership in any HI national hostel association, open to travelers of all ages, allows you to stay in HI-affiliated hostels at member rates (one-year membership is about $25 for adults; hostels run about $10–$25 per night). Members also have priority if the hostel is full; they're eligible for discounts around the world, even on rail and bus travel in some countries.

➤ ORGANIZATIONS: **Hostelling International—American Youth Hostels** (✉ 733 15th St. NW, Suite 840, Washington, DC 20005, ☎ 202/783–6161, FAX 202/783–6171). **Hostelling International—Canada** (✉ 400–205 Catherine St., Ottawa, Ontario K2P 1C3, ☎ 613/237–7884, FAX 613/237–7868). **Youth Hostel Association of England and Wales** (✉ Trevelyan

SMART TRAVEL TIPS

House, 8 St. Stephen's Hill, St. Albans, Hertfordshire AL1 2DY, ☎ 01727/855215 or 01727/845047, FAX 01727/844126). **Australian Youth Hostel Association** (✉ 10 Mallett St., Camperdown, NSW 2050, ☎ 02/9565-1699, FAX 02/9565-1325). **Youth Hostels Association of New Zealand** (✉ Box 436, Christchurch, New Zealand, ☎ 03/379-9970, FAX 03/365-4476). Membership in the U.S. $25, in Canada C$26.75, in the U.K. £9.30, in Australia $44, in New Zealand $24.

HOTELS

Wherever you look in South Florida, it seems, you'll find lots of plain, inexpensive motels and luxurious resorts, independents alongside national chains, and an ever-growing number of modern properties as well as quite a few timeless classics. In fact, since Florida has been a favored travel destination for some time, vintage hotels are everywhere, both grand edifices like the Breakers in Palm Beach, the Boca Raton Resort & Club in Boca Raton, the Biltmore in Coral Gables, and the Casa Marina in Key West as well as smaller, historic places.

All hotels listed have private bath unless otherwise noted.

➤ HOTEL AND MOTEL ASSOCIATION: **Florida Hotel & Motel Association** (200 W. College Ave., Box 1529, Tallahassee, FL 32301-1529, ☎ 850/224-2888).

➤ RESERVATION SERVICES: **Accommodations Express** (☎ 800/663-7666, FAX 609/525-0111). **Florida Hotel Network** (521 Lincoln Rd., Miami Beach, FL 33139, ☎ 800/538-3616, FAX 305/538-3616). **Florida Sunbreak** (169 Lincoln Rd., Miami Beach, FL 33139, ☎ 305/532-1516, FAX 305/781-1312).

➤ TOLL-FREE NUMBERS: **Adam's Mark** (☎ 800/444-2326). **Baymont Inns** (☎ 800/428-3438). **Best Western** (☎ 800/528-1234). **Choice** (☎ 800/221-2222). **Clarion** (☎ 800/252-7466). **Colony** (☎ 800/777-1700). **Comfort** (☎ 800/228-5150). **Days Inn** (☎ 800/325-2525). **Doubletree and Red Lion Hotels** (☎ 800/222-8733). **Embassy Suites** (☎ 800/362-2779).

Fairfield Inn (☎ 800/228-2800). **Forte** (☎ 800/225-5843). **Four Seasons** (☎ 800/332-3442). **Hilton** (☎ 800/445-8667). **Holiday Inn** (☎ 800/465-4329). **Howard Johnson** (☎ 800/654-4656). **Hyatt Hotels & Resorts** (☎ 800/233-1234). **Inter-Continental** (☎ 800/327-0200). **La Quinta** (☎ 800/531-5900). **Marriott** (☎ 800/228-9290). **Le Meridien** (☎ 800/543-4300). **Nikko Hotels International** (☎ 800/645-5687). **Omni** (☎ 800/843-6664). **Quality Inn** (☎ 800/228-5151). **Radisson** (☎ 800/333-3333). **Ramada** (☎ 800/228-2828). **Renaissance Hotels & Resorts** (☎ 800/468-3571). **Ritz-Carlton** (☎ 800/241-3333). **Sheraton** (☎ 800/325-3535). **Sleep Inn** (☎ 800/221-2222). **Westin Hotels & Resorts** (☎ 800/228-3000). **Wyndham Hotels & Resorts** (☎ 800/822-4200).

MAIL & SHIPPING

The fastest way to receive mail, assuming that you know where you will be staying, is to have it sent to that address. However, if you don't know exactly where you'll be, you can have mail sent to you care of General Delivery in the town where you'll be staying, remembering the zip code. Then you simply pick up your mail at that post office. This method works best in small towns, where prompt retrieval is more assured. Allow anywhere from a few days to a week or much longer for delivery of mail from overseas, depending on the origin.

MONEY MATTERS

Prices throughout this guide are given for adults. Substantially reduced fees are almost always available for children, students, and senior citizens. For information on taxes, *see* Taxes, *below.*

ATMS

Automatic Teller Machines (ATMs) are ubiquitous in South Florida. In addition to banks, you will find them at grocery store chains like Publix and Food Lion and in shopping malls big and small.

CREDIT CARDS

Should you use a credit card? A credit card allows you to delay payment and gives you certain rights as a consumer

(☞ Consumer Protection, *above*).Throughout this guide, the following abbreviations are used: **AE**, American Express; **D**, Discover; **DC**, Diners Club; **MC**, Master Card; and **V**, Visa.

NATIONAL PARKS

Look into discount passes to save money on park entrance fees. The Golden Eagle Pass ($50) gets you and your companions free admission to all parks for one year. (Camping and parking are extra). Both the Golden Age Passport ($10), for those 62 and older, and the Golden Access Passport (free), for travelers with disabilities, entitle holders to free entry to all national parks, plus 50% off fees for the use of many park facilities and services. You must show proof of age and of U.S. citizenship or permanent residency (such as a U.S. passport, driver's license, or birth certificate) and, if requesting Golden Access, proof of disability. All three passes are available at all national park entrances where entrance fees are charged. Golden Eagle and Golden Access passes are also available by mail.

➤ PASSES BY MAIL: **National Park Service** (✉ National Capitol Area Office, 1100 Ohio Dr. SW, Washington, DC 20242, ☎ 202/208–4747).

STATE PARKS

Florida's Department of Environmental Protection (DEP) is responsible for hundreds of historic buildings, landmarks, nature preserves, and parks. When requesting a free *Florida State Park Guide,* mention which parts of the state you plan to visit. For information on camping facilities at the state parks, ask for the free "Florida State Parks, Fees and Facilities" and "Florida State Parks Camping Reservation Procedures" brochures. Responding to cutbacks in its budget, the DEP established Friends of Florida State Parks, a citizen support organization open to all.

➤ STATE PARKS INFORMATION: **Florida Department of Environmental Protection** (Marjory Stoneman Douglas Bldg., MS 535, 3900 Commonwealth Blvd., Tallahassee, FL 32399-3000, ☎ 850/488–2850, FAX 850/488–

3947); **Friends of Florida State Parks** (☎ 850/488–8243).

PRIVATE PRESERVES

➤ FLORIDA SANCTUARY INFORMATION: **National Audubon Society** (Sanctuary Director, Miles Wildlife Sanctuary, R.R. 1, Box 294, W. Cornwall Rd., Sharon, CT 06069, ☎ 203/364–0048). **Nature Conservancy** (222 S. Westmonte Dr., Suite 300, Altamonte Springs, FL 32714, ☎ 407/682–3554; offices at 250 Tequesta Dr., Suite 301, Tequesta, FL 33469, ☎ 561/744–6668; 201 Front St., Suite 222, Key West, FL 33040, ☎ 305/296–3880; 225 E. Stuart Ave., Lake Wales, FL 33853, ☎ 941/678–1551; 625 N. Adams St., Tallahassee, FL 32301, ☎ 850/222–2473; Comeau Bldg., 319 Clematis St., Suite 611, West Palm Beach, FL 33401, ☎ 561/833–4226).

OUTDOORS & SPORTS

Recreational opportunities abound throughout South Florida. The Governor's Council on Physical Fitness and Sports puts on the Sunshine State Games each July in a different part of the state.

➤ GENERAL INFORMATION: **Florida Department of Environmental Protection** (Office of Greenways, MS 585, 3900 Commonwealth Blvd., Tallahassee, FL 32399-3000, ☎ 850/487–4784) for information on bicycling, canoeing, kayaking, and hiking trails.

➤ MARINE CHARTS: **Tealls, Inc.** (111 Saguaro La., Marathon, FL 33050, ☎ 305/743–3942, FAX 305/743–3942; $7.95 set, $3.60 each individual chart).

BIKING

Biking is a popular Florida sport. Rails to Trails, a nationwide group that turns unused railroad rights-of-way into bicycle and walking paths, has made great inroads in Florida. In addition, just about every town in Florida has its own set of bike paths and a bike rental outfit. For bike information, **check with Florida's Department of Transportation (DOT),** which publishes free bicycle trail guides, dispenses free touring information packets, and provides names of bike coordinators around the state.

SMART TRAVEL TIPS

SMART TRAVEL TIPS

➤ BICYCLE INFORMATION: **DOT state bicycle-pedestrian coordinator** (605 E. Suwannee St., MS 82, Tallahassee, FL 32399-0450, ☎ 850/488–1234).

CANOEING & KAYAKING

You can canoe or kayak along 1,550 mi of trails encompassing creeks, rivers, and springs. Both the DEP (☞ General Information, *above*) and outfitter associations provide information on trails and their conditions, events, and contacts for trips and equipment rental.

➤ OUTFITTERS AND OUTFITTING ASSOCIATIONS: **Canoe Outpost System** (2816 N.W. Rte. 661, Arcadia, FL 33821, ☎ 941/494–1215), comprising five outfitters. **Florida Professional Paddlesports Association** (Box 1764, Arcadia, FL 34265, ☎ no phone).

FISHING

In Atlantic and gulf waters, fishing seasons and other regulations vary by location and species. You will need to **buy one license for freshwater fishing and another license for saltwater fishing.** Nonresident fees for a saltwater license are $30. Nonresidents can purchase freshwater licenses good for seven days ($15) or for one year ($30). Typically, you'll pay a $1.50 surcharge at most any marina, bait shop, Kmart, Wal-Mart, or other license vendor.

➤ FISHING INFORMATION: **Florida Game and Fresh Water Fish Commission** (620 S. Meridian St., Tallahassee, FL 32399-1600, ☎ 850/488–1960) for the free *Florida Fishing Handbook* with license vendors, regional fishing guides, and educational bulletins.

HORSEBACK RIDING

Horseback riding is a popular sport outside of South Florida's metropolitan areas. There are trails around the state and even beaches on which you can ride.

➤ HORSEBACK RIDING INFORMATION: **Horse & Pony** (6229 Virginia La., Seffner, FL 33584, ☎ 813/621–2510).

JOGGING, RUNNING, & WALKING

Many towns have walking and running trails, and most of South Florida's beaches stretch on for miles, testing the limits of even the most stalwart runners and walkers. Local running clubs sponsor weekly public events.

➤ CLUBS & EVENTS: **Miami Runners Club** (7920 S.W. 40th St., Miami, FL 33155, ☎ 305/227–1500, FAX 305/220–2450) for South Florida events.

PARI-MUTUEL SPORTS

Miami has jai-alai frontons and greyhound-racing tracks. Patrons can bet on the teams or dogs or on televised horse races.

➤ SCHEDULES: Department of Business & Professional Regulations **Division of Pari-Mutuel Wagering** (8405 N.W. 53rd St., Suite C-250, Miami, FL 33166, ☎ 305/470–5675, FAX 305/470–5686).

TENNIS

Tennis is extremely popular in South Florida, and virtually every town has well-maintained public courts. In addition, many tennis tournaments are held in the state.

➤ TOURNAMENT AND EVENT SCHEDULES: **United States Tennis Association Florida Section** (1280 S.W. 36th Ave., Suite 305, Pompano Beach, FL 33069, ☎ 954/968–3434, FAX 954/968–3986; yearbook $11).

WILDERNESS & RECREATION AREAS

South Florida is studded with trails, rivers, and parks that are ideal for hiking, bird-watching, canoeing, bicycling, and horseback riding.

➤ PUBLICATIONS: **"Florida Trails: A Guide to Florida's Natural Habitats,"** available from Florida Tourism Industry Marketing Corporation (☞ Visitor Information, *below*), for bicycling, canoeing, horseback riding, and walking trails; camping; snorkeling and scuba diving; and Florida ecosystems. **Florida Wildlife Viewing Guide**, available from Falcon Press (Box 1718, Helena, MT 59624, ☎ 800/582–2665); $7.95 plus $3 shipping, by Susan Cerulean and Ann Morrow, for marked wildlife-watching sites. "Recreation Guide to District Lands," available from St. Johns River Water Management District (Box 1429, Palatka, FL 32178-1429); free for marine, wetland, and upland recreational areas.

PACKING

The Miami area is warm year-round and often extremely humid in summer months. Be prepared for sudden summer storms, but keep in mind that plastic raincoats are uncomfortable in the high humidity.

Dress is casual throughout the state, with sundresses, jeans, or walking shorts appropriate during the day; **bring comfortable walking shoes or sneakers** for theme parks. A few restaurants request that men wear jackets and ties, but most do not. Be prepared for air-conditioning working in overdrive.

You can generally swim year-round in peninsular Florida from about New Smyrna Beach south on the Atlantic coast. Be sure to **take a sun hat and sunscreen** because the sun can be fierce, even in winter and even if it is chilly or overcast.

In your carry-on luggage **bring an extra pair of eyeglasses or contact lenses** and **enough of any medication you take** to last the entire trip. You may also want your doctor to write a spare prescription using the drug's generic name, since brand names may vary from country to country. In luggage to be checked, **never pack prescription drugs or valuables.** To avoid customs delays, carry medications in their original packaging. And don't forget to copy down and carry addresses of offices that handle refunds of lost traveler's checks.

CHECKING LUGGAGE

How many carry-on bags you can bring with you is up to the airline. Most allow two, but not always, so make sure that everything you carry aboard will fit under your seat, and get to the gate early. Note that if you have a seat at the back of the plane, you'll probably board first, while the overhead bins are still empty.

If you are flying internationally, note that baggage allowances may be determined not by piece but by weight—generally 88 pounds (40 kilograms) in first class, 66 pounds (30 kilograms) in business class, and 44 pounds (20 kilograms) in economy.

Airline liability for baggage is limited to $1,250 per person on flights within the United States. On international flights it amounts to $9.07 per pound or $20 per kilogram for checked baggage (roughly $640 per 70-pound bag) and $400 per passenger for unchecked baggage. You can buy additional coverage at check-in for about $10 per $1,000 of coverage, but it excludes a rather extensive list of items, shown on your airline ticket.

Before departure **itemize your bags' contents** and their worth, and label the bags with your name, address, and phone number. (If you use your home address, cover it so that potential thieves can't see it readily.) Inside each bag **pack a copy of your itinerary.** At check-in **make sure that each bag is correctly tagged** with the destination airport's three-letter code. If your bags arrive damaged or fail to arrive at all, file a written report with the airline before leaving the airport.

PASSPORTS & VISAS

➤ U.K. CITIZENS: **U.S. Embassy Visa Information Line** (☎ 01891/200–290; calls cost 49p per minute, 39p per minute cheap rate) for U.S. visa information. **U.S. Embassy Visa Branch** (✉ 5 Upper Grosvenor Sq., London W1A 1AE) for U.S. visa information; send a self-addressed, stamped envelope. Write the **U.S. Consulate General** (✉ Queen's House, Queen St., Belfast BTI 6EO) if you live in Northern Ireland. Write the **Office of Australia Affairs** (✉ 59th fl., MLC Centre, 19-29 Martin Pl., Sydney NSW 2000) if you live in Australia. Write the **Office of New Zealand Affairs** (✉ 29 Fitzherbert Terr., Thorndon, Wellington) if you live in New Zealand.

PASSPORT OFFICES

The best time to apply for a passport or to renew is during the fall and winter. Before any trip, check your passport's expiration date, and, if necessary, renew it as soon as possible.

➤ AUSTRALIAN CITIZENS: **Australian Passport Office** (☎ 131–232).

➤ NEW ZEALAND CITIZENS: **New Zealand Passport Office** (☎ 04/494–0700 for information on how to apply; 04/474–8000 or 0800/225–050 in New Zealand for information on applications already submitted).

➤ U.K. CITIZENS: **London Passport Office** (☎ 0990/210–410) for fees and documentation requirements and to request an emergency passport.

SENIOR-CITIZEN TRAVEL

Since South Florida has a significant retired population, senior-citizen discounts are ubiquitous. To qualify for age-related discounts **mention your senior-citizen status up front** when booking hotel reservations (not when checking out) and before you're seated in restaurants (not when paying the bill). When renting a car ask about promotional car-rental discounts, which can be cheaper than senior-citizen rates.

➤ EDUCATIONAL PROGRAMS: **Elderhostel** (✉ 75 Federal St., 3rd fl., Boston, MA 02110, ☎ 877/426–8056, ℻ 877/426–2166).

STUDENTS IN FLORIDA

Students flock to the beaches of Florida during spring break, but there are also special tours for students year round.

➤ STUDENT I.D.S & SERVICES: **Council on International Educational Exchange** (CIEE, ✉ 205 E. 42nd St., 14th fl., New York, NY 10017, ☎ 212/822–2600 or 888/268–6245, ℻ 212/822–2699) for mail orders only, in the U.S. **Travel Cuts** (✉ 187 College St., Toronto, Ontario M5T 1P7, ☎ 416/979–2406 or 800/667–2887) in Canada.

TAXES

SALES TAX

Florida's sales tax is currently 6%, but local sales and tourist taxes can raise that number considerably, especially for certain items, such as lodging. Miami hoteliers, for example, collect roughly 12.5% for city

and resort taxes. It's best to **ask about additional costs up front,** to avoid a rude awakening.

TIME

Most of Florida is in the Eastern Time Zone.

TIPPING

Whether they carry bags, open doors, deliver food, or clean rooms, hospitality employees work to receive a portion of your travel budget. In deciding how much to give, **base your tip on what the service is and how well it's performed.**

In transit, tip an airport valet $1–$3 per bag, a taxi driver 15%–20% of the fare.

For hotel staff, recommended amounts are $1–$3 per bag for a bellhop, $1–$2 per night per guest for chambermaids, $5–$10 for special concierge service, $1–$3 for a doorman who hails a cab or parks a car, 15% of the greens fee for a caddy, 15%–20% of the bill for a massage, and 15% of a room service bill.

In a restaurant, give 15%–20% of your bill before tax to the server, 5%–10% to the maître d', 15% to a bartender, and 15% of the wine bill for a wine steward who makes a special effort in selecting and serving wine.

TOURS & PACKAGES

On a prepackaged tour or independent vacation everything is prearranged so you'll spend less time planning—and often get it all at a good price.

BOOKING WITH AN AGENT

Travel agents are excellent resources. But it's a good idea to collect brochures from several agencies because some agents' suggestions may be influenced by relationships with tour and package firms that reward them for volume sales. If you have a special interest **find an agent with expertise in that area;** ASTA (☞ Travel Agencies, *below*) has a database of specialists worldwide.

Make sure your travel agent knows the accommodations and other services of the place they're recommending. Ask about the hotel's location, room size, beds, and whether it has a pool, room service, or programs for children, if you care about these. Has your agent been there in person or sent others whom you can contact?

Do some homework on your own, too: Local tourism boards can provide information about lesser-known and small-niche operators, some of which may sell only direct.

BUYER BEWARE

Each year consumers are stranded or lose their money when tour operators—even large ones with excellent reputations—go out of business. So **check out the operator.** Ask several travel agents about its reputation, and try to **book with a company that has a consumer-protection program.** (Look for information in the company's brochure). In the United States, members of the National Tour Association and United States Tour Operators Association are required to set aside funds to cover your payments and travel arrangements in case the company defaults. It's also a good idea to choose a company that participates in the American Society of Travel Agent's Tour Operator Program (TOP); ASTA will act as mediator in any disputes between you and your tour operator.

Remember that the more your package or tour includes the better you can predict the ultimate cost of your vacation. Make sure you know exactly what is covered, and **beware of hidden costs.** Are taxes, tips, and transfers included? Entertainment and excursions? These can add up.

➤ TOUR-OPERATOR RECOMMENDATIONS: **American Society of Travel Agents** (☞ Travel Agencies, *below*). **National Tour Association** (NTA, ⌧ 546 E. Main St., Lexington, KY 40508, ☎ 606/226–4444 or 800/682–8886). **United States Tour Operators Association** (USTOA, ⌧ 342 Madison Ave., Suite 1522, New York, NY 10173, ☎ 212/599–6599 or 800/468–7862, FAX 212/599–6744).

TRAIN TRAVEL

Amtrak provides north–south service on two routes to the major cities of West Palm Beach, Fort Lauderdale, and Miami, with many stops in between on all routes.

➤ TRAIN INFORMATION: **Amtrak** (☎ 800/872–7245).

TRAVEL AGENCIES

A good travel agent puts your needs first. Look for an agency that has been in business at least five years, emphasizes customer service, and has someone on staff who specializes in your destination. In addition **make sure the agency belongs to a professional trade organization,** such as ASTA in the United States. If your travel agency is also acting as your tour operator *see* Buyer Beware *in* Tours & Packages, *above.*

➤ LOCAL AGENT REFERRALS: **American Society of Travel Agents** (ASTA, ☎ 800/965–2782 24-hr hot line, FAX 703/684–8319). **Association of Canadian Travel Agents** (⌧ 1729 Bank St., Suite 201, Ottawa, Ontario K1V 7Z5, ☎ 613/521–0474, FAX 613/521–0805). **Association of British Travel Agents** (⌧ 55–57 Newman St., London W1P 4AH, ☎ 0171/637–2444, FAX 0171/637–0713). **Australian Federation of Travel Agents** (⌧ Level 3, 309 Pitt St., Sydney 2000, ☎ 02/9264–3299, FAX 02/9264–1085). **Travel Agents' Association of New Zealand** (⌧ Box 1888, Wellington 10033, ☎ 04/499–0104, FAX 04/499–0786).

VISITOR INFORMATION

For general information about South Florida's attractions, contact the office below; welcome centers are located on I–10, I–75, I–95. For regional tourist bureaus and chambers of commerce see individual chapters.

➤ STATE: **Florida Tourism Industry Marketing Corporation** (Box 1100, 661 E. Jefferson St., Suite 300, Tallahassee, FL 32302, ☎ 850/487–1462, FAX 850/224–2938).

➤ IN THE U.K.: **ABC Florida** (Box 35, Abingdon, Oxon. OX14 4TB, ☎ 0891/600–555, 50p per minute; send £2 for vacation pack).

WEB SITES

The state of Florida is very visitor-oriented and has created a terrific

SMART TRAVEL TIPS

web site—www.flausa.com—with superb links to help you find out all you want to know. It's a wonderful place to learn about everything from fancy resorts to camping trips to car routes to beach towns.

WHEN TO GO

Florida is a state for all seasons, although most visitors prefer October–April, particularly in South Florida.

Winter remains the height of the tourist season, when South Florida is crowded with "snowbirds" fleeing cold weather in the North. (It did snow in Miami once in the 1970s, but since then the average snowfall has been exactly 00.00 inches.) Hotels, bars, discos, restaurants, shops, and attractions are all crowded. Hollywood and Broadway celebrities appear in sophisticated supper clubs, and other performing artists hold the stage at ballets, operas, concerts, and theaters.

For the college crowd, spring vacation is still the time to congregate in Florida; Fort Lauderdale, where city officials have refashioned the beachfront more as a family resort, no longer indulges young revelers, so it's much less popular with college students than it once was.

Summer in Florida, as smart budget-minded visitors have discovered, is often hot and very humid, but along the coast, ocean breezes make the season quite bearable and many hotels lower their prices considerably.

CLIMATE

What follows are average daily maximum and minimum temperatures for major cities in Florida.

KEY WEST (THE KEYS)

Jan.	76F	24C	May	85F	29C	Sept.	90F	32C
	65	18		74	23		77	25
Feb.	76F	24C	June	88F	31C	Oct.	83F	28C
	67	19		77	25		76	24
Mar.	79F	26C	July	90F	32C	Nov.	79F	26C
	68	20		79	26		70	21
Apr.	81F	27C	Aug.	90F	32C	Dec.	76F	24C
	72	22		79	26		67	19

MIAMI

Jan.	74F	23C	May	83F	28C	Sept.	86F	30C
	63	17		72	22		76	24
Feb.	76F	24C	June	85F	29C	Oct.	83F	28C
	63	17		76	24		72	22
Mar.	77F	25C	July	88F	31C	Nov.	79F	26C
	65	18		76	24		67	19
Apr.	79F	26C	Aug.	88F	31C	Dec.	76F	26C
	68	20		77	25		63	17

➤ FORECASTS: **Weather Channel Connection** (☎ 900/932–8437), 95¢ per minute from a Touch-Tone phone.

FESTIVALS AND SEASONAL EVENTS

➤ JAN.: Early in the month, **Polo Season** opens at the Palm Beach Polo and Country Club (☎ 561/793–1440). Mid-month, **Art Deco Weekend** spotlights Miami Beach's historic district with an Art Deco street fair, a 1930s-style Moon Over Miami Ball, and live entertainment (☎ 305/672–2014). **Martin Luther King Jr. Festivals** are celebrated throughout the state (☎ 407/246–2221). **Taste of the Grove Food and Music Festival** is a popular fund-raiser put on in Coconut Grove's Peacock Park by area restaurants (☎ 305/444–7270). In late January, **Miami Rivers Blues Festival** takes place on the south bank of the river next to Tobacco Road (☎ 305/374–1198).

➤ FEB.: The **Coconut Grove Art Festival,** mid-month, is the state's largest (☎ 305/447–0401). The **Florida Manatee Festival,** in Crystal River, focuses on both the river and the endangered manatee (☎ 352/795–3149). The **Miami Film Festival,** sponsored by the Film Society of America, is 10 days of international, domestic, and local films (☎ 305/377–3456). ➤ FEB.–MAR.: The **Winter Equestrian Festival,** at the Palm Beach Polo and Country Club in West Palm Beach, includes more than 1,000 horses and three grand-prix equestrian events (☎ 561/798–7000).

➤ APR.: The **Delray Affair,** in early April, is the biggest event in the area and features arts, crafts, and food (☎ 561/279–1880). ➤ LATE APR.–EARLY MAY: The **Conch Republic Celebration** honors the founding fathers of the Conch Republic, "the small island nation of Key West" (☎ 305/296–0123). ➤ MAY: The **Shell Air & Sea Show** draws more than 2 million to the Fort Lauderdale beachfront for performances by big names in aviation, such as the navy's Blue Angels and the air force's Thunderbirds (☎ 954/467–3555). In mid-May, the **Arabian Nights Festival,** in Opa-locka, is a mix of contemporary and fantasy-inspired entertainment (☎ 305/758–4166). ➤ JUNE: The **Miami-Bahamas Goombay Festival,** in Miami's Coconut Grove, celebrates the city's Bahamian heritage the first weekend of the month (☎ 305/443–7928 or 305/372–9966). ➤ JUNE–JULY: **Beethoven by the Beach,** in Fort Lauderdale, features Beethoven's symphonies, chamber pieces, and piano concertos performed by the Florida Philharmonic (☎ 954/561–2997).

➤ AUG.: The **Annual Wausau Possum Funday & Parade** is held in Possum Palace, Wausau, early in the month (☎ 904/638–7888).

➤ OCT.: The **Fort Lauderdale International Boat Show,** the world's largest show based on exhibit size, displays boats of every size, price, and description at the Bahia Mar marina and four other venues (☎ 954/764–7642). The **Fort Lauderdale International Film Festival** showcases independent cinema from around the world (☎ 954/563–0500). The **Cedar Key Seafood Festival** is held on Main Street in Cedar Key (☎ 352/543–5600). **Fantasy Fest,** in Key West, is a no-holds-barred Halloween costume party, parade, and town fair (☎ 305/296–1817).

➤ NOV.: The **Miami Book Fair International,** the largest book fair in the United States, is held on the Wolfson campus of Miami-Dade Community College (☎ 305/237–3032).

➤ EARLY NOV.–LATE FEB.: The **Orange Bowl and Junior Orange Bowl Festival,** in the Miami area, are best known for the King Orange Jamboree Parade and the Orange Bowl Football Classic but also include more than 20 youth-oriented events (☎ 305/371–3351).

➤ DEC.: **Winterfest Boat Parade** is on the Intracoastal Waterway, Fort Lauderdale (☎ 954/767–0686). At the end of the month, **Coconut Grove King Mango Strut** is a parody of the Orange Bowl Parade (☎ 305/445–1865).

1 DESTINATION: SOUTH FLORIDA

THE OTHER SIDE OF PARADISE

PERHAPS NO AREA in the United States is more misunderstood than South Florida. To the visitor, it may appear to be a seamless metropolis. From South Dade to North Palm Beach, communities bump into one another in a long strip wedged between the ocean and the Everglades. It's often hard to tell towns apart, unless you're in Boca Raton, where most of the buildings are pink. (My daughter once thought it was the corporate headquarters for Pepto-Bismol.) But behind this homogenous facade lie striking dichotomies. There are rich and poor, natural and overdeveloped, and amid it all, South Florida is at once paradise and paradox.

Renowned for its sandy beaches and sunny climate, South Florida is also criticized for its unbridled growth, which threatens the fragile environment that is one of its greatest attractions. Business leaders and top names in entertainment and sports have homes (or second homes) here, drawn by world-class dining, nightlife, and golf and other recreation opportunities. But this very chicness also draws scam artists, who give the region a reputation as the boiler room capital of the nation.

South Florida seems to have more than its share of waterside mansions, fast cars and boats, and designer drugs—often verging on wretched excess. But the region also attracts plenty of newcomers with some of the most affordable housing in the nation (and no state income tax). The quality of life is outstanding, and yet residents complain that it's hard to call South Florida home; recent development has yielded mostly cookie-cutter subdivisions and very few real neighborhoods.

Despite its shortcomings (and we haven't even mentioned hurricanes), the area continues to grow and prosper, attracting a United Nations of immigrants from Latin America and elsewhere, moneyed investors from Europe, high-tech entrepreneurs from across the United States, and retirees from everywhere. The area hums with the positives and negatives that result from this vibrant melting pot, and it works

hard to polish its image and fix its problems. After several high-profile crimes against travelers many years ago, both the police and the tourism industry stepped up programs to ensure visitor safety, and they seem to be paying off. Developers no longer get their plans rubber-stamped, and regional planners are now taking a hard look at the environmental impact of new development.

There will always be plenty to criticize. Two new professional sports arenas are open, complete with skyboxes and luxury suites, while many children attend school in portable classrooms. The Miami political scene is as zoolike as any Central Florida animal theme park. But there's also plenty to praise. Despite the vastly different characters of many South Florida communities, they do come together in time of need, as when Hurricane Andrew devasted much of South Dade in 1992, and in time of joy, as when the Marlins won the 1997 World Series.

And so South Florida remains one of the most popular U.S. vacation destinations, largely because there's always something going on. A friend who moved from Fort Lauderdale to North Carolina complained: "It's boring here. Mike Wallace never comes to Raleigh to do an investigative story. But it seems he's always in South Florida." Paradise may have its flaws, but most are the result of the change, growth, and interplay of cultures that make South Florida such a vibrant place.

–Alan Macher

NEW AND NOTEWORTHY

Miami and Miami Beach

There's so much building going on in Miami Beach that hard-hatted construction workers are nearly as prevalent as fashion models heading off to their next photo shoot.

Two decades ago, a decision to preserve Miami Beach's Art Deco District sparked a rebirth in South Beach and began a trend: renovating old properties along the aging, run-down strip. With hot new celebrity restaurants and clubs, SoBe became the place to see and be seen. Now, national hotel chains are getting into the act, renovating old properties and building new ones. This hotel boom means a wider choice for visitors.

For years, the only name hotel on the beach was the Fontainebleau Hilton. Today, the new **Miami Beach Marriott,** on Ocean Drive, and **Royal Palm Crowne Plaza Resort,** on Collins Avenue, join the Loews Miami Beach Hotel as the first major new hotels in 30 years. Other older hotels, often in disrepair, are being bought up and transformed. **Ritz-Carlton** is planning to pour $95 million into the old DiLido. **The Carlyle,** on Ocean Drive, is scheduled for a face-lift and will open in 2001 with a "futuristic" look. The aging **Deauville Hotel,** on Collins Avenue, was reopened after a $20 million upgrade and now flies the Radisson banner. This property maintains its 1950s appearance, keeping its marble lobby, gilded staircases, and circular banisters.

Over on the mainland, the NBA Miami Heat features a talent-rich lineup, a marquee coach in Pat Riley, and now a new home, **American Airlines Arena.** The arena sits downtown on Biscayne Bay near the entrance to the Port of Miami.

Visitors also have some new shopping choices in Miami-Dade. The **Dolphin Mall,** west of the Miami airport, expects to be open by the fall of 2000. If you're wondering what $250 million buys these days, it's 1.4 million square ft of retail outlets, theme restaurants, cafés, nightclubs, a 30-screen theater, and an amusement park. In South Miami, the **Shops at Sunset Place** has impressive entryways, winding paths, and a variety of retailers, making this the Main Street of the 21st century.

The Everglades

In Florida City, a new **aquarium** should be open by the year 2000.

Guests wanting to stay in the heart of the Everglades started checking into the **Miccosukee Resort & Convention Center** in June 1999.

Fort Lauderdale and Broward County

If you're looking for some trendy hangouts in Fort Lauderdale, try some of the new hot spots along Las Olas Boulevard, Beach Place, and **Las Olas Riverfront.** This complex along the New River offers a variety of shopping, dining, and entertainment choices. Outside are picturesque plazas and sweeping terraces with splashing fountains, making a tranquil spot for relaxing along the river. Inside is where the action is: There are 18 restaurants ranging from upscale to casual; the city's first downtown movie complex, with 23 screens and stadium seating; and a two-level spread of video and virtual-reality games. Recent additions to the dining scene here include China Grill Cafe, Murphy's Law, and Big Pink.

Not to be outdone by Miami-Dade, Broward County also sports a new arena— an 18,000-seat facility for the NHL Florida Panthers, located west of Fort Lauderdale in Sunrise. But don't let the name fool you. The **National Car Rental Center** is not where visitors pick up and return rental vehicles. The center also gives Broward County its first large-capacity indoor venue, drawing big-name performers like Billy Joel and Celine Dion.

World Fishing Center became an instant hit when it opened its doors in 1999. It's an angler's mecca on dry land, with an impressive collection of sportfishing exhibits and demonstrations, as well as the World Fishing Hall of Fame.

Palm Beach County

To keep up with its neighbors, West Palm Beach is planning its own new downtown entertainment, retail, and dining complex—**CityPlace**—scheduled to open in phases during the year 2000.

Perhaps the best example of a downtown renaissance in Palm Beach County is **Atlantic Avenue in Delray Beach.** It's become the home of trendy shops, restaurants, and music clubs, and special events like "Jazz on the Avenue." The success is spilling over into other neighborhoods, including Pineapple Grove, where the old Ocean City Lumber Co. has been transformed into a retail, entertainment, and cultural complex.

The Florida Keys

Hurricane Georges roared through the Florida Keys in September 1998, flooding and ripping apart waterfront hotels, businesses, and parks in Key West and the

Middle and Lower keys. In most cases, recovery was swift, with all but a few properties reopening within a few days or weeks. The most long-term visible effects are in the landscaping, once lush with mature trees, sea oats, and palms, but now thin or nonexistent. In one way, visitors will benefit from the storm: Many properties took the opportunity to renovate and upgrade.

Florida State Parks opened two new facilities. After nearly a six-month closing, Windley Key Fossil Reef State Geologic Site, in Islamorada, reopened with the new Alison Fahrer Environmental Education Center and improved trails. In the Middle Keys, Curry Hammock State Park, considered one of the best kayaking areas in the Keys, opened with a wide beach, bathhouse, and picnic tables.

In Key West, the **Historic Seaport at Key West Bight** officially debuted after a $30 million renovation of the 8.5-acre waterfront area. More than 100 land- and sea-based businesses are now open.

WHAT'S WHERE

The Everglades

"There are no other Everglades in the world," said Marjory Stoneman Douglas in her book *The Everglades: River of Grass.* The noted environmentalist who championed the cause of the Everglades, the 50-mi-wide stream that flows slowly through South Florida grasslands, died in 1998 at the age of 108, with much of her effort yet to be completed. As urban growth continues inland, the Everglades' future will be determined in coming decades. Meanwhile, hundreds of thousands of people visit Everglades National Park each year to see its spectacular beauty. Among its amazing flora and fauna are the manatee, the endangered Florida panther, more than 300 species of birds, and 1,000 kinds of flowering plants. Biscayne National Park, nearby, is the largest national park in the continental United States with living coral reefs.

The Florida Keys

This slender necklace of islands off the southern tip of Florida is strung together by 42 bridges along a 110-mi-long highway. From the underwater splendor of John Pennekamp Coral Reef State Park in the Upper Keys—called one of the world's most traveled-to dive and snorkel destinations—to the spectacular fireball sunsets at Mallory Square docks in Key West, visitors can be at one with nature in the Keys. The pace is slower, the style more casual, and the weather balmy and subtropical. Somehow, Key West manages to maintain its Old Florida charm, despite a wave of new upscale shops, franchise restaurants, and a steady stream of cruise ship passengers. Jimmy Buffett and family have moved to Palm Beach, but Margaritaville is still in Key West.

Fort Lauderdale and Broward County

Fort Lauderdale's 10-year effort to shed its image as a college spring break party town is finally paying off. Today, following a multimillion-dollar construction program, this city north of Miami has been transformed into an upscale destination with trendy shops and restaurants and a pedestrian-friendly beachfront. The hub of activity is along the 2-mi Las Olas corridor, anchored on the west by an arts district and on the east by a beach promenade. Instead of shutting down at 5, Las Olas Boulevard now has so many new sidewalk cafés, coffee shops, jazz clubs, movies, and bookstores that evening parking has become a problem.

Miami and Miami Beach

In the 1980s a stylized television cop show called *Miami Vice* brought notoriety to this southernmost of big Florida cities; South Beach put it on the map again in the 1990s with its revamping of the Art Deco District. At night, the trendy nightclub/restaurant strip along Ocean Drive bustles with a young crowd on the street, bumper-to-bumper cars, and jammed sidewalk cafés. The stomping ground for celebrities, the city has gone from an enclave of retired northeasterners to an international crossroads with a Latin beat. Miami's spice is in its neighborhoods. Don't miss Coconut Grove, the South Florida mainland's oldest settlement. It's chic and casual, full of bistros, cafés, and galleries. The crowded, noisy streets of Little Havana pulsate to the sounds of salsa, in contrast to the quiet, tree- and mansion-lined streets of stately Coral Gables.

Palm Beach and the Treasure Coast

For 100 years high society has made headlines in Palm Beach. Once a playground for the rich and famous (and infamous), Palm Beach County now has attractions for everyone. To keep up with the growing number of residents and visitors, the region is expanding its park system, renourishing its beaches, and improving roadways. From Boca Raton's Mizner Park north to Delray Beach's Atlantic Avenue and West Palm Beach's CityPlace (now under construction), the focus is on bringing people back to downtown. As for roads less traveled, the coast north of Palm Beach County, called the Treasure Coast, is also worth exploring. Comprising Martin, St. Lucie, and Indian River counties, it's dotted with nature preserves, fishing villages, and towns with active cultural scenes.

PLEASURES AND PASTIMES

Beaches

Warm weather and lots of sand make beaching a major South Florida activity. But if life's a beach, how do you find the one that suits you? Beaches in South Florida, from the Keys north to Jupiter, seem to have a personality all their own. At South Beach in Miami, young, in-shape model types often arrive on their in-line skates. Farther north along Miami Beach, you'll find families and foreign visitors. Bill Baggs Cape Florida State Recreation Area, on Key Biscayne, was rated one of the nation's top 20 beaches in 1998 by University of Maryland Professor Stephen Leatherman, also known as Dr. Beach. The wonderfully breezy park is also the site of the historic Cape Florida Lighthouse.

Since shedding its rowdy spring break image, Fort Lauderdale Beach has been reclaimed by families and many foreign visitors. With volleyball and basketball courts and a wide promenade for in-line skaters, it's also known as Workout Beach. Families from as far south as Miami-Dade County visit Boca Raton's Red Reef Park beach for snorkeling. It's an ideal place to introduce children to snorkeling because

the reef is so close to shore; the deepest water around the reef is 8 to 10 ft. Delray's public beach bustles with activity on weekends. After soaking up rays or playing volleyball, the crowd heads to nearby bars and restaurants that cater to beachgoers. If its location you want, Palm Beach Municipal Beach is but a short walk from the swank shops of Worth Avenue. Still farther north in Jupiter, Blowing Rocks Preserve attracts nature lovers. At high tide, you can watch the water rush through blowholes in the rock formations.

Returning south to the Florida Keys, coral reefs and prevailing currents prevent sand from building up. The few Keys beaches are small, narrow, and generally have little or no sandy bottom. An exception is the beach at Bahia Honda State Park, the largest natural sand beach in the Keys. It's a favorite spot for campers.

Although the state owns all beaches below the high-tide line, even in front of hotels and private resorts, gaining access to them can be a problem along much of Florida's coastline. You must pay to enter and/or park at most state, county, and local beachfront parks. Where hotels dominate the beach frontage, public parking may be limited or nonexistent.

Canoeing

The Everglades has areas suitable for flatwater wilderness canoeing that are comparable to spots in the Boundary Waters region of Minnesota. Another popular canoeing river is the Loxahatchee in north Palm Beach County. The river flows through Jonathan Dickinson State Park, where canoe rentals are available. The Florida Department of Environmental Protection provides maps and brochures on 1,550 mi of canoe trails in various parts of the state. Also contact individual city and county park and recreation departments or local chambers of commerce for information on canoe trails. The best time to canoe in Florida is winter—the dry season—when you're less likely to get caught in a torrential downpour or become a snack for mosquitoes.

Dining

South Florida has launched some big-league culinary stars. Restaurateurs like Fort Lauderdale's Mark Militello are nationally acclaimed, while others who got their start here—such as Douglas Rodriguez, formerly of Yuca when it was in Coral Gables—have gone on to glory in Manhattan.

South Florida serves up a diverse assortment of ethnic food. Latin American restaurants offer the distinctive national fare of Argentina, Brazil, Colombia, Cuba, El Salvador, Mexico, Nicaragua, and Puerto Rico, and it's also easy to find island specialties born of the Bahamas, Haiti, and Jamaica. A new fusion of tropical, Continental, and nouvelle cuisine—some call it Floribbean—has gained widespread popularity. It draws on exotic fruits, spices, and fresh seafood. Also in abundance, Asian cuisine no longer means just Chinese. Indian, Japanese, Pakistani, Thai, and Vietnamese specialties are now available. Continental cuisine (French, German, Italian, Spanish, and Swiss) is also well represented.

The region also has a high concentration of good waterfront restaurants—popular with both locals and visitors. Most menus are built around fresh seafood from local waters. They range from elegant, very pricy dining spots to casual, moderate-priced digs anchored next to fishing docks.

Every South Florida restaurant claims to make the best key lime pie. Pastry chefs and restaurant managers take the matter very seriously—they discuss the problems of getting good lime juice and maintaining top quality every day. Joe's Stone Crab in Miami Beach, for example, bakes nearly 30,000 pies annually, and key lime pie has been a staple on its menu for nearly all of the restaurant's 86 years. Traditional key lime pie is yellow, not green, with an old-fashioned graham cracker crust and meringue top. The filling should be tart and chilled but not frozen. Some restaurants make their pie with a pastry crust; most substitute whipped cream for the more temperamental meringue. Each pie will be a little different. Try several. After all, you're on vacation.

Fishing

Opportunities for saltwater fishing abound from the Keys all the way up the southeast Florida coast. Many seaside communities have municipal fishing piers that charge a modest admission to anglers (and usually a lower rate to spectators). These piers generally have a bait-and-tackle shop. It's also easy to find a boat-charter service that will take you out into deep water. Some of the best are in Islamorada, Marathon, and Key West in the Florida Keys, but popular charter fleets are also located at Fort Lauderdale's Bahia Mar docks, at the Hillsboro Inlet in north Broward County, and at the Boynton Beach inlet in Palm Beach County. Depending on your taste, budget, and needs, you can charter anything from an old wooden craft to a luxurious waterborne palace with state-of-the-art amenities.

For freshwater anglers, there's 448,000-acre Lake Okeechobee, the third-largest natural lake in the United States—home to bass, bluegill, speckled perch, and succulent catfish (which the locals call "sharpies"). In addition, parts of the Everglades in Palm Beach, Broward, and Miami-Dade counties are famed as the "river of bass." The best fishing here is found in the "flats," where canals turn into shallow, vegetation-filled marshes, a haven for bass. Many fishing camps on the fringes of the Everglades have guides for hire.

Golf

Except in the heart of the Everglades, you'll never be far from one of South Florida's golf courses. Palm Beach County, the state's leading golf locale, has 150 courses. Many of the best courses allow visitors to play without being members or hotel guests.

During the winter season, you should reserve tee times in advance. Ask about golf reservations when you make your lodging reservations.

Natural Areas

Although Florida is the fourth-most-populous state in the nation, more than 10 million acres of public and private recreation facilities are set aside in national forests, parks, monuments, reserves, and seashores; state forests and parks; county parks; and nature preserves owned and managed by private conservation groups. An active greenways development plan seeks to protect wildlife habitat as much as foster recreation.

On holidays and weekends crowds flock to the most popular parks—some on islands that are accessible only by boat. Come early or risk being turned away. Winter brings flocks of northern migratory birds along with migrating humans. Many resident species breed in the warm summer months, but others (such as the wood stork) time their breeding cycle to the winter dry season. Although mosquitoes are voracious and daily afternoon thundershowers add to the humidity in summer, it's during the early part of this season that sea turtles come ashore to lay their eggs and you're most likely to see frigate birds and other tropical species.

Pari-Mutuel Sports

South Florida has a variety of venues for sports on which you can lawfully bet. These include greyhound tracks, tracks for harness and Thoroughbred racing, and jai alai frontons.

Scuba Diving and Snorkeling

South Florida, and especially the Keys, attracts most of the state's divers and snorkelers. A multitude of dive shops schedule drift-, reef-, and wreck-diving trips all along the coast. The low-tech pleasures of snorkeling can be enjoyed throughout the Keys and elsewhere where shallow reefs hug the shore.

Shopping

ANTIQUES➤ Antiques lovers should explore U.S. 1 north of Dania Beach Boulevard in Dania, with its more than 150 shops; Southwest 28th Lane and Unity Boulevard in Miami, near the Coconut Grove Metrorail station; and the cluster of stores on South Dixie Highway in West Palm Beach.

CITRUS FRUIT➤ Fresh citrus is available most of the year, except in summer. Two kinds of citrus grow in Florida: the sweeter and more expensive Indian River fruit, from a thin ribbon of groves along the east coast, and the less costly fruit from the interior, south and west of Lake Okeechobee. A visit to a local grove can be a pleasant experience; many in western Broward and Palm Beach counties offer tours and educational programs.

Citrus is sold in ¼, ½, ¾, and full bushels. Many shippers offer special gift packages with several varieties of fruit, jellies, and other food items. Some prices include U.S. postage; others may not. Shipping may exceed the cost of the fruit. If you have a choice of citrus packaged in boxes or bags, take the boxes. They are easier to label and harder to squash.

NATIVE AMERICAN CRAFTS➤ Native American crafts are abundant in South Florida, where you'll find billowing dresses and shirts hand-sewn in striking colors and designs, handcrafted dolls, and beaded belts.

SEASHELLS➤ Shell shops, selling mostly kitschy items, abound throughout South Florida. The coral and other shells sold in the Florida Keys have been imported for sale because of restrictions on harvesting these materials.

FODOR'S CHOICE

Beaches

★ **Bahia Honda State Park, Bahia Honda Key.** Bahia Honda translates from Spanish as "deep bay," a good description of the waters surrounding this park with a natural sandy beach, unusual in the Keys. The beach extends on both gulf and ocean sides, and activities in the park abound, from hawk-watching to hiking. It's also a popular spot for weddings.

★ **Bill Baggs Cape Florida State Recreation Area, Key Biscayne.** After a $10 million restoration project, Cape Florida's 400-plus acres have been replanted with native vegetation. New fishing piers have been added, and a nature path is popular with bikers, skaters and parents pushing strollers. The beach is constantly buffeted by warm breezes and boasts a plethora of facilities, a historic lighthouse, and great views of sunsets and the Miami skyline.

★ **Fort Lauderdale Beach.** The area along Route A1A between Las Olas and Sunrise boulevards is a hot spot again, thanks to a pedestrian-friendly promenade and the absence of spring breakers. It's mostly frequented by families and foreign visitors.

★ **Spanish River Park, Boca Raton.** The renourished beach is connected to a large park by pedestrian tunnels under Route A1A. Filled with native vegetation, the park has nature trails and plenty of picnic tables and grills.

Comforts

★ **The Breakers, Palm Beach.** The building, originally built over a century ago to resemble an opulent Italian Renaissance palace, is remarkable, as is the resort's ability to balance old-world luxury with modern conveniences. Guest rooms have been recently renovated. $$$$

☆ **Delano Hotel, Miami Beach.** An air of surrealism hangs about this much-talked-about SoBe hotel, *the* hot spot for celebrities and other well-to-do visitors. $$$$

☆ **Little Palm Island.** On its own palm-fringed island 3 mi off the shores of Little Torch Key, this dazzling resort of thatch-roof villas on stilts provides a secluded, one-of-a-kind experience you could only have in the Keys. $$$$

☆ **La Casa Del Mar, Fort Lauderdale.** Bed-and-breakfasts are rare in Broward County, but this one located near the beach is a gem. $$

Flavors

☆ **Norman's, Coral Gables.** Chef Norman Van Aken turns out artful masterpieces of New World cuisine, combining bold tastes from Latin, American, Caribbean, and Asian traditions. $$$$

☆ **Cafe des Artistes, Key West.** Chef Andrew Berman's brilliant tropical version of French cuisine is served in a series of intimate dining rooms filled with tropical art and an upstairs outdoor patio. $$$–$$$$

☆ **Café L'Europe, Palm Beach.** You'd expect to find elegant dining in Palm Beach, and this doesn't disappoint. It's one of the area's most popular restaurants, noted for its European fine-dining experience and mood-setting atmosphere. $$$–$$$$

☆ **Mark's Las Olas, Fort Lauderdale.** Chef/owner Mark Militello offers dazzling Florida-style creations, adding flavors from the Mediterranean, Caribbean, and Southwest. Mark's latest outpost is at Mizner Park in Boca Raton. $$–$$$

☆ **Armadillo Cafe, Davie.** The atmosphere is as creative and fun as the award-winning southwestern-style South Florida seafood. $$

☆ **Tom's Place, Boca Raton.** Tom Wright serves up legendary barbecue ribs, friendly service, and moderate prices at this local landmark. $

Views

☆ **Everglades National Park from the tower on Shark Valley Loop.** This 50-ft observation tower yields a splendid panorama of the wide River of Grass as it sweeps southward toward the Gulf of Mexico.

☆ **Ocean Drive in the Art Deco District, Miami Beach.** Feast your eyes on brilliantly restored vintage Art Deco hotels at every turn. Since its restoration, this palm-lined beachfront has been hopping 24 hours a day.

☆ **Seven Mile Bridge, Marathon.** One of the world's longest, this Middle Keys bridge lifts you above the shimmering waters of ocean and bay, providing a spectacular blend of color and light. The only time it's closed to vehicles and open to pedestrians is during the Seven Mile Bridge Run in April.

☆ **Sunset scene at Mallory Square, Key West.** Here sunset draws street performers, vendors, and thousands of onlookers to Mallory Dock and the eponymous square nearby.

Historic Sites and Museums

☆ **Flagler Museum, Palm Beach.** Henry Flagler, the Standard Oil magnate, built Whitehall in 1901 as a gift for his wife. The building has been restored, and visitors can now get a glimpse of Palm Beach's gilded age. Also on the grounds is Flagler's private railroad car, refurbished in 1967.

☆ **Hemingway House, Key West.** The home where Ernest Hemingway wrote several of his famous novels remains Key West's most popular attraction.

☆ **Morikami Museum and Japanese Gardens, Delray Beach.** The leading U.S. center for Japanese and American cultural exchange is housed in a model of a Japanese imperial villa. On display is a permanent exhibition on the area's Yamato Colony, a turn-of-the-century settlement of immigrant Japanese farmers.

☆ **Museum of Discovery and Science, Fort Lauderdale.** Providing hands-on experiences, this playground for kids (and adults) contains fun, interactive exhibits on ecology, health, and other sciences.

☆ **Vizcaya Museum and Gardens, Coconut Grove.** The estate of industrialist James Deering, overlooking Biscayne Bay, has an Italian Renaissance–style villa containing Renaissance, Baroque, Rococo, and Neoclassical art and furniture.

FESTIVALS AND SEASONAL EVENTS

➤ DEC.: Lighted boat parades are common throughout South Florida during the holiday season. The biggest is the **Winterfest Boat Parade** on the Intracoastal Waterway, Fort Lauderdale (☎ 954/767–0686). In Key West, the Heritage House Museum holds a free **Christmas House Tour** late in the month (☎ 305/296–3573).

➤ JAN.: Early in the month, **Polo Season** opens at the Palm Beach Polo and Country Club (☎ 561/793–1440). Mid-month, **Art Deco Weekend** spotlights Miami Beach's historic district with an Art Deco street fair, a 1930s-style Moon Over Miami Ball, live entertainment, and tours of the district (☎ 305/672–2014). **Martin Luther King Jr. Festivals** are celebrated throughout South Florida, including Hollywood (☎ 954/921–3404). **Taste of the Grove Food and Music Festival** is a popular fund-raiser put on in Coconut Grove's Peacock Park by area restaurants (☎ 305/444–7270). The **South Florida Folk Festival** features national acts at Easterlin Park in Fort Lauderdale (☎ 954/384–2197). In late January, **Miami Rivers Blues Festival** takes place on the south bank of the river next to Tobacco Road (☎ 305/374–1198).

➤ FEB.: The **Coconut Grove Art Festival,** mid-month, is the state's largest, drawing nearly a million folks to the four-day event (☎ 305/447–0401). The **Miami Film Festival,** sponsored by the Film Society of America, is 10 days of international, domestic, and local films (☎ 305/377–3456). **Seminole Tribal Festival** draws participants from many tribes to Hollywood for a weekend of competitions and traditional dance and music (☎ 954/966–6300). **Florida Renaissance Festival,** in Hollywood, features jousting, human chess matches, and 600 costumed performers (☎ 954/776–1642).

➤ FEB.–MAR.: The **Winter Equestrian Festival,** at the Palm Beach Polo and Country Club in West Palm Beach, includes more than 1,000 horses and three grand-prix equestrian events (☎ 561/798–7000).

➤ MAR.: **Calle Ocho's street festival**—a celebration of Cuban life and culture—has become Miami's biggest (☎ 305/644–8888). The **Las Olas Art Festival** has been a fixture in downtown Fort Lauderdale for more than 25 years (☎ 954/525–5500). Taste some of the best food from Upper Keys restaurants at the

Taste of the Keys Bird Bash, a fund-raiser for the Florida Keys Wild Bird Rehabilitation Center, in Key Largo (☎ 305/453–9643). Boynton Beach's **G.A.L.A.** (Great American Love Affair) is a mid-month weekend of art and entertainment (☎ 561/742–6243).

➤ APR.: The **Delray Affair,** in early April, is the biggest event in the area and features arts, crafts, and food (☎ 561/278–0424). Near the end of the month, the **River Cities Festival,** a three-day event in Miami Springs and Hialeah, focuses attention on the Miami River and the need to keep it clean (☎ 305/887–1515). Downtown West Palm Beach rocks with music and fireworks during **SunFest,** a weekend-long street party (☎ 561/659–5980 or 800/786–3378).

➤ LATE APR.–EARLY MAY: The 10-day **Conch Republic Celebration** honors the founding fathers of the Conch Republic, "the small island nation of Key West" (☎ 305/296–8803).

➤ MAY: The **Air & Sea Show** draws more than 2 million to the Fort Lauderdale beachfront for a weekend of performances by big names in aviation, such as the navy's Blue Angels and the air force's Thunderbirds (☎ 954/467–3555). In mid-May, the **Arabian Nights Festival,** in Opa-locka, is a mix of contemporary and fantasy-inspired entertainment (☎ 305/758–4166).

➤ JUNE: The **Miami-Bahamas Goombay Festival,** in Miami's Coconut Grove, celebrates the city's Bahamian heritage the first weekend of the month (☎ 305/443–7928 or 305/372–9966).

➤ JULY: The **Fourth of July Festival,** on the Florida Atlantic University grounds in Boca Raton, features a concert by the Boca Pops, lots of tailgate parties, and, of course, fireworks (☎ 561/393–7806). For more than 20 years, the **Roots Cultural Festival,** at Pompey Park

in Delray Beach, has celebrated black pride and heritage (☎ 561/276–2099).

➤ OCT.: The **Fort Lauderdale International Boat Show,** the world's largest show based on exhibit size, displays boats of every size, price, and description at the Bahia Mar marina and four other venues (☎ 954/764–7642). The **Fort Lauderdale International Film Festival** showcases independent cinema from around the world (☎ 954/563–0500). **Fantasy Fest,**

in Key West, is a no-holds-barred Halloween costume party, parade, and town fair (☎ 305/296–1817).

➤ NOV.: The **Miami Book Fair International,** the largest book fair in the United States, is held on the Wolfson campus of Miami-Dade Community College (☎ 305/237–3258).

➤ EARLY NOV.–LATE FEB.: The **Orange Bowl** and **Junior Orange Bowl Festival,** in the Miami area, are best known for the King Orange Jamboree Parade and the Orange Bowl Football Classic (now played at ProPlayer Stadium) but also include more than 20 youth-oriented events (☎ 305/371–3351).

2 MIAMI AND MIAMI BEACH

Miami is arguably the most exotic city that Americans can visit without a passport. On a typical evening in South Beach, you'll witness the energy and passion of Rio, Monte Carlo, Havana, and Hemingway's Paris. Other neighborhoods also bring the world into clearer focus through diverse architecture, dining, and customs, sparking a renaissance for Miami and its sultry sister, Miami Beach, that's reminiscent of the cities' glory days in the 1920s.

Updated by
Gary
McKechnie

MIAMI IS DIFFERENT from any other city in America—or any city in Latin America for that matter, though it has a distinctly Latin flavor. Both logically and geologically, Miami shouldn't even be here. Resting on a paved swamp between the Everglades and the Atlantic Ocean, the city is subject to periodic flooding, riots, hurricanes, and the onslaught of swallow-size mosquitoes. Despite the downsides, however, Miami is a vibrant city that works and plays with vigor.

The Tequesta Indians called this area home long before Spain's gold-laden treasure ships sailed along the Gulf Stream a few miles offshore. Foreshadowing 20th-century corporations, they traded with mainland neighbors to the north and island brethren to the south. Today their descendants are the 150-plus U.S. and multinational companies whose Latin American headquarters are based in Greater Miami. For fans of international business and random statistics, Greater Miami is home to more than 40 foreign bank agencies, 11 Edge Act banks, 23 foreign trade offices, 31 binational chambers of commerce, and 53 foreign consulates.

For tourists, far more intriguing is Miami's developing profile as a cruise-ship port. Miami's six cruise lines and 21 cruise ships wisely avoid those pesky icebergs by carrying more than 3 million passengers a year to the sunny Caribbean and on over to Mexico. And if you've ever dreamed of traveling aboard a tramp steamer, head to the docks, and you'll also find a flood of cargo freighters. It's no surprise that more than 40% of all U.S. exports to South America, Central America, and the Caribbean travel through the Miami Customs District. Miami is the U.S. gateway to the southern hemisphere.

The city has seen a decade of big changes. In the late 1980s Miami Beach was an ocean-side geriatric ward. Today's South Beach residents have the kind of hip that doesn't break. The average age dropped from the mid-sixties in 1980 to a youthful early forties today. Toned young men outnumber svelte young women 2 to 1, and hormones are as plentiful as pierced tongues. At night the revitalized Lincoln Road Mall is in full swing with cafés and galleries and theaters, but it is also suffering vacancies due to rapidly rising rents. The bloom may not be off the rose, but cash-crazy entrepreneurs hoping to strike it rich on Miami's popularity are finding the pie isn't large enough to feed their financial fantasies. Those who have seen how high rents can crush a dream are heading to North Beach and the southern neighborhoods of South Beach, whose derelict buildings are a flashback to the pre-renaissance days of the 1980s. Perhaps this is where the next revival will take place (file this under insider information).

As you plan your trip, know that winter *is* the best time to visit, but if money is an issue, come in the off-season—after Easter and before October. You'll find plenty to do, and room rates are considerably lower. Summer brings many European and Latin American vacationers, who find Miami congenial despite the heat, humidity, and intense afternoon thunderstorms.

Regardless of when you arrive, once you're here, you'll suspect that you've entered Cuban air space. No matter where you spin your radio dial, virtually every announcer punctuates each sentence with an emphatic "COO-BAH!" Look around, and you'll see Spanish on billboards, hear it on elevators, and pick it up on the streets. But Miami sways to more than just a Latin beat. *Newsweek* called the city "America's

Casablanca," and it may be right. In addition to populations from Brazil, Colombia, El Salvador, Haiti, Jamaica, Nicaragua, Panama, Puerto Rico, Venezuela, and of course Cuba, there are also representatives from China, Germany, Greece, Iran, Israel, Italy, Lebanon, Malaysia, Russia, and Sweden—all speaking a veritable babel of tongues. Miami has accepted its montage of nationalities, and it now celebrates this cultural diversity through languages, festivals, world-beat music, and a wealth of exotic restaurants.

If you're concerned about Miami crime, you'll be glad to know that criminals are off the street—and seem to be running for public office. Forget about D.C. If you want weird politics, spread out a blanket and enjoy the show. Mayor Xavier Suarez was removed from office in March 1998 after a judge threw out absentee ballots that included votes from dead people. The Miami City Commission chairman was also removed following a voter fraud conviction, and a state senator was re-elected despite being under indictment for pocketing profits from sham home-health-care companies.

Corrupt politicians aside, Miami has its share of the same crimes that plague any major city. However, you'll be happy to know that the widely publicized crimes against tourists of the early '90s led to stepped-up and effective visitor-safety programs. Highway direction signs with red-sunburst logos are installed at ¼-mi intervals on major roads and lead directly to such tourist hot spots as Coconut Grove, Coral Gables, South Beach, and the Port of Miami. Patrol cars bearing the sunburst logo are driven by TOP (Tourist Oriented Police) Cops, who cruise heavily touristed areas and add a sense of safety. Identification that made rental cars conspicuous to would-be criminals has been removed, and multilingual pamphlets on avoiding crime are widely distributed. The precautions have had a positive impact. From 1992 to 1998 the number of tourist robberies in Greater Miami decreased more than 80%.

What *is* on the increase is Miami's film profile. In recent years Arnold Schwarzenegger and Jamie Lee Curtis filmed *True Lies* here, Al Pacino and Johnny Depp dropped by to shoot scenes for *Donnie Brasco*, Jim Carrey rose to stardom through the Miami-based *Ace Ventura: Pet Detective*, Robin Williams and Nathan Lane used two Deco buildings on Ocean Drive as their nightclub in *The Birdcage*, and Cameron Diaz discovered a new brand of hair gel in *There's Something About Mary*. All in all, it's a far cry from when Esther Williams used to perform water ballet in Coral Gables' Venetian Pool. Add to this mix daily fashion-magazine and TV shoots, and you'll see that Miami is made for the media.

It may be this synergy that prompted a slew of international celebrities to move or purchase homes here. Although Madonna and Sylvester Stallone are selling their houses, Al Pacino, Michael Caine, and Whitney Houston are here now. Three major-league sports franchises call Miami home, along with the Doral-Ryder Open Tournament, the Lipton Championships, and the culture-contributing Miami City Ballet and Florida Grand Opera. Miami played host to the Summit of the Americas in 1994 and to the Super Bowl in 1999. Nearly 10 million tourists arrive annually to see what's shaking in Miami-Dade County and discover a multicultural metropolis that invites the world to celebrate its diversity.

New and Noteworthy

There's so much construction going on in Miami, you'd suspect they're trying to tear down the town and put up a city. Tool belts are nearly as prevalent as bikinis, and building sounds echo everywhere.

One of the most noteworthy arrivals is the new **American Airlines Arena,** which sits downtown on Biscayne Bay near the entrance to the Port of Miami. Scheduled to open on December 31, 1999, this will be the new home of the NBA's Miami Heat. Up Biscayne Boulevard, the **Freedom Tower,** one of downtown's most prominent landmarks, is being restored by the Cuban American National Foundation to house its museum. **Parrot Jungle** is destined to give up its South Miami location for digs near Watson Island by the Port of Miami. The move is scheduled for mid-2000, although the date has changed several times.

The **Royal Palm Crowne Plaza Resort** is being promoted as the first African-American majority–owned four-star convention hotel in the United States. Planned for the spring of 2000, the 422-room, two-tower Collins Avenue hotel (near the new Loews) was designed by Arquitectonica, an internationally known Miami architectural firm. Over in the financial district, on Brickell Avenue, the new 21-story, $60 million **J. W. Marriott Hotel** is supposed to open in fall 1999, although early 2000 seems more likely. A new **Ritz-Carlton** may arrive in Coconut Grove by the end of 2000. Their next project is in SoBe, where $95 million will be poured into the less-than-impressive DiLido to bring it up to Ritz standards.

The **Dolphin Mall,** west of the Miami airport, expects to be open by fall 2000. If you're wondering what $250 million buys these days, it's 1.4 million square ft of retail outlets, theme restaurants, cafés, nightclubs, a 30-screen theater, and an amusement park. In South Miami the **Shops at Sunset Place** opened in the spring of 1999. Mighty impressive entryways, winding paths, and a variety of retailers make this the Main Street of the 21st century.

Pleasures and Pastimes

Beaches

Greater Miami has numerous free beaches to fit every style. A sandy, 300-ft-wide beach with several distinct sections extends for 10 mi from the foot of Miami Beach north to Haulover Beach Park. Amazingly, it's all man-made. Seriously eroded during the mid-1970s, the beach was restored in a $51.5 million project between 1977 and 1981 and remains an ongoing project for environmental engineers, who spiff up the sands every few years. Between 23rd and 44th streets, Miami Beach built boardwalks and protective walkways atop a dune landscaped with sea oats, sea grape, and other native plants whose roots keep the sand from blowing away. Farther north there's even a nude beach, and Key Biscayne adds more great strands to Miami's collection. Even if the Deco District didn't exist, the area's beaches would be enough to satisfy tourists.

Boating

It's not uncommon for traffic to jam at boat ramps, especially on weekend mornings, but the waters are worth the wait. If you have the opportunity to sail, do so. Blue skies, calm seas, and a view of the city skyline make for a pleasurable outing—especially at twilight, when the fabled "moon over Miami" casts a soft glow on the water. Key Biscayne's calm waves and strong breezes are perfect for sailing and windsurfing, and though Dinner Key and the Coconut Grove waterfront remain the center of sailing in Greater Miami, sailboat moorings and rentals sit along other parts of the bay and up the Miami River.

Miami's idle rich prefer attacking the water in sleek, fast, and nicotine-free cigarette boats, but there's plenty of less powerful powerboating to enjoy as well. Greater Miami has numerous marinas, and dockmasters can provide information on any marine services you may need. Ask for *Teall's Tides and Guides, Miami-Dade County,* and other nautical publications.

Dining

Miami cuisine is what mouths were made for. The city serves up a veritable United Nations of dining experiences, including dishes native to Spain, Cuba, and Nicaragua as well as China, India, Thailand, Vietnam, and other Asian cultures. Chefs from the tropics combine fresh, natural foods—especially seafood—with classic island-style dishes, creating a new American cuisine that is sometimes called Floribbean. Another style finding its way around U.S. restaurants is the Miami-born New World cuisine. The title comes from chefs who realized their latest creations were based on ingredients found along the trade routes discovered by early explorers of the "New World."

Nightlife

Miami has more clubs than a deck of cards, but the ones that command the most attention are those where people pose with less expression than Mona Lisa and where mirrored balls salvaged from the set of *Saturday Night Fever* spin as fast as the techno-pop CDs.

The heaviest concentration of these nightspots is in South Beach along Ocean Drive, Washington Avenue, and Lincoln Road Mall. Other nightlife centers on Little Havana, Coconut Grove, and the fringes of downtown Miami. Clubs offer jazz, reggae, salsa, various forms of rock, disco, and Top 40 sounds on different nights of the week—most played at a body-thumping, ear-throbbing volume. If you prefer to hear what people are saying, look for small lobby bars in Art Deco hotels. Throughout Greater Miami, bars and cocktail lounges in larger hotels operate nightly discos with live weekend entertainment. Many hotels extend their bars into open-air courtyards, where patrons dine and dance under the stars throughout the year. Some clubs refuse entrance to anyone under 21, others to those under 25, so if that is a concern, call ahead. It's also a good idea to ask in advance about cover charges; policies change frequently. And be warned: Even the most popular club can fall out of favor quickly. Ask your hotel's concierge, check Friday's *Miami Herald,* or grab a copy of *New Times,* an entertainment tabloid that includes listings of alternative clubs and live bands. With this and some insider info from locals, you should be able to tell what's hot and what's just a dying ember.

Spectator Sports

Greater Miami has franchises in basketball, football, and baseball. Thanks to Dan Marino's record-breaking accomplishments, fans still turn out en masse for the Dolphins, as they do for basketball's Heat and the 1997 World Series champion Marlins. Miami also hosts top-rated events in boat racing, jai alai, and tennis. Generally you can find daily listings of local events in the sports section of the *Miami Herald,* while Friday's "Weekend" section carries more detailed schedules and coverage.

Activities of the annual Orange Bowl and Junior Orange Bowl Festival take place from early November until well into the new year. Best known for its King Orange Jamboree Parade and the Federal Express/Orange Bowl Football Classic, the festival also includes two tennis tournaments. The Junior Orange Bowl Festival is the world's largest youth festival, with more than 20 events between November and January, including sports, cultural, and performing arts activities held throughout Miami-Dade County.

EXPLORING MIAMI AND MIAMI BEACH

If you had arrived here 40 years ago with Fodor's guide in hand, chances are you'd be thumbing through listings looking for alligator wrestlers and u-pick citrus groves. Well, things have changed. While Disney sidetracked families in Orlando, Miami was developing a grown-up attitude courtesy of *Miami Vice,* European fashion photographers, and historic preservationists. Nowadays the wildest ride is the city itself.

Climb aboard and check out the different sides of Greater Miami. Miami, on the mainland, is South Florida's commercial hub, while its sultry sister, Miami Beach (America's Riviera), encompasses 17 islands in Biscayne Bay. Seducing winter refugees with its warm sunshine, sandy beaches, shady palms, and ever-rocking nightlife, this is what most people envision when planning a trip to a trip to what they think of as Miami. These same visitors fail to realize that there's more to Miami Beach than the bustle of South Beach and its Deco District. Indeed there are quieter areas to the north, with names like Sunny Isles, Surfside, Bal Harbour, and—you guessed it—North Beach.

During the day downtown Miami has become the lively hub of the mainland city, now more accessible thanks to the Metromover extension (☞ Getting Around by Train *in* Miami and Miami Beach A to Z, *below*). Other major attractions include Coconut Grove, Coral Gables, Little Havana, and, of course, the South Beach/Art Deco District, but since these areas are spread out beyond the reach of public transportation, you'll have to drive. Rent a convertible if you can. There's nothing quite like wearing cool shades and feeling the wind in your hair as you drive across one of the causeways en route to Miami Beach. Take precautions if you wear a rug.

You're in luck: Finding your way around Greater Miami is easy if you know how the numbering system works—just as quantum mechanics is easy for physicists. Miami is laid out on a grid with four quadrants—northeast, northwest, southeast, and southwest—which meet at Miami Avenue and Flagler Street. Miami Avenue separates east from west, and Flagler Street separates north from south. Avenues and courts run north–south; streets, terraces, and ways run east–west. Roads run diagonally, northwest–southeast. But other districts—Miami Beach, Coral Gables, and Hialeah—may or may not follow this system, and along the curve of Biscayne Bay, the symmetrical grid may shift diagonally. It's best to buy a detailed map, stick to the major roads, and ask directions early and often. However, make sure you're in a safe neighborhood or public place when you seek guidance; cabbies and cops are good resources.

Numbers in the text correspond to numbers in the margin and on the Miami Beach; Downtown Miami; Miami, Coral Gables, Coconut Grove, and Key Biscayne; and South Dade maps.

Great Itineraries

IF YOU HAVE 3 DAYS

To recuperate from your journey, grab your lotion and head to the ocean, more specifically Ocean Drive on South Beach, where you can catch some rays while relaxing on the white sands. Afterward, take a guided or self-guided tour of the Art Deco District to see what all the fuss is about. Keep the evening free to socialize with the oh-so-trendy people who gather at Ocean Drive cafés. The following day drive through Little Havana to witness the heartbeat of Miami's Cuban culture (and snag a stogie) on your way south to Coconut Grove's Vizcaya. Wrap up the evening a few blocks away in Coconut Grove, enjoying its partylike atmosphere and many nightspots. On the last day head over to Coral Gables to take in the eye-popping display of 1920s Mediterranean Revival architecture in the neighborhoods surrounding the city center and the majestic Biltmore Hotel; then take a dip in the fantastic thematic Venetian Pool. That night indulge in an evening of fine dining at your choice of gourmet restaurants in Coral Gables.

IF YOU HAVE 5 DAYS

Follow the suggested three-day itinerary, and on day 4 add a visit to the beaches of Virginia Key and Key Biscayne, where you can take a diving trip or fishing excursion, learn to windsurf, or do absolutely nothing but watch the water. On day 5 step back to the 1950s with a cruise up Collins Avenue to some of the monolithic hotels, such as the Fontainebleau Hilton and Eden Roc; continue north to the swank shops of Bal Harbour; and return to South Beach for an evening of shopping, drinking, and outdoor dining at Lincoln Road Mall.

IF YOU HAVE 7 DAYS

A week gives you just enough time to experience fully the multicultural, cosmopolitan, tropical mélange that is Greater Miami and its beaches. On day 6 see where it all began. Use the Miami Metromover to ride above downtown Miami before touring the streets (if possible, on a tour with historian Dr. Paul George). Take time to visit the Miami-Dade Cultural Center, home of art and history museums. In the evening check out the shops and clubs at Bayside Marketplace. The final day can be used to visit South Miami, site of Parrot Jungle (for now), Fairchild Tropical Garden, and the new, commercial Shops at Sunset Place. Keep the evening free to revisit your favorite nightspots and get jiggy with your new pals, Madonna and Will Smith.

South Beach/Miami Beach

The hub of Miami Beach is South Beach (SoBe, to the truly hip), and the hub of South Beach is the 1-square-mi Art Deco District, fronted on the east by Ocean Drive and on the west by Alton Road. The story of South Beach has become the story of Miami. In the early 1980s South Beach's vintage hotels were badly run down, catering mostly to infirm retirees. But a group of visionaries led by Barbara Baer Capitman, a spirited New York transplant, saw this collection of buildings as an architectural treasure to be salvaged from a sea of mindless urban renewal. It was, and is, a peerless grouping of Art Deco architecture from the 1920s to 1950s, whose forms and decorative details are drawn from nature, the streamlined shapes of modern transportation and industrial machinery, and human extravagance.

Investors started fixing up the interiors of these hotels and repainting their exteriors with a vibrant pastel palette—a look made famous by *Miami Vice*. International bistro operators sensed the potential for a new café society. Fashion photographers and the media took note, and celebrities like singer Gloria Estefan; the late designer Gianni Versace, whose fashions captured the feel of the awakening city; and record executive Chris Blackwell bought a piece of the action.

As a result, South Beach now holds the distinction of being the nation's first 20th-century district on the National Register of Historic Places, with more than 800 significant buildings making the roll. But it hasn't all been smooth. Miami officials seem to lack the gene enabling them to appreciate residents who help the city. Barbara Capitman was well into her sixties when she stepped in front of bulldozers ready to tear down the Senator, a Deco hotel. Her reward for helping to save the

Deco District and laying the groundwork for a multibillion-dollar tourist trade is a side street named in her honor.

More recently, SoBe hoteliers were similarly rewarded for successfully renovating old or abandoned buildings by having their taxes quadrupled—an attempt by the local government to make up for the lack of tax revenues generated in other areas of Miami-Dade County. Nevertheless, SoBe continues to roll 24 hours a day. Photographers pose beautiful models for shoots, tanned skaters zip past palm trees, and tourists flock to see the action.

Yet Miami Beach is more than just SoBe. (The northern edge of South Beach is generally considered to be around 24th–28th streets, while Miami Beach itself extends well north.) It also consists of a collection of quiet neighborhoods where Little Leaguers play ball, senior citizens stand at bus stops, and locals do their shopping away from the prying eyes of visitors. Surprisingly, Miami Beach is a great walking town in the middle of a great city.

Several things are plentiful in SoBe: pierced body parts, cell phones, and meter maids. Tickets are given freely when meters expire, and towing charges are high. Check the meter to see when parking fees are required; times vary by district. From mid-morning on, parking is scarce along Ocean Drive. You'll do better on Collins or Washington avenues, the next two streets to the west. Fortunately, there are several surface parking lots south and west of the Jackie Gleason Theater, on 17th Street, and parking garages on Collins Avenue at 7th and 13th streets, on Washington Avenue at 12th Street, and west of Washington at 17th Street. Keep these sites in mind, especially at night, when cruising traffic makes it best to park your car and see SoBe on foot.

A Good Walk

The stretch of Ocean Drive from 1st to 23rd streets—primarily the 10-block stretch from 5th to 15th streets—has become the most talked-about beachfront in America. A bevy of Art Deco jewels hug the drive, while across the street lies palm-fringed **Lummus Park** ①, whose south end is a good starting point for a walk. Beginning early (at 8) gives you the pleasure of watching the awakening city without distraction. Sanitation men hose down dirty streets, merchants prepare window displays, bakers bake, and construction workers change the skyline one brick at a time. Cross to the west side of Ocean Drive, where there are many sidewalk cafés, and walk north, taking note of the Park Central Hotel, built in 1937 by Deco architect Henry Hohauser.

At 10th Street recross Ocean Drive to the beach side and visit the **Art Deco District Welcome Center** ② in the 1950s-era Oceanfront Auditorium. Here you can rent tapes or hire a guide for a Deco District tour.

Look back across Ocean Drive and take a look at the wonderful flying-saucer architecture of the Clevelander, at No. 1020. On the next block you'll see the late Gianni Versace's Spanish Mediterranean **Amsterdam Palace** ③. Graceful fluted columns stand guard at the Leslie (No. 1244) and **The Carlyle** ④. A few doors down, at No. 1300, is the Cardozo (☞ Lodging, *below*), which was recently brought up to super snuff by Miami icon/hotelier Gloria Estefan and her man, Emilio.

Walk two blocks west (away from the ocean) on 13th Street to Washington Avenue, where a mix of chic restaurants, avant-garde shops, delicatessens, produce markets, and nightclubs have spiced up a once-derelict neighborhood. Turn left on Washington and walk 2½ blocks south to the **Wolfsonian–FIU Foundation Gallery** ⑤, which showcases artistic movements from 1885 to 1945.

Provided you haven't spent too long in the museum, return north on Washington Avenue past 14th Street, and turn left on **Espanola Way** ⑥, a narrow street of Mediterranean Revival buildings, eclectic shops, and a weekend market. Continue west to Meridian Avenue and turn right. Three blocks north of Espanola Way is the redesigned **Lincoln Road Mall** ⑦, which is often paired with Ocean Drive as part of must-see South Beach.

The next main street north of Lincoln Road is 17th Street, and to the east is the Miami Beach Convention Center. Walk behind the massive building to the corner of Meridian Avenue and 19th Street to see the chilling **Holocaust Memorial** ⑧, a monumental record honoring the 6 million Jewish victims of the Holocaust.

Head east and return to Ocean Drive in time to pull up a chair at an outdoor café, order an espresso, and settle down for an evening of people-watching, SoBe's most popular pastime. If you've seen enough people, grab some late rays at one of the area's beaches, which offer different sands for different tans. You can go back to Lummus Park (*the* beach) or head north, where there's a boardwalk for walking but no allowance for skates and bicycles.

TIMING

To see only the Art Deco buildings on Ocean Drive, allow one hour minimum. Depending on your interests, schedule at least five hours and include a drink or meal at a café and browsing time in the shops on Ocean Drive, along Espanola Way, and at Lincoln Road Mall.

Start your walking tour as early in the day as possible. In winter the street becomes crowded as the day wears on, and in summer, afternoon heat and humidity can be unbearable, wilting even the hardiest soul. Finishing by mid-afternoon also enables you to hit the beach and cool your heels in the warm sand.

Sights to See

❸ **Amsterdam Palace.** In the early 1980s, before South Beach became the hotbed of chicness, the late Italian designer Gianni Versace purchased this run-down Spanish Mediterranean residence, built before the arrival of Deco. Today the home is an ornate three-story palazzo with a guest house and a copper-dome rooftop observatory and pool that were added at the expense of a 1950s hotel, the Revere. Its loss and the razing of the fabled Deco Senator became a rallying point for preservationists, who like to point out that although they lost a few, they saved 40. In July 1997 Versace was tragically shot and killed in front of his home. Like a tropical Ford's Theatre, this now attracts picture-taking tourists. Eerie. ⊠ *1114 Ocean Dr.*

❷ **Art Deco District Welcome Center.** Run by the Miami Design Preservation League, this clearinghouse in the Oceanfront Auditorium provides information about the buildings in the Art Deco District. A well-stocked gift shop sells 1930s–1950s Art Deco memorabilia, posters, and books on Miami's history. Several tours—covering Lincoln Road, Espanola Way, North Beach, the entire Art Deco District, and more—start here. You can choose to rent audiotapes for a self-guided tour, join the regular Saturday-morning or Thursday-evening walking tour, or take a bicycle tour, all providing detailed histories of the Deco hotels. ⊠ *1001 Ocean Dr., at Barbara Capitman Way,* ☎ *305/531–3484.* 🎟 *Free.* ☉ *Daily 11–6, open later Thurs.–Mon. in season.*

Bal Harbour. This tony community, known for its upscale shops (also known as "shoppes"), has a stretch of prime beach real estate, where wealthy condominium owners cluster during the winter. Look close,

20

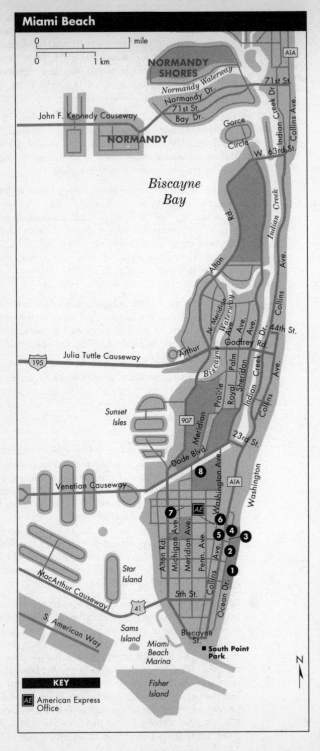

Miami Beach

and you may spy Bob Dole sunning himself outside his condo. ⊠ *Collins Ave. between 96th and 103rd Sts.*

Bass Museum of Art. A diverse collection of European art is the focus of this fortresslike museum made of keystone, a short drive north of SoBe's key sights. Works on display include *The Holy Family,* a painting by Peter Paul Rubens; *The Tournament,* one of several 16th-century Flemish tapestries; and works by Albrecht Dürer and Henri de Toulouse-Lautrec. An $8 million, three-phase expansion, expected to be completed shortly after 2000, will add a new wing, cafeteria, and theater, doubling the museum's size to nearly 40,000 square ft. ⊠ *2121 Park Ave.,* ☎ *305/673–7530.* ⌨ *$5.* ☉ *Tues.–Sat. 10–5, except 1–9 the 2nd and 4th Wed. of each month; Sun. 1–5.*

❹ **The Carlyle.** Built in 1941, this empty Deco building no longer functions as a hotel, but it's still popular as a movie location. Fans will recognize it and its neighbor, the Leslie, as the nightclub from *The Birdcage,* starring Robin Williams and Nathan Lane. ⊠ *1250 Ocean Dr.*

★ ❻ **Espanola Way.** The Mediterranean Revival buildings along this road were constructed in 1925 and frequented through the years by artists and writers. In the 1930s future bandleader Desi Arnaz strapped on a conga drum and started beating out a rumba rhythm at a nightclub that is now the Clay Hotel, a youth hostel. Since high rents have pushed some merchants out and vacant storefronts have resulted, try to visit this quaint avenue on a Sunday afternoon, when itinerant dealers and craftspeople set up shop to sell everything from garage-sale items to handcrafted bongo drums. Between Washington and Drexel avenues, the road has been narrowed to a single lane, and Miami Beach's trademark pink sidewalks have been widened to accommodate sidewalk cafés and shops selling imaginative clothing, jewelry, and art.

★ **Fontainebleau Hilton Resort and Towers.** For a sense of what Miami was like during the Fabulous '50s, take a drive north to see the finest example of SoBe's grandiose architecture. By the 1950s smaller Deco-era hotels were passé, and architects like Morris Lapidus got busy designing free-flowing hotels that affirmed the American attitude of "bigger is better." Even if you're not a guest, wander through the lobby and pool area just to feel the energy generated by an army of bellhops, clerks, concierges, and travelers. ⊠ *4441 Collins Ave.,* ☎ *305/538–2000.*

Haulover Beach Park. At this county park, far from the action of SoBe, you can see the Miami of 30 years ago. Pack a picnic, use the barbecue grills, or grab a snack at the concession stand. If you're into fitness, you may like the tennis and volleyball courts or paths designed for exercise, walking, and bicycling. If you're into cleanliness, take advantage of the shower facilities. The beach is nice for those who want water without long marches across hot sand, and Florida's only authorized clothing-optional beach lures people who want to tan every nook and cranny. Other offerings are kite rentals, kayak rentals, charter fishing excursions, and a par-3, nine-hole golf course. ⊠ *10800 Collins Ave., Sunny Isles,* ☎ *305/947–3525.* ⌨ *$3.50 per vehicle.* ☉ *Daily sunrise–sunset.*

❽ **Holocaust Memorial.** The focus of the memorial is a 42-ft-high bronze arm rising from the ground, with sculptured people climbing the arm seeking escape. Don't stare from the street. Enter the courtyard to see the chilling memorial wall and hear the eerie songs that seem to give voice to the victims. ⊠ *1933–1945 Meridian Ave.,* ☎ *305/538–1663.* ⌨ *Donation welcome.* ☉ *Daily 9–9.*

ART DECO HOTELS: MIAMI NICE

WITH APOLOGIES TO the flamingo, Miami's most recognizable icons are now the Art Deco hotels of South Beach. Their story begins in the 1920s, when Miami Beach was a winter playground of the rich, and grand themed hotels ruled. By the late '20s, however, shipping problems and a hurricane turned the boom to bust, and another approach to attract vacationers was needed.

In the early 1930s it was the turn of the middle class, which was drawn south by a more affordable version of paradise. New hotels were needed, and the architectural motif of choice became what we call Deco (for purists, Moderne), based on a sleek and cheerful look with geometric designs and creative colors. It was introduced in Paris in the '20s and later crossed the Atlantic.

In South Beach, architects added other shapes brought to America by industrial designers: streamlined, aerodynamic forms based on trains, ocean liners, and automobiles. Using a steel-and-concrete box as a foundation, architects dipped into this new grab bag of styles to accessorize their hotels. Pylons, spheres, cylinders, and cubes thrust out from facades and roofs. "Eyebrows," small ledges topping window frames, popped out of buildings like concrete caps. To soften sharp edges, designers added wraparound windows and curved corners, many ornamented with racing stripes. To reflect the beach locale, nautical elements were added: Portholes appeared in sets of three. Small etchings of seaweed, starfish, and rolling waves were plastered, painted, or etched on walls. Buildings looked ready to go to sea. Also taking advantage of the environment, sunlight, an abundant commodity, was brought indoors through glass blocks. But because there was no air-conditioning, coolness was achieved by planting shady palms and laying terrazzo tile.

Of course, everything has a life span, and the Deco hotels were no exception. Eventually, bold colors and creative accents became cliché, and ensuing decades saw owners hide their hotels beneath coats of plain white or beige paint. Deco still had its proponents, inspiring later architects, most notably Morris Lapidus, to create larger-than-life 1950s Deco hotels, such as the Fontainebleau and Eden Roc. But the days of small Deco hotels had passed. By the 1970s they were no longer welcoming tourists. . . or welcoming to look at. Most had matured into flophouses or dirt-cheap homes for retirees. Various plans ranging from leveling the buildings to legalizing gambling were proposed—and defeated.

THEN IN THE 1980S, an unusual confluence of people and events proved the area's salvation. The hyperactive cop show *Miami Vice*, set against the newly painted pastel facades of Ocean Drive, portrayed an exotic tropical appeal. European fashion photographers, restaurateurs, and entrepreneurs started using the area as a backdrop for models, cafés, and resurrected hotels. Above all, there was Barbara Baer Capitman, a senior citizen who reviewed South Beach's buildings and proposed it for the National Register of Historic Places. Thanks to her efforts and the ongoing drive of others to rescue, maintain, and improve these historic jewels, a new generation (yourself included) can experience the same tropical pleasures enjoyed by travelers of the 1930s.

NEED A
BREAK? If your feet are still holding up, head to the **Delano Hotel** (⊠ 1685 Collins Ave., ☎ 305/674–6400) for a drink. This surrealistic hotel, like a Calvin Klein ad come to life, continues to generate a buzz among SoBe's fashion models and hepcats.

★ ❼ **Lincoln Road Mall.** A playful redesign of this grande dame of Miami Beach overran its original $16 million budget, but the results were worth the extra bucks. The renovation spruced up the futuristic 1950s vision of Fontainebleau designer Morris Lapidus and added a grove of 20 towering date palms and five linear pools. Indicative of the road's resurgence is the restoration of dozens of buildings, including a former Jehovah's Witness hall that actor Michael Caine transformed into a restaurant. The best times to hit the road are during Sunday-morning farmers' markets and on weekend evenings, when cafés are bustling; art galleries, like Romero Britto's Britto Central, schedule openings; street performers take the stage; and bookstores, import shops, and clothing stores are open for late-night purchases. If things are slower when you arrive, credit SoBe's omnipresent high rents, which have forced many merchants out.

In the classical four-story Deco gem with friezes at 541–545 Lincoln Road, the **New World Symphony,** a national advanced-training orchestra led by Michael Tilson Thomas, rehearses and performs. To the west, the street is lined with chic food markets, cafés, and boutiques. Even farther west is the **South Florida Art Center,** home to one of the first arts groups to help resurrect the area. Still farther west (actually just a few blocks) is a black-and-white Deco movie house with a Mediterranean barrel-tile roof, which is now the **Colony Theater.** ⊠ *Lincoln Rd. between Collins Ave. and Alton Rd.*

☝ ❶ **Lummus Park.** Once part of a turn-of-the-century plantation owned by brothers John and James Lummus, this palm-shaded oasis on the beach side of Ocean Drive attracts beach-going families with its children's play area. Senior citizens predominate early in the day. Volleyball, in-line skating along the wide and winding sidewalk, and a lot of posing go on here, and officials don't enforce the law against topless female bathers, as long as everyone behaves with decorum. Gays like the beach between 11th and 13th streets. The lush foliage is a pleasing, natural counterpoint to the ultrachic atmosphere just across the street, where endless sidewalk cafés make it easy to come ashore for everything from burgers to quiche. Like New York's Central Park, this is a natural venue for big-name public concerts by such performers as Luciano Pavarotti and past Art Deco Weekend stars Cab Calloway and Lionel Hampton. ⊠ *East of Ocean Dr. between 5th and 15th Sts.*

North Beach. Families and those who like things quiet prefer this section of beach. Metered parking is ample right behind the dune and a block behind Collins Avenue along a pleasant, old shopping street. With high prices discouraging developers from SoBe, this area will no doubt see some redevelopment in years to come. However, without the cafés or 300-ft-wide beach to lure tourists, it may never match SoBe's appeal. ⊠ *Ocean Terr. between 73rd and 75th Sts.*

OFF THE
BEATEN PATH **OLETA RIVER STATE RECREATION AREA –** At more than 1,000 acres, this is the largest urban park in Florida. It's backed by lush tropical growth rather than hotels and offers interpretive talks, group and youth camping, 14 log cabins, kayak and canoe rentals, bicycle trails, and a fishing pier. Popular with outdoors enthusiasts, it also attracts dolphins, ospreys, and manatees, who arrive for the winter. ⊠ *3400 N.E. 163rd St., North Miami,* ☎ *305/919–1846.* ⊡ *$3.25 per vehicle with up to 8 people, $1 for pedestrians.* ☉ *Daily 8–sunset.*

SANFORD L. ZIFF JEWISH MUSEUM OF FLORIDA. This museum chronicles 230 years of the Jewish experience in Florida through lectures, films, storytelling, walking tours, and special events. If you've never seen a crate of kosher citrus, drop in. From the photo of a party girl in a seashell dress to ark ornaments from a Florida synagogue to a snapshot of Miss Florida 1885 (Mena Williams), exhibits reflect all things Jewish. Even the building is the former Congregation Beth Jacob Synagogue. ⊠ *301 Washington Ave.,* ☎ *305/672–5044.* ▨ *$5.* ☉ *Tues.–Sun. 10–5.*

South Pointe Park. From the 50-yard Sunshine Pier, which adjoins the 1-mi-long jetty at the mouth of Government Cut, you can fish while watching huge ships pass. No bait or tackle is available in the park. Facilities include two observation towers, rest rooms, and volleyball courts. ⊠ *1 Washington Ave.*

Surfside. *Parlez-vous français?* If you do, you'll feel quite comfortable in and around this community, a French Canadian enclave. Many folks have spent their winters along this stretch of beach (and elsewhere down to 72nd Street) for years. ⊠ *Collins Ave. between 88th and 96th Sts.*

❺ **Wolfsonian–FIU Foundation Gallery.** An elegantly renovated 1927 storage facility is now both a research center and home to the 70,000-plus-item collection of modern design and "propaganda arts" amassed by Miami native Mitchell Wolfson, Jr., a world traveler and connoisseur. Included in the museum's eclectic holdings, representing Art Moderne, Art Nouveau, Arts and Crafts, and other artistic movements, is a 1930s braille edition of Hitler's *Mein Kampf.* Exhibitions such as World's Fair designs and the architectural heritage of S. H. Kress add to the appeal. ⊠ *1001 Washington Ave.,* ☎ *305/531–1001.* ▨ *$5, free Thurs. 6–9.* ☉ *Mon.–Tues. and Fri.–Sat. 11–6, Thurs. 11–9, Sun. noon–5.*

Downtown Miami

Although steel-and-glass buildings have sprung up around downtown, the heart of the city hasn't changed much since the 1960s—except that it's a little seedier. Not surprising for a city that, though one of the country's greatest, has its share of political corruption, cronyism, nepotism, shortsightedness, and insensitivity. In 1997 a proposal to disband the city actually reached voters, but they voted overwhelmingly to keep it, flaws and all.

Nevertheless, by day there's plenty of activity downtown, as office workers and motorists crowd the area. Staid, suited lawyers and bankers share the sidewalks with Latino merchants wearing open-neck, intricately embroidered shirts called guayaberas. Fruit merchants sell their wares from pushcarts, young European travelers with backpacks stroll the streets, and foreign businesspeople haggle over prices in import-export shops, including more electronics and camera shops than you'd see in Tokyo. You hear Arabic, Chinese, Creole, French, German, Hebrew, Hindi, Japanese, Portuguese, Spanish, Swedish, Yiddish, and even a little English now and then. But what's best in the heart of downtown Miami is its Latinization and the sheer energy of Latino shoppers.

At night, however, downtown is sorely neglected. Except for Bayside Marketplace, the old Miami Arena, and the new American Airlines Arena, the area is deserted, and arena patrons rarely linger. Visitors spend little time here since most tourist attractions are in other neighborhoods, but there is a movement afoot to bring a renaissance to downtown. A new performing arts center and a CocoWalk-style pedestrian mall are expected in 2000.

Thanks to the Metromover (☞ Getting Around by Train *in* Miami and Miami Beach A to Z, *below*), which has inner and outer loops through downtown plus north and south extensions, this is an excellent tour to take by rail, and it's only 25¢ to boot. Attractions are conveniently located within about two blocks of the nearest station. Parking downtown is no less convenient or more expensive than in any other city, but the best idea is to park near Bayside Marketplace or leave your car at an outlying Metrorail station and take the train downtown.

A Good Tour

A smart place to start is at the Bayfront Park Metromover stop. There's plenty of parking in lots in the median of Biscayne Boulevard and slightly more expensive covered parking at the Bayfront Marketplace. If you want, you can wait until you return to walk through the **Mildred and Claude Pepper Bayfront Park** ⑨, but look south of the park, and you'll see the Hotel Inter-Continental Miami, which displays *The Spindle*, a huge sculpture by Henry Moore, in its lobby. West of Bayfront Park Station stands the tallest building in Florida, the **First Union Financial Center** ⑩.

Now it's time to board the Metromover northbound and take in the fine view of Bayfront Park's greenery, the bay beyond, the Port of Miami in the bay, and Miami Beach across the water. The next stop, College/Bayside, serves the downtown campus of **Miami-Dade Community College** ⑪, which has two fine galleries.

As the Metromover rounds the curve after the College/Bayside station, look northeast for a view of the vacant **Freedom Tower** ⑫, an important milepost in the history of Cuban immigration. You'll also catch a view of the *Miami Herald* building, home to columnists/authors Dave Barry and Carl Hiaasen.

Survey the city as the train works its way toward Government Center station. Look off to your right (north) as you round the northwest corner of the loop to see the round, windowless, pink **Miami Arena** ⑬.

Now it's time to see the city on foot. Get off at Government Center, a large station with small shops, restaurants, and a hair salon, in case you're looking shaggy. It's also where the 21-mi elevated Metrorail commuter system connects with the Metromover, so this is a good place to start your tour if you're coming downtown by train. Walk out the east doors to Northwest 1st Street, and head a block south to the **Miami-Dade Cultural Center** ⑭, which contains the city's main art museum, historical museum, and library and made an appearance in the movie *There's Something About Mary.*

After sopping up some culture, hoof it east down Flagler Street. On the corner is the **Dade County Courthouse** ⑮, whose pinnacle is accented by circling vultures. Now you're in the heart of downtown, where the smells range from pleasant (hot dog carts) to rancid (hot dog carts). If you cleaned up the streets and put a shine on the city, you'd see Miami circa 1950. Still thriving today, the downtown area is a far cry from what it was in 1896, when it was being carved out of pine woods and palmetto scrub to make room for Flagler's railroad. If you're in the market for jewelry, avoid the street peddlers and duck into the Seybold Building, at 36 Northeast 1st Street; it comprises 10 stories with 250 jewelers hawking watches, rings, bracelets, etc.

Just a few blocks from your starting point at the Bayfront Park Metromover station, duck into the **Gusman Center for the Performing Arts** ⑯, a stunningly beautiful movie palace that now serves as downtown Miami's concert hall. If there's a show on—even a bad one—get tickets. It's worth it just to sit in here.

When you get back to your car and the entrance to the Bayfront Marketplace, you can opt to hit the road, go shopping, or grab a brew at a bay-front bar.

TIMING

To walk and ride to the various points of interest, allow two hours. If you want to spend additional time eating and shopping at Bayside, allow at least four hours. To include museum visits, allow six hours.

Sights to See

🕲 **American Police Hall of Fame and Museum.** This museum exhibits more than 11,000 law enforcement–related items, including weapons, a jail cell, and an electric chair, as well as a 400-ton marble memorial listing the names of more than 6,000 police officers killed in the line of duty since 1960. ⊠ *3801 Biscayne Blvd.,* ☎ *305/573–0070.* 🎟 *$6.* ☉ *Daily 10–5:30.*

⓯ **Dade County Courthouse.** Built in 1928, this was once the tallest building south of Washington, D.C. Unlike Capistrano, turkey vultures—not swallows—return to roost here in winter. ⊠ *73 W. Flagler St.*

⓾ **First Union Financial Center.** The tallest building in Florida is this 55-story structure. Unfortunately, there's no observation deck, but a 1-acre plaza graced by towering palms can be a nice place to rest your feet. ⊠ *200 S. Biscayne Blvd.*

⓬ **Freedom Tower.** In the 1960s this imposing Spanish Baroque structure was used by the Cuban Refugee Center to process more than 500,000 Cubans who entered the United States after fleeing Fidel Castro's regime. Built in 1925 for the *Miami Daily News,* it was inspired by the Giralda, an 800-year-old bell tower in Seville, Spain. Preservationists were pleased to see the tower restored to its original grandeur in 1988, but the building remains vacant awaiting the arrival of a proposed Cuban museum. ⊠ *600 Biscayne Blvd.*

★ ⓰ **Gusman Center for the Performing Arts.** Carry an extra pair of socks when you come here; the beauty of this former movie palace will knock yours clean off. Restored as a concert hall, it resembles a Moorish courtyard on the inside, with twinkling stars in the sky. You can catch performances by the Florida Philharmonic and movies of the Miami Film Festival. If the hall is closed, call the office and they may let you in. ⊠ *174 E. Flagler St.,* ☎ *305/374–2444 administration, 305/372–0925 box office.*

⓭ **Miami Arena.** Currently the home of the NBA's Miami Heat (at least until the new American Airlines Arena opens by the bay), the arena also hosts a variety of other sports and entertainment events. ⊠ *701 Arena Blvd.,* ☎ *305/530–4444.*

⓫ **Miami-Dade Community College.** The campus houses two fine galleries: The larger, third-floor **Centre Gallery** hosts various photography, painting, and sculpture exhibitions, and the fifth-floor **Frances Wolfson Art Gallery** houses smaller photo exhibits. ⊠ *300 N.E. 2nd Ave.,* ☎ *305/237–3278.* 🎟 *Free.* ☉ *Mon.–Thurs. 9–4:30.*

★ 🕲 ⓮ **Miami-Dade Cultural Center.** Containing three important cultural resources, this 3-acre complex is one of the focal points of downtown. From books to paintings to history, you'll find it all right here. The **Miami Art Museum** (☎ 305/375–3000) displays a permanent collection as well as putting on major touring exhibitions of work by inter-

Downtown Miami

Dade County
Courthouse, **15**

First Union
Financial Center, **10**

Freedom Tower, **12**

Gusman Center for
the Performing
Arts, **16**

Miami Arena, **13**

Miami-Dade
Community
College, **11**

Miami-Dade Cultural
Center, **14**

Mildred and Claude
Pepper Bayfront
Park, **9**

national artists, focusing on work completed since 1945. Open Tuesday–Friday 10–5 and weekends noon–5, the museum charges $5 admission. At the **Historical Museum of Southern Florida** (☎ 305/375–1492), visitors are treated to pure Floridiana, including an old Miami streetcar, cigar labels, and a railroad exhibit as well as a display on prehistoric Miami. Admission is $5, and hours are Monday–Wednesday and Friday–Saturday 10–5, Thursday 10–9, and Sunday noon–5. The **Main Public Library** (☎ 305/375–2665), which is open Monday–Wednesday and Friday–Saturday 9–6, Thursday 9–9, and Sunday 1–5, contains nearly 4 million holdings and offers art exhibits in the auditorium and second-floor lobby. ✉ *101 W. Flagler St.*

❾ Mildred and Claude Pepper Bayfront Park. This oasis among the skyscrapers borders the Bayfront Marketplace, making it a natural place for a pre- or post-shopping walk. An urban landfill in the 1920s, it became the site of a World War II memorial in 1943, which was revised in 1980 to include the names of victims of later wars. Japanese sculptor Isamu Noguchi redesigned the park before his death in 1989 to include two amphitheaters, a memorial to the *Challenger* astronauts, and a fountain honoring the late Florida congressman Claude Pepper and his wife. At the park's north end, the Friendship Torch was erected to honor JFK during his presidency and was dedicated in 1964. ✉ *Biscayne Blvd. between 2nd and 3rd Sts.*

Little Havana

Nearly 40 years ago the tidal wave of Cubans fleeing the Castro regime flooded into an older neighborhood west of downtown Miami. Don't expect a sparkling and lively reflection of 1950s Havana, however. What you will find are ramshackle motels and cluttered storefronts. With a million Cubans and other Latinos—making up more than half the metropolitan population—dispersed throughout Greater Miami, Little Havana and neighboring East Little Havana remain magnets for Hispanics and Anglos alike, who come to experience the flavor of traditional Cuban culture. That culture, of course, functions in Spanish. Many Little Havana residents and shopkeepers speak little or no English.

A Good Tour

From downtown go west on Flagler Street across the Miami River to Teddy Roosevelt Avenue (Southwest 17th Avenue) and pause at **Plaza de la Cubanidad** ⑰, on the southwest corner. The plaza's monument is indicative of the prominent role of Cuban history and culture here.

Turn left at Douglas Road (Southwest 37th Avenue), drive south to **Calle Ocho** ⑱ (Southwest 8th Street), and turn left again. You are now on the main commercial thoroughfare of Little Havana. After you cross Unity Boulevard (Southwest 27th Avenue), Calle Ocho becomes a one-way street eastbound through the heart of Little Havana.

At Avenida Luis Muñoz Marín (Southwest 15th Avenue), stop at **Domino Park** ⑲, where elderly Cuban men pass the day with their black-and-white play tiles. The **Brigade 2506 Memorial** ⑳, commemorating the victims of the unsuccessful 1961 Bay of Pigs invasion, stands at Memorial Boulevard (Southwest 13th Avenue). A block south are several other monuments relevant to Cuban history, including a bas-relief of and quotations by José Martí.

TIMING

If the history hidden in the monuments is your only interest, set aside one hour. Allow more time to stop along Calle Ocho for a strong cup of Cuban coffee or to shop for a cigar made of Honduran tobacco hand-rolled in the United States by Cubans.

Sights to See

⓴ Brigade 2506 Memorial. To honor those who died in the Bay of Pigs invasion, an eternal flame burns atop a simple stone monument with the inscription CUBA—A LOS MARTIRES DE LA BRIGADA DE ASALTO ABRIL 17 DE 1961. The monument also bears a shield with the Brigade 2506 emblem, a Cuban flag superimposed on a cross. ⊠ *S.W. 8th St. and S.W. 13th Ave.*

⓲ Calle Ocho. In Little Havana's commercial heart, experience such Cuban customs as hand-rolled cigars or sandwiches piled with meats and cheeses. Though it all deserves exploring, if time is limited, try the stretch from Southwest 14th to 11th avenues. ⊠ *S.W. 8th St.*

⓳ Domino Park. Officially known as Maximo Gomez Park, this is a major gathering place for elderly, guayabera-clad Cuban males, who, after 40 years, still pass the day playing dominoes while arguing anti-Castro politics. ⊠ *S.W. 8th St. and S.W. 15th Ave.* ☉ *Daily 9–6.*

⓱ Plaza de la Cubanidad. Redbrick sidewalks surround a fountain and monument with the words of José Martí, a leader in Cuba's struggle for independence from Spain and a hero to Cuban refugees and immigrants in Miami. The quotation, LAS PALMAS SON NOVIAS QUE ESPERAN (The palm trees are girlfriends who will wait), counsels hope and fortitude to the Cubans. ⊠ *W. Flagler St. and S.W. 17th Ave.*

Coral Gables

If not for George E. Merrick, Coral Gables would be just another suburb. Merrick envisioned an American Venice, with canals and gracious homes spreading across the community. In 1911 his minister father died, and Merrick inherited 1,600 acres of citrus and avocado groves; by 1921 he had upped that to 3,000 acres. Using this as a foundation, Merrick began designing a city based on centuries-old prototypes from Mediterranean countries. He began planning lush landscaping, magnificent entrances, and broad boulevards named for Spanish explorers, cities, and provinces. His uncle, Denman Fink, helped Merrick crystallize his artistic vision, and he hired architects trained abroad to create themed neighborhood villages, such as Florida pioneer, Chinese, French city, Dutch South African, and French Normandy. The result was a planned community with Spanish Mediterranean architecture that justifiably calls itself the City Beautiful—a moniker it acquired by following the Garden City method of urban planning in the 1920s.

That's the good news. The bad news is that, unfortunately for Merrick, the devastating no-name hurricane of 1926 and the Great Depression prevented him from fulfilling many of his plans. He died at 54, working for the post office. His city languished until after World War II but then grew rapidly. Today Coral Gables has a population of about 41,000. In its bustling downtown, more than 140 multinational companies maintain headquarters or regional offices, and the University of Miami campus in the southern part of Coral Gables brings a youthful vibrancy: The median age of residents is 36.

Like much of Miami, Coral Gables has realized the aesthetic and economic importance of historic preservation and has passed a Mediterranean design ordinance, rewarding businesses for maintaining their building's architectural style. Even the street signs (ground-level markers that are hard to see in daylight, impossible at night) are preserved

Miami, Coral Gables, Coconut Grove, and Key Biscayne

ATLANTIC

KEY BISCAYNE

Cape Florida Lighthouse

KEY

AE American Express Office

3 miles

3 km

Alhambra Water Tower, **18**
Barnacle State Historic Site, **37**
Bill Baggs Cape Florida State Recreation Area, **41**
Biltmore Hotel, **25**
Brigade 2506 Memorial, **20**

Calle Ocho, **18**
Coral Gables City Hall, **22**
Coral Gables Congregational Church, **26**
Coral Gables Merrick House and Gardens, **28**
Crandon Park, **40**

De Soto Plaza and Fountain, **24**
Domino Park, **19**
Fairchild Tropical Garden, **31**
Matheson Hammock Park, **32**
Miami City Hall, **35**

Miami Museum of Science and Space Transit Planetarium, **34**
Miami Seaquarium, **39**
Miracle Mile, **21**
Old Rickenbacker Causeway Bridge, **38**
Parrot Jungle, **30**

Plaza de la Cubanidad, **17**
Plymouth Congregational Church, **36**
University of Miami, **29**
Venetian Pool, **23**
Vizcaya Museum and Gardens, **33**

due to their historical value. They're worth the inconvenience, if only to honor the memory of Merrick.

A Good Tour

Heading south on downtown's Brickell Avenue, turn right onto Coral Way—also marked as Southwest 13th Street—and stay on Coral Way even as it turns into Southwest 3rd and Southwest 22nd avenues. An arch of banyan trees prepares you for the grand entrance onto **Miracle Mile** ㉑, the heart of downtown Coral Gables. Park your car and take time to explore on foot.

When you've seen enough, continue driving west, passing the 1930s Miracle Theater on your left, which now serves as home of the Actors' Playhouse. Keep heading west, cross LeJeune Road, and bear left onto Biltmore Way, catching an eyeful of the ornate Spanish Renaissance **Coral Gables City Hall** ㉒.

Past several blocks of nondescript condos, Biltmore Way becomes Andalusia, whereupon you should look for De Soto Boulevard and turn left. If you can't read the hard-to-decipher street markers, follow the more prominent signs to the Venetian Pool and the Biltmore. A few blocks up on your left, you'll see the gates surrounding the exotic and unusual Merrick-designed **Venetian Pool** ㉓, created from an old coral quarry. There's parking on your right. Immediately ahead of you is the Merrick-designed **De Soto Plaza and Fountain** ㉔.

As in many areas of Coral Gables, there's a traffic circle surrounding the fountain. Head to 12 o'clock (the opposite side of the fountain) and stay on De Soto for a magnificent vista and entrance to the, yes, Merrick-designed and reborn **Biltmore Hotel** ㉕. On your right, before you reach the hotel, you'll see the **Coral Gables Congregational Church** ㉖, one of the first churches in this planned community. After visiting the hotel, double back to the fountain, this time circling to 9 o'clock and Granada Way. Several blocks away you'll arrive at the Granada Golf Course, where you turn left onto North Greenway. As you cruise up the street, notice the stand of banyan trees that separates the fairways. At the end of the course the road makes a horseshoe bend, but instead cross Alhambra to loop around the restored **Alhambra Water Tower** ㉗, a city landmark dating from 1924. By the way, it's Merrick designed.

Return to Alhambra and follow it straight to the next light (Coral Way), where you can turn left and ogle beautifully maintained Spanish homes from the 1920s. Although there's only a small sign to announce it, the **Coral Gables Merrick House and Gardens** ㉘, Merrick's boyhood home, is at Coral Way and Toledo Street. If you love planned development, stop in to pay your respects. Parking is behind the house.

Afterward, take a right on Coral Way, followed by a left on Granada, which winds south past Bird Road and eventually to Ponce de León Boulevard. Turn right and follow it to the entrance of the main campus of the **University of Miami** ㉙. Turn right at the first stoplight (Stanford Drive) to enter the campus, and park in the lot on your right designated for visitors to the Lowe Art Museum.

You may have noticed that this tour contains some backtracking. Unfortunately, no matter how you navigate Coral Gables, directions get confusing. This tour takes in the highlights first and lets you fill out the balance of your day as you see fit. Now bow to your partner, and bow to your corner, and promenade home.

TIMING

Strolling Miracle Mile should take slightly more than an hour—about 63 minutes—unless you plan to shop (and you should). In that case, allow four hours. Save time for a refreshing dip at the Venetian Pool, and plan to spend at least an hour getting acquainted with the Biltmore—longer if you'd like to order a drink and linger poolside. If you can pull yourself away from the lap of luxury, allow an hour to visit the University of Miami campus (if you're into college campuses).

Sights to See

㉗ Alhambra Water Tower. In 1924 this city landmark stored water and was clad in a decorative Moresque, lighthouselike exterior. After more than 50 years of disuse and neglect, the windmill-like tower was completely restored in 1993 with a copper-rib dome and multicolored frescoes. Pretty impressive when you consider its peers are merely steel containers. ⊠ *Alhambra Circle, Greenway Ct., and Ferdinand St.*

㉕ Biltmore Hotel. Bouncing back from dark days as an army hospital, this hotel has become the jewel of Coral Gables. After extensive renovations it reopened in 1992 and hosted the Summit of the Americas in 1994. Its 16-story tower, like the Freedom Tower in downtown Miami, is a replica of Seville's Giralda Tower. To the west is the Biltmore Country Club, a richly ornamented Beaux Arts–style structure with a superb colonnade and courtyard; it was reincorporated into the hotel in 1989. Free tours are offered. ⊠ *1200 Anastasia Ave.,* ☏ *305/445–1926.* ⊘ *Tours Sun. 1:30, 2:30, and 3:30.*

㉒ Coral Gables City Hall. Far more attractive than today's modular city halls, this 1928 building has a three-tier tower topped with a clock and a 500-pound bell. A mural by Denman Fink (George Merrick's uncle and artistic adviser), inside the dome ceiling on the second floor, depicts the four seasons. (Although not as well known as Maxfield Parrish, Fink demonstrated a similar utopian vision.) Also on display are paintings, photos, and ads touting 1920s Coral Gables. ⊠ *405 Biltmore Way,* ☏ *305/446–6800.* ⊘ *Weekdays 8–5.*

NEED A BREAK?

Whether you want to relax or grab an on-the-go snack, you can't miss with **Wrapido** (⊠ 2334 Ponce de León Blvd., ☏ 305/443–1884), Florida's first wrapper restaurant. The funky, upbeat atmosphere shows signs of SoHo, and the healthy wraps, soups, and smoothies are made from scratch. Strawberry Fields, the restaurant's best-selling smoothie, is prepared with fresh bananas, strawberries, apple juice, and low-fat yogurt.

㉖ Coral Gables Congregational Church. The parish was organized in 1923, and with George Merrick as a charter member (and donor of the land), this small church became the first in the city. Rumor has it Merrick built it in honor of his father, a Congregational minister. The original interiors are still in magnificent condition. ⊠ *3010 De Soto Blvd.,* ☏ *305/448–7421.* ⊘ *Weekdays 8:30–4:30, services Sun. 9:15 and 10:45.*

㉘ Coral Gables Merrick House and Gardens. In 1976 the city of Coral Gables acquired George Merrick's boyhood home. Restored to its 1920s appearance, it contains Merrick family furnishings and artwork. The lush and lazy tropical atmosphere suggests the inspiration for George's masterpiece: Coral Gables. ⊠ *907 Coral Way,* ☏ *305/460–5361.* ▣ *House $2, grounds free.* ⊘ *House Wed. and Sun. 1–4, grounds daily 8–sunset, also by appointment.*

㉔ De Soto Plaza and Fountain. Water flows from the mouths of four sculpted faces on a classical column on a pedestal in this Denman Fink–designed fountain from the early 1920s. The closed eyes of the face looking west symbolize the day's end. ⊠ *Granada Blvd. and Sevilla Ave.*

㉑ **Miracle Mile.** This upscale yet neighborly stretch of retail stores is actually only ½ mi long. Appealing to residents who predated Miami's resurgence, it has managed to maintain its 1960s premall existence. Cafeterias mingle with high-tone jewelers, and independent bookstores share customers with major book chains. The street appears to have the world's greatest concentration of bridal shops, and for support, florists fill in many of the neighboring storefronts. ⊠ *Coral Way between S.W. 37th Ave. (Douglas Rd.) and S.W. 42nd Ave. (LeJeune Rd.).*

㉙ **University of Miami.** With almost 14,000 full-time, part-time, and noncredit students, UM is the largest private research university in the southeast. Walk around campus and visit the **Lowe Art Museum,** which has a permanent collection of 8,000 works that include Renaissance and Baroque art, American paintings, Latin American art, and Navajo and Pueblo Indian textiles and baskets. The museum also hosts traveling exhibitions. ⊠ *1301 Stanford Dr.,* ☎ *305/284–3535 or 305/284–3536.* ⊡ *$5.* ☉ *Tues.–Wed. and Fri.–Sat. 10–5, Thurs. noon–7, Sun. noon–5.*

★ ☝ ㉓ **Venetian Pool.** Sculpted from a rock quarry in 1923 and fed by artesian wells, this 825,000-gallon municipal pool remains quite popular due to its themed architecture—a fantasized version of a waterfront Italian village—created by Denman Fink. The pool has earned a place on the National Register of Historic Places and showcases a nice collection of vintage photos depicting 1920s beauty pageants and swank soirees held long ago. Paul Whiteman played here, Johnny Weissmuller and Esther Williams swam here, and you should, too. A snack bar, lockers, and showers make this must-see user-friendly as well. ⊠ *2701 De Soto Blvd.,* ☎ *305/460–5356.* ⊡ *$5, free parking across De Soto Blvd.* ☉ *Weekends 10–4:30; plus June–Aug., weekdays 11–7:30; Sept.–Oct. and Apr.–May, Tues.–Fri. 11–5:30; and Nov.–Mar., Tues.–Fri. 10–4:30.*

South Miami

South of Miami and Coral Gables is a city called South Miami, which is not to be confused with the region known as South Dade. A pioneer farm community, it grew into a suburb but retains its small-town charm. Fine old homes and stately trees line Sunset Drive, a city-designated Historic and Scenic Road to and through the town. A local chamber of commerce provides a free map listing u-pick farms where your fresh fruit can be blended in with a creamy milk shake. All this could change slightly, however, with the arrival of the Shops at Sunset Place, a retail complex larger than Coconut Grove's CocoWalk—big digs for a quiet town.

A Good Tour

Drive south from Sunset Drive on Red Road (watching for the plentiful orchid merchants), and turn right just before Killian Drive (Southwest 112th Street) into the 13-acre grounds of **Parrot Jungle** ㉚, one of Greater Miami's oldest and most popular commercial tourist attractions.

From Parrot Jungle follow Red Road ⅓ mi south and turn left on scenic Old Cutler Road, which curves north along the uplands of southern Florida's coastal ridge toward the 83-acre **Fairchild Tropical Garden** ㉛. Just north of the gardens, Old Cutler Road traverses Dade County's lovely **Matheson Hammock Park** ③②. From here you can follow the road back to U.S. 1, heading north to Miami.

TIMING

Most people should allow at least half a day to see these three natural attractions, but dedicated ornithologists and botanists will want to leave a full day. Driving from SoBe should take only 25 minutes—longer during afternoon rush hour.

Sights to See

③① **Fairchild Tropical Garden.** Comprising 83 acres, this is the largest tropical botanical garden in the continental United States. Eleven lakes, a rain forest, and lots of flowers, including orchids, mountain roses, bellflowers, coral trees, bougainvillea, and fire trees, make it a garden for the senses—and there's special assistance for deaf guests. As covering the whole garden would make for a very long walk, take the free guided tram tour, which leaves on the hour. Spicing up the social calendar are garden sales, theatrical performances, moonlight strolls, and symphony concerts. A combination bookstore–gift shop is a popular source for books on gardening and horticulture, ordered by botanists the world over. ✉ *10901 Old Cutler Rd.,* ☎ *305/667–1651.* ⌨ *$8.* ☉ *Daily 9:30–4:30.*

③② **Matheson Hammock Park.** In the 1930s the Civilian Conservation Corps developed this 100-acre tract of upland and mangrove swamp on land donated by a local pioneer, Commodore J. W. Matheson. The park, Miami-Dade County's oldest and most scenic, features a bathing beach and changing facilities. In 1997 the marina was expanded to include 243 slips, 71 dry-storage spaces, a bait-and-tackle shop, and a restaurant. Noticeably absent are fishing and diving charters, although there is a sailing school. ✉ *9610 Old Cutler Rd., Coral Gables,* ☎ *305/ 665–5475.* ⌨ *Parking for beach and marina $3.50 per car, $8 per car with trailer, $6 per bus and RV; limited free upland parking.* ☉ *Daily 6–sunset; pool lifeguards winter, daily 8:30–5; summer, weekends 8:30–6.*

③⓪ **Parrot Jungle.** One of South Florida's original tourist attractions, Parrot Jungle opened in 1936 and is now home to more than 1,100 exotic birds, who look for handouts from visitors. The tone is kitschy (in the tradition of Florida favorites Silver Springs and Cypress Gardens) but oddly peaceful and exotic after you've experienced the urban jungle. Once you've photographed the postcard-perfect Caribbean flamingos and watched a trained-bird show, stroll among orchids and other flowering plants nestled in ferns, bald cypress, and massive live oaks. An imminent move (sometime in mid-2000) will take the birds to a new home on Watson Island, across from the Port of Miami, but this park will be preserved as some type of wildlife sanctuary. ✉ *11000 S.W. 57th Ave.,* ☎ *305/666–7834.* ⌨ *$13.95.* ☉ *Daily 9:30–6, last admission 5; café daily 8–5.*

Coconut Grove

South Florida's oldest settlement, the Grove was inhabited as early as 1834 and established by 1873, two decades before Miami. Its early settlers included Bahamian blacks, "Conchs" (white Key Westers, many originally from the Bahamas), and New England intellectuals. They built a community that attracted artists, writers, and scientists to establish winter homes. By the end of World War I more people listed in *Who's Who* gave addresses in Coconut Grove than any other place in the country.

To this day Coconut Grove reflects its pioneers' eclectic origins. Posh estates mingle with rustic cottages, modest frame homes, and stark modern dwellings, often on the same block. To keep Coconut Grove a village in a jungle, residents lavish affection on exotic plantings while battling to protect remaining native vegetation.

The historic center of the Village of Coconut Grove went through a hippie period in the 1960s, a laid-back funkiness in the 1970s, and a teenybopper invasion in the early 1980s. Today the tone is upscale and urban, with a mix of galleries, boutiques, restaurants, bars, and sidewalk cafés. On weekends the Grove is jam-packed with both locals and tourists shopping at the Streets of Mayfair, CocoWalk, and small boutiques. Parking can be a problem, especially on weekend evenings, when police direct traffic and prohibit turns at some intersections to prevent gridlock. Be prepared to walk several blocks from the periphery into the heart of the Grove.

A Good Tour

From downtown Miami take Brickell Avenue south and follow the signs pointing to Vizcaya and Coconut Grove. If you're interested, keep your eyes peeled to see where Madonna lived, at 3029 Brickell, and Sylvester Stallone's old estate, the faux-finished yellow house with blue trim and huge gates a few doors south on the corner of Brickell and Southwest 32nd. Turn right on Southwest 32nd and then left at the next street.

Although the road is called South Miami Avenue here, it soon turns into South Bayshore Drive. With either name, it's the easiest route into the village. Continue south and watch on your left for the entrance to the don't-miss **Vizcaya Museum and Gardens** ㉝, an estate with an Italian Renaissance–style villa. Less than 100 yards down the road on your right is the **Miami Museum of Science and Space Transit Planetarium** ㉞, a participatory museum with animated displays for all ages.

The road switches from four lanes to two and back again as you approach the village. If you're interested in the history of air travel, take a quick detour down Pan American Drive to see the 1930s Art Deco Pan Am terminal, which has been horribly renovated inside to become **Miami City Hall** ㉟. You'll also see the Coconut Grove Convention Center, where antiques, boat, and home shows are held, and Dinner Key Marina, where seabirds soar and sailboats ride at anchor.

With 28 waterfront acres of Australian pine, lush lawns, and walking and jogging paths, the bayside David T. Kennedy Park makes one more pleasant stop before it's time to hit the village. South Bayshore Drive heads directly into McFarlane Road, which takes a sharp right into the center of the action. If you can forsake instant gratification, turn left on Main Highway and drive less than ½ mi to Devon Road and the interesting **Plymouth Congregational Church** ㊱ and its gardens.

Return to Main Highway and travel northeast toward the historic Village of Coconut Grove. As you reenter the village center, note on your left the Coconut Grove Playhouse. On your right, beyond the benches and shelter, is the entrance to the **Barnacle State Historic Site** ㊲, a pioneer residence built by Commodore Ralph Munroe in 1891. After getting your fill of history, relax and spend the evening mingling with Coconut Grove's artists and intellectuals.

TIMING
Plan on devoting from six to eight hours to enjoy Vizcaya, other bayfront sights, and the village's shops, restaurants, and nightlife.

Sights to See

37 **Barnacle State Historic Site.** The oldest Miami home still on its original foundation rests in the middle of 5 acres of native hardwood and landscaped lawns surrounded by flashy Coconut Grove. Built by Florida's first snowbird—New Yorker Commodore Ralph Munroe—the home features many original furnishings, a broad sloping roof, and deeply recessed verandas that channel sea breezes into the house. If your timing is right, you may catch one of the monthly Moonlight Concerts. ⊠ *3485 Main Hwy.,* ☎ *305/448–9445.* ⊠ *$1, concerts $5.* ⊘ *Fri.– Sun. 9–4; tours 10, 11:30, 1, and 2:30, but call ahead; group tours (10 or more) Mon.–Thurs. by reservation; concerts on day near full moon 6 PM–9 PM, but call ahead.*

NEED A BREAK?   Although **Joffrey's Coffee Co.** (⊠ 3434A Main Hwy., ☎ 305/448–0848) is a chain, it's still a nice place to drop by for a cappuccino, espresso, tea, or chilled coffee from morning to midnight. Tables at the sidewalk café enable you to critique the trendies that inhabit the neighborhood. Muffins, bagels, and cakes bring the bill to about $5.

35 **Miami City Hall.** Built in 1934 as the terminal for the Pan American Airways seaplane base at Dinner Key, the building retains its nautical-style Art Deco trim. Sadly, the interior is generic government, but a 1938 Pan Am menu on display (with filet mignon, *petit pois au beurre,* and Jenny Lind pudding) lets you know Miami officials appreciate from whence they came. ⊠ *3500 Pan American Dr.,* ☎ *305/250–5400.* ⊘ *Weekdays 8–5.*

☝ **34** **Miami Museum of Science and Space Transit Planetarium.** This museum is chock-full of hands-on sound, gravity, and electricity displays for children and adults alike. A wildlife center houses native Florida snakes, turtles, tortoises, and birds of prey. Outstanding traveling exhibits appear throughout the year, and virtual reality, life-science demonstrations, and Internet technology are on hand every day. The spinning 1933 Pan Am globe—once the focal point of the airline's terminal—is now the focal point of the museum's lobby. ⊠ *3280 S. Miami Ave.,* ☎ *305/ 854–4247 museum; 305/854–2222 planetarium information hotline.* ⊠ *Museum, planetarium, and wildlife center $9; laser-light rock-and-roll concert $6.* ⊘ *Daily 10–6.*

36 **Plymouth Congregational Church.** Opened in 1917, this handsome coral-rock structure resembles a Mexican mission church. The front door, made of hand-carved walnut and oak with original wrought-iron fittings, came from an early 17th-century monastery in the Pyrenees. Also on the 11-acre grounds are the first schoolhouse in Miami-Dade County (one room), which was moved to this property, and the site of the original Coconut Grove waterworks and electric works. ⊠ *3400 Devon Rd.,* ☎ *305/444–6521.* ⊘ *Weekdays 9–4:30, Sun. service 10 AM.*

★ **33** **Vizcaya Museum and Gardens.** Of the 10,000 people living in Miami between 1912 and 1916, about 1,000 of them were gainfully employed by Chicago industrialist James Deering to build this $20 million neoclassical winter residence. Once comprising 180 acres, the grounds now cover a still-substantial 30-acre tract, including a native hammock and more than 10 acres of formal gardens and fountains overlooking Biscayne Bay. The house, open to the public, contains 70 rooms, 34 of which are filled with paintings, sculpture, antique furniture, and other decorative arts dating from the 15th through the 19th centuries and representing the Renaissance, Baroque, rococo, and neoclassical styles. So unusual and impressive is Vizcaya, its guest list has included Ronald Reagan, Pope John Paul II, Queen Elizabeth II, Bill Clinton, and Boris Yeltsin. It's a shame the guided tour can be far less impressive and interesting than the home's guest list and surroundings. ⊠ *3251 S. Miami Ave.,* ☎ *305/250–9133.* 🎟 *$10.* ⊙ *House and ticket booth daily 9:30–4:30, garden daily 9:30–5:30.*

Virginia Key and Key Biscayne

Government Cut and the Port of Miami separate the city's dense urban fabric from two of its playground islands, Virginia Key and Key Biscayne. Parks occupy much of both keys, providing facilities for golf, tennis, softball, picnicking, and sunbathing, plus uninviting but ecologically valuable stretches of dense mangrove swamp. Key Biscayne's long and winding roads are great for rollerblading and bicycling, and its lush, lazy setting provides a respite from the buzz-saw tempo of SoBe.

A Good Tour

To reach Virginia Key and Key Biscayne take the Rickenbacker Causeway ($1 per car) across Biscayne Bay from the mainland at Brickell Avenue and Southwest 26th Road, about 2 mi south of downtown Miami. The causeway links several islands in the bay.

The William M. Powell Bridge rises 75 ft above the water to eliminate the need for a draw span. The panoramic view from the top encompasses the bay, keys, port, and downtown skyscrapers, with Miami Beach and the Atlantic Ocean in the distance. Just south of the Powell Bridge, a stub of the **Old Rickenbacker Causeway Bridge** ㊳, built in 1947, is now a fishing pier with a nice view.

Immediately after crossing the Rickenbacker Causeway onto Virginia Key, you'll see a long strip of bay front popular with windsurfers and jet skiers. Nearby rest rooms and a great view of the curving shoreline make this an ideal place to park and have your own tailgate party. Look for the gold dome of the **Miami Seaquarium** ㊴, one of the country's first marine attractions. Opposite the causeway from the Seaquarium, a road leads north to Virginia Key Beach and the adjacent Virginia Key Critical Wildlife Area, which is often closed to the public to protect nesting birds.

From Virginia Key the causeway crosses Bear Cut to the north end of Key Biscayne and becomes Crandon Boulevard. The boulevard bisects 1,211-acre **Crandon Park** ㊵, which has a popular Atlantic Ocean beach and nature center. On your right are entrances to the Crandon Park Golf Course and the Tennis Center at Crandon Park, home of the Lipton Championships. Keep your eyes open for pure Miami icons: coconut palms and iguana-crossing signs.

From the traffic circle at the south end of Crandon Park, Crandon Boulevard continues to the **Bill Baggs Cape Florida State Recreation Area** ㊶, a 460-acre park containing, among other things, the brick Cape Florida Lighthouse and light keeper's cottage.

Follow Crandon Boulevard back to Crandon Park through Key Biscayne's downtown village, where shops and a 10-acre village green cater mainly to local residents. On your way back to the mainland, pause as you approach the Powell Bridge to admire the Miami skyline. At night the brightly lighted NationsBank Tower looks like a clipper ship running under full sail before the breeze.

TIMING

Set aside the better part of a day for this tour, double that if you're into beaches, fishing, and water sports.

Sights to See

★ **④①** **Bill Baggs Cape Florida State Recreation Area.** Thanks to great beaches, blue-green waters, amenities, sunsets, and a lighthouse, this park at Key Biscayne's southern tip is worth the drive. Since Hurricane Andrew, it has returned better than ever, with new boardwalks, 18 picnic shelters, and a café that serves beer, wine, and meals ranging from hot dogs to lobster. An additional 54 acres of wetlands were acquired in 1997, and a marina is on the drawing board. A stroll or ride along walking and bicycle paths and boardwalks provides wonderful views of Miami's dramatic skyline. Also on site are bicycle and skate rentals, a playground, fishing piers, and kayak rental. Guided tours of the cultural complex and the ☾ **Cape Florida Lighthouse**, South Florida's oldest structure, are offered, but call for availability. The lighthouse was erected in 1845 to replace an earlier one destroyed in an 1836 Seminole attack, in which the keeper's helper was killed. Climb 118 steps to visit a replica of the keeper's house. ✉ *1200 S. Crandon Blvd.,* ☎ *305/361–5811 or 305/361–8779.* 🎫 *$4 per vehicle with up to 8 people; $1 per person on bicycle, bus, motorcycle, or foot.* ☉ *Daily 8–sunset, tours Thurs.–Mon. 10 and 1.*

④⓪ **Crandon Park.** This laid-back park in northern Key Biscayne is popular with families, and many educated beach enthusiasts rate the 3½-mi county beach here among the top 10 beaches in North America. The sand is soft, there's a great view of the Atlantic, and parking is both inexpensive and plentiful. So large is this park that it includes a marina, golf course, tennis center, and ball fields. At the north end of the beach is the free **Marjory Stoneman Douglas Biscayne Nature Center** (☎ 305/642–9600). Explore a variety of natural habitats by taking a tour that includes dragging nets through sea-grass beds to catch, study, and release such marine creatures as sea cucumbers, seahorses, crabs, and shrimp. Nature center hours vary, so call ahead. ✉ *4000 Crandon Blvd.,* ☎ *305/361–5421.* 🎫 *$3.50 per vehicle.* ☉ *Daily 8–sunset.*

☾ **③⑨** **Miami Seaquarium.** This old-fashioned attraction has six daily shows featuring sea lions, dolphins, and Lolita, a killer whale. (Lolita's tank is small for seaquariums—just three times her length—and so some wildlife advocates are trying to get her back to sea.) Exhibits include a shark pool, a 235,000-gallon tropical-reef aquarium, and manatees. Glass-bottom boats take tours of Biscayne Bay. Want to get your feet (and everything else) wet? The Water and Dolphin Exploration program (WADE) enables you to swim with dolphins during a two-hour session. Reservations are required. ✉ *4400 Rickenbacker Causeway,* ☎ *305/361–5705.* 🎫 *$20.95, WADE $125, parking $3.* ☉ *Daily 9:30–6, last admission 4:30; WADE Wed.–Sun. 8:30 and noon.*

③⑧ **Old Rickenbacker Causeway Bridge.** Here you can watch boat traffic pass through the channel, pelicans and other seabirds soar and dive, and dolphins cavort in the bay. Park at its entrance, about a mile from the tollgate, and walk past anglers tending their lines to the gap where the center draw span across the Intracoastal Waterway was removed. ✉ *South of Powell Bridge.*

DINING

By Kendall Hamersly

So successful have Miami's better restaurants been that the local dining scene has attracted worldwide attention. The city is a cradle of culinary imagination, where international and indigenous flavors collide in delicious inspiration. Dining in Miami is also an essential part of nightlife, whether in the Cuban restaurants on Calle Ocho or in the

Miami Area Dining

ATLANTIC OCEAN

MIAMI BEACH

KEY

AE American Express
Office

N

Astor Place, **23**
Balan's, **11**
Blue Door at
 Delano, **17**
Café Barcelona, **46**
Café Prima Pasta, **5**
Café Tu Tu Tango, **49**
Captain's Tavern, **52**

Chef Allen's, **1**
China Grill, **27**
Darbar, **43**
East Coast
 Fisheries, **33**
11th St. Diner, **22**
El Rancho Grande, **15**
Fishbone Grill, **34**
The Forge, **8**

Giacosa, **42**
Grillfish, **19**
The Heights, **45**
Hy-Vong Vietnamese
 Cuisine, **40**
Joe's Stone Crab
 Restaurant, **29**
Johnny V's, **10**
Katana, **6**

Las Culebrinas, **36**
Lemon Twist, **7**
Le Pavillon, **32**
Los Ranchos, **31**
Mezzanotte, **20**
Mozart Stube, **38**
Mykonos, **48**
Nemo, **28**
News Café, **25**

Noodles of Asia
 (NOA), **14**
Norman's, **41**
Osteria del Teatro, **18**
Pacific Time, **12**
Perricone's
 Marketplace, **35**
Shula's Steak House, **2**
Siam Lotus Room, **51**

Specchio, **4**
Spiga, **21**
Sushi Republic, **3**
Tap Tap, **26**
Thai Toni, **24**
Tony Chan's
 Water Club, **30**
Tropical Chinese
 Restaurant, **50**

Two Sisters, **39**
Van Dyke Café, **13**
Versailles, **37**
Victor's Café, **47**
Wolfie's, **9**
Yuca, **16**

exclusive eateries of South Beach. The sizzle in Miami's food scene means fierce competition among restaurateurs, such that hopefuls open and failures close almost every week. Restaurants listed here have passed the test of time, but you might double-check by phone before you set out for the evening. At many of the hottest spots, you'll need a reservation to avoid a long wait for a table. And when you get your check, note whether a gratuity is already included; most restaurants add 15% (ostensibly for the convenience of and protection from the many Latin-American and European tourists who are used to this practice in their homelands), but you can reduce or supplement it depending on your opinion of the service.

Coconut Grove

Greek

$–$$$ ✕ **Mykonos.** Since 1973 this busy Miami fixture has brightened the intersection at Five Points (in the Roads section of town) with a beautiful exterior mural of the Aegean. Inside, a sparkling blue-and-white setting is dressed up with Greek travel posters. Specialties include gyros, moussaka, marinated lamb and chicken, calamari and octopus sautéed in wine and onions, and sumptuous Greek salads thick with feta cheese and briny olives. Vegetarian moussaka, eggplant roll, lasagna, and a Greek-style omelet are also on the menu. ⊠ *1201 Coral Way*, ☎ *305/856–3140. AE, DC, MC, V. No lunch Sun.*

Latin

$–$$ ✕ **Café Tu Tu Tango.** Local artists set up their easels in the rococo-modern arcades of this café-lounge on the second story of Coconut Grove's highly popular CocoWalk. The artistic concept follows through to the menu, which allows you to pick appetizers as if you were selecting paints from a palette. A never boring parade of people passes by outside, while inside, guests graze on chips, dips, breads, and spreads. House specials include frittatas, crab cakes, *picadillo* empanadas (pastries stuffed with spicy ground beef and served with cilantro sour cream), and chicken and shrimp orzo paella, all to be enjoyed with some of the best sangria in the city. ⊠ *3015 Grand Ave. (CocoWalk)*, ☎ *305/529–2222. AE, MC, V.*

Coral Gables

Austrian

$$–$$$ ✕ **Mozart Stube.** It's Oktoberfest year-round at this Austrian *schnitzelhaus.* The Bitburger flows early and often as you peruse a menu loaded down with heavy but scrumptious food. Start with a light garlic soup or maybe some snails in a lagoon of butter and garlic. A terrific side of German potato salad, homemade slaw, and more precedes ultrameaty entrées like veal shank, roast duckling, medallions of filet mignon in peppercorn-mushroom sauce, and of course wurst and schnitzel. The Black Forest cake is legendary. ⊠ *325 Alcazar Ave.*, ☎ *305/446–1600. AE, D, DC, MC, V.*

Contemporary

$$$–$$$$ ✕ **The Heights.** Food as design is the rule at this stylish Gables spot, ★ but there's integrity, too. Pan-seared Sonoma Valley foie gras with clove-spiked caramelized pear, chile-spiced corn cake, toasted walnuts with port, and red chile drizzlers seems almost too much to take until you eat it. You'll feel the same about the wheat-berry salad with chile-crusted barbecue quail and jalapeño-orange sauce or the organic greens with apple cider vinaigrette, sweet roast garlic, and toasted *pepitas* (little pumpkin seeds). Tuna gets a crust of New Mexican chile, served with

cactus tempura and Japanese-style soy-ponzu sauce, and sea bass is glazed with *achiote* (a yellow-orange Mexican spice) and served with jicama, asparagus, and a citrus beurre blanc. And there's more—pumpkin pie with pink-peppercorn ice cream—making for heady Heights indeed. ⊠ *2530 Ponce de León Blvd.,* ☎ *305/461–1774. AE, D, DC, MC, V.*

Eclectic

$$$$ ✕ **Norman's.** This elegantly casual restaurant, which has won as many
★ awards as it has customers, turns out gourmet cuisine with an edge. Nationally acclaimed chef Norman Van Aken has created a buzz by perfecting the art of New World cuisine—a combination rooted in Latin, North American, Caribbean, and Asian influences. Bold tastes are delivered in every dish, whether it's a simple black-and-white bean soup with sour cream, chorizo, and tortillas or a rum-and-pepper-painted grouper on a mango-*habanero mojo* sauce. From the comfortable decor to the staff that never seems harried even when all seats are filled (usually every minute between opening and closing), Norman's has captured the essence of Miami dining. ⊠ *21 Almeria Ave.,* ☎ *305/446–6767. AE, DC, MC, V. Closed Sun. No lunch Sat.*

$$–$$$ ✕ **Two Sisters.** Competition among Coral Gables restaurants means the food here has to be better than fantastic. This restaurant, on the ground floor of the Hyatt Regency, approaches nirvana. Though the mood is understated, the Pacific Rim–inspired dishes have definite pizzazz. Entrées such as wok-cooked tangled shrimp with jungle curry, rice ribbons, and coconut glaze or the jerk marinated snapper with red onion confit and ginger butter might make you consider a vacation in the South Pacific. But stay in South Florida with your attentive servers and experience incredibly delicious desserts. ⊠ *50 Alhambra Plaza,* ☎ *305/441–1234. AE, MC, V.*

Indian

$–$$ ✕ **Darbar.** Owner Bobby Nangia's impeccably arranged Darbar (Royal Court, in English) is the leader among Miami's Indian restaurants. Surrounded by portraits of turbaned maharajas, witness flavors rise as if in a dance from the *bangan bharta* (eggplant mashed with onions, tomatoes, herbs, and spices and baked in a tandoori oven). The menu focuses on northern Indian, or frontier, cuisine—various kebabs, tandoori platters, and *tikkas* (chicken or lamb marinated in yogurt and spices and cooked tandoori style)—although there are also curries from different regions and *biryani* specialties prepared with basmati rice and garnished with boiled egg, tomato, nuts, and raisins. Everything, including the delectable Indian breads, is cooked to order. ⊠ *276 Alhambra Circle,* ☎ *305/448–9691. AE, DC, MC, V. No lunch Sun.*

Italian

$$$–$$$$ ✕ **Giacosa.** Named for one of Puccini's librettists, Giacosa is both superbly evocative and just plain superb. The thickly carpeted room resembles a smart Venetian salon, courtesy of fresh flowers and chair cushions with designs inspired by tapestries. From the moment they place your napkin in your lap to the moment they discreetly present your check, the smooth staff is the standard of competence. While you contemplate your choices, a server whisks a tower of airy pita bread with a carafe of olive oil to your table. A salad *tricolore* imparts the bitter kiss of arugula; pastas, veal, and fresh seafood are all prepared for peak taste. Whenever you request it, Parmesan is freshly grated on the plate. ⊠ *394 Giralda Ave.,* ☎ *305/445–5858. AE, DC, MC, V. No lunch weekends.*

$$–$$$ ✕ **Caffe Abbracci.** Although the kitchen closes at midnight, the last wave of weekend customers—usually Brazilians—is still partying to flamenco or salsa music at 2 AM. The graciously Deco setting overflows with flowers, and the light above each table operates on an individual dimmer. After the cold and hot antipasti—various carpaccios, porcini mushrooms, calamari, grilled goat cheese, shrimps, mussels—come festive entrées. Most pasta is made fresh, so consider sampling two or three, maybe with pesto sauce, Gorgonzola, and fresh tomatoes. Room for dessert? Napoleons and tiramisu are made here daily, and there's always a choice of fresh fruit tarts. ⊠ *318 Aragon Ave.,* ☎ *305/441–0700. Reservations essential. AE, DC, MC, V. No lunch weekends.*

Spanish

$ ✕ **Café Barcelona.** In a room with high ceilings and coral walls, gilt-framed art and slender ceiling lamps with tiny, green fluted shades impart a rich glow. The result is an ambience that's part art gallery and part private home. Exceptional food matches the exceptional mood, and in a city where fresh fish has gotten priced off the deep end, entrées here range a good $5 below comparable dishes at the top restaurants. The chef does a sea bass in sea salt for two, a traditional codfish with garlic confit, and a grouper in a clay pot with seafood sauce, as well as lamb, duck, and several affordable rice dishes, including three types of paella. The *crema Catalana,* a version of flan, is not to be missed. ⊠ *160 Giralda Ave.,* ☎ *305/448–0912. AE, D, DC, MC, V.*

Downtown Miami

Chinese

$$–$$$$ ✕ **Tony Chan's Water Club.** One of a pair of outstanding Chinese restaurants, this beautiful dining room just off the lobby of the high-rise DoubleTree Grand Hotel looks onto a bay-side marina. Filled with art and detailed with chrome, the long room is modern rather than stereotypically Chinese. On the menu of more than 200 appetizers and entrées are minced quail tossed with bamboo shoots and mushrooms wrapped in lettuce leaves. Indulge in a seafood spectacular of shrimp, conch, scallops, fish cakes, and crabmeat tossed with broccoli in a bird's nest, or go for pork chops sprinkled with green pepper in a black bean–garlic sauce. A lighter favorite is steamed sea bass with ginger and garlic. ⊠ *1717 N. Bayshore Dr.,* ☎ *305/374–8888. AE, D, DC, MC, V.*

Contemporary

$$$ ✕ **Le Pavillon.** The mahogany, jade marble, and leather appointments of the dining room in the Hotel Inter-Continental evoke the conservative air of an English private club. Beautiful floral displays enhance the mood as the attentive staff serves regional American fare from a limited but frequently changing menu, including items low in calories, cholesterol, and sodium. Specialties are char-grilled bluefin tuna fillet, poached yellowtail snapper, panfried corn-fed squab, roasted free-range chicken, spring lamb, and roasted fillet of milk-fed veal. For a light dessert try red-berry soup with vanilla ice cream. The wine list is extensive. ⊠ *100 Chopin Plaza,* ☎ *305/577–1000, ext. 4494; 305/577–1000, ext. 4494 or 4462. AE, DC, MC, V. Closed Sun. No dinner.*

Italian

$$–$$$ ✕ **Perricone's Marketplace.** The emerging neighborhood along Brickell Avenue south of the Miami River seems to be swelling with Italian restaurants. This one, housed in a 120-year-old barn brought down from Vermont by the owner, is the biggest and most popular among them. The recipes are ancient, too, handed down grandmother to mother to daughter, and the cooking is simple and good. Next door, a deli carries a selection of wine that you can bring to the table for a small corkage fee. Enjoy a glass with homemade minestrone; a generous antipasto; linguine with a sauté of jumbo shrimp, fresh asparagus, and chopped tomatoes; or gnocchi with four cheeses. The homemade

tiramisu and fruit tart are top-notch. ⊠ *15 S.E. 10th St.,* ☎ *305/374–9449. AE, MC, V. Beer and wine only. Closed Sun. No lunch Sat.*

Latin

$–$$$ ✕ **Los Ranchos.** Owner Carlos Somoza, nephew of Nicaragua's late president Anastasio Somoza, sustains the tradition of Managua's original Los Ranchos by serving Argentine-style beef—lean, grass-fed tenderloin with chimichurri. Nicaragua's own sauces are a tomato-based marinara and the fiery *cebollitas encurtidas,* with jalapeño and pickled onion. Specialties include chorizo and *cuajada con maduro* (skim cheese with fried bananas). Don't look for veggies or brewed decaf, but there is live entertainment. ⊠ *Bayside Marketplace, 401 Biscayne Blvd.,* ☎ *305/375–8188 or 305/375–0666;* ⊠ *2728 Ponce de León Blvd., Coral Gables,* ☎ *305/446–0050;* ⊠ *Kendall Town & Country, 8505 Mills Dr., Kendall (South Miami),* ☎ *305/596–5353;* ⊠ *The Falls, 8888 S.W. 136th St., Suite 303, South Miami,* ☎ *305/238–6867;* ⊠ *125 S.W. 107th Ave., Little Managua (West Dade),* ☎ *305/221–9367. AE, DC, MC, V.*

Seafood

$$–$$$$ ✕ **East Coast Fisheries.** This friendly family-owned restaurant and retail fish market on the Miami River offers fresh Florida seafood caught by its own 38-boat fleet in the Keys. From tables along the second-floor balcony, watch the cooks prepare your dinner in the open kitchen below. Specialties include a complimentary fish-pâté appetizer, blackened pompano with owner Peter Swartz's personal herb-and-spice recipe, lightly breaded fried grouper, and a homemade key lime pie. ⊠ *360 W. Flagler St.,* ☎ *305/372–1300. AE, MC, V. Beer and wine only.*

$–$$ ✕ **Fishbone Grill.** The artsy humor of this place is evident in the menus, each of which bears a different magazine cover, but the fish here is nononsense and impeccably fresh. Start with hearty, cheesy, cakelike jalapeño corn bread, served alongside a small salad with your entrée. Smoked salmon mousse with French bread is tasty, too, as is gazpacho. Order your fresh fish from a blackboard, and have it grilled, blackened, sauteed, baked, Française-style, or Oriental. Pizzas are available, too, as is a mean cioppino, the San Francisco–style fish stew in a tomato base. ⊠ *650 S. Miami Ave.,* ☎ *305/530–1915. AE, MC, V. Beer and wine only. No dinner Sun.*

Little Havana

Cuban

$$–$$$ ✕ **Victor's Café.** The look of this popular restaurant was inspired by ★ *casonas,* the great houses of colonial Cuba. The mood is old Havana, with Cuban art and antiques and a glass-covered fountain courtyard; come on Friday afternoon, when the tapas bar is packed and lunch often lasts until dusk, in Cuban fashion. A Cuban immigrant, owner Victor del Corral runs the place with his daughter, Sonia Zaldivar, and her son Luis. Hot appetizers, such as a puff pastry filled with aromatically herbed lump crabmeat or savory cassava turnover filled with Florida lobster, can be enough for a meal. Truly jumbo shrimp come with yam quenelles in a creamy champagne sauce sprinkled with salmon roe. Entrées come with rice and black beans, and romantic music plays nightly. ⊠ *2340 S.W. 32nd Ave.,* ☎ *305/445–1313. AE, MC, V.*

$–$$ ✕ **Versailles.** Cubans meet to dine on Calle Ocho in what is quite possibly the most garish budget restaurant you'll ever see. It's all mirrors and candelabras and hairdos and tuxedoed waiters, with hundreds of seats and a tremendous din. The food is terrific, especially classics like *ropa vieja* (Cuban-style shredded beef), arroz con pollo, *palomilla* steak, *sopa de platanos* (plantain soup), ham shank, and roast pork. To achieve a total experience, have the town's strongest Cuban coffee and a terrific flan or sweet *tres leches* to finish. ⊠ *3555 S.W. 8th St.,* ☎ *305/444–0240. AE, D, DC, MC, V.*

Spanish

$–$$ ✕ **Las Culebrinas.** A Spanish *tapaceria* ("house of little plates") is a place to live each meal as if it were your last, with much wine, much fun, much noise, and much food. Tapas are not small at all; some are entrée size, such as a succulent mix of garbanzos with ham, sausage, red peppers, and oil, or the Spanish tortilla, a giant Frisbee-shape omelet. Entrée-wise, indulge in tender fillet of crocodile, fresh fish, grilled pork, and more. For dessert, there's a bit of a show—crema Catalana, a puffy cream caramelized at the table with, you guessed it, a blowtorch. ⊠ *4700 W. Flagler St.,* ☎ *305/445–2337. AE, MC, V. Beer and wine only.*

Vietnamese

$–$$ ✕ **Hy-Vong Vietnamese Cuisine.** Beer-savvy proprietor Kathy Manning
★ serves a half-dozen top brews (Double Grimbergen, Moretti, and Spaten, among them) at this plain little restaurant, and magic pours forth from the tiny kitchen. Come before 7 to avoid a wait. Favorites include spring rolls of ground pork, cellophane noodles, and black mushrooms wrapped in homemade rice paper; whole fish panfried with *nuoc mam*, a garlic-lime fish sauce; and thinly sliced pork barbecued with sesame seeds and fish sauce and served with bean sprouts, rice noodles, and slivers of carrots, almonds, and peanuts. ⊠ *3458 S.W. 8th St.,* ☎ *305/446–3674. No credit cards. Closed Mon. and 2 wks in Aug. No lunch.*

Miami Beach North of South Beach

Continental

$$$–$$$$ ✕ **The Forge.** Often compared to a museum, this landmark restaurant, which bills itself as "the Versailles of steak," stands behind a facade like that of a 19th-century Parisian mansion. Each intimate dining salon has its own historical artifacts, including a chandelier that hung in James Madison's White House. The wine cellar contains 380,000 bottles—including more than 500 dating from 1822 (and costing as much as $35,000) and recorked in 1989 by experts from Domaines Barons de Rothschild. In addition to steak, specialties include Norwegian salmon served over fresh garden vegetables with spinach vinaigrette and free-range Wisconsin duck roasted with black currants. For dessert try the blacksmith pie. This place is a hot party spot on Wednesday night, and the adjoining club, Jimmy'z at the Forge, is very popular with the rich and famous. ⊠ *432 Arthur Godfrey Rd.,* ☎ *305/538–8533. AE, DC, MC, V. No lunch.*

Italian

$–$$ ✕ **Café Prima Pasta.** As many Italian restaurants in Miami are run by
★ Argentines as by Italians. One of the best is this cozy spot in the emerging North Beach neighborhood. Consistently intense flavors, high-quality ingredients, and just plain good cooking are the key. Service can be disjointed and erratic, but you forget it all upon delivery of fresh-made bread with a dipping oil of garlic, parsley, virgin olive oil, and crushed red pepper. Also good are carpaccio, antipasto, pasta *e fagioli* (a soup with pasta and beans), and a gigantic platter of pasta with seafood. Have a legendary tiramisu to finish. ⊠ *414 71st St.,* ☎ *305/ 867–0106. No credit cards.*

$–$$ ✕ **Specchio.** Homemade pastas and sauces, rich soups, and luscious meats draw a sophisticated before- and after-theater crowd to this brightly lit, fun dining room. You can buy art right off the wall, but it's better to devote most of your attention to the brilliant food. Chomp on crusty bread with chopped tomato, garlic, and basil as you select from a broad menu. Grilled vegetables are a light starter, as are cream-free pureed vegetable soups and an arugula salad with crabmeat and avocado. Beef gets real-food treatment with *tagliata di manzo al rosmarino* (sliced sirloin steak with rosemary and arugula), or try black-ink linguine with shrimp and fresh tomato. ✉ *9485 Harding Ave., Surfside,* ☎ *305/865–5653. MC, V.*

Japanese

$–$$ ✕ **Sushi Republic.** This tiny spot lies on the main drag of Surfside, a resort area that straddles an Annette Funicello–style past and a Euro-tourist future. Here you'll find one of the freshest and tastiest sushi spreads in town, along with cooked items that excel. Try *shumai* (soft shrimp dumplings with ponzu sauce), whole fried softshell crab, and succulent salmon teriyaki. Among rolls, the Tiger Woods roll—tuna rolled with cream cheese and topped with avocado and salmon—is a hole in one. Cool nights call for a steaming noodle soup like *nabeyaki udon,* a broth laden with udon noodles, eggs, mushrooms, and big pieces of shrimp tempura. ✉ *9583 Harding Ave., Surfside,* ☎ *305/867–8036. AE, D, DC, MC, V. Closed Mon. No lunch Sun.*

$ ✕ **Katana.** Here's a sushi spot where you not only eat the fish, you catch it. An oval moat is the centerpiece of the tiny (only 30 seats) bar. It's filled with little wooden boats that circle the moat and deliver bits of sushi on color-coded plates. Pluck the plates that appeal to you and pay by the plate at the end. What could be more fun? Gimmicks aside, this is tasty sushi and a real value for a quick, quick bite. Best are rainbow rolls (California rolls with thin-sliced tuna, salmon, and avocado arrayed on top); *futomaki* (pickled Japanese vegetables rolled with rice and seaweed) with spinach, crab, and egg; and simple, fresh sashimi of tuna or salmon. But go early: Katana is packed every night. ✉ *920 71st St.,* ☎ *305/864–0037. AE, MC, V. Closed Mon. No lunch.*

Mediterranean

$–$$ ✕ **Lemon Twist.** From the start—a complimentary bowl of green and black olives with virgin olive oil, garlic, lemon, cayenne pepper, lavender, and thyme—you know you're in for South Beach style in a quiet North Beach setting. The model-pretty crowd makes the pilgrimage north to visit this French-Mediterranean spot. Try an excellent gazpacho with condiments you add at the table, a nosh of roasted vegetables with lemony cream, and meaty entrées including a beautiful pounded chicken breast with lemon and butter. One luscious side dish to look for is baked potato casserole au gratin; also keep an eye out for lasagna with salmon in lobster-tomato bisque. ✉ *908 71st St.,* ☎ *305/868–2075. AE, MC, V. No lunch.*

North Miami Beach and North Dade

Contemporary

$$$–$$$$ ✕ **Chef Allen's.** In this Art Deco world of glass block, art, neon trim, ★ and fresh flowers, your gaze remains riveted on the kitchen. Chef Allen Susser designed it with a picture window 25 ft wide, so you can watch him create contemporary American masterpieces from a menu that changes nightly. After a salad of baby greens and warm wild mushrooms or a rock-shrimp hash with roasted corn, consider *orecchiette* pasta with sun-dried tomatoes, goat cheese, spinach, and toasted pine nuts; swordfish with conch-citrus couscous, macadamia nuts,

and lemon; or grilled lamb chops with eggplant timbale and a three-nut salsa. A favorite dessert is the double-chocolate soufflé with lots of nuts. New is Chef Allen's Gourmet to Go, a takeout place with excellent food at grocery store–deli prices. Take home a bottle of Chef Allen's mango ketchup as a tasty souvenir. ⊠ *19088 N.E. 29th Ave., Aventura,* ☎ *305/935–2900. AE, DC, MC, V.*

Steak

$$–$$$$ ✕ **Shula's Steak House.** Prime rib, fish (including dolphin), and award-winning steaks are almost an afterthought to the icons in this shrine for the NFL-obsessed, located at the club part of Don Shula's Hotel & Golf Club (☞ Lodging, *below*). Dine in a woody setting with a fireplace, surrounded by memorabilia of retired coach Don Shula's perfect 1972 season with the Miami Dolphins, including game footballs, assistant coach Howard Schnellenberger's pipe, and a playbook autographed by President Richard Nixon. Polish off the 48-ounce porterhouse steak and achieve a sort of immortality—your name on a plaque and an autographed picture of Shula. Also for fans, there's shula's steak 2 (lowercase borrowed from espn2), a sports celebrity hangout in the resort's hotel section, as well as a branch at the Alexander Hotel (☞ Lodging, *below*), in Miami Beach. ⊠ *7601 N.W. 154th St., Miami Lakes,* ☎ *305/820–8102. AE, DC, MC, V.*

South Beach

American

$–$$ ✕ **11th Street Diner.** Come here to relive the sights, sounds, and smells of the '50s, without the artificial ambience of James Dean cutouts and poodle skirts. Since serving its first plate of meat loaf in 1992, the diner has become a low-priced, unpretentious hangout for locals. The best time to visit is weekend mornings, when the stragglers from the night before and early birds with their morning papers converge for conversation. At this busy, bustling eatery in a 1948 Deco-style dining car, you can grab a corner booth and order a cherry cola, a blue-plate special, or a milk shake and pretend you've traveled back in time. ⊠ *11th St. and Washington Ave.,* ☎ *305/534–6373. AE, MC, V.*

Café

$–$$ ✕ **News Café.** An Ocean Drive landmark, this 24-hour café attracts
★   a big crowd around the clock with snacks, light meals, drinks, and the sidewalk people parade. There's a bar with 12 stools in back, but most diners prefer sitting outside, where they can feel the salt breeze and gawk at the human scenery. Offering a little of this and a little of that—bagels, pâtés, chocolate fondue, sandwiches, and a terrific wine list—this joint has something for everyone. In 1997 the café spawned a new location—twice as large—in Coconut Grove; by 2000 the owners hope to open another, on Biscayne Boulevard. ⊠ *800 Ocean Dr.,* ☎ *305/538–6397;* ⊠ *2901 Florida Ave., Coconut Grove,* ☎ *305/774–6397. AE, DC, MC, V.*

Caribbean

$–$$ ✕ **Tap Tap.** South Beach style is in full flower at this Haitian bar/restaurant on the northern fringe of SoFi, the part of South Beach south of 5th Street. It's an art gallery and concert venue as well as the Beach's only spot to try spicy, fascinating Haitian cuisine. Luxuriate in a bowl of pumpkin chowder, with *calabaza* (a Caribbean pumpkin), chayote, and yam, plus the ever-present scotch bonnet pepper. Conch fritters come with *malanga* fritters and a cooling watercress sauce. Goat is simmered in a sauce made of tomato and chayote; shrimp are creole and tender; and fish is whole and served with a spicy fruit salsa. To finish, dip into the delectable coconut custard with almonds and cream. ⊠ *819 5th St., ☎ 305/672–2898. AE, DC, MC, V. No lunch.*

Contemporary

$–$$ ✕ **Johnny V's.** "Cowboy chef" Johnny Vinzencz, ringleader at Astor Place (☞ *below*), has a casual place here. Diner design belies gourmet aspirations, and some menu items are even duplicated from the swanky Astor at a much lower price. Southwestern flavors, such as barbecue, chilies, smoked meats, and roasted corn, predominate—each one a revelation. Homemade soups change daily. Mango inspires coleslaw, and handmade potato chips are spicy. If you're hungry, dig into the Miami Thanksgiving—herb-roasted turkey with plantain stuffing and mango-cranberry chutney. The fainter of heart won't find relief with the smoked turkey sandwich, which is nearly unfinishable, but after the main course the bold will be tempted by the Double Mac Daddy Brownie, as big and caloric as it sounds. Walk out the door with a jar of pickles, salsa, sauce, chutney, oil, stock, or ketchup to go. ⊠ *1671 Alton Rd., ☎ 305/534–2433. AE, MC, V.*

$–$$ ✕ **Van Dyke Café.** Just as its parent, News Café, draws the fashion crowd, this offshoot attracts the artsy crowd. Of course, tourists like it, too. In the restored 1924 Van Dyke Hotel, this place seems even livelier than its Ocean Drive counterpart, with pedestrians passing by on the Lincoln Road Mall and live jazz playing upstairs every evening. The kitchen serves three meals daily, featuring dishes from mammoth omelets with home fries to soups and grilled dolphin sandwiches to basil-grilled lamb and pasta dishes. There's an impressive list of wines and desserts. ⊠ *846 Lincoln Rd., ☎ 305/534–3600. AE, DC, MC, V.*

Cuban

$$–$$$$ ✕ **Yuca.** Top-flight Cuban dining can be had at this bistro-chic restau-
★ rant on Lincoln Road. Yuca, the potatolike staple of Cuban kitchens, also stands for the kind of Young Urban Cuban-Americans who frequent the place. The food rises to high standards: traditional corn tamales filled with conch and a spicy jalapeño and creole cheese pesto, the namesake yuca stuffed with *mamacita's picadillo* and dressed in wild mushrooms on a bed of sautéed spinach, and plantain-coated dolphin with a tamarind tartar sauce. Featured desserts include classic Cuban rice pudding in an almond basket and coconut pudding in its shell. Friday- and Saturday-evening entertainment is provided by Albita, a popular Cuban chanteuse. ⊠ *501 Lincoln Rd., ☎ 305/532–9822. AE, DC, MC, V.*

Delicatessen

$ ✕ **Wolfie's.** If there's one place in Miami that screams New York, this is it. A bakery featuring giga-caloric desserts, steaming bowls of matzo ball soup, and sandwiches stacked high with pastrami make you feel like you're eating in Brooklyn. If you want to see what Miami looked like 40 years ago, sidle up to the counter or share a round booth in Celebrity Corner. Open 24 hours, this is a perfect place to soak up some local color or satisfy a late-night craving for corned beef. ⊠ *2038 Collins Ave., ☎ 305/538–6626. D, DC, MC, V.*

Eclectic

$$$$ ✕ **Blue Door at Delano.** In a hotel where style reigns supreme, service
★ and meals at its restaurant are in fact quite good. Acclaimed chef Claude Troisgros combines the flavors of classic French cuisine with South American influences to create dishes like the Big Raviole, filled with taro-root mousseline and white-truffle oil, and *boeuf au manioc* (a beef tenderloin in a cabernet sauce and yuca biscuit). The dessert menu showcases such selections as a Brazilian coffee and sweet chocolate mousse as well as banana puff pastry with strawberries and cin-

namon. Equally pleasing is dining with the crème de la crème of Miami (and New York and Paris) society. *Bon appétit!* ✉ *1685 Collins Ave.,* ☎ *305/674–6400. Reservations essential. AE, D, DC, MC, V.*

$$$–$$$$ ✕ **Astor Place.** The Hotel Astor had already earned a reputation for
★ exceptional service, so it was only natural that its basement-turned-bright-and-airy-restaurant followed suit. Chef Johnny Vinzencz wows diners with his "New Floridian Barbecue," centered on grilled meats, tropical fruits, and such Floridian ingredients as *boniato* (a big, white, potatolike tuber) and stone crab. He puts creative spins on appetizers like yellowtail snapper soft tacos and entrées that include ancho-cinnamon pork tenderloin and skillet-steamed sea bass. Critics nationwide have admired the signature short stack of wild-mushroom pancakes drizzled with balsamic syrup. The lunch menu is just as interesting as dinner's. ✉ *956 Washington Ave.,* ☎ *305/672–7217. AE, DC, MC, V.*

$$$–$$$$ ✕ **China Grill.** This crowded, noisy place has no view, but that doesn't
★ detract from its popularity or that of the original China Grill in New York. Jack Nicholson, Joe Pesci, and other celebs are regulars—perhaps hoping to live the dream of finishing the Grill's 38-ounce porterhouse steak. Contrary to what you might think, chef Ephraim Kadish turns out not Chinese food but rather "world cuisine," in portions large and meant for sharing. Crispy duck with caramelized black vinegar sauce and scallion pancakes is a nice surprise, as is pork and beans with green apple and balsamic mojo. Don't miss the broccoli rabe dumpling starter, the wild-mushroom pasta entrée, or the flash-fried crispy spinach that shatters when eaten. ✉ *404 Washington Ave.,* ☎ *305/534–2211. AE, DC, MC, V. No lunch Sat.*

$$$–$$$$ ✕ **Nemo.** Back in 1994, chef Michael Schwartz took a chance open-
★ ing this restaurant in the struggling south end of SoBe. Today, however, Nemo is receiving raves from gourmands, and the neighborhood—fueled by luxury condominium and hotel projects—is emerging as SoBe's next hot spot. So get here while you can still find a table. The open-air atmosphere, bright colors, copper fixtures, and tree-shaded courtyard lend casual comfort, and a menu that blends Caribbean, Japanese, and Southeast Asian influences promises an explosion of cultures in each bite. Popular appetizers include garlic-cured salmon rolls with *tabiko* caviar and wasabi mayo and crispy prawns with spicy salsa *cruda.* Favorite entrées? Try the wok-charred salmon or the grilled Indian-spiced pork chop—and there's more where those came from. Nemo also serves up a terrific Sunday brunch. ✉ *100 Collins Ave.,* ☎ *305/532–4550. AE, MC, V.*

$$$–$$$$ ✕ **Pacific Time.** Packed nearly every night, this superb eatery owned
★ by chef Jonathan Eismann has a high blue ceiling and banquettes, accents of mahogany and brass, plank floors, and an open-window kitchen. The brilliant American-Asian cuisine includes such entrées as cedar-roasted salmon, rosemary-roasted chicken, and dry-aged Colorado beef grilled with shiitake mushrooms. The cuttlefish appetizer and the Florida pompano entrée are masterpieces. Rice dishes, potatoes, and vegetables are à la carte; however, a pretheater prix-fixe dinner ($20), served 6–7, comes with a noodle dish, Szechuan mixed grill, and grilled ginger chicken. Desserts (around $7) include a fresh pear-pecan spring roll. There's an extensive California wine list. Pacific Time/Next Door, a casual satellite restaurant a door to the west, has the same excellent food and service for a bit less. ✉ *915 Lincoln Rd.,* ☎ *305/534–5979. AE, DC, MC, V.*

$–$$ ✕ **Balan's.** The British are coming, all right—to Lincoln Road and this low-priced, stylish spot. However, aside from breakfast and desserts, this outpost of an English chain bears scant stamp of the mother country. Instead, a fusion of Mediterranean, Middle Eastern, and Thai delights the fashionable crowd here. Try deep-fried goat cheese and mushrooms in a beer and caraway bread crust; Moroccan chicken with a spicy, spicy sauce; sea bass over oven-roasted Italian tomatoes and sautéed potato slices; or sirloin steak with balsamic glaze and black lentils. The place is especially busy at breakfast. ⊠ *1022 Lincoln Rd.,* ☎ *305/534–9191. AE, D, MC, V.*

Italian

\$\$–\$\$\$ ✕ **Mezzanotte.** Sometime between 6 and 10, this big square room with a square bar transforms from an empty catering hall to a New Year's Eve party. Many weekend nights you'll see guests—and staff— dancing on tabletops. Trendoids call for cappellini with fresh tomato and basil; calamari in clam juice, garlic, and red wine; or scallopini with mushroom, pepper, and white wine. In the off-season lobster specials are a great deal. Top off your meal with a *dolci* such as a fresh napoleon, chocolate mousse, or tiramisu. Chic and intimate, Mezzanotte is known for fine food at moderate prices. ⊠ *1200 Washington Ave.,* ☎ *305/673–4343;* ⊠ *3390 Mary St., Coconut Grove,* ☎ *305/ 448–7677. AE, D, DC, MC, V. No lunch in Miami Beach.*

\$\$–\$\$\$ ✕ **Osteria del Teatro.** Thanks to word of mouth, this northern Italian
★ restaurant is constantly full. Orchids grace the tables in the intimate gray-on-gray room with a low laced-canvas ceiling, Deco lamps, and the most refined clink and clatter along Washington Avenue's re- markable restaurant row. You'll start with large hunks of homemade bread lightly toasted. Then try an appetizer such as grilled Portobello mushrooms topped with fontina cheese and served over a bed of arugula with a green peppercorn–brandy sauce. For the main course, one standout is the linguine sautéed with chunks of jumbo shrimp, roasted peppers, capers, black olives, fresh diced tomato, and herbs in a tangy garlic–olive oil sauce. ⊠ *1443 Washington Ave.,* ☎ *305/538– 7850. AE, DC, MC, V. Closed Tues. No lunch.*

\$\$–\$\$\$ ✕ **Spiga.** When you need a break from Miami's abundant exotic fare, savor the modestly priced Italian standards that are served with flair in this small, pretty place. Homemade is the hallmark here, and pas- tas and breads are fresh daily. Carpaccio *di salmone* (thinly sliced salmon with mixed greens) is a typical appetizer, and the *zuppa di pesce* (fish soup) is unparalleled. Entrées include ravioli *di vitello ai funghi shitaki,* homemade ravioli stuffed with veal and sautéed with shiitake mushrooms. The cozy restaurant has become a neighborhood favorite where customers sometimes bring in CDs for their personal enjoyment. ⊠ *1228 Collins Ave.,* ☎ *305/534–0079. AE, D, DC, MC, V.*

Mexican

\$–\$\$ ✕ **El Rancho Grande.** The location (just off Lincoln Road) and the menu (mainstream Mexican) have made this neighborhood restaurant pop- ular with locals and earned it a slew of "best" awards in area dining polls. Prices are reasonable, and service is casual and laid-back. Beef *flautas,* chicken enchiladas, *taquitas,* and more are served in a cantina- style setting. This is a good option for a quick and inexpensive meal. ⊠ *1626 Pennsylvania Ave.,* ☎ *305/673–0480. AE, MC, V.*

Pan-Asian

\$\$ ✕ **Noodles of Asia (NOA).** This inexpensive house of noodles once again proves that South Beach takes style seriously. Green-glass etchings, stained wood ceilings, gleaming metal stairwell walls, brushed metal stairs, and burlap-covered booths all contribute to a modern-art-museum look. Food is similarly artistic, but portions can be scant. All entrées feature some sort of noodle, representing a pan-Asian array from Malaysia, China, Thailand, Vietnam, Japan, and other countries. Most dishes are rather spicy, and some are fantastic: smoky pork dumplings, Vietnamese-style grape leaves with beef and lemongrass, Thai beef salad. Various sorbets are the best choices for dessert. ⊠ *801 Lincoln Rd.,* ☎ *305/925–0050. AE, MC, V.*

Seafood

$$$–$$$$ ✕ **Joe's Stone Crab Restaurant.** "Before SoBe, Joe Be," touts this fourth-generation family restaurant with a chest-puffing facade at the base of Washington Avenue. Joe's attracts phenomenal crowds despite stubbornly refusing reservations, so go prepared to wait—up to an hour to register for a table, perhaps another *three* to sit down. Depending on the crowd, the wait can be convivial or contentious. The center-piece of the menu is, of course, stone crab: About a ton of claws are served daily with drawn butter, lemon wedges, and piquant mustard sauce. Save room for dessert—key lime pie or apple pie with a crumb-pecan topping. If you can't stand loitering hungrily while self-impor-tant patrons try to grease the maître d's palm, go next door for Joe's takeout. ⊠ *227 Biscayne St.,* ☎ *305/673–0365; 305/673–4611 for take-out; 800/780–2722 for overnight shipping. Reservations not accepted. AE, D, DC, MC, V. Closed Sept. 1–Oct. 15. No lunch Sun.–Mon.*

$–$$$ ✕ **Grillfish.** An eclectic crowd of over-it locals and Bermuda-shorted tourists get along happily at this dramatically Deco-style spot in the heart of South Beach. They watch as delicacies emerge from a busy, open, stainless-steel kitchen. Delicious takes on grilled fish grace the tables—perhaps simple grilled tuna, seared outside, rosy pink inside, and just how you like it. Or get the seafood quesadilla if it's available. Some of the world's best fried calamari, with marinara, shows up, and squid over pasta with marinara is a tasty bargain. ⊠ *1444 Collins Ave.,* ☎ *305/538–9908. AE, DC, MC, V.*

Thai

$$ ✕ **Thai Toni.** Enjoy upscale dining in an exceptional restaurant with bamboo floors and teakwood tables that bring to mind Laos, Vietnam, and other Southeast Asian countries. Mellow Thai Singha beer com-plements the spicy jumping squid appetizer with chili paste and hot pepper or the hot, hot pork. Choose from a large variety of inexpen-sive noodle, fried-rice, and vegetarian dishes or such traditional entrées as beef and broccoli, basil duck, or hot-and-spicy deep-fried whole snap-per with basil leaves and mixed vegetables. Fresh whole fish fillets are specialties. The homemade lemonade is distinctly tart. ⊠ *890 Wash-ington Ave.,* ☎ *305/538–8424. AE, MC, V. No lunch.*

South Miami

Seafood

$$–$$$$ ✕ **Captain's Tavern.** This family fish house has an unusually interest-ing menu fortified with Caribbean and South American influences. The decor may be hokey, with paneled walls and witty sayings on plaques hung here and there, but the food can fascinate. Beyond good versions of the typical fare—conch chowder and conch fritters—you'll find a Portuguese fish stew, fish with various tropical fruits, a delightful black-bean soup, and oysters in cream sauce with fresh rosemary, not to mention decadent desserts. ⊠ *7495 S.E. 98th St.,* ☎ *305/661–4237. AE, MC, V.*

Thai

$–$$ ✕ **Siam Lotus Room.** This aqua-color piece of motel architecture isn't much to look at, but it's great eating; in fact, it's one of South Florida's best Thai restaurants. Jump at the chance to eat spicy jumping squid and savory, coconut-silky *tom kar pla,* a fish soup. Spicy bamboo shoots with shrimp, beef, chicken, and pork is fantastic, as is a bub-bly yellow curry. All the other basics are here, from basil, garlic, and red-curry treatments for various meats to whole fried snapper. For dessert the Thai donut makes a light-sweet finish. Try it with thick, creamy Thai iced coffee. ⊠ *6388 S. Dixie Hwy.,* ☎ *305/666–8134. AE, MC, V.*

West Miami

Chinese

$–$$ ✕ **Tropical Chinese Restaurant.** This big, lacquer-free room feels as open and busy as a railway station. You'll find unfamiliar items on the menu—early spring leaves of snow pea pods, for example, which are sublimely tender and flavorful. The extensive menu is filled with tofu combinations, poultry, beef, and pork, as well as tender seafood. A dim sum lunch is served from great carts. In the big, open kitchen 10 chefs prepare everything as if for dignitaries. ⊠ *7991 S.W. 40th St.,* ☎ *305/ 262–7576 or 305/262–1552. AE, DC, MC, V.*

LODGING

Few urban areas can match Greater Miami's diversity of accommodations. South Beach alone had more than 2,000 rooms, even before the 1998 arrival of the Loews Miami Beach Hotel boosted that number by another 800. Miami offers hundreds of hotels, motels, resorts, spas, and B&Bs, with prices ranging from $12 a night in a dormitory-style hostel to $2,000 a night in a luxurious presidential suite (if you can swing it, take the suite). Although some hotels (especially on the mainland) have adopted steady year-round rates, many adjust their rates to reflect seasonal demand. The peak occurs in winter, with a dip in summer (prices are often more negotiable than rate cards let on).

You'll find the best values between Easter and Memorial Day (which is actually a delightful time in Miami but a difficult time for many people to travel) and in September and October (the height of hurricane season). Keep in mind that Miami hoteliers collect roughly 12.5%—ouch—for city and resort taxes; parking fees can run up to $16 per evening; and tips for bellhops, valet parkers, concierges, and housekeepers add to the expense. Some hotels actually tack on an automatic 15% gratuity. All told, you can easily spend 25% more than your room rate to sleep in Miami.

Coconut Grove

$$$$ 🏨 **Grand Bay Hotel.** Combining the classical elegance of Greece, a
★ stepped facade that looks vaguely Aztec, a hint of the South, and a brush of the tropical, this hotel is like no other in South Florida. Guest rooms are filled with superb touches, such as antique sideboards that hold house phones and matched woods variously inlaid and fluted. Whoopi, Schwarzenegger, and Willis have all stayed here, perhaps enjoying the easterly views that look over the bay. Afternoon tea is served. ⊠ *2669 S. Bayshore Dr., 33133,* ☎ *305/858–9600 or 800/327–2788,* ℻ *305/ 859–2026. 132 rooms, 49 suites. Restaurant, 2 bars, pool, beauty salon, hot tub, massage, saunas, health club, concierge. AE, DC, MC, V.*

$$$$ 🏨 **Mayfair House.** This European-style luxury hotel sits within the Streets of Mayfair, an exclusive open-air shopping mall just steps from the heart of the Grove. A cross between a business hotel and romantic getaway, it has public areas done in Art Nouveau instead of Art Deco. Soft, flowing lines are reflected in Tiffany windows, polished mahogany, marble, imported ceramics and crystal, and an impressive glassed-in elevator. The individually furnished suites have outdoor terraces fac-

Miami Area Lodging

KEY

AE American Express Office

ATLANTIC OCEAN

MIAMI BEACH

NORTH MIAMI BEACH

NORTH MIAMI

Miami

The Albion, **18**
Alexander Hotel, **7**
Banana Bungalow, **12**
Bay Harbor Inn, **6**
Bayliss, **20**
Biltmore Hotel, **36**
Cadet Hotel, **12**
Cardozo, **23**

Casa Grande, **30**
Cavalier, **22**
Days Inn Convention Center, **13**
Delano Hotel, **16**
Don Shula's Hotel & Golf Club, **5**
Doral Golf Resort and Spa, **32**

Eden Roc, **9**
Essex House, **28**
Fontainebleau Hilton Resort and Towers, **11**
Grand Bay Hotel, **38**
Hotel Astor, **29**
Hotel Impala, **24**

Hotel Place St. Michel, **35**
Hyatt Regency Miami, **33**
Indian Creek Hotel, **10**
Kenmore, **27**
Loews Miami Beach Hotel, **19**

Mayfair House, **37**
Nassau Suite Hotel, **21**
National Hotel, **17**
Newport Beachside Resort, **4**
Ocean Front Hotel, **25**
Pelican, **31**

Raleigh Hotel, **14**
Sheraton Biscayne Bay, **34**
Sonesta Beach Resort Key Biscayne, **39**
Suez Oceanfront Resort, **3**
Thunderbird, **2**

The Tides, **26**
Turnberry Isle Resort & Club, **1**
Wyndham Miami Beach Resort, **8**

ing the street, screened by vegetation and wood latticework. Each has a relatively small Japanese hot tub on the balcony or a Roman tub inside, and 10 have antique pianos. A rooftop recreation area is peaceful (although the miniature lap pool is odd for such a large hotel), and the quiet Orchid Bar, a ground-floor lounge, attracts a trendy clientele. If you can't sleep, go downstairs and chat with the 24-hour concierge. ⊠ *3000 Florida Ave., 33133,* ☎ *305/441–0000 or 800/433–4555,* ℻ *305/447–9173. 179 suites. Restaurant, bar, snack bar, pool, hot tubs, sauna, concierge. AE, D, DC, MC, V.*

Coral Gables

$$$$ 🏨 **Biltmore Hotel.** Miami's grand boom-time hotel has undergone two
★   renovations since 1986 but still manages to recapture a bygone era. Now owned by the city of Coral Gables and operated by Westin, the 1926 Biltmore rises like a sienna-color wedding cake in the heart of a residential district. The vaulted lobby has hand-painted rafters on a twinkling sky-blue background. Large guest rooms are done in a restrained Moorish style, and for slightly more than the average rate ($2,550) you can book the Everglades (a.k.a. Al Capone) Suite—President Clinton's room when he's in town. Each month a visiting French chef drops by to surprise diners and teach Biltmore chefs something new, and the Cellar Club offers fine wines and premium cigars. ⊠ *1200 Anastasia Ave., 33134,* ☎ *305/445–1926 or 800/727–1926,* ℻ *305/ 913–3159. 237 rooms, 38 suites. Restaurant, bar, café, pool, sauna, spa, 18-hole golf course, 10 lighted tennis courts, health club, concierge, meeting rooms. AE, DC, MC, V.*

$$–$$$ 🏨 **Hotel Place St. Michel.** Art Nouveau chandeliers suspended from
★   vaulted ceilings grace the public areas of this intimate boutique hotel in the heart of downtown. Built in 1926, the historic low-rise was restored between 1981 and 1986 and yet again after a 1995 fire. Within easy walking distance of the Miracle Mile, the charming inn is filled with the scent of fresh flowers, circulated by paddle fans. Its fine restaurant is an undeniable asset. Each room has its own dimensions, personality, and antiques imported from England, Scotland, and France, although plusher beds would be a more welcome accent. A complimentary Continental breakfast is served. ⊠ *162 Alcazar Ave., 33134,* ☎ *305/444–1666 or 800/848–4683,* ℻ *305/529–0074. 24 rooms, 3 suites. Restaurant, bar. AE, DC, MC, V.*

Downtown Miami

$$$–$$$$ 🏨 **Sheraton Biscayne Bay.** When you arrive at the entrance, you'll have a hard time believing that this waterfront establishment is on busy Brickell Avenue. A short drive through a grove of oak trees will calm you down. As at most large hotels, the lobby is designed for business (as is the conference center) and features a bar, restaurant, and gift shop, but the back patio and green space softens the experience. Rooms have all the accoutrements you'd expect: irons, hair dryers, voice mail. Thank management for providing self-parking for those who want it (valets are standing by), although you will pay a fee. ⊠ *495 Brickell Ave., 33131,* ☎ *305/373–6000 or 800/284–2000,* ℻ *305/374–2279. 598 rooms, 14 suites. Restaurant, bar, pool, exercise room, meeting rooms, parking (fee). AE, DC, MC, V.*

$$–$$$$ 🏨 **Hyatt Regency Miami.** The blend of leisure and business has positioned the Hyatt well for the downtown renaissance that began with the opening of the new Miami Avenue Bridge in 1996 and continues with the upsurge in business at the Port of Miami and the arrival of the American Airlines Arena. If your vacation is based on boats, basketball, or business, you can't do much better. The distinctive public spaces are more colorful than businesslike, and guest rooms are done in an unusual combination of avocado, beige, and blond. Rooms yield views of the river or port, and not surprisingly the best ones occupy the upper floors. The James L. Knight International Center is accessible without stepping outside, as is the downtown Metromover and its Metrorail connection. ⊠ *400 S.E. 2nd Ave., 33131,* ☎ *305/358–1234,* FAX *305/358–0529. 615 rooms, 25 suites. Restaurant, bar, pool. AE, D, DC, MC, V.*

Key Biscayne

$$$$ 🏨 **Sonesta Beach Resort Key Biscayne.** This excellent resort with a great
★ seaside setting is now more tropical than ever, offering stunning sea views from east-facing units. Rooms are done in a sand tone with fabrics in emerald, purple, gold, and ruby. Villas are actually three-bedroom homes with full kitchen and screened pool. The property's size, Olympic pool, activities, and Just Us Kids program (9 AM–10 PM) make it a good family getaway. Don't miss the museum-quality modern art, especially Andy Warhol's drawings of rock star Mick Jagger in the hotel's disco bar, Desires. The 750-ft beach, one of Florida's best, has a wide variety of recreational opportunities, including catamarans and sailing lessons. ⊠ *350 Ocean Dr., 33149,* ☎ *305/361–2021 or 800/766–3782,* FAX *305/361–3096. 284 rooms, 15 suites, 3 villas. 3 restaurants, 3 bars, snack bar, pool, massage, steam rooms, 9 tennis courts (3 lighted), aerobics, health club, beach, windsurfing, parasailing, children's program. AE, D, DC, MC, V.*

Miami Beach North of South Beach

$$$$ 🏨 **Alexander Hotel.** Amid the high-rises of the mid-Beach district, this
★ 16-story hotel exemplifies the elegance of Miami Beach. It has immense suites furnished with antiques and reproductions, each with a terrace yielding ocean or bay views and each with a living and dining room, kitchen, and two baths. The beachside Aqua Sports Center provides wave runners, catamarans, paddleboats, and volleyball courts. With the addition of the Aveda salon and an outpost of Shula's Steak House, you can pamper your body and your appetite without leaving the property. Beware of mandatory gratuities attached to everything from valet parking to bellhop and maid service to deliveries. ⊠ *5225 Collins Ave., 33140,* ☎ *305/865–6500 or 800/327–6121,* FAX *305/341–6553. 150 1- and 2-bedroom suites. Restaurant, coffee shop, 2 pools, beauty salon, exercise room, volleyball, beach, dock, boating, jet skiing. AE, D, DC, MC, V.*

$$$$ 🏨 **Eden Roc.** Who knows why this grand 1950s hotel designed by Morris Lapidus is overshadowed by the larger, more prominent Fontainebleau (☞ *below*)? From the moment you enter, the free-flowing lines of its nautical Deco architecture make you feel casual and comfortable. In the late '90s a major renovation added three new ballrooms and meeting facilities, as well as an indoor basketball court and a rock-climbing wall for fitness and motivation. The resort's yacht is available for oceangoing meetings. The 55,000-square-ft Spa of Eden usually runs full tilt, while Dolphins coach Jimmy Johnson's beachside sports bar caters to those who prefer lifting weights 16 ounces at a time. Rooms blend a touch of the '50s with informal '90s elegance. ⊠ *4525 Collins Ave., 33140,* ☎ *305/531–0000 or 800/327–8337,* FAX *305/674–5555. 346 rooms. 2 restaurants, sports bar, pool, massage, spa, basketball, exercise room, racquetball, meeting rooms. AE, MC, V.*

$$$$ 🏨 **Fontainebleau Hilton Resort and Towers.** This big, busy, and ornate grand dame is scheduled to wrap up a complete overhaul by 2000. Corridors, guest rooms, suites, pools, recreation areas, and the building's exterior have been spiffed up with new carpet, wall coverings, lighting, and furnishings. Tower rooms, already luxurious, are now even more exclusive, with upgraded linens, multiline phones, fax, minibars, a personal concierge, and Italian marble baths. Room decor varies throughout the property, from the 1950s to contemporary—very contemporary. Even the smallest room is large by Miami standards, as are the convention facilities, which rank second only to the city-owned convention center. A 40,000-square-ft beachside spa is ideal for self-indulgence. Guests enjoy complimentary admission to the hotel's *Club Tropigala*, a Vegas-style floor show with a Latin twist. ⊠ *4441 Collins Ave., 33140,* ☎ *305/538–2000 or 800/548–8886,* ℻ *305/531–9274. 1,146 rooms, 60 suites. 12 restaurants, 3 bars, 2 pools, saunas, spa, 7 lighted tennis courts, health club, volleyball, beach, windsurfing, boating, parasailing, children's programs, convention center. AE, D, DC, MC, V.*

$$$$ ☲ **Wyndham Miami Beach Resort.** Of the great Miami Beach hotels,
★   this 18-story glass tower remains a standout. A renovation completed in 1998 upgraded the lobby, pool, facade, sleeping rooms, meeting rooms, and landscaping. Warm-tone guest rooms are filled with nice details: mini-refrigerator; three layers of drapes, including blackout curtains; big closets; and bathrooms with high-quality toiletries and a magnifying mirror. Two presidential suites were designed in consultation with the Secret Service, and a rooftop meeting room offers views of bay and ocean. Free transportation to Doral Golf Resort and Spa is provided. ⊠ *4833 Collins Ave., 33140,* ☎ *305/532–3600 or 800/203–8368,* ℻ *305/534–7409. 378 rooms, 46 suites. 2 restaurants, 2 bars, pool, tennis court, exercise room, beach, helipad, meeting rooms. AE, D, DC, MC, V.*

$$–$$$$ ☲ **Indian Creek Hotel.** Not as grand as the North Beach behemoths or as hectic as the Ocean Drive offerings, this 1936 Pueblo Deco jewel may just be Miami's most charming and sincere lodge—and it gets nicer every year. Owner Marc Levin rescued the inn by adding a cozy dining room with an eclectic and appetizing menu, relandscaping a lush pool and garden, and restoring rooms using Deco furniture, much of it discovered in the basement. Items were cleaned, reupholstered, and put on display, helping the hotel win the Miami Design Preservation League's award for outstanding restoration. Suites have refrigerators, cable TV, VCR/CD players, and modem capabilities; safe-deposit boxes are available. The hotel restaurant now flows outside to a secluded poolside dining area—yet another comforting touch. Stay a while, and manager Zammy Migdal and his staff will have you feeling like family. ⊠ *2727 Indian Creek Dr., 33140,* ☎ *305/531–2727,* ℻ *305/531–5651. 61 rooms. Restaurant, pool, concierge. AE, D, DC, MC, V.*

North Miami, North Miami Beach, and North Dade

$$$$ ☲ **Turnberry Isle Resort & Club.** Finest of the grand resorts, Turnberry
★   is a tapestry of islands and waterways on 300 superbly landscaped acres by the bay. Choose from the Yacht Club, on the Intracoastal Waterway; the intimate Marina Hotel; a beautiful three-wing Mediterranean-style annex; and the Addison Mizner–style Country Club Hotel. Oversize rooms have light woods and earth tones, large curving terraces, Jacuzzis, honor bars, and safes. The marina has moorings for 117 boats up to 150 ft long, there's a free shuttle to the beach club and the Aventura Mall, and Robert Trent Jones stopped by to design two tropical golf courses. A new seven-story building, adding 128 rooms, offices, and a terrace restaurant, opens in 1999. ⊠ *19999 W. Country Club Dr., Aventura 33180,* ☎ *305/936–2929 or 800/223-6800,* ℻ *305/933–6560. 300 rooms, 40 suites. 7 restaurants, 5 bars, 4 pools,*

saunas, spa, steam rooms, driving range, 2 18-hole golf courses, 24 tennis courts (18 lighted), health club, jogging, racquetball, beach, dive shop, docks, windsurfing, boating, helipad. AE, D, DC, MC, V.

$$$–$$$$ ☷ **Bay Harbor Inn.** Although the inn's not on the ocean, the tranquil Indian Creek flowing outside is sure to soothe. Rooms with queen- and king-size beds are quite pleasant, baths are large, and you receive a complimentary breakfast each morning. One of the nicest features is your own front porch, where you can sit with a book or drink or both and view the village of Bal Harbour, just a five-minute walk away. The restaurant here (Islands) is very nice, but it's also pleasant to walk around the corner to a small Italian restaurant (Da Vinci's) or over the bridge to Surfside for a wider selection of neighborhood bars and eateries. One caveat: The hotel staff is largely composed of students from Johnson & Wales University, so service is enthusiastic but not flawlessly professional. ⊠ *9601 E. Bayshore Dr., Bal Harbour 33154,* ☎ *305/868–4141,* FAX *305/867–9094. 22 rooms, 23 suites. Restaurant, bar, pool. AE, DC, MC, V.*

$$$–$$$$ ☷ **Newport Beachside Resort.** The nicest place to stay in Sunny Isles,
★ and more upscale than most, is this combination time share/hotel. While mom or dad is in Miami on business, the family can enjoy the beach and the plentiful activities. Check out the fishing pier, the kids' center (with diversions from painting to videos), or the midday calypso entertainment. The pool area is perfectly suited for enjoying the sun, and the large, bright lobby is brightened further by colorful macaws. The tropical rooms feature king-size beds, mini-refrigerators, and microwaves; one- and two-bedroom suites are similar but are much larger and include a marble bath. The resort even has a travel agency, though once you check in you'll never have to leave. ⊠ *16701 Collins Ave., Sunny Isles 33160,* ☎ *305/949–1300 or 800 327–5476,* FAX *305/947–5873. 300 rooms, 20 suites. Restaurant, sports bar, pool, wading pool, exercise room, beach, dive shop, jet skiing, fishing, nightclub, concierge, meeting rooms, travel services. AE, DC, MC, V.*

$$$ ☷ **Don Shula's Hotel & Golf Club.** This low-rise resort is part of Miami Lakes, a planned town about 14 mi northwest of downtown. Opened in 1962, the golf club includes a championship course, a lighted executive course, and a golf school. All club rooms have balconies, and the theme is English traditional, rich in leather and wood. The hotel, on the other hand, has a typical Florida-tropics look—light pastels and furniture of wicker and light wood. In both locations the best rooms are near the lobby for convenient access; ask for a room away from the elevators. Sixteen executive two-bedroom suites (geared for extended stays) were opened in early 1999. ⊠ *6840 Main St., Miami Lakes 33014,* ☎ *305/821–1150 or 800/247–4852,* FAX *305/820–8190. 269 rooms, 32 suites. 5 restaurants, 2 bars, 2 pools, saunas, steam rooms, driving range, 2 golf courses, 9 lighted tennis courts, aerobics, basketball, health club, racquetball, volleyball. AE, DC, MC, V.*

$$–$$$ ☷ **Thunderbird.** One of the nicest finds in North Beach, this hotel is well priced for such a clean and neat place. Right off the bat the lobby—warmer than Deco and with an attractive chandelier and staircase—puts you at ease. The good vibes continue in the rooms, done in a typical Miami tropical floral style but particularly bright, especially those that open to the courtyard. Accommodating four people at no extra charge, rooms include a mini-refrigerator; a few efficiencies are also available. Outdoors is even more appealing. The tropical courtyard, tennis courts, and an Olympic-size pool create a miniature oasis, and the tiki bar is a perfect place to watch the waves. A supermarket across the street is an added convenience. ⊠ *18401 Collins Ave., North Miami Beach 33139,* ☎ *305/931–7700 or 800/327–2044,* FAX *305/932–7521. 180 rooms. Restaurant, 2 bars, 2 pools, beauty salon,*

2 tennis courts, exercise room, coin laundry, dry cleaning. AE, D, DC, MC, V.

$$ 🏨 **Suez Oceanfront Resort.** Several miles north of Miami Beach, along what's known as Motel Row, the carousel-striped, family-run Suez stands out from the area's pricier but nondescript motels. Look beyond the tacky sphinx statuary to the quiet, gardenlike lounge and the landscaped palm courtyard. Rooms have Chinese-style furniture and dazzling color, offsetting generally small spaces. Those in the north wing, with parking-lot views, are the smallest and least expensive. Modified American Plan availability, refrigerators in all rooms, kitchens in some, free laundry service, and special kids' rates make this an especially good value, popular with Europeans. ⊠ *18215 Collins Ave., Sunny Isles 33160,* ☎ *305/932–0661 or 800/327–5278; 800/432–3661 in FL;* FAX *305/937–0058. 196 rooms. Restaurant, bar, freshwater and saltwater pools, wading pool, lighted tennis court, shuffleboard, volleyball, beach, playground, laundry service. AE, DC, MC, V.*

South Beach

$$$$ 🏨 **The Albion.** The owners of this resurrected hotel just off Lincoln Road brought it back in style, hiring Carlos Zapata to update the 1939 nautical Art Deco building by Igor Polevitzky. The focal point is a two-story lobby, which sweeps into a secluded courtyard and is framed by a flowing indoor waterfall. A prosperous young and young-at-heart crowd of hip but friendly types makes up the clientele; they like to gather at the mezzanine-level pool, which is unusual for its depth (9 ft), its artificial beach (Florida's first), and portholes that allow courtyard strollers an underwater view of swimmers. The blond-wood Fallabella Bar recalls the styling of Heywood-Wakefield, and the Pantry offers breakfast and sandwiches overlooking the pool or lobby. Guest rooms are minimalist in design though filled with what travelers expect: data ports, two-line phones, minibars, and stereos. The owners of the chic Cuban restaurant Yuca (☞ Dining, *above*) also run Maya, the restaurant here. ⊠ *1650 James Ave., Miami Beach 33139,* ☎ *305/913–1000 or 888/665–0008,* FAX *305/674–0507. 85 rooms, 9 suites. 2 restaurants, bar, pool, exercise room. AE, D, DC, MC, V.*

$$$$ 🏨 **Casa Grande.** The first of SoBe's new top-flight hotels, this is still
★ one of the best, with the level of quality characteristic of Chris Blackwell's other five Island Outpost hotels in Miami: the Tides and the Cavalier (☞ *below*), the Leslie, the Marlin, and the Kent. The lobby's teak, tile, and recessed lighting create a warm and relaxing look. Luxurious suites capture the fashionable air of Ocean Drive yet reflect fine taste. Done in Balinese-inspired teak and mahogany, units have dhurrie rugs, beautiful Indonesian fabrics and artifacts, two-poster beds with ziggurat turns, full kitchens with fine European utensils, and large baths—practically unheard of in the Deco District—adorned with green decorator tiles. Goodies range from a daily newspaper and in-room coffee to fresh flowers and evening turndown with Italian chocolates. Insulated windows keep the noise from Ocean Drive revelers at bay. Book early for peak periods. ⊠ *834 Ocean Dr., Miami Beach 33139,* ☎ *305/672–7003 or 800/688–7678,* FAX *305/673–3669. 34 suites. Café, laundry service and dry cleaning, concierge. AE, D, DC, MC, V.*

$$$$ 🏨 **Delano Hotel.** If Calvin Klein had teamed with Salvador Dalí to build
★ a hotel, this weird—really weird—wonderful, and slightly snooty property would be it. Tourists marvel at the lobby hung with massive, white billowing drapes and try to act casual while watching for U2, Elvis Costello, George Clooney, Michael Keaton, and Spike Lee (an actual week's roster of celebrity guests). Fashion models and men of in-

dependent means gather beneath cabanas, pose by the pool, and sniff fragrances wafting in from the orchard. Business travelers are offered comprehensive executive services, guests can access 1,500 videos, and men and women have the run of a rooftop bathhouse and solarium on alternating schedules. Although the standard rooms are of average size, their stark whiteness makes them appear larger. The gift shop carries magazines you wouldn't want your parents to see. The real appeal here is the surrealism. ⊠ *1685 Collins Ave., Miami Beach 33139,* ☎ *305/672–2000 or 800/555–5001,* 𝔽𝔸𝕏 *305/532–0099. 184 rooms, 24 suites. Restaurant, bar, pool, spa, health club, business services. AE, D, DC, MC, V.*

$$$$ 🏨 **Loews Miami Beach Hotel.** Miami has been waiting for a major new beachfront luxury hotel for 30 years. Although others have been renovated, this 18-story, 800-room gem was built from the blueprints up. Not only did Loews manage to snag 99 ft of oceanfront, it took over the vacant St. Moritz next door and restored it to its original 1939 Art Deco splendor, adding another 100 rooms to the complex. The resort features kids' programs (SoBe Kids Camp), a health spa, and 85,000 square ft of meeting space with a 28,000-square-ft ocean-view grand ballroom. Dining, too, is a pleasure, courtesy of the Argentinian-inspired Gaucho Room, Preston's SoBe Coffee Bar, and Hemisphere Lounge. But won't someone please do something about those garish uniforms? ⊠ *1601 Collins Ave., Miami Beach 33139,* ☎ *305/604–1601,* 𝔽𝔸𝕏 *305/531–8677. 743 rooms, 57 suites. 4 restaurants, 2 bars, lobby lounge, pool, spa, beach, children's programs, meeting rooms. AE, D, DC, MC, V.*

$$$$ 🏨 **National Hotel.** This resurrected 1939 shorefront hotel reopened in 1997 and took a few years to work out the kinks. Miami Beach's longest (205 ft) tropical pool sparkles at night with illuminated messages and logos, and its presence makes a perfect backdrop for the film crews who work here almost daily. With curtains closed, poolside rooms could be generic Holiday Inn, displaying little of the flair of other recent arrivals. Rooms in the main building are far more appealing, however, and the interiors approach a higher level of creativity. Applause is in order for preserved pieces, such as the original dining-room chandelier and furniture, as well as such modern in-room amenities as ironing boards, safes, data ports, and robes. Another notable is the intimate 1930s-style Press Room cigar bar and meeting room. Unfair, however, is the $16-per-day parking fee. ⊠ *1677 Collins Ave., Miami Beach 33139,* ☎ *305/532–2311 or 800/327–8370,* 𝔽𝔸𝕏 *305/534–1426. 115 rooms, 39 suites. Restaurant, bar, pool, beach, concierge, meeting rooms, parking (fee). AE, DC, MC, V.*

$$$$ 🏨 **The Tides.** Miami hotels like white, and this one is no exception.
★ The nice twist here is the added features that owner Chris Blackwell introduced with a flawless renovation. Some touches are small—spyglasses in each room (fitting since they all face the ocean), a blackboard for messages to maids. Others are large—every room has a king-size bed, capacious closets, and generous post-Moderne baths, the result of turning 115 rooms into 45 suites. Elvis would have liked the blackout curtains and private VIP entrance. The downstairs lobby is large and austere (and white), and facilities include a reading room, hypercool terrace dining, and a mezzanine pool where women can go topless (total nudity is "undesirable"). Wondering what's happening in the outside world? Request a newspaper, which you can read beside Ocean Drive's only Olympic-size pool. If you're bored with the pool, the entire Atlantic Ocean is a short walk away. This hotel is generating a buzz, so check it out, hipsters. ⊠ *1220 Ocean Dr., Miami Beach 33139,* ☎ *305/604–5000 or 800/688–7678,* 𝔽𝔸𝕏 *305/604–5180. 45 suites. Restaurant, café, pool, exercise room. AE, D, DC, MC, V.*

$$$–$$$$ ⊞ **Cardozo.** Perhaps it's because this hotel is owned by Gloria and Emilio Estefan that there's such lively and loud music in the lobby. (Unfortunately, on weekend nights loud music from the disco can still be heard in the otherwise quiet and comfortable rooms.) The Estefans completed the hotel's makeover in 1998, deciding—wisely—to forsake cold tile floors for the warmth of the building's original hardwood. Leopard-print blankets and large baths with mosaic-tile sinks give rooms a warm African tint, but the terra-cotta walls cool things off. Whether you opt for a standard room or suite, you'll have room to spread out. Units feature minibar and TV/VCR/CD, and views from oceanfront rooms are impressive (especially from Number 202). The staff is just as pleasant as the hotel's design. ⊠ *1300 Ocean Dr., Miami Beach 33139,* ☎ *305/535–6500,* ℻ *305/673–8609. 44 rooms, 7 suites. Restaurant, bar. AE, DC, MC, V.*

$$$–$$$$ ⊞ **Essex House.** Already adequate before renovation, the hotel annexed the building next door and prettied it up with 20 large suites, putting the Essex House well above average. All the work put into the suites, which are reached by crossing a tropical courtyard, has paid off: Each includes a wet bar, king-size bed, pullout sofa, 100-square-ft bathroom, refrigerator, and hot tub. Rooms are no slouches, either. Club chairs, custom carpet and lighting, mahogany entertainment units and matching desks, marble tubs, two phone lines, computer data ports, and voice mail make them like the home office you wish you had built. Although the hotel is in the heart of the city, sound-absorbing windows keep things quiet, just as the free Continental breakfast keeps your stomach quiet, too. ⊠ *1001 Collins Ave., Miami Beach 33139,* ☎ *305/534–2700 or 800/553–7739,* ℻ *305/532–3827. 59 rooms, 20 suites. Bar, pool. AE, D, DC, MC, V.*

$$$–$$$$ ⊞ **Hotel Astor.** How does yet another Art Deco hotel stand out from
★   the crowd? This one does it by double-insulating walls against noise and offering such luxuries as ambient low-voltage lighting, thick towels, down pillows, paddle fans, and a seductive pool. The renovation also included expansion of guest rooms and baths and the addition of custom-milled French furniture, blackout Roman shades, and sleek sound and video systems. A tasteful, muted color scheme and the most comfortable king-size beds imaginable make for eminently restful rooms, and excellent service eliminates any worries about practical matters. The Astor Place restaurant (☞ Dining, *above*) is exceptional. Those in the know come to be pampered at this lavishly understated hotel two blocks from the frenzy of Ocean Drive. ⊠ *956 Washington Ave., Miami Beach 33139,* ☎ *305/531–8081 or 800/270–4981,* ℻ *305/531– 3193. 40 rooms. Restaurant, bar, pool, massage. AE, MC, V.*

$$$–$$$$ ⊞ **Hotel Impala.** One of the nicest inns in the area, this former store-
★   front for drug dealers was reborn in a stunning tropical Mediterranean Revival style that distinguishes it from the Art Deco pack. Iron, mahogany, and stone on the inside are in synch with the sporty white-trim ocher exterior and quiet courtyard. Rooms, among the cleanest in SoBe, are elegant, comfortable, and complete, with a TV/VCR/stereo and a stock of CDs and videos. It's all very European, from mineral water and orchids to the Mediterranean-style armoires, Italian fixtures, heavy ornamental drapery rods, and Spanish surrealist art above white-on-white, triple-sheeted modified Eastlake sleigh beds. Everything from wastebaskets to towels to toilet paper is of extraordinary quality. This place definitely has great *feng shui.* ⊠ *1228 Collins Ave., Miami Beach 33139,* ☎ *305/673–2021 or 800/646–7252,* ℻ *305/673–5984. 17 rooms, 3 suites. Restaurant, bar. AE, DC, MC, V.*

$$$–$$$$ ☎ **Ocean Front Hotel.** If the street signs didn't read Ocean Drive, you might suspect you were whiling away the day on the Riviera. The tropical French feel is evident when you enter the shaded, bougainvillea-draped courtyard and see diners enjoying a complimentary casual breakfast in the hotel's brasserie. Two buildings connected by this courtyard contain many pleasant surprises. The comfortable rooms (which average 425 square ft each) are highlighted by soft beds, authentic 1930s Art Deco pieces, large foldout couches, and clean, spacious baths. Add to this wet bars with refrigerators, TV/VCR/CD players, and two phone lines with data-port access. If you spring for the penthouse suite, be sure to settle on the balcony and grab an eyeful of ocean. Blessedly, rooms have soundproofed windows. ⊠ *1230–38 Ocean Dr., Miami Beach 33139,* ☎ *305/672–2579,* FAX *305/672–7665. 4 rooms, 23 suites. Restaurant, bar, concierge. AE, D, DC, MC, V.*

$$$–$$$$ ☎ **Raleigh Hotel.** Hidden behind a thick veil of tropical foliage is one of SoBe's nicest oceanfront hotels. Among the first Art Deco District hotels to be renovated, it added Victorian accents (hallway chandeliers and in-room oil paintings) to soften the hard Deco edges. The hotel has been a consistent favorite of fashion photogs and production crews, who appreciate state-of-the-art rooms with three phones and two lines. Even standard rooms are spacious, and suites are more so. Each unit offers a VCR, radio/CD/cassette player, safe, and refrigerator stocked to your taste. The gorgeous fleur-de-lis pool is the focal point year-round, but especially on December 31, when synchronized swimmers dive in at the stroke of midnight. If you prefer salt with your water, sample the 300-ft beach. Other pluses are the lobby coffee bar, a romantic restaurant (Tiger Oak Room), and the 1940s-style Martini Bar. ⊠ *1775 Collins Ave., Miami Beach 33139,* ☎ *305/534–6300 or 800/848–1775,* FAX *305/538–8140. 107 rooms, 1176 suites. Restaurant, bar, pool, beach, laundry service. AE, DC, MC, V.*

$$$ ☎ **Pelican.** Dazzling, brilliant spaces with Art Deco–inspired frivolity result from the transformation from another tired Ocean Drive home for the elderly into pop-eyed digs for the gay, hip, and adventurous. Rooms, with names like Leafforest, Best Whorehouse, People from the 1950s, and Cubarrean, are all different, but all have small sleeping chambers and triple-size bathrooms with outrageous industrial piping. Best Whorehouse envelops you in black silk and thoroughly red-flocked wallpaper flecked with gold. Ornaments are bordello extravagant: a heart-shape red-velvet chair, hideously aqua night tables, whorish art, and griffins with voluptuous mammaries. Each room comes with its own cylindrical entertainment center. Room for room, Pelican outweirds even the Delano. Guests have included JFK Jr. and Yoko Ono. ⊠ *826 Ocean Dr., Miami Beach 33139,* ☎ *305/673–3373 or 800/773–5422,* FAX *305/673–3255. 22 rooms, 5 suites. Restaurant, café, concierge. AE, DC, MC, V.*

$$–$$$$ ☎ **Cavalier.** Chris Blackwell is consistent. In any of his Island Outpost hotels (☞ Casa Grande *and* the Tides, *above*), you can count on a clean room, good service, and creative surroundings. In most cases you can expect to pay dearly for the privilege, but not here if you get a standard room. Rooms start at a Miami-modest $125 and include TV/VCR, CD, safe, minibar, queen-size bed, and access to the pool at the Tides. Batik fabrics, the requisite Deco furniture, and vintage B&W photos set the mood. Suites get an ocean view and king-size bed. And talk about location: You're right across the street from that great big Atlantic. ⊠ *1320 Ocean Dr., Miami Beach 33139,* ☎ *305/604–5064 or 800/688–7678,* FAX *305/531–5543. 43 rooms, 4 suites. Concierge, meeting rooms. AE, DC, MC, V.*

$$–$$$ 🏨 **Nassau Suite Hotel.** The sister property of the Bayliss (☞ *below*), this relative bargain offers huge studio suites at a third of the price demanded by Ocean Drive properties. The original 1937 floor plan of 50 rooms gave way to 22 spacious and smart-looking suites. King-size beds, fully equipped kitchens, hardwood floors, white wood blinds, voice mail, data ports, plush sofas, free local calls, mini-refrigerators. . . why they don't charge more is a mystery, though there's no 24-hour staff. The hotel is in the heart of the action yet quiet enough to give travelers the rest they need. Note: This three-floor hotel has no elevator and no bellhop. ⊠ *1414 Collins Ave., Miami Beach 33139,* ☎ *305/531–3755 or 888/305–4683,* FAX *305/673–8609. 22 suites. Concierge. AE, D, DC, MC, V.*

$$ 🏨 **Cadet Hotel.** Clark Gable stayed in Room 225 when he came to Miami for Army Air Corps training in the 1940s. Although this Lincoln Road district lodging doesn't have the glamour to attract stars today, it's still a clean, friendly, and perfectly placed little hotel. Just a few minutes' walk from the Theater of the Performing Arts and the convention center and five minutes from the ocean, it's about half the cost of an Ocean Drive hotel. The other big difference is a staff that doesn't act like it's doing you a favor by letting you stay here. Bright without glitz, the Cadet features soft pastels in the lobby, blues and creams in rooms. Ordinary furniture is mixed but not necessarily matched—nor is it crummy. Tiled baths have tubs, and a complimentary breakfast is served in the lobby or on the terrace. ⊠ *1701 James Ave., Miami Beach 33139,* ☎ *305/672–6688 or 800/432–2338,* FAX *305/532–1676. 44 rooms. AE, D, DC, MC, V.*

$$ 🏨 **Days Inn Convention Center.** Nothing flashy and nothing trashy, this link in a chain is a fairly pleasant one. The lobby is bright and floral, with a fountain and a gift shop that remind you that this is one of many, not one of a kind. Standard hotel rooms include in-room safes and cable TV; deluxe rooms throw in impressive views of the ocean. If you're more concerned about your wallet than your image, this can be a good bet. Though you can find lodgings at the same rates with more character, here you will find everything you'd expect at a franchise (including a pool)—all literally seconds from the beach, the boardwalk, and the Bass Museum. ⊠ *100 21st St., Miami Beach 33139,* ☎ *305/ 538–6631 or 800/451–3345,* FAX *305/674–0954. 172 rooms. Restaurant, pool, beach, laundry service. AE, D, DC, MC, V.*

$$ 🏨 **Kenmore.** Understated comfort is the hallmark of this hotel, part of an entire block of accommodations known collectively as the Park Washington Resort. Although other Art Deco hostelries accessorize to achieve a 1930s feel, this place seems to have captured the essence of the period on its own. The lobby's glass-block facade, the courtyard bar, and inviting patio furniture complement rooms that are clean but not overly spacious. Tropical-theme rooms have twin- or king-size beds and a refrigerator. On a very active street the Kenmore has a privacy that's surprising. A quiet pool hidden behind a low wall allows you to tan in an Adirondack chair without being subject to voyeurs. It's only a short walk to the clubs and shops of SoBe, and you get a free breakfast, to boot. ⊠ *1020–1050 Washington Ave., Miami Beach 33139,* ☎ *305/532–1930 or 888/424–1930,* FAX *305/972–4666. 60 rooms. Restaurant, bar, pool. AE, DC, MC, V.*

$–$$ 🏨 **Bayliss.** Paul Crowley is Chris Blackwell on a budget. With no recording empire to support him, he reinvests his hotel profits to make his guests as comfortable as possible. At his properties (☞ Nassau Suite Hotel, *above*), the clean and bright rooms are abnormally large and surprisingly inexpensive—you may even think you've rented a house when you check into an efficiency or apartment here. And not only are the bedrooms large; so, too, are the kitchens (not in standard rooms), sitting rooms, and baths. An easy three blocks west of the ocean, the Bayliss is in a residential neighborhood that's comfortably close to—but far enough away from—the din of the Art Deco District. You can't do much better than this, if you don't mind carrying your own bags. ⊠ *500 14th St., Miami Beach 33139,* ☎ *305/531–3755 or 888/ 305–4683,* ℻ *305/673–8609. 12 rooms, 7 suites. Coin laundry. AE, DC, MC, V.*

$ 🏨 **Banana Bungalow.** This may seem like a university dormitory—indeed, some rooms have dorm-style bunk beds for about $14 a night—but the cleanliness, friendliness, and abundance of activities make this lodge worth checking into, especially for hard-core student travelers. A large pool, the bungalow's social center, is surrounded by a patio bar, Ping-Pong table, game room, outdoor grills, a café, and an activity board announcing kayak rentals, scenic flights, and beach volleyball games held across the street. Some may be put off by the smell of the brackish canal nearby and the recently increased prices, but for others it's a small price to pay for a small price to stay. ⊠ *2360 Collins Ave., Miami Beach 33139,* ☎ *305/538–1951 or 800/746–7835,* ℻ *305/531– 3217. 40 private rooms, 20 dorm-style rooms, all with bath. Bar, café, pool, Ping-Pong, billiards, recreation room, video games. MC, V.*

West Dade

$$$$ 🏨 **Doral Golf Resort and Spa.** This 650-acre golf-and-tennis resort has made major renovations, adding a lighter tone to the eight separate three- and four-story lodges nestled beside golf courses. At the world-renowned spa, a 148,000-square-ft paradise, massages from head to foot, European facials, aroma scrubs and wraps, stress reduction, hypnotherapy, and several dozen other indulgences rejuvenate the mind, body, and soul. Dining ranges from a sports bar to an informal trattoria to an elegant restaurant, Windows on the Green. The famed Blue Monster course has been redesigned, and the other four 18-hole courses were increased in size and difficulty, which makes things tougher on guests as well as the pros who compete in the annual $2 million Doral-Ryder Open Tournament. In 1999 Blue Lagoon, an extravagant water play area, opened at the resort. ⊠ *4400 N.W. 87th Ave., 33178-2192,* ☎ *305/592–2000 or 800/713–6725,* ℻ *305/594– 4682. 694 rooms, 48 suites. 4 restaurants, 3 bars, 4 pools, spa, driving range, 99 holes of golf, 10 tennis courts (4 lighted), health club, jogging, fishing, pro shop. AE, D, DC, MC, V.*

NIGHTLIFE AND THE ARTS

For information on what's happening around town, Greater Miami's English-language daily newspaper, the **Miami Herald,** publishes reliable reviews and comprehensive listings in its "Weekend" section on Friday and in the "Lively Arts" section on Sunday. Call ahead to confirm details. *El Nuevo Herald* is the paper's Spanish version.

If you read Spanish, check **Diario Las Américas,** the area's largest independent Spanish-language paper, for information on the Spanish theater and a smattering of general performing arts news.

A good source of information on the performing arts and nightspots is the calendar in **Miami Today,** a free weekly newspaper available each Thursday in downtown Miami, Coconut Grove, and Coral Gables. The best, most complete source is the **New Times,** a free weekly distributed throughout Miami-Dade County each Thursday. Various tabloids reporting on Deco District entertainment and the Miami social scene come and go. **Ocean Drive** outglosses everything else. **Wire** reports on the gay community.

The free **Greater Miami Calendar of Events** is published twice a year by the Miami-Dade County Cultural Affairs Council (✉ 111 N.W. 1st St., Suite 625, 33128, ☎ 305/375–4634).

Real Talk/WTMI (93.1 FM, ☎ 305/856–9393) provides classical concert information in on-air reports three times daily at 7:30, 12:50, and 6:30. Call the station if you miss the report.

You can find out about activities from Miami's **Arts & Entertainment Hotline** (☎ 305/557–5600), but it takes a while to reach a human. The **Greater Miami Convention & Visitors Bureau** (☎ 305/539–3000 or 800/283–2707) publishes a comprehensive list of dance venues, theaters, and museums as well as a seasonal guide to cultural events.

The Arts

Miami's performing arts aficionados will tell you they survive quite nicely, thank you, despite the area's historic inability to support a county-based professional symphony orchestra. But in recent years this community has begun to write a new chapter in its performing arts history.

In addition to established music groups, several churches and synagogues run classical-music series with international performers. In theater, Miami offers English-speaking audiences an assortment of professional, collegiate, and amateur productions of musicals, comedy, and drama. Spanish theater also is active.

The not-for-profit **Concert Association of Florida** (✉ 555 17th St., Miami Beach 33139, ☎ 305/532–3491), led by Judith Drucker, presents classical arts, music, and dance in venues throughout Miami-Dade and Broward counties. It boasts of presenting the world's greatest music and dance—Itzhak Perlman, Isaac Stern, Baryshnikov, Pavarotti, and the Russian National Ballet.

To order tickets for performing arts events by telephone, call **Ticketmaster** (☎ 305/358–5885). **Ticket Madness** (☎ 305/460–3188) promises half-price tickets for same-day performances.

Arts Venues

What was once a 1920s movie theater has become the 465-seat **Colony Theater** (✉ 1040 Lincoln Rd., Miami Beach 33139, ☎ 305/674–1026). The city-owned performing arts center features dance, drama, music, and experimental cinema.

If you have the opportunity to attend a concert, ballet, or touring stage production at the **Gusman Center for the Performing Arts** (✉ 174 E. Flagler St., Miami 33131, ☎ 305/374–2444 for administration; 305/372–0925 for box office), do so. Originally a movie palace, this 1,700-plus-seat theater is as far from a mall multiplex as you can get. The stunningly beautiful hall resembles a Moorish courtyard, with twinkling stars and rolling clouds skirting across the ceiling and Roman statues guarding the wings.

Not to be confused with the ornate Gusman theater, **Gusman Concert Hall** (✉ 1314 Miller Dr., Coral Gables 33146, ☎ 305/284–2438) is a 600-seat facility on the University of Miami campus. Presenting primarily recitals and concerts by students, it has good acoustics and plenty of room, but parking is a problem when school is in session.

Acoustics and visibility are perfect for all 2,700 seats in the **Jackie Gleason Theater of the Performing Arts** (TOPA, ✉ 1700 Washington Ave., Miami Beach 33139, ☎ 305/673–7300). A pleasant walk from the heart of SoBe, TOPA hosts the Broadway Series, with five or six major productions annually; guest artists, such as David Copperfield, Stomp, and Shirley MacLaine; and classical-music concerts.

Midway between Coral Gables and downtown Miami, the **Miami-Dade County Auditorium** (✉ 2901 W. Flagler St., Miami 33135, ☎ 305/545–3395) satisfies patrons with nearly 2,500 comfortable seats, good sight lines, and acceptable acoustics. Opera, concerts, and touring musicals are usually on the schedule, and past performers have included David Helfgott and Celia Cruz.

Dance

The **Miami City Ballet** (✉ 905 Lincoln Rd., Miami Beach 33139, ☎ 305/532–7713 or 305/532–4880) has risen rapidly to international prominence since its arrival in 1985. Under the direction of Edward Villella (a principal dancer with the New York City Ballet under George Balanchine), Florida's first major, fully professional resident ballet company has become a world-class ensemble. The company re-creates the Balanchine repertoire and introduces works of its own during its September–March season. Performances are held at the Jackie Gleason Theater of the Performing Arts; the Broward Center for the Performing Arts; Bailey Concert Hall, also in Broward County; the Raymond F. Kravis Center for the Performing Arts; and the Naples Philharmonic Center for the Arts.

Film

Alliance Film/Video Project (✉ Sterling Building, Suite 119, 927 Lincoln Rd. Mall, Miami Beach 33139, ☎ 305/531–8504) presents cutting-edge international cinema and art films, with special midnight shows. Movies—or should we say *films*—are $6, less at matinees.

Screenings of new films from all over the world—including some made here—are held as part of the **Miami Film Festival** (✉ 444 Brickell Ave., Suite 229, Miami 33131, ☎ 305/377–3456). Each year more than 45,000 people descend on the eye-popping Gusman Center for the Performing Arts to watch about 25 movies over 10 days in late January and early February.

Music

From October to May **Friends of Chamber Music** (✉ 44 W. Flagler St., Suite 1725, Miami 33130, ☎ 305/372–2975) presents a series of chamber concerts by internationally known guest ensembles, such as the Emerson and Guarneri quartets. Concerts are held at the Gusman Concert Hall at the University of Miami, with tickets averaging about $20.

Because Greater Miami has no resident symphony orchestra, the **New World Symphony** (✉ 541 Lincoln Rd., Miami Beach 33139, ☎ 305/673–3331 or 305/673–3330), a unique advanced-training orchestra conducted by Michael Tilson Thomas, helps fill the void. Since 1986 musicians ages 22–30 who have finished their academic studies have performed here before moving on to other orchestras. With luck, you may arrive while one of the 60–75 coaches is here to help students. Past "coaches" (and guest conductors) have included Leonard Bernstein and Georg Solti.

Opera

South Florida's leading company, the **Florida Grand Opera** (✉ 1200 Coral Way, Miami 33145, ☎ 305/854–1643) presents five operas each year in the Miami-Dade County Auditorium, featuring the Florida Philharmonic Orchestra (Stewart Robinson, musical director). The series brings such luminaries as Placido Domingo and Luciano Pavarotti (Pavarotti made his American debut with the company in 1965 in *Lucia di Lammermoor*). Operas are sung in the original language, with English subtitles projected above the stage.

Theater

Actors' Playhouse (✉ 280 Miracle Mile, Coral Gables 33134, ☎ 305/444–9293), a year-round professional Equity company, presents family fare—musicals, comedies, and dramas—that's mostly good quality, in the very cool 600-seat Miracle Theater. The 1940s-era movie house received a $6 million renovation in the late '90s. Productions of musical theater for younger audiences began in the 300-seat Children's Balcony Theatre in 1997.

Built in 1926 as a movie theater, the **Coconut Grove Playhouse** (✉ 3500 Main Hwy., Coconut Grove 33133, ☎ 305/442–4000 or 305/442–2662) became a legitimate theater in 1956 and is now owned by the state of Florida. The Spanish rococo Grove fixture stages tried-and-true Broadway plays and musicals as well as experimental productions in its main theater and cabaret-style/black box Encore Room. Although onetime Coconut Grove coffee bar singer Jimmy Buffett premiered his play *Don't Stop the Carnival* at the playhouse, its most popular event occurred in 1996, when David Letterman hosted an on-the-road *Late Show* here. Parking is $4 during the day, $5 in the evening.

The **GableStage** (✉ 1200 Anastasia Ave., Coral Gables 33134, ☎ 305/446–1116) presents classic and contemporary theater in a beautiful 154-seat hall at the Biltmore Hotel.

The **Gold Coast Theatre Company** (✉ 345 W. 37th St., Miami Beach 33140, ☎ 305/538–5500), in Miami since 1989, performs a combination of physical theater, mime, and vaudeville comedy. The touring company performs year-round; call to find its current venue.

The **New Theatre** (✉ 65 Almeria Ave., Coral Gables 33134, ☎ 305/443–5909) is a year-round showcase for contemporary and classical plays. Packed houses and critical acclaim are a testament to the skill of Havana-born artistic director Rafael de Acha.

On the campus of the University of Miami, **Ring Theater** (✉ 1380 Miller Dr., Coral Gables 33124, ☎ 305/284–3355) is the 311-seat hall of UM's Department of Theatre Arts. Six plays a year are performed.

SPANISH THEATER

Spanish theater prospers, although many companies have short lives. About 20 Spanish companies perform light comedy, puppetry, vaudeville, and political satire. To locate them, read the Spanish newspapers. When you call, be prepared for a conversation in Spanish—few box-office personnel speak English.

The 255-seat **Teatro de Bellas Artes** (✉ 2173 S.W. 8th St., Miami 33135, ☎ 305/325–0515), on Calle Ocho, presents eight Spanish plays and musicals year-round. Midnight musical follies and female impersonators round out the showbiz lineup.

Nightlife

Bars and Lounges

COCONUT GROVE

CocoWalk presents three different but all potentially decadent drinking establishments. Drinking cold beer and gorilla-size margaritas in the middle of the Grove is part of the fun at **Fat Tuesday** (✉ 3015 Grand Ave., ☎ 305/441–2992). With more flavors than in a roll of Life Savers, the bar offers up drinks called 190 Octane (190-proof alcohol), Swampwater (also 190 proof), and Grapeshot (a meager 151-proof rum and bourbon concoction). Can you say, "designated driver"? **Hooters** (✉ 3015 Grand Ave., ☎ 305/442–6004) and its well-known distractions will take you back to high school, but now you have credit cards to keep the party going. A few drinks can lower the inhibitions of even the most reserved and tone-deaf person. This explains the magic of **Howl at the Moon Saloon** (✉ 3015 Grand Ave., ☎ 305/441–4411), where dueling pianists get the crowd worked up with sing-alongs. Imagine Ferrante and Teicher on pep pills, and you can picture this place.

The **Hungry Sailor** (✉ 3064½ Grand Ave., ☎ 305/444–9359) serves up Jamaican-English food, British beer, rock on Monday and Tuesday, and reggae from Thursday through Sunday. Hit it on Thursday night and order a round of 1¢ beers. Yes, they're a penny a pop. Bring a quarter and buy a case. The **Taurus Steak House** (✉ 3540 Main Hwy., ☎ 305/448–0633) is an unchanging oasis in the trendy Grove. The bar, built of native cypress in 1919, draws an over-30 singles crowd nightly. A band plays from Tuesday through Saturday.

CORAL GABLES

Two Irishmen missed the Emerald Isle so they opened **John Martin's Restaurant and Irish Pub** (✉ 253 Miracle Mile, ☎ 305/445–3777). It serves up fish-and-chips, bangers and mash, shepherd's pie, and all the accoutrements of a Dublin pub—plus the requisite pints of Guinness, Harp, Bass, and other ales. In a building that dates from 1926, **Stuart's Bar-Lounge** (✉ 162 Alcazar Ave., ☎ 305/444–1666), inside the charming Hotel Place St. Michel, was named one of the best new bars of 1987 by *Esquire,* and it's still favored by locals. The style is fostered by beveled mirrors, mahogany paneling, French posters, pictures of old Coral Gables, and Art Nouveau lighting. Stuart's is closed Sunday.

MIAMI

Tobacco Road (✉ 626 S. Miami Ave., ☎ 305/374–1198), opened in 1912, holds Miami's oldest liquor license: Number 0001! Upstairs, in space occupied by a speakeasy during Prohibition, blues bands perform nightly, accompanied by single-malt scotch and bourbon.

MIAMI BEACH

Blue Steel (✉ 2895 Collins Ave., ☎ 305/672–1227) is a cool but unpretentious hangout with pool tables, darts, live music, comfy old sofas, and beer paraphernalia. Open-mike night is Friday, and there's a jam on Monday. German *Vogue* liked it so much they named it the "hippest and hottest" club in SoBe. At **The Clevelander** (✉ 1020 Ocean Dr., ☎ 305/531–3485), a giant pool-bar area attracts revelers for happy hour drink specials and live music. *Ach du lieber!* Here since 1926, **Mac's Club Deuce** (✉ 222 14th St., ☎ 305/673–9537) must be doing something right. This is a South Beach gem where top international models pop in to have a drink, listen to the jukebox, and shoot some pool (surprising, considering the working-class atmosphere). All you get late at night are minipizzas, but the pizzazz lasts long. In a nondescript motel row with nudie bars, baby stores, and bait-and-tackle shops, **Molly Malone's** (✉ 166 Sunny Isles Blvd., ☎ 305/948–9143) is the only cool, down-to-earth spot that thrives in this neighborhood. The Irish pub, a big local fave, has a traditional European look, with oak paneling, live Irish music on Friday, and acoustic sounds Saturday. **Rose's Music Bar & Lounge** (✉ 754 Washington Ave., ☎ 305/532–0228) is a casual neighborhood bar with Monday-night football and Friday-night blues. An ATM and 5 PM–5 AM hours mean you can muscle up to the bar *and* save money on a hotel room. **Zeke's Road House** (⊠ 625 Lincoln Rd., ☎ 305/532–0087) arrived just before Lincoln Road got its spit and polish (when it was just spit). A neighborhood bar that transcends trends, it's hidden amid revitalized buildings but keeps it simple with sandwiches and draft beers such as Chester, Harp, and Ybor Gold.

Dance Clubs

KEY BISCAYNE

Stefano's of Key Biscayne (⊠ 24 Crandon Blvd., ☎ 305/361–7007) is a northern Italian restaurant with a disco that changes formats nightly: Thursday, Latin; Friday, ladies' night; Saturday, standard disco; and Sunday, oldies. There's a cover charge Friday and Saturday.

MIAMI BEACH

South Beach is headquarters for nightclubs that start late and stay open until the early morning. The clientele is largely a mix of freak-show rejects, sullen male models, and sultry women.

Amnesia (⊠ 136 Collins Ave., ☎ 305/531–5535), open Thursday–Sunday, specializes in mega-events, but be warned: Tea dances here are nothing like those in Mayberry. Formats range from Friday's Reggae Island Dance to Saturday's techno music and Sunday's gay night. The indoor/outdoor venue is like a luxurious amphitheater in the tropics, complete with rain forest, what used to be called go-go dancers, and frenzied dancing in the rain when showers pass over the open-air ground-level club. Here since 1993, this is one of the old-timers—but still a fave. One look at the padded walls of another venue, and you'll think you've entered an asylum; but rest assured: You're only at **Bash** (⊠ 655 Washington Ave., ☎ 305/538–2274). With two DJs spinning dance music—sometimes reggae, sometimes Latin, plenty of loud disco, and world-beat sounds—the party is always going full tilt. You can catch some fresh air by heading to the patio, which is overshadowed by a towering parking garage and a chicken-wire ceiling. The scene is just as lively, but it's strangely calming to be outside. As in other clubs, the posing doesn't stop. If you're anxious to enter one of the three VIP rooms, strike a pose and try joining the chic crowd. The **Bermuda Bar & Grille** (⊠ 3509 N.E. 163rd St., ☎ 305/945–0196) is way north of SoBe but worth the drive if you want to hang with the locals. Rock radio stations do remote broadcasts, and hard liquor and bottled beer are favored over silly drinks with umbrellas. The music is as loud as the setting is large—two floors and seven bars—and hours run 4 PM–6 AM. Male bartenders wear knee-length kilts, while female bartenders are in matching minis. The atmosphere and crowd, though, are stylish, and there's a big tropical-forest scene, booths you can hide in, and pool tables to dive into. The joint is closed from Sunday through Tuesday.

Chaos (⊠ 743 Washington Ave., ☎ 305/674–7350) presents themed evenings from Wednesday's LoveSexy and Thursday's World Tour to Fashion Friday and Saturday evening's Total Chaos. It must be hot: One night it hosts Playboy models, and the next George Foreman's here celebrating his birthday. If Desi Arnaz were still around, he wouldn't recognize **Club Lua** (⊠ 409 Espanola Way, ☎ 305/534–0061), one of the places where he played in the '30s. Dark as night, the tomblike club changes formats from retro to gothic to hip-hop depending on the night. The still hot, still happenin' **Groove Jet** (⊠ 323 23rd St., ☎ 305/532–2002) breaks new ground by featuring DJs from the worldwide musical underground. (If you're not in tune with the subtle nuances of techno pop, however, it'll all sound the same.) Since the club's open 11 PM–5 AM, you'll have plenty of time to break your eardrums with hypnotic dance music played in three rooms. Just remember to say, "I'll be home late, Mom!" To avoid a cover, hit this one on Thursday night. **Liquid** (✉ 1437–39 Washington Ave., ☎ 305/532–9154), open 10 PM–5 AM, is a high-energy dance club with themed evenings. Thursday's NFA is hip-hop, Friday brings the Kingdom, Saturday welcomes top New York DJs, Sunday is Manwich Night (for gays), and Monday throbs to funk and soul during Fat Black Pussycat. Weekdays' staid conventioneers give way to the chic crowd on weekends.

Designed like a sultan's palace, the very classy and elegant **Living Room at the Strand** (✉ 671 Washington Ave., ☎ 305/532–2340) draws A-list celebs and sheiks who drop $1,000 tips. If your bankroll hasn't risen to that level, just shoot a game of pool or have dinner before the club crowd arrives. After dinner the club hops with techno pop. There's great service all around, and the comfortable couches are a welcome addition. A truly frightening evening can be spent at the **Shadow Lounge** (✉ 1532 Washington Ave., ☎ 305/531–9411), where the club kids look like mannequins come to life. By mixing Berlin of the '30s with Havana of the '50s and New York of the '70s, it creates a weird atmosphere that attracts Miami's crème de la creepy. If you can't take it and are afraid you'll whimper like a beaten puppy, stay home and watch *The Twilight Zone* instead. SoBe's warhorse, **Warsaw Ballroom** (✉ 1450 Collins Ave.) has outlasted most other clubs, becoming an institution. Once Gianni Versace's party central, it boasts a guest list that's included Madonna, Sean Penn, Jack Nicholson, and Dennis Rodman. The 9:30 PM–5 AM hours (Wednesday–Saturday only) turn a traditional work schedule on its head. Though most nights are becoming gay, there's still an occasional straight night with hip-hop and disco. Beware of cover charges ranging from $7 on up to $40 to cover the occasional $12,000-a-night DJ.

Jazz

MIAMI BEACH

Jazid (✉ 1342 Washington Ave., ☎ 305/604–9798) is the place for blues and jazz from swing to traditional jazz. Performers change nightly, but the intimate candlelit atmosphere and no-cover policy remain constant. More restaurant than jazz club, **Van Dyke Café** (✉ 846 Lincoln Rd., ☎ 305/534–3600) serves music on the second floor seven nights a week. Its location on the Lincoln Road Mall makes it a great spot to take a break during an evening shopping excursion.

Nightclub

MIAMI BEACH

You can dine as you watch the show at the Fontainebleau Hilton's **Club Tropigala** (✉ 4441 Collins Ave., ☎ 305/672–7469), which tries to blend modern Vegas with 1950s Havana. The four-tier round room is decorated with orchids, banana leaves, and philodendrons to create an indoor tropical jungle. The performances themselves can be less satisfying, sometimes consisting of disappointing writing, choreography, and acting. Hotel guests are comped, but others pay a $20 cover. Reservations are suggested, and men should wear jackets.

OUTDOOR ACTIVITIES AND SPORTS

In addition to contacting the addresses below directly, you can get tickets to major events from **Ticketmaster** (☎ 305/358–5885).

Auto Racing

Hialeah Speedway, the area's only independent raceway, holds stock-car races on a ⅓-mi asphalt oval in a 5,000-seat stadium. Don't be fooled: The enthusiasm of the local drivers makes this as exciting as Winston

Cup races. Five divisions of cars run weekly. The Marion Edwards, Jr., Memorial Race, for late-model cars, is held in November. The speedway is on U.S. 27, ¼ mi east of the Palmetto Expressway (Route 826). ⊠ *3300 W. Okeechobee Rd., Hialeah,* ☎ *305/821–6644.* ⊇ *$10, special events $15.* ⊘ *Late Jan.–early Dec., Sat.; gates open at 5, racing 7–11.*

Baseball

Although the **Florida Marlins** (⊠ 2267 N.W. 199th St., Miami 33056, ☎ 305/626–7400) team that won the 1997 World Series was split up soon afterward, games are still as exciting as baseball can be. Home games are played at Pro Player Stadium, which is 16 mi northwest of downtown. On game days the Metro-Dade Transit Agency runs buses to the stadium.

Basketball

The NBA's **Miami Heat** (⊠ 1 S.E. 3rd Ave., Miami 33131, ☎ 305/577–4328) were Atlantic Division champs for the 1996–97 and 1997–98 seasons. Their reward, it would seem, is the new 20,000-seat, waterfront American Airlines Arena (scheduled to open December 31, 1999), which features a scoreboard with special effects and indoor fireworks. Home games are held November–April.

Biking

Perfect weather and flat terrain make Miami-Dade County a popular place for cyclists. A free color-coded map highlighting the cyclability of local roads as well as bike shops, parks, safety tips, and the routes of bike rack–equipped buses make it even better. The map is available from area bike shops and from the **Miami-Dade County Bicycle Coordinator** (⊠ Metropolitan Planning Organization, 111 N.W. 1st St., Suite 910, Miami 33128, ☎ 305/375–4507, ext. 1735), whose purpose in life is to share with you the glories of Miami's bicycle-friendly roads. For information on dozens of monthly group rides, contact the **Everglades Bicycle Club** (⊠ Box 430282, South Miami 33243-0282, ☎ 305/598–3998). For bike rentals check out the **Miami Beach Bicycle Center** (MBBC; ⊠ 601 5th St., Miami Beach, ☎ 305/674–0150), in business since 1975. MBBC's proximity to Ocean Drive and the ocean itself make it worth the $20 per day (or $5 per hour), which includes a helmet, lock, and basket on a mountain bike or cruiser. Tours of the Deco District are offered twice a month.

Boating

The popular full-service **Crandon Park Marina** is a one-stop shop for all things ocean-y. You can embark on deep-sea fishing or scuba-diving excursions, dine at a marina restaurant, or rent powerboats through **Club Nautico** (⊠ 5420 Crandon Blvd., Key Biscayne, ☎ 305/361–9217; also ⊠ 2560 Bayshore Dr., Coconut Grove, ☎ 305/858–6258), a national powerboat rental company. Half- to full-day rentals range from $109 to $419, or you can buy a membership, which costs a bundle at first but saves around 60% on future rentals. ⊠ *4000 Crandon Blvd., Key Biscayne,* ☎ *305/361–1281.* ⊘ *Office daily 8–6.*

Named for an island where early settlers had picnics, **Dinner Key Marina** is Greater Miami's largest, with nearly 600 moorings at nine piers. There is space for transients and a boat ramp. ⊠ *3400 Pan American Dr., Coconut Grove,* ☎ *305/579–6980.* ⊘ *Daily 7 AM–11 PM.*

Haulover Marine Center is low on glamour but high on service. It offers a bait-and-tackle shop, marine gas station, and boat launch. ⊠ *15000 Collins Ave., Miami Beach,* ☎ *305/945–3934.* ⊘ *Bait shop and gas station open 24 hours.*

Although **Matheson Hammock Park** has no charter services, it does have 243 slips and boat ramps. It also has **Castle Harbor** (☎ 305/665–4994), a sailing school that relocated here from Coconut Grove in 1998. In operation since 1949, it offers sailboat rentals for those with U.S. Sailing certification as well as classes held in outdoor—and very warm—Seminole Indian–style chickees. When you're ready to rent, take your pick of boats ranging from 23 ft to 41 ft. ⊠ *9610 Old Cutler Rd., Coral Gables,* ☎ *305/665–5475.* ⊙ *Daily 6–sunset.*

A happening waterfront mecca, **Miami Beach Marina** is the nearest marina to the Deco District, about a 15-minute walk away. It has restaurants, charters, boat and vehicle rentals, a complete marine hardware store, dive shop and excursions, large grocery store, fuel dock, concierge services, and 400 slips accommodating vessels up to 190 ft. Facilities include air-conditioned rest rooms, washers and dryers, U.S. Customs clearing, and a heated pool. One charter outfit here is family-owned **Florida Yacht Charters** (☎ 305/532–8600 or 800/537–0050). After completing a checkout cruise and paperwork, slap down a deposit and take off for the Keys or Bahamas on a catamaran, sailboat, or motor yacht. Charts, lessons, and captains are available if needed. Call for a comprehensive info kit. ⊠ *300 Alton Rd., Miami Beach,* ☎ *305/673–6000 for marina.* ⊙ *Daily 7–6.*

Dog Racing

In the middle of Little Havana, **Flagler Greyhound Track** has dog racing during its June–November season and a poker room that's open when the track is running. Closed-circuit TV brings harness-racing action here as well. The track is five minutes east of Miami International Airport, off Dolphin Expressway (Route 836) and Douglas Road (Northwest 37th Avenue). ⊠ *401 N.W. 38th Ct., Miami,* ☎ *305/649–3000.* ☞ *$1, clubhouse $3, parking 50¢–$2.* ⊙ *Racing daily 7:30, plus Tues.–Wed. and Sat. 12:30.*

Fishing

Before there was fashion, there was fishing. Deep-sea fishing is still a major draw, and anglers drop a line for sailfish, kingfish, dolphin, snapper, wahoo, grouper, and tuna. Smaller charter boats can cost $350–$400 for a half day and provide everything but food and drinks. If you're on a budget, you might be better off paying around $25 for passage on a larger fishing boat. Rarely are they filled to capacity. Most charters have a 50-50 plan, which allows you to take (or sell) half your catch while they do the same. Nearby general stores sell such essentials as fuel, tackle, sunglasses, and beer. Don't let them sell you a fishing license, however; a blanket license should cover all passengers.

Crandon Park Marina (⊠ 4000 Crandon Blvd., Key Biscayne, ☎ 305/361–1281) has earned an international reputation for knowledgeable captains and good catches. Heading out to the edge of the Gulf Stream (about 3 to 4 mi), you're sure to wind up with something on your line—although sailfish is one fish that's catch and release. Many ocean-fishing charters sail out of **Haulover Park** (⊠ 10800 Collins Ave., Miami Beach), including **Blue Waters Sportfishing Charters** (☎ 305/944–4531), four boats in the **Kelley Fleet** (☎ 305/945–3801), *Therapy IV* (☎ 305/945–1578), and about 10 additional charter services. Among the charter services at the **Miami Beach Marina** (⊠ 300 Alton Rd., MacArthur Causeway, Miami Beach) is **Reward Fleet** (☎ 305/372–9470). It operates two boats at moderate prices: $28 per person including bait, rod, reel, and tackle, less for kids.

Football

Despite the resignation of legendary coach Don Shula in 1995, fans keep coming to watch the NFL's **Miami Dolphins**—probably still waiting for a repeat of the 17–0 record of 1972 (a record that still stands). The team plays at the former Joe Robbie Stadium, renamed Pro Player Stadium in honor of a sports apparel company and a $20 million check. The state-of-the-art stadium, which has 75,000 seats and a grass playing surface, is on a 160-acre site 16 mi northwest of downtown Miami, 1 mi south of the Miami-Dade–Broward County line and accessible from I–95 and Florida's Turnpike. On game days the Metro-Dade Transit Agency runs buses to the stadium. ⊠ 2269 N.W. 199th St., Miami 33056, ☎ 305/620–2578. ⊙ Box office weekdays 8:30–6, also Sat. during season.

After calling the venerable Orange Bowl home for many years, the **University of Miami Hurricanes** (⊠ 1 Hurricane Dr., Coral Gables 33146, ☎ 305/284–2263), once contenders for the top collegiate ranking, are playing their home games at Pro Player Stadium (☞ above) from September to November.

Golf

Greater Miami has more than 30 private and public courses. Fees at most courses are higher on weekends and in season, but you can save money by playing weekdays and after 1 PM or 3 PM (call to find out when afternoon or twilight rates go into effect). That said, costs are reasonable to play in such an appealing setting as Miami.

To get the **"Golfer's Guide for South Florida,"** which includes information on most courses in Miami and surrounding areas, call ☎ 800/864–6101. The cost is $3.

The 18-hole championship **Biltmore Golf Course** (⊠ 1210 Anastasia Ave., Coral Gables, ☎ 305/460–5364), known for its scenic layout, has been restored to its original Donald Ross design, circa 1925. Greens fees range from $39 to $59 in season, and the gorgeous hotel makes a scenic backdrop. The **California Golf Club** (⊠ 20898 San Simeon Way, North Miami Beach, ☎ 305/651–3590) has an 18-hole course made challenging by a tight front nine and three of the area's toughest finishing holes. Eighteen holes will set you back between $40 and $50. Overlooking the bay, the **Crandon Park Golf Course** (⊠ 6700 Crandon Blvd., Key Biscayne, ☎ 305/361–9129), formerly the Links at Key Biscayne, is a top-rated public course in a beautiful tropical setting. Expect to pay around $90 for a round. **Don Shula's Hotel & Golf Club** (⊠ 7601 Miami Lakes Dr., Miami Lakes, ☎ 305/820–8106) has one of the longest championship courses in Miami (7,055 yards), a lighted par-3 course, a golf school, and more than 100 tournaments a year. Weekdays you can play for about $65, $90 on weekends. With four championship courses and one executive course, the **Doral Golf Resort and Spa** (⊠ 4400 N.W. 87th Ave., Doral, ☎ 305/592–2000 or 800/713–6725) is known for the Blue Monster course and the annual Doral-Ryder Open Tournament, with $2 million in prize money. If you're ready for the challenge, you'll pay fees of $110 to $240—less after 3.

Now operated by the city of Coral Gables, the **Granada Golf Course** (⊠ 2001 Granada Blvd., Coral Gables, ☎ 305/460–5367) is the oldest nine-hole course in Florida and costs only $16.25 with cart, $11 walking. If you aren't quite in Tiger Woods's league, you may enjoy the large fairways, minimal bunkers, and lack of water hazards. Then again, the par-36 layout is a respectable 3,001 yards. **Normandy Shores Golf Course** (⊠ 2401 Biarritz Dr., Miami Beach, ☎ 305/868–6502) is good for seniors, with some modest slopes and average distances. The

Turnberry Isle Resort & Club (⊠ 19999 W. Country Club Dr., Aventura, ☎ 305/933–6929) has 36 holes designed by Robert Trent Jones. The South Course's 18th hole is a killer, and the course is very expensive, but since it's private, you won't be able to play unless you're a hotel guest.

Horse Racing

The **Calder Race Course,** opened in 1971, is Florida's largest glass-enclosed, air-conditioned sports facility. It often has an unusually extended season, from late May to early January, though it's a good idea to call the track for specific starting and wrap-up dates, since Calder, Hialeah Park, and Gulfstream Park rotate their race dates. Each year between November and early January, Calder holds the Tropical Park Derby for three-year-olds. The track is on the Miami-Dade–Broward County line near I–95 and the Hallandale Beach Boulevard exit, ¾ mi from Pro Player Stadium. ⊠ *21001 N.W. 27th Ave., Miami,* ☎ *305/625–1311.* ☞ *$2, clubhouse $4, parking $1–$4.* ⊙ *Gates open at 11, racing 12:30–5.*

A superb setting for Thoroughbred racing, **Hialeah Park** has 228 acres of meticulously landscaped grounds surrounding paddocks and a clubhouse built in a classic French-Mediterranean style. Since it opened in 1925, Hialeah Park has survived hurricanes and now seems likely to survive even changing demographics, as the racetrack crowd has steadily moved north and east. Although Hialeah tends to get the less prestigious racing dates from March to May, it still draws crowds. The park is open year-round for free sightseeing, during which you can explore the gardens and admire the park's breeding flock of Cuban flamingos. Metrorail's Hialeah Station is on the grounds. ⊠ *2200 E. 4th Ave., Hialeah,* ☎ *305/885–8000.* ☞ *Weekdays, grandstand $1, clubhouse $2; weekends, grandstand $4, clubhouse $4; parking $1– $4.* ⊙ *Gates open at 10:30, racing 1–5:30.*

Jai Alai

Built in 1926, the **Miami Jai-Alai Fronton,** a mile east of the airport, is America's oldest fronton. It presents 13 games—14 on Friday and Saturday—some singles, some doubles. This game, invented in the Basque region of northern Spain, is the world's fastest. Jai-alai balls, called pelotas, have been clocked at speeds exceeding 170 mph. Players ducking from the pelotas have been clocked at 175 mph. The game is played in a 176-ft-long court, and players literally climb the walls to catch the ball in a cesta—a woven basket—with an attached glove. You can bet on a team to win or on the order in which teams will finish. Dinner is available. ⊠ *3500 N.W. 37th Ave., Miami,* ☎ *305/633–6400.* ☞ *$1, reserved seats $2, Courtview Club $5.* ⊙ *Mon., Wed., and Fri.– Sat. noon–5 and 7–midnight, Thurs. 7–midnight, Sun. 1–6.*

Jogging

There are numerous places to run in Miami, but these recommended jogging routes are considered among the most scenic and the safest: in Coconut Grove, along the pedestrian-bicycle path on South Bayshore Drive, cutting over the causeway to Key Biscayne for a longer run; from the south shore of the Miami River, downtown, south along the sidewalks of Brickell Avenue to Bayshore Drive, where you can run alongside the bay; in Miami Beach, along Bay Road (parallel to Alton Road) or on the sidewalk skirting the Atlantic Ocean, opposite the cafés of Ocean Drive; and in Coral Gables, around the Riviera Country Club golf course, just south of the Biltmore Country Club. A good source of running information is the **Miami Runners Club** (⊠ 7920 S.W. 40th St., Miami, ☎ 305/227–1500), although the volunteer group often has an answering machine on. An even better source may be **Foot Works**

(✉ 5724 Sunset Dr., South Miami, ☎ 305/667–9322), a running-shoe store that's open every day. Since 1971 it has hosted races and marathon training.

Scuba Diving and Snorkeling

Though winter storms can cause dive boats to vary their schedules, summer diving conditions in Greater Miami have been compared to those in the Caribbean. Chances are excellent you'll come face to face with a flood of tropical fish. One option is to find real reefs, such as Fowey, Triumph, Long, and Emerald, in 10- to 15-ft dives that are perfect for snorkelers and beginning divers. On the edge of the continental shelf a little more than 3 mi out, these reefs are ¼ mi from depths greater than 100 ft. Another option is to paddle around the tangled prop roots of the mangrove trees that line the coast, peering at the fish, crabs, and other creatures hiding there.

Perhaps the most unusual option, however, is to dive on one of the local artificial reefs. In 1981 Dade County's Department of Environmental Resources Management (DERM) started sinking tons of limestone boulders and more than 65 tankers, trawlers, tugs, a water tower, two M-60 tanks, and a 727 jet to create a "wreckreational" habitat where divers can swim with yellow tang, barracudas, nurse sharks, snappers, eels, and groupers. Most dive shops sell a book listing the location of these wrecks.

Information on wreck diving can be obtained from the Miami Beach Chamber of Commerce's **WaterSports Marketing Council** (✉ 1920 Meridian Ave., Miami Beach, ☎ 305/672–1270 or 888/728–2262), composed of hotels and dive shops involved in finding big stuff to sink.

Bubbles Dive Center (✉ 2671 S.W. 27th Ave., Miami, ☎ 305/856–0565), an all-purpose dive shop with PADI affiliation, runs night and wreck dives. Its boat, *Divers Dream,* is kept on Watson Island on MacArthur Causeway. **Divers Paradise of Key Biscayne** (✉ 4000 Crandon Blvd., Key Biscayne, ☎ 305/361–3483) has a complete dive shop and diving-charter service inside a trailer next to the Crandon Park Marina. On offer are equipment rental and PADI-affiliated scuba instruction. A 3½-day accelerated course ($399) is available for beginners. The PADI-affiliated **Diving Locker** (✉ 223 Sunny Isles Blvd., North Miami Beach, ☎ 305/947–6025) offers full sales, service, and repairs, plus three-day and three-week international certification courses as well as more advanced certifications. Wreck and reef sites are reached aboard fast and comfortable six-passenger dive boats.

Spa

Housed in a small coral building in SoBe, **White** bills itself as a salon, spa, and café, so you can walk in dirty, tired, and hungry and walk out completely satisfied. A destination for wealthy retirees and hot young models, it offers everything from body wraps and massages to cuts, makeovers, and pedicures. An Hour of Power will set you back $240. ✉ *900 Collins Ave., Miami Beach,* ☎ *305/538–0604.* ☼ *Tues. 11–8, Wed. 11–7, Thurs.–Fri. 11–9, Sat.–Mon. 11–6.*

Tennis

Greater Miami has more than a dozen tennis centers open to the public, and countywide nearly 500 public courts are open to visitors. Nonresidents are charged an hourly fee. If you're on a tight schedule, try calling in advance, as some courts take reservations on weekdays.

Biltmore Tennis Center has 10 hard courts and the added bonus of being located at the beautiful Biltmore Hotel (☞ Lodging, *above*). ✉ *1150 Anastasia Ave., Coral Gables,* ☎ *305/460–5360.* ▱ *Day rate $4.30,* *night rate $5 per person per hour.* ⊙ *Weekdays 8* AM–*10* PM, *weekends 8–8.*

Very popular with locals, **Flamingo Tennis Center** has 19 clay courts smack dab in the middle of Miami Beach. ⊠ *1000 12th St., Miami Beach,* ☎ *305/673–7761.* ⊞ *Day rate $2.67, night rate $3.20 per person per hr.* ⊙ *Weekdays 8* AM–*9* PM, *weekends 8–8.*

North Shore Tennis Center, within the North Shore Park, has six clay and five hard courts. ⊠ *350 73rd St., Miami Beach,* ☎ *305/993–2022.* ⊞ *Day rate $2.66, night rate $3.20 per person per hr.* ⊙ *Weekdays 8* AM–*9* PM, *weekends 8–7.*

The $18 million, 30-acre **Tennis Center at Crandon Park** is one of America's best. Included are 2 grass, 8 clay, and 17 hard courts. Reservations are required for night play. The only time courts are closed to the public is during the Lipton Championships (☎ 305/442–3367), held for 11 days each spring. The tournament is one of the best attended in the world, and with prize money nearing $5 million, it has the cash clout to attract players like Michael Chang, Pete Sampras, Venus Williams, and Martina Hingis. It's played in a 14,000-seat stadium. ⊠ *7300 Crandon Blvd., Key Biscayne,* ☎ *305/365–2300.* ⊞ *Laykold courts day rate $3, night rate $5 per person per hr; clay courts $6 per person per hour.* ⊙ *Daily 8* AM–*9* PM.

Windsurfing

New lightweight boards and smaller sails make learning windsurfing easier. The safest and most popular windsurfing area in city waters is south of town at Windsurfer Beach, just beyond the Rickenbacker Causeway on your way to Key Biscayne. Miami Beach's best windsurfing is at 1st Street just north of the Government Cut jetty and at 21st Street. You can also windsurf from Lummus Park at 10th Street and around 3rd, 14th, and 21st streets.

Sailboards Miami, just past the tollbooth for the Rickenbacker Causeway, claims to be the largest windsurfing school in the United States. It rents equipment, offers year-round lessons, and promises to teach anyone within two hours. ⊠ *Key Biscayne,* ☎ *305/361–7245.* ⊞ *1 hr $20, 10 hrs $150, 2-hr lesson $49.* ⊙ *Daily 10–5:30.*

SHOPPING

Visitors to Greater Miami are never more than 15 minutes from a major shopping area and the familiar *ca-ching* of a cash register. Miami-Dade County has more than a dozen major malls, an international free-trade zone, and hundreds of miles of commercial streets lined with stores and small shopping centers. Latin neighborhoods contain a wealth of Latin merchants and merchandise, including children's *vestidos de fiesta* (party dresses) and men's guayaberas (a pleated, embroidered tropical shirt), conveying the feel of a South American *mercado* (market).

Malls

Aventura Mall (⊠ 19501 Biscayne Blvd., Aventura) has more than 250 shops anchored by Macy's, Lord & Taylor, JCPenney, Sears, and Bloomingdale's. Who else is there? Guess. And a Disney Store and Banana Republic and . . . and . . . A recent expansion, which nearly doubled the mall's size, now accommodates a 24-screen theater, a Cheesecake Factory, Rainforest Café, China Grill, Burdines, and—surprise—a Starbucks. In a tropical garden setting, **Bal Harbour Shops** (⊠ 9700 Collins Ave., Bal Harbour) is a swank collection of 100 shops, boutiques, and department stores, such as Chanel, Gucci, Cartier, Fendi, Bruno Magli, Neiman Marcus, and Florida's largest Saks Fifth Avenue.

It was named by fashionable *Elle* magazine as one of the top five shopping collections in the United States. **Bayside Marketplace** (⊠ 401 Biscayne Blvd., Miami), the 16-acre shopping complex on Biscayne Bay, has more than 150 specialty shops, entertainment, tour-boat docks, and a food court. It's open late (10 during the week, 11 on Friday and Saturday), but its restaurants stay open even later. It's a nice place for a bayside drink, and the cafés and bars will only get more popular when the neighboring arena opens for basketball.

A complex of clapboard, coral-rock, and stucco buildings, **Cauley Square** (⊠ 22400 Old Dixie Hwy., Goulds) was erected in 1907–20 as housing for railroad workers who built and maintained the line to Key West. Crafts, clothing, and antiques shops are well represented. The heartbeat of Coconut Grove, **CocoWalk** (⊠ 3015 Grand Ave., Coconut Grove) has three floors of nearly 40 specialty shops (Victoria's Secret, the Gap, Banana Republic, among others) that stay open almost as late as the popular restaurants and clubs. Kiosks with cigars, beads, incense, herbs, and other small items are scattered around the ground level, while the restaurants and nightlife (e.g., Hooters, Fat Tuesday, an AMC theater) are upstairs. If you're ready for an evening of people-watching, this is the place.

The oldest retail mall in the county, **Dadeland** (⊠ 7535 N. Kendall Dr., Miami) is always upgrading. It sits at the south side of town close to the Dadeland North and Dadeland South Metrorail stations. Retailers include Saks Fifth Avenue, JCPenney, Lord & Taylor, more than 175 specialty stores, 17 restaurants, and the largest Burdines, Limited, and Limited Express in Florida. When it opens in fall 2000, the $250 million **Dolphin Mall** (⊠ Rte. 836 and Florida's Turnpike, Miami), 5 mi west of the airport, will offer plenty of less-expensive shopping, including Marshall's, Oshman's Super Sports, and Saks off Fifth, plus a Regal Cinema. The **Falls** (⊠ 8888 S.W. 136th St., at U.S. 1, Miami), which derives its name from the several waterfalls inside, is the most upscale mall on the south side of the city. It contains a Macy's and Bloomingdale's as well as another 50 specialty stores, restaurants, and a 12-theater multiplex.

The downtown **Omni International Mall** (⊠ 1601 Biscayne Blvd., Miami) rises vertically alongside the atrium of the Crowne Plaza Miami, whose eye-popping feature is an old-fashioned carousel. Among its 75 shops are a JCPenney, many restaurants, and 10 movie screens. You'll find **Paseos** (⊠ 3301 Coral Way, Coral Gables) as you roll into Coral Gables on Coral Way. The plain but imposing exterior hides a collection of shops, cafés, and movie theaters. To compete with trendy Coconut Grove, the **Shops at Sunset Place** (⊠ U.S. 1 and Red Rd. [S.W. 57th Ave.], South Miami) is larger than CocoWalk. The three-story, 519,000-square-ft, family-oriented center upped the ante for entertainment complexes with a 24-screen multiplex, IMAX theater, Barnes & Noble, Virgin Megastore, F.A.O. Schwarz, NikeTown, and Game-Works (a Spielberg-movie-inspired virtual-reality attraction wrapped into a restaurant). **Streets of Mayfair** (⊠ 2911 Grand Ave., Coconut Grove) is an active, bustling group of shops both day and night. Thanks to its Grove setting, along with the News Café, Planet Hollywood, the Limited, Borders, and a few dozen other shops and restaurants, this is a safe bet. Entertainment is provided by an improv comedy club, a 10-screen theater, and the Iguana Cantina, a nightclub, martini bar, and pool room.

Outdoor Markets

Coconut Grove Farmers Market (⊠ Grand Ave., 1 block west of Mac-Donald Ave. [S.W. 32nd Ave.], Coconut Grove), open Saturday 8–2, originated in 1977 and was the first in the Miami area. The **Espanola Way Market** (⊠ Espanola Way, Miami Beach), Sunday noon–9, has been a city favorite since its debut in 1995. Scattered among the hand-crafted items and flea market merchandise, musicians beat out Latin rhythms on bongos, conga drums, steel drums, and guitars. Food vendors sell inexpensive Latin snacks and drinks. Each Saturday morning from mid-January to late March, some 25 produce and plant vendors sell herbs, fruits, fresh-squeezed juices, chutneys, cakes, and muffins at the **Farmers Market at Merrick Park** (⊠ LeJeune Rd. [S.W. 42nd Ave.] and Biltmore Way, Coral Gables). Regular features include gardening workshops, children's activities, and cooking demonstrations offered by Coral Gables' master chefs. More than 500 vendors sell a variety of goods at the **Flagler Dog Track** (⊠ 401 N.W. 38th Ct., Miami), every weekend 9–4. The **Lincoln Road Farmers Market** (⊠ Lincoln Rd. between Meridian and Euclid Aves., Miami Beach), open Sunday November–March, brings about 15 local produce vendors coupled with plant workshops and children's activities. With 1,200 dealers, **Opa-Locka/Hialeah Flea Market** (⊠ 12705 N.W. 47th Ave., Miami) is one of the largest in South Florida. Though it's open seven days, weekends are best. From 10 to 5 on the second and fourth Sundays of each month, locals set up the **Outdoor Antique and Collectibles Market** (⊠ Lincoln and Alton Rds., Miami Beach). The eclectic goods should satisfy post-Impressionists, Deco-holics, Edwardians, Bauhausers, and Gothic, atomic, and '50s junkies.

Shopping Districts

The shopping is great on a two-block stretch of **Collins Avenue** (⊠ Between 6th and 8th Aves., Miami Beach). Vidal Sassoon, Nicole Miller, Nike, Kenneth Cole, Guess, and Banana Republic are among the high-profile tenants, and a parking garage is just a block away. The busy **Lincoln Road Mall** is just a few blocks from the beach and convention center, making it popular with locals and tourists. Despite some empty storefronts caused by escalating rents, there's still an energy to shopping here. Creative merchandise, galleries, and a Sunday-morning antiques market can be found among the theaters and cool cafés.

There are 500 garment manufacturers in Miami and Hialeah, and many sell their clothing locally in the **Miami Fashion District** (⊠ 5th Ave. east of I–95, between 25th and 29th Sts., Miami), making Greater Miami the fashion marketplace for the southeastern United States, the Caribbean, and Latin America. Most of the more than 30 factory outlets and discount fashion stores are open Monday–Saturday 9–5. The **Miami International Arts and Design District** (⊠ Between N.E. 38th and N.E. 42nd Sts. and between Federal Hwy. and N. Miami Ave., Miami), also known as 40th Street, contains some 225 wholesale stores, showrooms, and galleries specializing in interior furnishings, decorative arts, and a rich mix of exclusive and unusual merchandise. Don't expect to find a flood of shoppers here; the surrounding neighborhood keeps many tourists away. **Miracle Mile** (⊠ Coral Way between 37th and 42nd Aves., Coral Gables) consists of some 160 shops along a wide, tree-lined boulevard. Shops range from posh boutiques to bargain basements, from beauty salons to chain restaurants. As you go west, the quality increases.

Specialty Stores

ANTIQUES

A&J Unique Deco (⊠ 2000 Biscayne Blvd., Miami, ☎ 305/576–5170) is constantly rotating its inventory of Deco furniture, collected from Europe and the United States. In a world of reproductions, this is the real thing: 5,000 square ft of cool armoires, dressers, beds, and bars.

Alhambra Antiques Center (✉ 3640 Coral Way, Miami, ☎ 305/446–1688) is a collection of four antiques dealers that sell high-quality decorative pieces from Europe. **Architectural Antiques** (✉ 2500 S.W. 28th La., Coconut Grove, ☎ 305/285–1330) carries large and eclectic items—railroad crossing signs, statues, English roadsters—in a setting so cluttered that shopping here becomes an adventure promising hidden treasures for the determined.

BOOKS

Like others in the superstore chain, **Barnes & Noble** (✉ 152 Miracle Mile, Coral Gables, ☎ 305/446–4152) manages to preserve the essence of a neighborhood bookstore by encouraging customers to pick a book off the shelf and lounge on a couch without being hassled. A well-stocked magazine and national/international news rack and an espresso bar–café complete the effect. Greater Miami's best English-language bookstore, **Books & Books, Inc.** (✉ 296 Aragon Ave., Coral Gables, ☎ 305/442–4408; ✉ Sterling Bldg., 933 Lincoln Rd., Miami Beach, ☎ 305/532–3222) specializes in books on the arts, architecture, Florida, and contemporary and classical literature. At the Coral Gables location, a true old-fashioned bookstore, collectors enjoy browsing through the rare-book room upstairs, which doubles as a photography gallery. There are frequent poetry readings and book signings. The Lincoln Road shop always has a desk filled with intriguing discounted tomes. If being in the Grove prompts you to don a beret, grow a goatee, and sift through a volume of Kerouac, head to **Borders** (✉ Grand Ave. and Mary St., Coconut Grove, ☎ 305/447–1655) at the Streets of Mayfair. Its 100,000 book titles, 70,000 CDs, 10,000 video titles, and more than 2,000 periodicals and newspapers in 10 languages from 15 countries make it seem like the southern branch of the Library of Congress.

CHILDREN'S BOOKS AND TOYS

F.A.O. Schwarz (✉ 9700 Collins Ave., Bal Harbour Shops, Bal Harbour, ☎ 305/865–2361; ✉ 19501 Biscayne Blvd., Aventura Mall, Aventura, ☎ 305/692–9200; ✉ 5701 Sunset Dr., Shops at Sunset Place, South Miami, ☎ 305/668–2300) has three area stores. **A Likely Story** (✉ 5740 Sunset Dr., South Miami, ☎ 305/667–3730) has been helping Miamians choose books and educational toys appropriate to children's interests and stages of development since 1978.

CIGARS

Although Tampa is Florida's true cigar capital, Miami's Latin population is giving it a run for its money. Smoking anything even remotely affiliated with a legendary Cuban has boosted the popularity of Miami cigar stores and the small shops where you can buy cigars straight from the press.

The **Cigar Connection** (✉ 534 Lincoln Road Mall, Miami Beach, ☎ 305/531–7373) is hoping to capture the trendy tastes of pedestrians strolling on Lincoln Road. Carrying such premium cigars as the Arturo Fuente Opus X and Paul Garmirians, the shop also serves coffees and cappuccino. With soft terra-cotta and ochre tones suggestive of an Italian villa, **Condal & Peñamil** (✉ 741 Lincoln Road Mall, Miami Beach, ☎ 305/604–9690) is Miami's most beautiful cigar bar. In addition to carrying the traditional ashtrays, cutters, and humidors, C&P has a "cigar cave" with a private salon, enabling you to complement your smoke with a coffee or cocktail. In the heart of Little Havana, **El Credito** (✉ 1106 S.W. 8th St., Miami, ☎ 305/858–4162 or 800/726–9481) seems to have been transported from the Cuban capital lock, stock, and stogie. Rows of workers at wooden benches rip through giant tobacco leaves, cut them with rounded blades, wrap them tightly, and press them in vises. Dedicated smokers like Robert De Niro, Gregory Hines, and George Hamilton have found their way here to pick up a $90 bundle or peruse the *gigantes, supremos,* panatelas, and Churchills available in natural or maduro wrappers.

It's the only cigar shop on Miracle Mile, but that's not the sole reason to drop by **Giorgio's Cigars** (✉ 210 Miracle Mile, Coral Gables, ☎ 305/448–2992 or 888/833–8819). The standard lineup (Espinosa, Arturo Fuente, Macanudo, Partagas, et al.) is complemented by a large humidor, coffee bar, nice leather sofas, and a cheesy nude painting. There's added applause for the friendly staff. **Havana Ray's** (✉ 3111 Grand Ave., Coconut Grove, ☎ 305/446–4003 or 800/732–4427) continues a cigar-making dynasty that began in 1920s Cuba. The Quirantes family's devotion to cigars has resulted in this cozy Streets of Mayfair shop, where you can buy cigars and related accouterments. **Smokers' Notch** (✉ 425 Washington Ave., Miami Beach, ☎ 305/534–4090) has a terrific location (across from the China Grill), which means celebs (Nicholson) and regular folks (you) can drop in for an after-dinner smoke or stock up on pipe tobacco, cutters, humidors, cigar mags, and more than 100 cigar brands, including Sweet Millionaires (flavored cigars). **South Beach Cigar Cafe** (✉ 710 Washington Ave., No. 9, Miami Beach, ☎ 305/673–3002) has expanded beyond simple cigars to carry imported wines and beers, gourmet espresso and coffee, sandwiches, and croissants. But the real draw is cigars made on the premises or imported from the Dominican Republic, Nicaragua, and Honduras.

COLLECTIBLES

CJ's Animation Art Gallery (✉ 279 Miracle Mile, Coral Gables, ☎ 305/529–1700) carries animation and cel art from Warner Brothers, Disney, and Marvel artists. Prices range from $20 to thousands of dollars, with some pieces on consignment. **Gotta Have It! Collectibles** (✉ 504 Biltmore Way, Coral Gables, ☎ 305/446–5757) will make fans of any kind break out in a cold sweat. Autographed sports jerseys, canceled checks from the estate of Marilyn Monroe, fabulously framed album jackets signed by all four Beatles, and an elaborate autographed montage of all the *Wizard of Oz* stars are among this intriguing shop's museum-quality collectibles. Looking for an Einstein autograph? A Jack Nicklaus–signed scorecard? Look no farther. And if they don't have the autograph you desire, fear not—they'll track one down.

DECORATIVE AND GIFT ITEMS

American Details (✉ 3107 Grand Ave., Coconut Grove, ☎ 305/448–6163) sells colorful, trendy arts and crafts handmade by American artists. Jewelry and handblown glass are popular sellers. The **Indies Company** (✉ 101 W. Flagler St., Miami, ☎ 305/375–1492), the Historical Museum of Southern Florida's gift shop, offers interesting artifacts reflecting Miami's history, including some inexpensive reproductions. The collection of books on Miami and South Florida is impressive.

ESSENTIALS

Wall-to-wall merchandise is found at the **Compass Market** (✉ 860 Ocean Dr., Miami Beach, ☎ 305/673–2906), a cute and cozy basement shop that carries all the staples you'll need, especially if you're staying in an efficiency. The market stocks sandals, souvenirs, cigars, deli items, umbrellas, newspapers, and produce. If the heat of Miami gets you hot and bothered, try **Condom USA** (✉ 3066 Grand Ave., Coconut Grove, ☎ 305/445–7729) on for size. Sexually oriented games and condoms are sold by the gross. If you're easily offended, stay away. If you're easily aroused, stay the night.

JEWELRY

Easily overlooked in the quick pace of downtown, the 10-story **Seybold Building** (⊠ 36 N.E. 1st St., Miami, ☎ 305/374–7922) is filled from bottom to top with more than 250 independent jewelry companies. Diamonds, bracelets, necklaces, and rings are sold in a crowded, lively setting. Word is that competition makes prices flexible, but it's closed Sunday. **Stones of Venice** (⊠ 550 Biltmore Way, Coral Gables, ☎ 305/444–4474), operated by a three-time winner of the DeBeers Diamond Award for jewelry, sells affordable creations. Customers have included Elliott Gould, Pope John Paul II, and film director Barbet Schroeder.

LIGHTING

If you thought designers just keep coming up with the same old stuff, check out **Lunatika** (⊠ 900 Lincoln Rd., Miami Beach, ☎ 305/534–8585). It lights up SoBe with funky, creative lighting from chandeliers to wall sconces to floor lamps. Prices range from a $35 desk clock to a dizzying color-changing clock for $3,000. One look and you'll say, "Yowsa!"

SIDE TRIP

South Dade

Although the population of these suburbs southwest of Dade County's urban core was largely dislocated by Hurricane Andrew in 1992, little damage is evident today. Indeed, FEMA grants and major replanting have made the area better than ever. All attractions—many of which are especially interesting for kids—have reopened, and a complete exploration of them would probably take two days. Keep an eye open for hand-painted signs announcing agricultural attractions, such as orchid farms, fruit stands, u-pick farms, and horseback riding.

🕙 ㊷ Aviation enthusiasts touch down at **Weeks Air Museum** to view some 15 planes of World War II vintage. Sadly, Hurricane Andrew destroyed the World War I aircraft, and those from World War II suffered damage as well. What you will find are extensive videos, a 707 cockpit you can peer into, and a nose section of a B-29 Superfortress. The museum is inside Tamiami Airport. ⊠ 14710 S.W. 128th St., ☎ 305/233–5197. ☞ $7.95. ☉ Daily 10–5.

🕙 ㊸ One of the only zoos in the United States in a subtropical environment, the first-class, 290-acre **Metrozoo** is state of the art. Inside the cageless zoo, some 800 animals roam on islands surrounded by moats. Major attractions include the Tiger Temple, where white tigers roam, and the African Plains exhibit, where giraffes, ostriches, and zebras graze in a simulated habitat. There are also koalas, Komodo dragons, and other animals whose names begin with a K. Paws, a petting zoo for children, features three shows daily; during the Wildlife Show, trained animals demonstrate natural behavior on cue. Kids can touch Florida animals such as alligators and possums at the Ecology Theater. ⊠ 12400 Coral Reef Dr. (S.W. 152nd St.), ☎ 305/251–0401. ☞ $8, 45-min tram tour $2. ☉ Daily 9:30–5:30, last admission 4.

🕙 ㊹ Historic railroad cars on display at the **Gold Coast Railroad Museum** include a 1949 *Silver Crescent* dome car and the *Ferdinand Magellan,* the only Pullman car constructed specifically for U.S. presidents. It was used by Franklin Delano Roosevelt, Harry Truman, Dwight Eisenhower, and Ronald Reagan. On weekends, a train ride is included in the price of admission to the museum, which is next to the zoo. ⊠ 12450 Coral

South Dade

Reef Dr. (S.W. 152nd St.), ☎ *305/253–0063.* 🖃 *$5.* ⊘ *Weekdays 11–3, weekends 11–4.*

☺ ④⑤ Still a kitschy attraction for adults, **Monkey Jungle** claims to be home to more than 300 monkeys representing 25 species—including orangutans from Borneo and Sumatra and golden lion tamarins from Brazil. Unfortunately, it's showing its age with empty cages, sad-looking monkeys, and shows performed without showmanship. Perhaps the most fun is feeding monkeys who scurry across the fences overhead, hauling up peanuts you place in a metal cup. ⊠ *14805 Hainlin Mill Dr. (S.W. 216th St.),* ☎ *305/235–1611.* 🖃 *$13.50.* ⊘ *Daily 9:30–5, last admission 4.*

④⑥ The 35-acre **Redland Fruit & Spice Park** has been a Dade County treasure since 1944, when it was opened as a 20-acre showcase of tropical fruits and vegetables. Two of the park's three historic buildings were ruined by Hurricane Andrew, as well as about half its trees and plants, but it's now back in full swing. Plants are now grouped by country of origin and include more than 500 economically important varieties of exotic fruits, herbs, spices, nuts, and poisonous plants from around the world. A sampling reveals 80 types of bananas, 30 varieties of grapes, and 100 kinds of citrus fruits. The park store offers many varieties of tropical-fruit products, jellies, seeds, aromatic teas, and reference books. ⊠ *24801 Redland Rd. (S.W. 187th Ave.),* ☎ *305/247–5727.* 🖃 *$3.50.* ⊘ *Daily 10–5, tours daily 1 and 3.*

☺ ④⑦ **Coral Castle of Florida** was born when 26-year-old Edward Leedskalnin, a Latvian immigrant, was left at the altar by his 16-year-old fiancée. She went on with her life, while he went off the deep end and began carving a castle out of coral rock. It's hard to believe that Eddie, only 5 ft tall and 100 pounds, could maneuver tons of coral rock single-handedly. Built between 1920 and 1940, the 3-acre castle is one of

South Florida's original tourist attractions. There is a 9-ton gate a child could open, an accurate working sundial, and a telescope of coral rock aimed at the North Star. This weird, wonderful place is the inspiration for Billy Idol's *Sweet Sixteen*. ⊠ *28655 S. Dixie Hwy.,* ☎ *305/248–6344 or 305/248–6345.* ⊠ *$7.75.* ☉ *Sun.–Thurs. 9–7, Fri.–Sat. 9–8.*

MIAMI AND MIAMI BEACH A TO Z

Arriving and Departing

By Boat

If you enter the United States in a private vessel along the Atlantic Coast south of Sebastian Inlet, you must call the **U.S. Customs Service** (☎ 800/432–1216 near Miami; 305/536–5263 otherwise). Customs clears most boats of less than 5 tons by phone, but you may be directed to a marina for inspection.

The **Port of Miami** (⊠ 1015 North American Way, Miami, ☎ 305/347–4860 or 305/371–7678) bills itself as the "cruise capital of the world," appropriate since its 21 cruise ships (with several more due by 2001) and six cruise lines accommodate more than 3 million passengers a year—representing one out of every three North American cruise passengers. Containing car rental agencies and a limousine service, the port connects passengers to the Bahamas, Mexico, Jamaica, Europe, and around the world. Cruise lines operating out of the port are **Carnival Cruise Lines** (☎ 305/599–2600), **Cunard Line, Ltd.** (☎ 305/463–3000), **Discovery Cruise Lines** (☎ 800/937–4477), **Norwegian Cruise Lines** (☎ 305/436–4000 or 800/327–7030), **Premier Cruise Lines** (☎ 305/358–5122), and **Royal Caribbean Cruise Lines** (☎ 305/539–6000 or 800/255–4373).

By Bus

Greyhound (☎ 800/231–2222) buses stop at four terminals in Greater Miami (⊠ 700 Biscayne Blvd., Miami; ⊠ 4111 N.W. 27th St., Miami; ⊠ 16560 N.E. 6th Ave., North Miami; ⊠ 20505 S. Dixie Highway, South Miami) and at Miami International Airport.

By Car

The main highways into Greater Miami from the north are Florida's Turnpike (a toll road) and I–95. From the northwest take I–75 or U.S. 27 into town. From the Everglades, to the west, use the Tamiami Trail (U.S. 41), and from the south use U.S. 1 and the Homestead Extension of Florida's Turnpike.

By Plane

Miami International Airport (MIA, ☎ 305/876–7000), 6 mi west of downtown Miami, is the only airport in Greater Miami that provides scheduled service. With a daily average of 1,400 flights, it handled more than 35 million passengers in 1997, nearly half of them international travelers. MIA is also the nation's busiest airport for international freight. Altogether more than 120 airlines serve 200 cities and five continents with nonstop or one-stop service. MIA has 102 aircraft gates and eight concourses.

Anticipating continued growth, the airport has begun a more than $4 billion expansion program that is expected to be completed by 2005. Passengers will mainly notice rebuilt and expanded gate and public areas, which should reduce congestion.

A greatly underused convenience for passengers who have to get from one concourse to another in this long, horseshoe-shape terminal is the amazingly convenient moving walkway, on the skywalk level (third floor), with access points at every concourse. Also available on site is the 259-room **Miami International Airport Hotel** (✉ Concourse E, upper level, ☎ 305/871–4100), which has the Top of the Port restaurant on the seventh floor and the Port Lounge on the eighth. MIA, the first to offer duty-free shops, now boasts 18, carrying liquors, perfumes, electronics, and various designer goods.

Heightened security at MIA has meant that it's suggested you check in 90 minutes before departure for a domestic flight, two hours for an international flight. Services for international travelers include 24-hour multilingual information and paging phones and currency conversion booths throughout the terminal. There is an information booth with a multilingual staff across from the 24-hour currency exchange at the entrance of Concourse E on the upper level. Other tourist information centers are at the customs exit, Concourse E, lower level (daily 5 AM–11 PM); customs exit, Concourse B, second level (daily 11–11); Concourse G, lower level (daily 11–7); Concourse D, lower level (daily 11–11); and Satellite Terminal (daily 11–7).

Airlines that fly into MIA include **Aeroflot** (☎ 888/340–6400), **Aerolineas Argentinas** (☎ 800/333–0276), **AeroMexico** (☎ 800/237–6639), **AeroPeru** (☎ 800/777–7717), **Air Aruba** (☎ 800/882–7822), **Air Canada** (☎ 800/776–3000), **Air France** (☎ 800/237–2747), **Air Jamaica** (☎ 800/523–5585), **Alitalia** (☎ 800/223–5730), **American/American Eagle** (☎ 800/433–7300), **American TransAir** (☎ 800/225–2995), **Avensa** (☎ 800/428–3672), **Avianca** (☎ 800/284–2622), **Aviateca** (☎ 800/327–9832), **Bahamasair** (☎ 800/222–4262), **British Airways** (☎ 800/247–9297), **BWIA** (☎ 305/371–2942), **Cayman Airways** (☎ 800/422–9626), **Comair** (☎ 800/354–9822), **Continental** (☎ 800/525–0280), **Delta** (☎ 800/221–1212), **El Al** (☎ 800/223–6700), **Finnair** (☎ 800/950–5000), **Gulfstream International** (☎ 800/992–8532), **Guyana Airways** (☎ 800/242–4210), **Iberia** (☎ 800/772–4642), **LAB** (☎ 800/327–7407), **Lacsa** (☎ 800/225–2272), **Lan Chile** (☎ 800/735–5526), **Lauda Air** (☎ 800/588–8399), **LTU** (☎ 800/888–0200), **Lufthansa** (☎ 800/645–3880), **Martinair Holland** (☎ 800/366–4655), **Mexicana** (☎ 800/531–7921), **Northwest** (☎ 800/225–2525), **Paradise Island** (☎ 800/786–7202), **Saeta** (☎ 800/827–2382), **Servivensa** (☎ 800/428–3672), **South African Airways** (☎ 800/722–9675), **Taca** (☎ 800/535–8780), **Tower Air** (☎ 800/348–6937), **Transbrasil** (☎ 800/872–3153), **TWA** (☎ 800/221–2000), **United** (☎ 800/241–6522), **US Airways/US Airways Express** (☎ 800/428–4322), **Varig** (☎ 800/468–2744), and **Virgin Atlantic** (☎ 800/862–8621).

Pan Am Air Bridge (✉ 1000 MacArthur Causeway, Miami, ☎ 305/373–1120 or 800/424–2557) is starting over where the original Pan Am began—with seaplane flights. Departing from Watson Island, the 30- to 60-minute rides to Bimini, Paradise Island, and Walkers Cay in the Bahamas are exciting, anachronistic, and somewhat cramped. Still, if you've got an extra $200–$250, a round-trip could be quite fun.

BETWEEN THE AIRPORT AND CENTER CITY

By Bus: The county's **Metrobus** (☎ 305/770–3131) still costs $1.25, though equipment has improved. From Concourse E on the ground level, you can take Bus 7 to downtown (weekdays 5:30 AM–9 PM every 40 minutes; weekends 6:30 AM–7:30 PM every 40 minutes), Bus 37 south to Coral Gables and South Miami (6 AM–10 PM every 30 minutes) or north to Hialeah (5:30 AM–11:30 PM every 30 minutes), Bus J south to Coral Gables (6 AM–12:30 AM every 30 minutes) or east to Miami Beach (4:30 AM–11:30 PM every 30 minutes), and Bus 42 to Coconut Grove (5:30 AM–7:20 PM hourly). Some routes change to 60-minute schedules after 7 PM and on weekends, so be prepared to wait or call the information line for exact times.

By Limousine: Miami has more than 100 limousine services, though they're frequently in and out of business. If you rely on the Yellow Pages, look for a company with a street address, not just a phone. Offering 24-hour service, **Club Limousine Service** (⊠ 12050 N.E. 14th Ave., Miami 33161, ☎ 305/893–9850; 800/824–4820; 800/325–9834 in FL) has shuttle vans and minibuses as well as limos. One of the oldest companies in town is **Vintage Rolls Royce Limousines of Coral Gables** (⊠ 4501 Monserrate St., Coral Gables 33146, ☎ 305/444–7657 or 800/888–7657), which operates a 24-hour reservation service and provides chauffeurs for privately owned, collectible Rolls-Royces from the 1940s.

By Taxi: Except for the flat-fare trips described below, cabs cost $3.25 for the first mile, $2 a mile after that, plus a $1 toll for trips originating at MIA or the Port of Miami. Approximate fares from MIA include $17 to Coral Gables or downtown Miami, $31 to Key Biscayne. In addition, Miami's regulatory commission has established flat rates for five zones of the city, four of which are listed here: $24 to between 63rd Street and the foot of Miami Beach (including South Beach); $41 to Golden Beach and Sunny Isles, north of Haulover Beach Park; $34 to between Surfside and Haulover Beach Park; and $29 to between 63rd and 87th streets. These fares are per trip, not per passenger, and include tolls and $1 airport surcharge but not tip. The approximate fare between MIA and the Port of Miami is $18.

For taxi service to destinations in the immediate vicinity, ask a uniformed county taxi dispatcher to call an **ARTS** (Airport Region Taxi Service) cab for you. These special blue cabs offer a short-haul flat fare in two zones. An inner-zone ride is $7; the outer-zone fare is $10. The area of service is north to 36th Street, west to the Palmetto Expressway (77th Avenue), south to Northwest 7th Street, and east to Douglas Road (37th Avenue). Maps are posted in cab windows on both sides.

By Van: SuperShuttle (☎ 305/871–2000 from MIA; 954/764–1700 from Broward [Fort Lauderdale]; 800/874–8885 from elsewhere) vans transport passengers between MIA and local hotels, the Port of Miami, and even individual residences on a 24-hour basis. At MIA the vans pick up at the ground level of each concourse (look for clerks with yellow shirts, who will flag one down). The company's service area extends from Palm Beach to Monroe County (including the Lower Keys). Drivers provide narration en route. Service from MIA is available around the clock on demand; for the return it's best to make reservations 24 hours in advance, although the firm will try to arrange pickups within Miami-Dade County on as little as four hours' notice. The cost from MIA to downtown hotels runs $9–$10; to the beaches it can be $11–$16 per passenger, depending on how far north you go. Additional members of a party pay a lower rate for many destinations, and children under three ride free with their parents. There's a pet transport fee of $10 for animals in kennels.

By Train

Amtrak (☎ 800/872–7245) runs three trains daily between New York City and Miami (⊠ 8303 N.W. 37th Ave., ☎ 305/835–1223 for recorded arrival and departure information; 800/368–8725 for shipping); the trains make several stops along the way.

Tri-Rail (⊠ 1 River Plaza, 305 S. Andrews Ave., Suite 200, Fort Lauderdale, ☎ 800/874–7245) is Florida's only commuter train system. Daily runs connect Miami with Broward and Palm Beach, stopping at 18 stations along the 70-mi route. Fares are established by zones, with prices ranging from $2 to a high of $9.25 round-trip. Tri-Rail connects with Miami's Metrorail, so you may not have to drive at all.

Getting Around

Greater Miami resembles Los Angeles in its urban sprawl and traffic. You'll need a car to visit many attractions and points of interest. Some are accessible via the public transportation system, run by a department of the county government—the **Metro-Dade Transit Agency,** which consists of 650 Metrobuses on 70 routes, the 21-mi Metrorail elevated rapid-transit system, and the Metromover, an elevated light-rail system. Free maps and schedules are available. ⊠ *Government Center Station, 111 N.W. 1st St., Miami 33128,* ☎ *305/654–6586 for Maps by Mail; 305/770–3131 for route information weekdays 6 AM–10 PM and weekends 9–5.*

By Bus

Metrobus stops are marked by blue-and-green signs with a bus logo and route information. The frequency of service varies widely, so call in advance to obtain specific schedules. The fare is $1.25 (exact change), transfers 25¢; 60¢ with 10¢ transfers for people with disabilities, senior citizens (65 and older), and students. Some express routes carry surcharges of $1.50. Reduced-fare tokens, sold 10 for $10, are available from Metropass outlets. Lift-equipped buses for people with disabilities are available on 16 routes, including one from the airport that links up with many routes in Miami Beach as well as Coconut Grove, Coral Gables, Hialeah, and Kendall. All but four of these routes connect with Metrorail. Those unable to use regular transit service should call **Special Transportation Services** (☎ 305/263–5400) for information on such services as curb-to-curb van pickup.

By Car

In general, Miami traffic is the same as in any other big city, with the same rush hours and the same likelihood that parking garages will be full at peak times. Many drivers who aren't locals and don't know their way around might turn and stop suddenly, or drop off passengers where they shouldn't. Some drivers are short-tempered and will assault those who cut them off or honk their horn.

Motorists need to be careful, even when their driving behavior is beyond censure, however, especially in rental cars. Despite the removal of identifying marks, cars piled with luggage or otherwise showing signs that a tourist is at the wheel remain prime targets for thieves. Your best bet is to "follow the sun"; major (and safer) travel routes are marked by huge sunburst logos, which connect to tourist hot spots like the Deco District. Stick with these, and you should get where you need to go fairly easily and quickly. The city has also initiated a TOP (Tourist Oriented Police) Cops program to assist tourists with directions and safety. For more safety advice on driving in Miami, *see* Driving *in* Smart Travel Tips A to Z.

By Taxi

One cab "company" stands out immeasurably above the rest. It's actually a consortium of drivers who have banded together to provide good service, in marked contrast to some Miami cabbies, who are rude, unhelpful, unfamiliar with the city, or dishonest, taking advantage of visitors who don't know the area. To plug into this consortium—they don't have a name, simply a number—call the **dispatch service** (☎ 305/888–4444)—although they can be hard to understand over the phone. If you have to use another company, try to be familiar with your route and destination. For information call the **Metro-Dade Passenger Transportation Regulatory Service** (☎ 305/375–2460), also known as the Hack Bureau. It takes complaints and monitors all for-hire vehicles.

Starting in 1998, fares were set at $3.25 per first mile and $2 every mile after, with no additional charge for up to five passengers, luggage, and tolls. Taxis can be hailed on the street, although you may not always find one when you need one—it's better to call for a dispatch taxi or have a hotel doorman hail one for you. Some companies with dispatch service are **Central Taxicab Service** (☎ 305/532–5555), **Diamond Cab Company** (☎ 305/545–5555), **Metro Taxicab Company** (☎ 305/888–8888), **Miami-Dade Yellow Cab** (☎ 305/633–0503), **Society Cab Company** (☎ 305/757–5523), **Super Yellow Cab Company** (☎ 305/888–7777), **Tropical Taxicab Company** (☎ 305/945–1025), and **Yellow Cab Company** (☎ 305/444–4444). Many now accept credit cards; inquire when you call.

By Train

Elevated **Metrorail** (☎ 305/770–3131) trains run from downtown Miami north to Hialeah and south along U.S. 1 to Dadeland, daily 5:30 AM–midnight. Trains run every five minutes in peak hours, every 15 minutes at other times. The fare is $1.25. Transfers, which cost 25¢, must be bought at the first station entered. Parking at train stations costs $2.

Metromover (☎ 305/770–3131) has two loops that circle downtown Miami, linking major hotels, office buildings, and shopping areas. The system spans 4½ mi, including the 1½-mi Omni Extension, with six stations to the north, and the 1-mi Brickell Extension, with six stations to the south. Quite convenient and amazingly cheap, it beats walking all around downtown. Service runs daily every 90 seconds, 6 AM–midnight. The fare is 25¢. Transfers to Metrorail are $1.

By Trolley

The best thing to arrive in Miami Beach since sand, the **Electro-Wave** (☎ 305/843–9283) is a fleet of *free* electric trolleys running every few minutes up and down Washington Avenue between 5th and 17th streets. New service continues south of 5th Street, west to Alton Road, and over by the Miami Beach Marina. Considering the great lengths between SoBe attractions, it'll save a lot of shoe leather. Trolleys operate Monday–Wednesday 8 AM–2 AM, Thursday–Saturday 8 AM–4 AM, and Sunday and holidays 10 AM–2 AM.

By Water Taxi

A **water taxi service** (☎ 954/467–6677), inaugurated in 1988 in Fort Lauderdale, began Miami area operations in 1993. Canopied boats, 28 ft and longer, run between Miami Beach and the Bayside Marketplace. Routes cover downtown restaurants and the Watson Island airboat station. Taxi hours vary by season, with average fares from Bayside Marketplace of $3.50 one-way and $6 round-trip to waterfront stops in Miami and $7 one-way and $13 round-trip to Miami Beach. An all-day pass is $15.

Contacts and Resources

Emergencies

Dial **911** for police or ambulance. You can dial free from pay phones.

AMBULANCE

Randle Eastern Ambulance Service Inc. (⊠ 7255 N.W. 19th St., Suite C, Miami 33126, ☎ 305/718–6400) operates at all hours, although in an emergency they'll direct you to call 911.

DENTISTS

East Coast District Dental Society (✉ 420 S. Dixie Hwy., Suite 2E, Coral Gables, ☎ 305/667–3647) is open weekdays 9–4:30 for dental referral. After hours stay on the line and a recording will direct you to a dentist. Services include general dentistry, endodontics, periodontics, and oral surgery.

DOCTORS

Dade County Medical Association (✉ 1501 N.W. North River Dr., Miami, ☎ 305/324–8717) is open weekdays 9–5 for medical referral.

HOSPITALS

Miami has 32 hospitals and more than 34,000 health-care professionals. The following hospitals have 24-hour emergency rooms.

In Miami Beach: **Miami Heart Institute** (✉ 4701 N. Meridian Ave., Miami Beach, ☎ 305/672–1111; 888/432–7848 physician referral), **Mt. Sinai Medical Center** (✉ Off Julia Tuttle Causeway, I–195 at 4300 Alton Rd., Miami Beach, ☎ 305/674–2121; 305/674–2200 emergency; 305/674–2273 physician referral), and **South Shore Hospital & Medical Center** (✉ 630 Alton Rd., Miami Beach, ☎ 305/672–2100).

In the north: **Parkway Regional Hospital** (✉ 160 N.W. 170th St., North Miami Beach, ☎ 305/651–1100; 800/833–8005 physician referral).

In central Miami: **Coral Gables Hospital** (✉ 3100 Douglas Rd., Coral Gables, ☎ 305/445–8461; 305/444–2100 physician referral), **Jackson Memorial Hospital** (✉ 1611 N.W. 12th Ave., near Dolphin Expressway, Miami, ☎ 305/585–1111; 305/585–6901 emergency; 305/243–5757 physician referral), **Mercy Hospital** (✉ 3663 S. Miami Ave., Coconut Grove, ☎ 305/854–4400; 305/285–2171 emergency; 305/285–2929 physician referral), and **Pan American Hospital** (✉ 5959 N.W. 7th St., Miami, ☎ 305/264–1000, ext. 6125 emergency; 305/264–5118 physician referral).

In the south: **Baptist Hospital of Miami** (✉ 8900 N. Kendall Dr., Miami, ☎ 305/596–1960; 305/596–6556 emergency; 305/596–6557 physician referral) and **South Miami Hospital** (✉ 6200 S.W. 73rd St., South Miami, ☎ 305/661–4611; 305/662–8181 emergency; 305/596–6557 physician referral).

LATE-NIGHT PHARMACIES

Eckerd Drug (✉ 1825 Miami Gardens Dr. NE, at 185th St., North Miami Beach, ☎ 305/932–5740) is open until midnight. **Eckerd Drug** (✉ 200 Lincoln Rd., Miami Beach, ☎ 305/532–6978) has a pharmacy open until 8 PM weekdays, 6 PM Saturday. Also in South Beach, **Walgreen** (✉ 524 Jefferson Ave., Miami Beach, ☎ 305/531–7688) has a pharmacy open until 10 PM weekdays, 6 PM weekends. The following are open 24 hours: **Eckerd Drug** (✉ 9031 S.W. 107th Ave., Miami, ☎ 305/274–6776) and **Walgreens** (✉ 500-B W. 49th St., Palm Springs Mall, Hialeah, ☎ 305/557–5468; ✉ 2750 W. 68th St., Hialeah, ☎ 305/828–0268; ✉ 12295 Biscayne Blvd., North Miami, ☎ 305/893–6860; ✉ 5731 Bird Rd., Miami, ☎ 305/666–0757; ✉ 1845 Alton Rd., Miami Beach, ☎ 305/531–8868; ✉ 791 N.E. 167th St., North Miami Beach, ☎ 305/652–7332).

Car Rentals

The following agencies have booths near the baggage-claim area on MIA's lower level: **Alamo** (☎ 800/468–2583), **Avis** (☎ 800/331–1212), **Budget** (☎ 800/527–0700), **Dollar** (☎ 800/800–4000), **Hertz** (☎ 800/654–3131), and **National** (☎ 800/227–7368). Avis and Budget have offices at the Port of Miami.

If money is no object, check out **Excellence Luxury Car Rental** (☎ 305/ 526–0000). As the name implies, you can rent some wheels (a Ferrari, perhaps?) to cruise SoBe and pretend you're Don Johnson. If you can't find the excellent car you want, you can rent a Dodge Viper, BMW, Hummer, Jag, Porsche, or Rolls from **Exotic Cars** (☎ 888/541–1789). Airport pickup is provided.

Guided Tours

BOAT TOURS

Bay Ex.Cape (⊠ 401 Biscayne Blvd., ☎ 305/373–7001) cruises in air-conditioned comfort past Millionaires' Row and the Venetian Islands during bilingual excursions that depart from the Bayside Marketplace at 11, 1, 3, 5, and 7.

Heritage of Miami II (⊠ 401 Biscayne Blvd., ☎ 305/442–9697) offers sightseeing cruises on board a two-masted, 85-ft topsail schooner. Tours start and end at Bayside Marketplace. One-hour sails cost $10 per person, and two-hour sails are $15. Tours loop through lower Biscayne Bay, with views of the Vizcaya Museum and Gardens; the homes of Madonna, Sly, Luciano, and Whitney; the Port of Miami; and several residential islands. It's a little money for a lot of fun.

Island Queen, Island Lady, and **Pink Lady** (⊠ 401 Biscayne Blvd., ☎ 305/379–5119) are 150-passenger double-decker tour boats docked at Bayside Marketplace. They go on daily 90-minute narrated tours of the Port of Miami and Millionaires' Row, costing $12. Refreshments are available.

Casino gambling is illegal in Florida, which explains the popularity of **SeaKruz** (⊠ 300 Alton Rd., Miami Beach, ☎ 305/538–8300). For $15 you can travel into international waters and drop cash into craps, roulette, blackjack, and even pai gow—whatever floats your boat! If you're annoyed by mediocre food, cigarette smoke, and the hell's bells of slots, it'll be a loooong trip. Cruises depart from the Miami Beach Marina.

HISTORICAL TOURS

Art Deco District Tour (⊠ 1001 Ocean Dr., Bin L, Miami Beach 33139, ☎ 305/672–2014), operated by the Miami Design Preservation League, is a 90-minute guided walking tour ($6) departing from the league's welcome center at the Oceanfront Auditorium at 10:30 AM Saturday and 6:30 PM Thursday. Private group tours can be arranged with advance notice. You can go at your own pace with a self-guided $5 audio tour, which takes roughly an hour. The league also sells the *Art Deco District Guide,* a book of six detailed walking or driving tours of the Art Deco District. A two-hour bike tour leaves from the **Miami Beach Bicycle Center** (⊠ 601 5th St., Miami Beach, ☎ 305/ 674–0150) at 10:30 on the first and third Sundays of the month. Led by a guide from the Miami Design Preservation League, this tour costs $15 including a rental bike, $6 with your own bike.

Deco Tours Miami Beach (⊠ 420 Lincoln Rd., Suite 412, Miami Beach, ☎ 305/531–4465) offers walking tours of the Art Deco District, with 24-hour notice for reservations preferred. These 90-minute tours, which cost $15, depart from the National Hotel, on Collins Avenue. Tours of the city are conducted in vans and buses.

Professor Paul George (⊠ 1345 S.W. 14th St., Miami, ☎ 305/858–6021), a history professor at Miami-Dade Community College and past president of the Florida Historical Society, leads a variety of walking tours as well as boat tours and tours that make use of the Metrorail and Metromover. Pick from tours covering downtown, historic neighborhoods, cemeteries, Coconut Grove, and the Miami River. They start Saturday at 10 and Sunday at 11 at various locations, depending on the tour, and generally last about 2½ hours. Call for each weekend's schedule and for additional tours by appointment. The fee is $15.

Coconut Grove Rickshaw centers its operations at CocoWalk. Two-person rickshaws scurry along Main Highway in Coconut Grove's Village Center, nightly 7 PM–midnight. You can take a 10-minute ride through Coconut Grove or a 20-minute lovers' moonlight ride to Biscayne Bay; prices start at $5 per person.

Motorcycle Rentals

American Road Collection (⊠ 3970 N.W. 25th St., Miami, ☎ 305/871–1040 or 888/736–8433) rents new Harleys for half days, full days, or longer.

Services for People with Hearing Impairments

Fire, police, medical, rescue (☎ 305/595–4749 TDD; 305/595–6263 voice; 911 voice).

Operator and directory assistance (☎ 800/855–1155 TDD).

Deaf Services of Miami (⊠ 9100 S. Dadeland Blvd., Suite 104, Miami 33156; ☎ 305/668–3323 TDD; 305/668–4407 voice; 305/668–4693 24-hour hot line; 305/806–6090 24-hour emergency numerical pager for interpreters).

Florida Relay Service (☎ 800/955–8771 TDD; 800/955–8770 voice).

Visitor Information

Greater Miami Convention & Visitors Bureau (⊠ 701 Brickell Ave., Suite 2700, Miami 33131, ☎ 305/539–3063 or 800/283–2707). Satellite tourist information centers are at **Bayside Marketplace** (⊠ 401 Biscayne Blvd., Miami 33132, ☎ 305/539–2980) and **South Dade Visitor Information Center** (⊠ 160 U.S. 1, Florida City 33034, ☎ 305/245–9180 or 800/388–9669, FAX 305/247–4335).

Coconut Grove Chamber of Commerce (⊠ 2820 McFarlane Rd., Coconut Grove 33133, ☎ 305/444–7270, FAX 305/444–2498). **Coral Gables Chamber of Commerce** (⊠ 50 Aragon Ave., Coral Gables 33134, ☎ 305/446–1657, FAX 305/446–9900). **Florida Gold Coast Chamber of Commerce** (⊠ 1100 Kane Concourse, Suite 210, Bay Harbor Islands 33154, ☎ 305/866–6020) serves the beach communities of Bal Harbour, Bay Harbor Islands, Golden Beach, North Bay Village, Sunny Isles, and Surfside. **Greater Miami Chamber of Commerce** (⊠ 1601 Biscayne Blvd., Miami 33132, ☎ 305/350–7700, FAX 305/374–6902). **Greater North Miami Chamber of Commerce** (⊠ 13100 W. Dixie Hwy., North Miami 33181, ☎ 305/891–7811, FAX 305/893–8522). **Greater South Dade/South Miami Chamber of Commerce** (⊠ 6410 S.W. 80th St., South Miami 33143-4602, ☎ 305/661–1621, FAX 305/666–0508). **Key Biscayne Chamber of Commerce** (⊠ Key Biscayne Bank Bldg., 95 W. McIntyre St., Key Biscayne 33149, ☎ 305/361–5207). **Miami Beach Chamber of Commerce** (⊠ 1920 Meridian Ave., Miami Beach 33139, ☎ 305/672–1270, FAX 305/538–4336). **Surfside Tourist Board** (⊠ 9301 Collins Ave., Surfside 33154, ☎ 305/864–0722 or 800/327–4557, FAX 305/861–1302).

3 THE EVERGLADES

South Florida's wide, slow-moving "River of Grass"—the largest roadless expanse in the United States—is home to Everglades National Park and spectacular plant and animal life found no place else in the country. Nearby Biscayne National Park protects living coral reefs, mangroves, undeveloped islands, a shallow bay, and all the wild things that come with them. Both areas, within minutes of Miami's metropolis, maintain a fragile balance between humans and nature.

Updated by
Diane P.
Marshall

THE ONLY METROPOLITAN AREA in the United States with two national parks in its backyard is Miami. Everglades National Park, created in 1947, was meant to preserve the slow-moving "River of Grass"—a freshwater river 50 mi wide but only 6 inches deep, flowing from Lake Okeechobee through marshy grassland into Florida Bay. Along the Tamiami Trail (U.S. 41), marshes of cattails extend as far as the eye can see, interspersed only with hammocks or tree islands of bald cypress and mahogany, while overhead southern bald eagles make circles in the sky. A wide variety of trees and flowers, including ferns, orchids, and bromeliads, share the brackish waters with otters, turtles, marsh rabbits, and occasionally that gentle giant, the West Indian manatee. Not so gentle, though, is the saw grass. Deceptively graceful, these tall, willowy sedges have small sharp teeth on the edges of their leaves.

Biscayne National Park, established as a national monument in 1968 and 12 years later expanded and designated a national park, is the nation's largest marine park and the largest national park within the continental United States with living coral reefs. A small portion of the park's almost 274 square mi consists of mainland coast and outlying islands, but 96% is under water, much of it in Biscayne Bay. The islands contain lush, heavily wooded forests with an abundance of ferns and native palm trees. Of particular interest are the mangroves and their tangled masses of stiltlike roots and stems that thicken the shorelines. These "walking trees," as locals sometimes call them, have striking curved prop roots, which arch down from the trunk, while aerial roots drop from branches. These trees draw freshwater from saltwater and create a coastal nursery capable of sustaining all types of marine life.

Unfortunately, Miami's backyard is threatened by suburban sprawl and agriculture. What results is competition among environmental, agricultural, and developmental interests. The biggest issue is water. Originally, alternating floods and dry periods maintained wildlife habitat and regulated the water flowing into Florida Bay. The brackish seasonal flux sustained a remarkably vigorous bay, including the most productive shrimp beds in American waters, with thriving mangrove thickets and coral reefs at its Atlantic edge. The system nurtured sea life and attracted anglers and divers. Starting in the 1930s, however, a giant flood-control system began diverting water to canals running to the gulf and the ocean. As you travel Florida's north–south routes, you cross this network of canals symbolized by a smiling alligator representing the South Florida Water Management District, ironically known as "Protector of the Everglades."

The unfortunate side effect of flood control has been devastation of the wilderness. Park visitors decry diminished bird counts (a 90% reduction over 50 years); the black bear has been eliminated; and the Florida panther is nearing extinction. In 1997 the nonprofit group American Rivers again ranked the Everglades among the most threatened rivers of North America. Meanwhile, the loss of freshwater has made Florida Bay more salty, devastating breeding grounds and creating dead zones where pea green algae has replaced sea grasses and sponges.

Even as the ecosystem fades, new policies, still largely on paper, hold promise. Some 40% of what is commonly called Big Cypress Swamp was established as Big Cypress National Preserve in 1974 to protect the watershed of Everglades National Park. Some 22 government agencies and a host of conservation groups and industries are working on restoration plans. Some of the 40,000 acres of filtration marshes that will remove harmful agricultural nutrients before they enter the protected wetlands have been constructed as part of the Everglades Forever Act. Within the next decade farming must sharply reduce its phosphorus runoff, and the U.S. Army Corps of Engineers, which maintains Florida's flood-control system, proposes restoring a more natural flow of water into the Everglades and its related systems. Although the future of the natural system hangs uncertainly as engineers and ecologists battle over what to do and when to do it, there are promising signs.

New and Noteworthy

In Florida City, a new **aquarium** should be open by the year 2000.

Guests wanting to stay in the heart of the Everglades started checking into the **Miccosukee Resort & Convention Center** in June 1999.

Pleasures and Pastimes

Biking and Hiking

In the Everglades there are several nice places to ride and hike. The Shark Valley Loop Road (15 mi round-trip) makes a good bike trip. "Foot and Canoe Trails of the Flamingo Area," a leaflet, lists others. Inquire about insect conditions before you go and plan accordingly, stocking up on insect repellent, sunscreen, and water, as necessary.

Boating and Canoeing

One of the best ways to experience the Everglades is by boat, and almost all of Biscayne National Park is accessible only by water. Boat rentals are available in both parks. Rentals are generally for half day (four hours) and full day (eight hours).

In the Everglades the 99-mi inland Wilderness Trail between Flamingo and Everglades City is open to motorboats as well as canoes, although powerboats may have trouble navigating the route above Whitewater Bay. Flat-water canoeing is best in winter, when temperatures are moderate, rainfall is minimal, and mosquitoes are tolerable. You don't need a permit for day trips, but tell someone where you're going and when you expect to return. Getting lost is easy, and spending the night without proper gear can be unpleasant, if not dangerous.

On the Gulf Coast you can explore the nooks, crannies, and mangrove islands of Chokoloskee Bay, as well as many rivers near Everglades City. The Turner River Trail, a good day trip, passes through mangrove, dwarf cypress, coastal prairie, and freshwater slough ecosystems of Everglades National Park and Big Cypress National Preserve.

Dining

With a few exceptions, dining centers on low-key mom-and-pop places that serve hearty home-style food and small eateries specializing in local fare: seafood, conch, alligator, turtle, and frogs' legs. Native American restaurants add another dimension, serving local favorites as well as catfish, Indian fry bread (a flour-and-water dough), pumpkin bread, Indian burgers (ground beef browned, rolled in fry-bread dough, and deep-fried), and tacos (fry bread with chili, lettuce, tomato, and shredded cheddar cheese on top). Restaurants in Everglades City appear to operate with a "captive audience" philosophy: Prices run high, service is mediocre, and food preparation is uninspired. The closest good restaurants are in Naples, 35 mi northwest.

Although both Everglades and Biscayne national parks are wilderness areas, there are restaurants within a short drive. Most are between Miami and Shark Valley along the Tamiami Trail (U.S. 41), in the Homestead–

Florida City area, in Everglades City, and in the Florida Keys along the Overseas Highway (U.S. 1). The only food service in either park is at Flamingo, in the Everglades, but many independent restaurants will pack picnics. (You can also find fast-food establishments on the Tamiami Trail east of Krome Avenue and along U.S. 1 in Homestead–Florida City.)

Fishing

Largemouth bass are plentiful in freshwater ponds, while snapper, redfish, and sea trout are caught in Florida Bay. The mangrove shallows of the Ten Thousand Islands, along the gulf, yield tarpon and snook. Whitewater Bay is also a favorite spot. Note: The state has issued health advisories for sea bass, largemouth bass, and other freshwater fish, especially those caught in the canals along the Tamiami Trail, due to their high mercury content. Signs are posted throughout the park, and consumption should be limited.

Exploring the Everglades

The southern tip of the Florida peninsula is largely taken up by Everglades National Park, but land access to it is primarily by two roads: The main park road traverses the southern Everglades from the gateway towns of Homestead and Florida City to the outpost of Flamingo, on Florida Bay. In the northern Everglades you can take the Tamiami Trail (U.S. 41) from the Greater Miami area in the east to the western park entrance in Everglades City. In far southeastern Florida, Biscayne National Park lies almost completely offshore. As a result, most sports and recreational opportunities in both national parks are based on water, the study of nature, or both, so even on land, be prepared to get a bit damp on the region's marshy trails.

Though relatively compact, as compared with the national parks of the West, these parks still require a bit of time to see. The narrow, two-lane roads through the Everglades make for long travel, whereas it's the necessity of sightseeing by boat that takes time at Biscayne.

Numbers in the text correspond to numbers in the margin and on the Everglades and Biscayne National Parks map.

Great Itineraries

IF YOU HAVE 1 DAY

You'll have to make a choice—the Everglades or Biscayne. If you want quiet and nature, go with the Everglades. If you're interested in boating or underwater flora and fauna, Biscayne is your best bet. Either way, you'll experience a little of what's left of the "real" Florida.

For a day in Everglades National Park, begin in **Florida City** ⑭, gateway to the park and site of a museum on Florida pioneer life. Head to the **Ernest F. Coe Visitor Center** ① for an overview of the park and its ecosystems and continue to the **Royal Palm Visitor Center** ② for a look at several unique plant systems. Then go to **Flamingo** ③, where you can rent a boat or take a tour of Florida Bay.

If Biscayne is your preference, begin at **Convoy Point** ⑮ for an orientation before forsaking dry land. Sign up for a snorkel or dive trip or an outing on a glass-bottom boat, or explore an island.

IF YOU HAVE 3 DAYS

With three days you can explore both the northern and southern Everglades as well as Biscayne National Park. Start in the north by driving west along the Tamiami Trail, stopping at **Everglades Safari Park** ④ for an airboat ride; at **Shark Valley** ⑥ for a tram tour, walk, or bicycle trip; at the **Miccosukee Indian Village** ⑦ for lunch; at the **Big Cy-**

press Gallery ⑧ to see Clyde Butcher's photographs; and then at the **Ochopee post office** ⑩, before ending in ⚅ **Everglades City** ⑫, home of the Gulf Coast Visitor Center. From here you can visit historic Smallwood's Store on Chokoloskee Island and watch the sunset. Day two is for exploring the south. Return east on the Tamiami Trail to **Homestead** ⑬, pausing at Everglades Air Tours to take a sightseeing trip before following the one-day Everglades itinerary above and overnighting in ⚅ **Florida City** ⑭. Biscayne National Park is the subject of day three. If you plan to scuba or take the glass-bottom boat, get an early start. You can explore the visitor center at **Convoy Point** ⑮ when you return and finish your day checking out sights in Florida City and Homestead. Snorkel trips leave later, giving you time to see Florida City and Homestead, have lunch, and learn about the park's ecosystem at the visitor center first. Be warned that though you can fly and then scuba dive, you can't dive and then fly within 24 hours. So if you're flying out, reverse the days' sequence accordingly.

IF YOU HAVE 5 DAYS

Follow day one above, spending the night in ⚅ **Everglades City** ⑫. Begin the second day with a canoe, kayak, or boat tour of the Ten Thousand Islands. In the late afternoon take a walk on the boardwalk at **Fakahatchee Strand State Preserve** ⑪ to see rare epiphytic orchids or on a 2½-mi trail at the Big Cypress National Preserve. Drive east to Coopertown and take a nighttime ride with Ray Cramer's Everglades Airboat Tours. Spend the night in ⚅ **Florida City** ⑭. Day three is spent at Biscayne National Park, then sightseeing in **Homestead** ⑬ and **Florida City** ⑭ as suggested above. Begin day four at Everglades Air Tours in Homestead; then browse the antiques shops along Krome Avenue before picking up a picnic lunch and seeing some of South Dade's other nearby attractions. On day five, augment your picnic lunch with goodies from the remarkable fruit stand Robert Is Here, before heading to the southern portion of Everglades National Park, as described above.

When to Tour the Everglades

Winter is the best time to visit Everglades National Park. Temperatures and mosquito activity are low to moderate, low water levels concentrate the resident wildlife around sloughs that retain water all year, and migratory birds swell the avian population. Winter is also the busiest time in the park. Make reservations and expect crowds at Flamingo, the main visitor center (known officially as the Ernest F. Coe Visitor Center), and Royal Palm.

In spring the weather turns hot and rainy, and tours and facilities are less crowded. Migratory birds depart, and you must look harder to see wildlife. Be careful with campfires and matches; this is when the wildfire-prone saw grass prairies and pinelands are most vulnerable.

Summer brings intense sun and billowing clouds unleashing torrents of rain almost every afternoon. Start your outdoor activities early to avoid the rain and the sun's strongest rays, and use sunscreen. Water levels rise and wildlife disperses. Mosquitoes hatch, swarm, and descend on you in voracious clouds. (Carrying mosquito repellent is a good idea at any time of year, but it's a necessity in summer.) Europeans constitute 80% of the summer visitors.

Even if you're not lodging in Everglades National Park, try to stay until dusk, when dozens of bird species feed around the ponds and trails. While shining a flashlight over the water in marshy areas, look for two yellowish-red reflections above the surface—telltale alligator signs.

EVERGLADES NATIONAL PARK

11 mi southwest of Homestead, 45 mi southwest of Miami International Airport.

The best way to experience the real Everglades is to get your feet wet, like paddling a canoe into the River of Grass to stay in a backcountry campsite. Most visitors won't do that, however. Luckily, there are several ways to see the wonders of the park with dry feet. Take a boat tour in Everglades City or Flamingo, ride the tram at Shark Valley, or walk the boardwalks along the main park road. And there's more to see than natural beauty. Miccosukee Indians operate a range of attractions and restaurants worthy of a stop.

Admission to Everglades National Park is valid at all entrances for seven days. Coverage below begins in the southern Everglades, followed by the northern Everglades, starting in the east and ending in Everglades City.

The Main Park Road

The main park road (Route 9336) travels from the main visitor center to Flamingo, across a section of the park's eight distinct ecosystems: hardwood hammock, freshwater prairie, pineland, freshwater slough, cypress, coastal prairie, mangrove, and marine-estuarine. Highlights of the trip include a dwarf cypress forest, the ecotone (transition zone) between saw grass and mangrove forest, and a wealth of wading birds at Mrazek and Coot Bay ponds. Boardwalks, looped trails, several short spurs, and observation platforms allow you to stay dry.

❶ The **Ernest F. Coe Visitor Center,** at park headquarters, houses numerous interactive exhibits and films. Stand in a simulated blind and peer through a spyglass to watch birds in the wild; though it's actually a film, the quality is so good you'll think you're outside. Move on to a bank of telephones to hear differing viewpoints on the Great Water Debate. There's a 15-minute film on the park, two movies on hurricanes, and a 45-minute wildlife film for children. Computer monitors present a schedule of daily ranger-led activities park-wide as well as information on canoe rentals and boat tours. In the Everglades Discovery Shop you can browse through lots of neat nature, science, and kids' stuff and pick up the insect repellent you forgot. The center provides information on the entire park. ✉ *11 mi southwest of Homestead on Rte. 9336,* ☎ *305/242–7700.* 🎟 *Park $10 per car, $5 per pedestrian or bicyclist, $5 per motorcycle.* ☉ *Daily 8–5.*

❷ The **Royal Palm Visitor Center** is a must for anyone who wants to experience the real Everglades. You can stroll along the Anhinga Trail boardwalk or follow the Gumbo Limbo Trail through a hardwood hammock. The visitor center has an interpretive display, a bookstore, and vending machines. ✉ *4 mi west of Ernest F. Coe Visitor Center on Rte. 9336,* ☎ *305/242–7700.* ☉ *Daily 8–5.*

Flamingo

❸ *38 mi southwest of Ernest F. Coe Visitor Center.*

Here at the far end of the main road you'll find a cluster of buildings containing a visitor center, lodge, restaurant and lounge, gift shop, marina, and bicycle rentals, plus an adjacent campground. Tour boats narrated by interpretive guides, fishing expeditions of Florida Bay, and canoe and kayak trips all leave from here. Nearby is Eco Pond, one of the most popular wildlife observation areas.

The Everglades and Biscayne National Parks

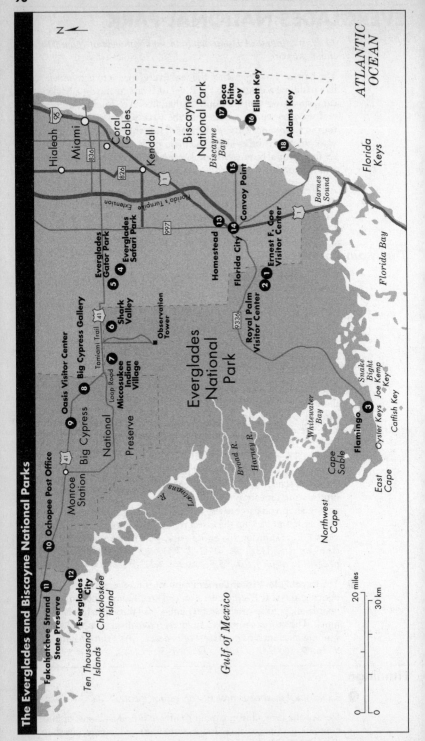

The **Flamingo Visitor Center** provides an interactive display and has natural history exhibits in the Florida Bay Museum. Check the schedule for ranger-led activities, such as naturalist discussions, evening programs in the campground amphitheater, and hikes along area trails. ☎ *305/ 242–7700.* ◯ *Daily 8–5.*

Dining and Lodging

$–$$ ✕ **Flamingo Restaurant.** The grand view, convivial lounge, and casual style are great. Big picture windows on the visitor center's second floor overlook Florida Bay, revealing soaring eagles, gulls, pelicans, terns, and vultures. Dine at low tide to see birds flock to the sandbar just offshore. Though the restaurant, which serves palatable seafood, pasta, and grills, is only open in high season, the marina store is open all year for pizza, sandwiches, and salads. ✉ *Flamingo Lodge, 1 Flamingo Lodge Hwy.,* ☎ *941/695–3101. AE, D, DC, MC, V. Closed May–Oct.*

$$ ▦ **Flamingo Lodge, Marina & Outpost Resort.** This simple low-rise motel is the only lodging inside the park. Accommodations are basic but well kept, and an amiable staff helps you adjust to bellowing alligators, roaming raccoons, and ibis grazing on the lawn. Rooms have contemporary furniture, floral bedspreads, and art prints of bird life. Though they face Florida Bay, they don't necessarily look out over it. Bathrooms are small. Cottages, in a wooded area on the margin of a coastal prairie, have kitchenettes and accommodate up to six people. Reservations are essential in winter; Continental breakfast is included from May to October. Some facilities, like the restaurant, are seasonal. ✉ *1 Flamingo Lodge Hwy., 33034,* ☎ *941/695–3101 or 800/600–3813,* ℻ *941/695–3921. 103 rooms, 24 cottages, 1 suite. Restaurant, bar, snack bar, pool, coin laundry. AE, D, DC, MC, V.*

$ ⚠ **Everglades National Park.** Three developed campgrounds and group campsites have drinking water, sewage dump station, and rest rooms. Some also have picnic tables, grills, cold-water showers, and tent and trailer pads. Long Pine Key has 108 drive-up sites; Flamingo has 234 drive-up sites, 64 walk-in sites, and cold showers; and Chekika has 20 sites, warm showers, and a sulfur spring where you can swim. Pets are allowed. From late November through April sites at Long Pine Key and Flamingo are available through a reservation system, but the rest of the year all sites are first-come, first served. In addition, deep in the park are 48 backcountry sites, many inland with some on the beach. Three are accessible by land, the others by canoe; 16 have *chickees* (raised wooden platforms with thatched roofs). Most have chemical toilets. Several are within an easy day's canoeing of Flamingo; five are near Everglades City. You'll need to carry your food, water, and supplies in; carry out all trash. You'll also need a site-specific permit, available on a first-come, first-served basis from the Flamingo or Gulf Coast Visitor Center (☞ Contacts and Resources *in* Everglades A to Z, *below,* for both). Developed sites are free June–August and $14 the rest of the year, groups pay $28, and backcountry sites cost $10 or more depending on group size. ☎ *305/242–7700 or 305/251–0371; 800/365–2267 for campsite reservations. 471 sites. Picnic areas. No credit cards.*

Outdoor Activities and Sports

BIKING

Flamingo Lodge, Marina & Outpost Resort (☎ 941/695–3101) rents bikes for $14 a day and $8 per half day.

BOATING

The marina at **Flamingo Lodge, Marina & Outpost Resort** (☎ 941/695–3101) rents power skiffs for $90 per day and $65 per half day, four Carolina skiffs for $155 per day, as well as fully furnished and outfitted houseboats that sleep up to six. Rates (two-day minimum) run $475 without air-conditioning for two days, $575 with air-conditioning for two days. Several private boats are also available for charter. There are two ramps, one for Florida Bay, the other for Whitewater Bay and the backcountry. The hoist across the plug dam separating Florida Bay from the Buttonwood Canal can take boats from 16 ft to 26 ft long. A small store sells food, camping supplies, bait and tackle, propane, and fuel.

CANOEING AND KAYAKING

The Everglades has six well-marked canoe trails in the Flamingo area, including the south end of the 99-mi Wilderness Trail from Everglades City to Flamingo. **Flamingo Lodge, Marina & Outpost Resort** (☎ 941/695–3101) rents canoes in two sizes: small (up to two paddlers) and family size (up to four). Small canoes rent for $32 per day and $22 per half day; family-size run $40 and $30, respectively. Single-person kayaks cost $43 per day and $27 per half day; doubles rent for $54 and $38, respectively.

FISHING

Flamingo Lodge, Marina & Outpost Resort (☎ 941/695–3101) helps arrange charter fishing trips for two to six persons. The cost is $300 a day for up to two people, $25 each additional person.

Tamiami Trail

141 mi from Miami to Fort Myers.

In 1915, when officials decided to build an east–west highway linking Miami to Fort Myers and continuing north to Tampa, someone suggested calling it the Tamiami Trail. In 1928 the road became a reality, cutting through the Everglades and altering the natural flow of water and the lives of the Miccosukee Indians who eked out a living fishing, hunting, and frogging here.

Today the traffic screams through Everglades National Park, Big Cypress National Preserve, and Fakahatchee Strand State Preserve. The landscape is surprisingly varied, changing from hardwood hammocks to pinelands, then abruptly to tall cypress trees dripping with Spanish moss and back to coastal prairie. Those who slow to take in the scenery can see alligators sunning themselves along the banks of roadside canals and in the shallow waters, hundreds of waterbirds, chickee huts, people fishing, Native American villages, and airboats parked at roadside enterprises.

Businesses along the trail give their addresses either based on their distance from Krome Avenue, Florida's Turnpike, and Miami on the east coast or Fort Myers and Naples on the west coast or by mile marker. Between Miami and Fort Myers the road goes by several names, including Tamiami Trail, U.S. 41, and, at the Miami end, Southwest 8th Street.

❹ Attractions at **Everglades Safari Park** include a jungle trail, an educational alligator show and wrestling demonstration, a wildlife museum, airboat rides (included in admission), and a restaurant and gift shop. Climb the observation platform and take in the beauty of the Glades. ⊠ *26700 Tamiami Trail, 9 mi west of Krome Ave.,* ☎ *305/226–6923 or 305/223–3804.* ☞ *$15.* ⊙ *Daily 8:30–5.*

❺ At **Everglades Gator Park,** you can hold a baby alligator while friends snap a photo, squirm in a "reptilium" of venomous and nonpoisonous native snakes, or learn about Native Americans of the Everglades through a reproduction of a Miccosukee village. The park also features airboat tours, fishing charters, and RV campsites as well as a gift shop and restaurant. ⊠ *24050 Tamiami Trail, 12 mi west of Florida's Turn-*

*pike, ☎ 305/559–2255 or 800/559–2205. ⊠ Free, tours $12. ☉ Daily
9–sunset.*

⑥ Though **Shark Valley** is the national park's north entrance, no roads
here lead to other parts of the park. The only route is a paved 15-mi
loop (you can walk, bicycle, or take a tram tour); at the half-way point
there's a concrete observation tower built by an oil company in the
early 1940s. Climb the ramp that spirals skyward 50 ft. From there
everything as far as the eye can see is the vast River of Grass. Expect
to see all kinds of waterbirds as well as alligators warming themselves
along the banks and on the road (most quickly move out of the way).
Just behind the bike rental area, a short boardwalk trail meanders
through the saw grass. A small visitor center features rotating exhibits, a bookstore, and park rangers ready to answer questions. ⊠
*23.5 mi west of Florida's Turnpike, ☎ 305/221–8776. ⊠ Park $8 per
car, $4 per pedestrian, bicyclist, or motorcyclist. ☉ Visitor center daily
8:30–5:30.*

⑦ At the **Miccosukee Indian Village,** Miccosukee families prepare food
and make crafts, on sale at the cultural center. Informative alligator-
wrestling shows as well as airboat rides and a restaurant are other attractions. The Everglades Music & Craft Festival falls on a July
weekend, and the weeklong Indian Arts Festival is in late December.
⊠ *Just west of Shark Valley entrance, 25 mi west of Florida's Turnpike, ☎ 305/223–8380. ⊠ $5, rides $7. ☉ Daily 9–5.*

⑧ Clyde Butcher does for the River of Grass what Ansel Adams did for
the West, and you can check out his stunning photographs at his **Big
Cypress Gallery,** in the Big Cypress National Preserve. Working with
large-format black-and-white film, Butcher captures every blade of grass,
barb of feather, and flicker of light. Volunteers lead "Muck-About"
swamp tours at the gallery's annual Labor Day weekend open house,
during which there are also tours of the dark room and slide shows by
naturalists and historians. Other events, special exhibits, lectures,
tours, photo expeditions, and slide presentations are given throughout the year. ⊠ *52388 Tamiami Trail, 37 mi west of Miami, 45 mi east
of Naples, ☎ 941/695–2428. ⊠ Free, $20 suggested donation for Big
Cypress Preserve Boardwalk Fund on Labor Day weekend. ☉ Fri.–
Mon. 9:30–5.*

⑨ Pause at the **Oasis Visitor Center** to learn about the national park's northern neighbor, the Big Cypress National Preserve. Through the 1950s
and early 1960s, the world's largest cypress-logging industry prospered
in the Big Cypress Swamp. The industry died out in the 1960s, and
the government began buying parcels. Today part of the swamp, which
encompasses more than 729,000 acres, has become this national preserve. Its variegated pattern of wet prairies, ponds, marshes, sloughs,
and strands provides a sanctuary for a variety of wildlife, but because
of a politically dictated policy of balanced land use—"use without
abuse"—the watery wilderness is devoted to research and recreation
as well as preservation. The preserve allows—in limited areas—hunt-
ing, off-road vehicle (airboat, swamp buggy) use by permit, and cattle grazing. The 8-mi Turner River Canoe Trail begins here and crosses
through Everglades National Park before ending in Chokoloskee Bay,
near Everglades City. Hikers can join the Florida National Scenic Trail,
which runs north–south through the preserve for 31 mi. The visitor
center provides a schedule of myriad seasonal ranger-led and self-
guided activities, such as campfire talks, bike hikes, slough slogs, and
canoe excursions. Seven primitive campsites are available on a first-
come, first-served basis. ⊠ *50 mi west of Miami, 20 mi west of Shark
Valley, ☎ 941/695–4111. ⊠ Free. ☉ Daily 8:30–4:30.*

⑩ The tiny **Ochopee post office** is the smallest post office in North America. Buy a picture postcard of the little one-room shack and mail it to a friend, thereby helping to keep this picturesque spot in business. ⊠ *75 mi west of Miami, Ochopee,* ☎ *941/695–4131.* ⊙ *Weekdays 9:30–noon and 12:30–4, Sat. 9:30–11:30.*

⑪ The ½-mi boardwalk at the **Fakahatchee Strand State Preserve** affords an opportunity to see rare plants, bald cypress, and North America's largest stand of native royal palms and largest concentration and variety of epiphytic orchids. ⊠ *Rte. 29 and Tamiami Trail; ranger station 3 mi north of Tamiami Trail on Rte. 29, Box 548, Copeland 34137,* ☎ *941/695–4593.* ▣ *Free.* ⊙ *Daily 8–sunset.*

Dining and Lodging

$ ✕ **Coopertown Restaurant.** For more than a half century this rustic eatery just into the Everglades west of Miami has been full of Old Florida style—not to mention alligator skulls, stuffed alligator heads, and gator accessories. House specialties are frogs' legs and alligator tail prepared breaded or deep-fried, and they're available for breakfast, lunch, or dinner. You can also order more conventional selections, such as catfish, shrimp, or sandwiches. ⊠ *22700 S.W. 8th St., Miami,* ☎ *305/226–6048. MC, V. Beer only.*

$ ✕ **Joanie's Blue Crab Cafe.** Movie set designers could not have designed
★ a more quintessential 1950s-style swamp café and country store than this landmark restaurant diagonally across from the Ochopee post office. The decor consists of wood-plank floors, open rafters hung with cobwebs, stuffed owls, postcards from around the globe, and kitschy gator art. Joanie, the chief cook and bottle washer, came here in 1987. Tony, her partner and "crab-ologist," picks the fresh blue crabs—up to 372 pounds in a weekend—that they catch each day to go into sandwiches, soups, and stuffed shrimp. Although the steamed crabs and crab sandwich served on a kaiser roll are the stars, the fresh sautéed vegetables—not always on the menu, but ask anyway—are delicious, too. A new screened deck will house a draft beer and wine bar. ⊠ *50 mi west of Florida's Turnpike, Ochopee,* ☎ *941/695–2682. No credit cards.*

$ ✕ **Miccosukee Restaurant.** Murals depict Native American women cooking and men engaged in a powwow in this Native American restaurant at the Miccosukee Indian Village. Favorites are catfish and frogs' legs breaded and deep-fried, Indian fry bread, pumpkin bread, and Indian burgers and tacos. Breakfast is served daily, but weekends bring a breakfast buffet (8–noon) featuring meats, eggs, breads, and lots more. ⊠ *25 mi west of Florida's Turnpike,* ☎ *305/223–8380 ext. 332. MC, V.*

$ ✕ **Pit Bar-B-Q.** The intense aroma of barbecue and blackjack-oak smoke will overwork your salivary glands. Order at the counter, pick up your food when called, and eat at one of the indoor or outdoor picnic tables. Specialties include barbecued chicken and ribs with a tangy sauce, french fries, coleslaw, and a fried biscuit as well as catfish and frogs' legs deep-fried in vegetable oil. Heed the scribbled message on the blackboard menu not to cross the grass median out front. It's an $85 fine if you're caught. ⊠ *16400 Tamiami Trail, Miami,* ☎ *305/226–2272. AE, MC, V.*

$$–$$$ ▦ **Miccosukee Resort & Convention Center.** If location is everything, then this new resort at the crossroads of Tamiami Trail and Krome Avenue is a gold mine. Like an oasis, it's the only facility for miles, situated to attract visitors going to the Everglades, driving across the state, or looking for casino action. Most units have a view of Everglades sawgrass and wildlife. However, a pool, 8,500-sq-ft kids' play area, teen video center, gaming complex, tours to Everglades National Park and the Miccosukee Indian Village, shops, live entertainment, places to eat,

and shuttles to area malls are enough to distract guests from staring out the window. ⌧ *500 S.W. 177th Ave., Miami 33194,* ☏ *305/221–8623 or 877/242–6464. 256 rooms, 46 suites. 2 restaurants, deli, indoor pool, beauty salon, sauna, spa, exercise room, casino, nightclub, video games, children's programs, convention center, meeting rooms, travel services, airport shuttle. AE, D, DC, MC, V.*

$ ⚠ **Everglades Gator Park.** Popular with the RV set, the park has full hookups for as many as 80 vehicles in addition to airboats, Everglades attractions, and a small store. You can rent a campsite by the night ($25), week ($100), or month ($350) or store your RV in the short-term area. ⌧ *24050 S.W. 8th St., Miami,* ☏ *305/559–2255 or 800/559–2205;* ⌧ *mailing address: 13800 S.W. 8th St., Box 107, Miami 33184. 80 sites. Restaurant, lake, fishing. D, MC, V.*

Outdoor Activities and Sports

Shark Valley Tram Tours (⌧ Shark Valley, ☏ 305/221–8455) rents bikes daily 8:30–4 (last rental at 3) for $3.85 per hour.

Shopping

At the **Miccosukee Indian Village** (⌧ Just west of Shark Valley entrance, 25 mi west of Florida's Turnpike, ☏ 305/223–8380), you can buy Native American crafts, including beadwork, moccasins, dolls, pottery, baskets, and patchwork fabric and clothes, as well as kitschy Florida souvenirs.

Everglades City

⑫ *35 mi southeast of Naples, 83 mi west of Miami.*

The western gateway to Everglades National Park, this community, just off the Tamiami Trail, has been around since the late 19th century, when Barron Collier, a wealthy advertising man, bought a lot of land and formed Collier County with the town of Everglades as county seat. Collier built a company town to house workers for his numerous projects, including construction of the Tamiami Trail. The town grew rapidly and prospered until the Depression and World War II, and in 1953 it changed its name to Everglades City. Today the biggest draw is the park, especially the canoeing, fishing, and bird-watching excursions you can take within it. (Airboat tours, though also popular, do not operate within the park.) The annual Seafood Festival, held the first weekend of February, attracts 60,000–75,000 visitors to eat seafood, hear nonstop music, and buy crafts.

The **Gulf Coast Visitor Center,** at the Everglades' western entrance, offers interpretive exhibits about local flora and fauna. Backcountry campers can purchase the required permits, and for those in need of a little more guidance, there are naturalist-led boat trips. The center offers access to the Ten Thousand Islands region along the Gulf of Mexico, but there are no roads from here to other sections of the park. ⌧ *Rte. 29,* ☏ *941/695–3311.* 🎫 *Park free.* ☉ *Mid-Nov.–mid-Apr., daily 7:30–5; reduced hrs mid-Apr.–mid-Nov.*

The new **Museum of the Everglades** chronicles the 2,000-year history of human habitation in the southwestern Everglades. It's housed in the only remaining unaltered structure original to the town of Everglades, where it opened in 1927 as the town's laundry. In addition to artifacts, photographs, and a 1923 model of the town, there are traveling exhibits, lectures, and works by local artists. ⌧ *105 W. Broadway,* ☏ *941/695–0008.* 🎫 *$2.* ☉ *Tues.–Sat. 11–4.*

SMALLWOOD'S STORE – Ted Smallwood pioneered this last American frontier in 1906 and built a 3,000-square-ft pine trading post raised on pilings in Chokoloskee Bay. Smallwood's granddaughter Lynn McMillin reopened it in 1989, after it had been closed several years, and installed a small gift shop and museum chock-full of original goods from the store; historic photographs; Indian clothing, furs, and hides; and area memorabilia. In March a festival celebrates the nearly 100-year relationship the store has had with local Native Americans. ⊠ *360 Mamie St., Chokoloskee Island,* ☎ *941/695-2989.* ⊠ *$2.50.* ☉ *Dec.–May, daily 10–5; May–Nov., daily 10–4.*

Dining and Lodging

$–$$ ✕ **Everglades Seafood Depot.** This 1928 Spanish-style stucco structure on Lake Placid has had many lives. It began as the old Everglades depot, was part of the University of Miami, appeared in the film *Winds Across the Everglades,* and has housed several restaurants. Today veteran restaurateur Billy Potter serves up well-prepared seafood—from shrimp and grouper to frogs' legs and alligator—any way you like it, and the staff is eager to please. For big appetites there are generously portioned entrées that include soup or salad, potato or rice, and warm, fresh-baked biscuits. If you aren't very hungry, choose the smaller "lunch-able appetites" portion, which includes potato, slaw, and a biscuit. ⊠ *102 Collier Ave.,* ☎ *941/695–0075, MC, V.*

$–$$ ✕ **Oar House Restaurant.** With wood paneling, picnic table–style booths, and a mishmash of fishing and Glades decor, the first full-service eatery in town has the ambience of a diner. The menu features a blend of seafood and such local specialties as frogs' legs, turtle, conch, and gator. To its credit, the service is friendly, prices are very reasonable, the food is fried in canola and corn oils, and most dishes can be grilled or broiled, if you prefer. It's open for breakfast, and there is a lounge. ⊠ *305 Collier Ave.,* ☎ *941/695–3535. AE, D, MC, V.*

$ ✕ **Ivey House Restaurant.** Home-style meals are served every night at 6 (call for a reservation by 4 if you're not a guest of the hotel). The nightly changing menu features a mix of meat and vegetarian selections. For $10–$15 you can dine on barbecued chicken with potatoes, vegetable, salad, pineapple upside-down cake, and coffee or tea, and on Mexican night the fare is chicken fajitas, tortillas, beans, rice, flan, and coffee or tea. ⊠ *107 Camellia St.,* ☎ *941/695–3299. MC, V. Closed May–Oct.*

$$ 🏨 **Rod and Gun Club.** With a veranda, dark cypress fixtures, and a nautical theme, this landmark inn is like a time-warp trip back to the '20s, when wealthy hunters, anglers, and yachting parties from all over the world came to Florida for the winter season. The old guest rooms above the restaurant and bar aren't open anymore, but you can stay in comfortable cottages (no phone, however). The food is more than passable. Breakfast, lunch, and dinner are still served in the original dining room or on the wide veranda, and as in olden days, if you catch a "keeper," the chef will prepare it for your dinner. ⊠ *200 Riverside Dr., Box 190, 34139,* ☎ *941/695–2101. 17 rooms. Restaurant, bar, pool, 2 tennis courts, fishing. No credit cards.*

$–$$ 🏨 **On the Banks of the Everglades.** Built in 1923, this lodging takes its name from the building it occupies, the former Bank of Everglades. Patty Flick Richards and her father, Bob Flick, created minirooms for single travelers ($35–$40), spacious rooms, suites, and efficiencies with queen- or king-size beds and stylish coordinating linens, wall coverings, and draperies. Suites and efficiencies have private baths and kitchens (the staff does the dishes); a few single rooms share a women's or men's bath. Amenities include hair dryers and in-room ironing boards. At night you can snack on popcorn and watch movies in the parlor. A breakfast of baked goods, cereal, fresh fruit, juices, and coffee and tea is served in the bank's vault. There is no smoking. Tennis rackets are provided for use on the public courts next door. ✉ *201 W. Broadway, Box 455, 34139,* ☎ *941/695–3151 or 888/431–1977,* ℻ *941/695–3335. 8 units (3 share baths). Bicycles. AE, D, MC, V.*

$ 🏠 **Ivey House B&B.** This clean, friendly bargain is run by the folks who operate North American Canoe Tours (NACT), David and Sandee Harraden. The shotgun-style cracker house was once a boardinghouse for workers building the Tamiami Trail. Today's guests are well educated, well traveled, and in tune, as shown by the new annex, whose rooms have modem connections so "guests can hook up their laptop computers to stay in touch with their families." In the evening people talk about adventures and do jigsaw puzzles in the living room. Family-style dinners ($10–$15) often end with homemade apple pie. Guests save 10% on NACT canoe, kayak, and powerboat rentals. ✉ *107 Camellia St., 34139,* ☎ *941/695–3299,* ℻ *941/695–4155. 30 rooms, 20 with bath, 1 2-bedroom cottage. Bicycles, recreation room, library. MC, V. Closed May–Oct.*

Outdoor Activities and Sports

BIKING

North American Canoe Tours (✉ Ivey House, 107 Camellia St., ☎ 941/695–4666) rents bikes for $3 per hour, $15 per day (free for Ivey House guests).

BOATING

North American Canoe Tours (✉ Ivey House, 107 Camellia St., ☎ 941/695–4666) rents 16-ft Carolina skiffs with a 25-horsepower outboard, cooler, map, anchor, and safety equipment for $70 for a half day, $110 for a full day.

CANOEING AND KAYAKING

Everglades National Park Boat Tours (✉ Gulf Coast Visitor Center, ☎ 941/695–2591; 800/445–7724 in FL) rents 17-ft Grumman canoes for day and overnight use. Rates are $20 per day. Car shuttle service is provided for canoeists paddling the Wilderness Trail, and travelers with disabilities can be accommodated. **North American Canoe Tours** (✉ Ivey House, 107 Camellia St., ☎ 941/695–4666) is an established source for canoes, sea kayaks, and guided Everglades trips (November–April). Canoes cost $25 the first day, $20 for each day thereafter, while kayaks are $35–$55 per day. Half-day rentals are available. Car shuttles for canoeists paddling the Wilderness Trail are $135 with NACT canoe rental or $170 if you're using your own, plus the $10 park entrance fee.

GATEWAY TOWNS

The farm towns of Homestead and Florida City, flanked by Everglades National Park on the west and Biscayne National Park to the east, provide the closest visitor facilities to the parks. (The area's better restaurants are in Homestead, but the best lodgings are in Florida City.) The towns date from early in the century, when Henry Flagler extended his railroad to Key West but soon decided that farming would do more for rail revenues than ferrying passengers.

Homestead

🔢 *30 mi southwest of Miami.*

When Hurricane Andrew tore across South Florida with winds approaching 200 mph, it ripped apart lives and the small community of

Homestead. The city rebuilt itself, redefining its role as the "Gateway to the Keys" and attracting hotel chains, a shopping center, sports complex, and residential development. The historic downtown area has become a preservation-driven Main Street city. Krome Avenue (Route 997), which cuts through the city's heart, is lined with restaurants and antiques shops.

West of north–south Krome Avenue, miles of fields grow fresh fruits and vegetables. Some are harvested commercially. Others have U-PICK signs, inviting families to harvest their own. Stands that sell farm-fresh produce abound.

In addition to its agricultural legacy, the town has an eclectic flavor, attributable to its population mix: descendants of pioneer Crackers, Hispanic growers, and farmworkers as well as latter-day northern retirees. Until Hurricane Andrew the military had a huge presence at Homestead Air Force Base. The economy still suffers from its loss.

With a saltwater atoll pool that's flushed by tidal action, **Homestead Bayfront Park,** adjacent to Biscayne National Park, is popular among local families as well as anglers and boaters. Highlights include a playground, ramps for people with disabilities (including a ramp that leads into the swimming area), a picnic pavilion with grills, showers, and rest rooms. ⊠ *9698 S.W. 328th St.,* ☎ *305/230–3034.* ☞ *$3.50 per passenger vehicle, $8 per vehicle with boat, $6 per RV.* ☼ *Sunrise–sunset.*

To find out about more area attractions, *see* the South Dade side trip *in* Chapter 2.

Dining

$ ✕ **El Toro Taco.** This family-run area institution features a rustic atmo-
★ sphere, good Mexican food in generous servings, homemade tortilla chips (sometimes a little greasy), and friendly service. Selections range from tasty favorites like beef or chicken fajitas, enchiladas, tamales, burritos, and tacos to more traditional Mexican dishes like *mole de pollo,* which combines cooking chocolate and spices with chicken. Desserts include *tres leches* (a cake soaked in a syrup of three types of milk—evaporated, sweetened condensed, and heavy cream) and flan. You can order spicing from mild to tongue challenging. The restaurant is also open for breakfast. ⊠ *1 S. Krome Ave.,* ☎ *305/245–8182. D, MC, V. BYOB.*

$ ✕ **Tiffany's.** What looks like a converted pioneer house with a high-pitched roof and lattice under a big banyan tree is in reality a cluster of shops and this casual restaurant. The decor is frilly nouveau Victorian, with teaberry-color tablecloths and floral place mats, and the atmosphere is quaint but noisy. Featured entrées include hot crabmeat au gratin and asparagus rolled in ham with hollandaise sauce. Among the homemade desserts, choose from a very tall carrot cake, strawberry whipped-cream cake, and a harvest pie with double crust that has layers of apples, cranberries, walnuts, raisins, and a caramel topping. Sunday brunch is served, too. ⊠ *22 N.E. 15th St.,* ☎ *305/246–0022. MC, V. Closed Mon. No dinner.*

Outdoor Activities and Sports

AUTO RACING

The **Miami-Dade Homestead Motorsports Complex** (⊠ 1 Speedway Blvd., 33035, ☎ 305/230–7223) is a state-of-the-art facility with two tracks: a 2.21-mi continuous road course and a 1½-mi oval. There's a schedule of year-round manufacturer and race-team testing, club racing, and other national events.

BOATING

Boaters give high ratings to the facilities at **Homestead Bayfront Park.**
The 174-slip marina has a ramp, dock, bait-and-tackle shop, fuel station, ice, dry storage, and boat hoist, which can handle vessels up to 25 ft long with lifting rings. The park also has a tidal swimming area.
✉ 9698 S.W. 328th St., ☎ 305/230–3033. ☞ $3.50 per passenger vehicle, $8 per vehicle with boat, $6 per RV, $10 hoist. ☉ Sunrise–sunset.

Shopping

In addition to Homestead Boulevard (U.S. 1) and Campbell Drive (Southwest 312th Street and Northeast 8th Street), **Krome Avenue** is popular for shopping. In the heart of old Homestead, it has a brick sidewalk and many antiques stores.

Florida City

⑭ *2 mi southwest of Homestead.*

Florida's Turnpike ends in this southernmost town on the peninsula, spilling thousands onto U.S. 1 and eventually west to Everglades National Park, east to Biscayne National Park, or south to the Florida Keys. As the last civilization before 18 mi of mangroves and water, this stretch of U.S. 1 is lined with fast-food eateries, service stations, hotels, bars, dive shops, and restaurants.

Like Homestead, Florida City has roots planted in agriculture, as shown by the hundreds of acres of farmland west of Krome Avenue and a huge farmers' market that processes produce to be shipped around the country. Plans to build a new aquarium and IMAX theater, which will eventually show a film on Everglades and Biscayne national parks, were delayed after the sponsor, Destination Cinema, was purchased by *National Geographic.* But it should open sometime in 2000.

In the **Florida Pioneer Museum,** a former station agent's house, you can pore over a collection of articles from daily life that evokes the area's homestead period on the last frontier of mainland America. Items recall a time when Henry Flagler's railroad vaulted the development of the Florida Keys all the way to Key West, and Homestead and Florida City were briefly the take-charge supply outposts. A caboose outside, which dates from the days of the old Florida East Coast Railway station, is one of a few wooden cars left in the country. It's staffed by volunteers, so call first. ✉ 826 N. Krome Ave., ☎ 305/246–9531. ☞ $1. ☉ Daily 1–5.

Dining and Lodging

$$–$$$ ✕ **Mutineer Restaurant.** Former Sheraton Hotels builder Allan Bennett created this roadside steak and seafood restaurant with an indoor-outdoor fish and duck pond in 1980, back when Florida City was barely on the map. Etched glass divides the bilevel dining rooms, where striped-velvet chairs, stained glass, and a few portholes set the scene; in the lounge are an aquarium and nautical antiques. The big menu offers 18 seafood entrées plus another half-dozen daily seafood specials, as well as game, ribs, and steaks. There's live music Friday and Saturday evenings. ✉ 11 S.E. 1st Ave. (U.S. 1 and Palm Dr.), ☎ 305/245–3377. AE, D, DC, MC, V.

$–$$$ ✕ **Richard Accursio's Capri Restaurant and King Richard's Room.** Lo-
★ cals have been dining here—one of the oldest family-run restaurants in Miami-Dade County—since 1958. Outside it's a nondescript building in the middle of a big parking lot. Inside there are dark wood paneling and heavy wooden furniture. The tasty fare ranges from pizza

with light, crunchy crusts and ample toppings to mild, meaty conch chowder. Mussels come in garlic or marinara sauce, and the yellowtail snapper *française* is a worthy selection. More than a half-dozen early bird entrées are offered 4:30–6:30 for $9.45, including soup or salad and potato or spaghetti. ⊠ *935 N. Krome Ave.,* ☎ *305/247–1544. AE, MC, V.*

$ ✕ **Farmers' Market Restaurant.** Although it's in the farmers' market and serves fresh vegetables, this restaurant's specialty is seafood. A family of fishermen runs the place, so fish and shellfish are only hours from the sea. Catering to the fishing and farming crowd, it opens at 5:30, serving pancakes, jumbo eggs, and fluffy omelets with home fries or grits. The lunch and dinner menus have shrimp, fish, steaks, and conch baskets, as well as burgers, salads, and sandwiches. Normally the fish comes fried, but you can ask for it broiled or grilled. ⊠ *300 N. Krome Ave.,* ☎ *305/242–0008. No credit cards.*

$$ 🏨 **Best Western Gateway to the Keys.** This two-story motel sits well back from the highway and contains such amenities as full closets, a heat lamp in the bathroom, and complimentary Continental breakfast. Standard rooms have two queen-size beds or one king-size bed. More expensive rooms come with wet bar, refrigerator, microwave, and coffeemaker. Otherwise it's a standard modern motel with floral prints and twin reading lamps. ⊠ *1 Strano Blvd., 33034,* ☎ *305/246–5100,* ℻ *305/242–0056. 114 units. Pool, coin laundry, dry cleaning. AE, D, DC, MC, V.*

$$ 🏨 **Hampton Inn.** This two-story motel just off the highway has good clean rooms (including a post–Hurricane Andrew wing) and public-friendly policies, including free Continental breakfast, local calls, and movie channels. All rooms have at least two upholstered chairs, twin reading lamps, a desk and chair, coffeemaker, and an iron and ironing board. Units are color-coordinated and carpeted. Baths have tub-showers. ⊠ *124 E. Palm Dr., 33034,* ☎ *305/247–8833 or 800/426–7866,* ℻ *305/247–6456. 123 units. Pool. AE, D, DC, MC, V.*

Shopping

Prime Outlets at Florida City (⊠ 250 E. Palm Dr.) has more than 50 discount stores plus a small food court. **Robert Is Here** (⊠ 19200 Palm Dr. [S.W. 344th St.], ☎ 305/246–1592), a remarkable fruit stand, sells vegetables, fresh-fruit milk shakes, 10 flavors of honey, more than 100 flavors of jams and jellies, fresh juices, salad dressings, and some 40 kinds of tropical fruits, including carambola, litchi, egg fruit, monstera, sapodilla, soursop, sugar apple, and tamarind. The stand started in 1960, when seven-year-old Robert sat at this spot selling his father's bumper crop of cucumbers. Now Robert ships around the world, and everything is first quality. Seconds are given to needy area families. The stand opens at 8 and never closes earlier than 7.

BISCAYNE NATIONAL PARK

Occupying 180,000 acres along the southern portion of Biscayne Bay, south of Miami and north of the Florida Keys, this national park is 96% underwater, and its altitude ranges from 4 ft above sea level to 10 fathoms, or 60 ft, below. Contained within it are four distinct zones, which from shore to sea are mangrove forest along the coast, Biscayne Bay, the undeveloped upper Florida Keys, and coral reefs.

Mangroves line the mainland shore much as they do elsewhere in South Florida. Biscayne Bay functions as a lobster sanctuary and a nursery for fish, sponges, and crabs. Manatees and sea turtles frequent its warm, shallow waters. Lamentably, the bay is under assault from forces similar to those in Florida Bay.

To the east, about 8 mi off the coast, lie 44 tiny keys, stretching 18 nautical mi north–south and accessible only by boat. There is no commercial transportation between the mainland and the islands, and only a handful can be visited: Elliott, Boca Chita, Adams, and Sands keys. The rest either are wildlife refuges, are too small, or have rocky shores or waters too shallow for boats. It's best to explore the Keys between December and April, when the mosquito population is relatively quiescent.

Another 3 mi east of the Keys, in the ocean, lies the park's main attraction—the northernmost section of Florida's living tropical coral reefs. Some are the size of a student's desk, others as large as a football field. You can take a glass-bottom boat ride to see this underwater wonderland, but you really have to snorkel or scuba dive to appreciate it fully. A diverse population of colorful fish—angelfish, gobies, grunts, parrot fish, pork fish, wrasses, and many more—flits through the reefs.

More than 170 species of birds have been seen around the park. Though all the Keys offer excellent birding opportunities, Jones Lagoon, south of Adams Key, between Old Rhodes Key and Totten Key, is one of the best. It's approachable only by nonmotorized craft.

Convoy Point

🚯 *9 mi east of Florida City, 30 mi south of downtown Miami.*

Reminiscent of area pioneer homes, the **Convoy Point Visitor Center** is a wooden building with a metal roof and wide veranda from which you can look out across mangroves and Biscayne Bay and see the Miami skyline. Inside is a museum, where hands-on and historical exhibits and videos explore the park's four ecosystems. Among the facilities are a 50-seat auditorium, the park's canoe and tour concessioner, rest rooms with showers, a ranger information area, and gift shop. A short trail and boardwalk lead to a jetty and launch ramp. This is the only area of the park accessible without a boat. ⊠ *9700 S.W. 328th St., Homestead,* ☎ *305/230–7275.* 🎫 *Free.* ☉ *Daily 8:30–5.*

Outdoor Activities and Sports

CANOEING

Biscayne National Underwater Park, Inc. (⊠ Convoy Point Visitor Center, ☎ 305/230–1100), the park's official concessioner, has half a dozen canoes for rent on a first-come, first-served basis. Prices are $8 an hour, $22 for four hours.

SCUBA DIVING AND SNORKELING

Biscayne National Underwater Park, Inc. (⊠ Convoy Point Visitor Center, Box 1270, Homestead 33090, ☎ 305/230–1100) rents equipment and conducts snorkel and dive trips aboard the 45-ft *Boca Chita.* Snorkel trips ($27.95) leave daily at 1:30 and include mask, fins, snorkel, and vest. Trips include 1¼ hours on reefs and wrecks. Two-tank scuba trips, which leave at 9 on weekdays, 8:30 on weekends, cost $35. Complete gear rental is $37, and instruction is available. Even with a reservation (recommended), you should arrive 45 minutes before departure.

Elliott Key

16 *9 mi east of Convoy Point.*

This key, accessible only by boat (on your own or by special arrangement with the concessioner), has a rebuilt boardwalk made from recycled plastic and two nature trails with tropical plant life. Take an informal, ranger-led nature walk or walk its 7-mi length on your own along a rough path through a hammock. Videos shown at the ranger station describe the island. Facilities include rest rooms, fresh water, showers (cold), grills, and a campground. Pets are allowed on the island but not on trails.

A 30-ft-wide sandy beach about a mile north of the harbor on the west (bay) side of the key is the only one in the national park. Boaters like to anchor off it to swim. For day use only, it has picnic areas and a short trail that follows the shore and cuts through the hammock.

Lodging

$ 🏕 **Biscayne National Park.** Elliott Key has 40 primitive campsites, for which there are neither fees nor reservations. Just bring plenty of insect repellent. The park concessioner runs boats to the key periodically to drop off campers ($21 round-trip) because there is no regular ferry service or boat rental. There is a $10-per-night charge for docking private vessels.

Boca Chita Key

17 *10 mi northeast of Convoy Point.*

This island was once owned by Mark C. Honeywell, former president of Minneapolis's Honeywell Company. There is no fresh water, but grills, campsites (details similar to those at Elliott Key), and rest rooms are available. Access is by private boat only. No pets are allowed.

Adams Key

18 *9 mi southeast of Convoy Point.*

This small key, a stone's throw off the western tip of Elliott Key, is open for day use and has picnic areas, rest rooms, dockage, and a short trail that runs along the shore and through a hardwood hammock. Access is by private boat.

THE EVERGLADES A TO Z

Arriving and Departing

By Boat

If you're entering the United States by pleasure boat, you must phone **U.S. Customs** (☎ 800/432–1216) either from a marine phone or on first arriving ashore.

By Car

From Miami the main highways to the area are U.S. 1, the Homestead Extension of Florida's Turnpike, and Krome Avenue (Route 997 [old U.S. 27]).

By Plane

Miami International Airport (MIA) is 34 mi from Homestead and 83 mi from Flamingo in Everglades National Park.

BETWEEN THE AIRPORT AND TOWNS

Airporter (☎ 800/830–3413) runs shuttle buses three times daily off-season, four times daily in winter, that stop at the Hampton Inn in Florida City on their way between MIA and the Florida Keys. Shuttle service, which takes about an hour, runs 6:10–5:20 from Florida City, 7:30–6 from the airport. Reserve in advance. Pickups can be arranged for all baggage-claim areas. The cost is $20 one-way.

Greyhound Lines (☎ 800/231–2222) buses from MIA to the Keys make a stop in Homestead (⊠ 5 N.E. 3rd Rd., ☎ 305/247–2040) four times a day. Buses leave from Concourse E, lower level, and cost $8 one-way, $16 round-trip.

SuperShuttle (☎ 305/871–2000) operates 11-passenger air-conditioned vans to Homestead. Service from MIA is available around the clock; booths are outside most luggage areas on the lower level. For the return to MIA, reserve 24 hours in advance. The one-way cost is $28 per person for the first person, $12 for each additional person at the same address.

Getting Around

By Boat

Bring aboard the proper *NOAA Nautical Charts* before you cast off to explore park waters. The charts run $15–$15.95 at many marine stores in South Florida, at the Convoy Point Visitor Center in Biscayne National Park, and at Flamingo Marina in the Everglades.

The annual **Waterway Guide** (southern regional edition) is widely used by boaters. Bookstores all over South Florida sell it, or you can order it directly from the publisher (⊠ Intertec Publishing, Book Department, Box 12901, Overland Park, KS 66282-2901, ☎ 800/233–3359) for $36.95 plus $3 shipping and handling.

By Car

To reach Everglades National Park's Ernest F. Coe Visitor Center and Flamingo, head west on Route 9336 in Florida City and follow signs. From Homestead the Ernest F. Coe Visitor Center is 11 mi; Flamingo is 49 mi.

The north entrance of Everglades National Park at Shark Valley is reached by taking the Tamiami Trail about 20 mi west of Krome Avenue.

To reach the west entrance of Everglades National Park at the Gulf Coast Visitor Center in Everglades City, take Route 29 south from the Tamiami Trail.

To reach Biscayne National Park from Homestead, take U.S. 1 or Krome Avenue to Lucy Street (Southeast 8th Street) and turn east. Lucy Street becomes North Canal Drive (Southwest 328th Street). Follow signs for about 8 mi to the park headquarters.

By Taxi

Cab companies servicing the area include **Action Express Taxi** (☎ 305/743–6800) and **South Dade Taxi** (☎ 305/256–4444).

Contacts and Resources

Car Rentals

Agencies in the area include **A&A Auto Rental** (⊠ 30005 S. Dixie Hwy., Homestead 33030, ☎ 305/246–0974), **Budget** (⊠ 29949 S. Dixie Hwy., Homestead 33030, ☎ 305/248–4524 or 800/527–0700), and **Enterprise Rent-a-Car** (⊠ 29130 S. Dixie Hwy., Homestead 33030, ☎ 305/246–2056 or 800/736–8222).

Emergencies

Dial **911** for police, fire, or ambulance. If you are a TTY caller, tap the space bar or use a voice announcer to identify yourself. In the national parks, rangers answer police, fire, and medical emergencies: **Biscayne** (☎ 305/247–7272) or **Everglades** (☎ 305/247–7272). **Florida Marine Patrol** (☎ 305/795–2145), a division of the Florida Department of Natural Resources, maintains a 24-hour telephone service for reporting boating emergencies and natural-resource violations. **Miami Beach Coast Guard Base** (✉ 100 MacArthur Causeway, Miami Beach, ☎ 305/535–4300 or 305/535–4314) responds to local marine emergencies and reports of navigation hazards. The base broadcasts on VHF-FM Channel 16. The **National Weather Service** (☎ 305/229–4522) supplies local forecasts.

HOSPITALS

Hospital emergency line (☎ 305/596–6556). **SMH Homestead Hospital** (✉ 160 N.W. 13th St., Homestead, ☎ 305/248–3232; 305/596–6557 physician referral).

Guided Tours

The National Park Service organizes a variety of free programs, typically focusing on native wildlife, plants, and park history. At Biscayne National Park, for example, rangers give informal tours of Elliott and Boca Chita keys, which you can arrange in advance, depending on ranger availability. Contact the respective visitor centers for details.

AIRBOAT TOURS

In Everglades City, **Captain Doug's Florida Boat Tours** (✉ 200 Rte. 29, ☎ 941/695–4400; 800/282–9194 in FL) runs 30- to 40-minute backcountry tours ($12.95) aboard custom-designed jet airboats. Even more popular, however, are one-hour tours ($30) through mangrove trails on a six-passenger airboat. The smaller boat allows visitors to get up close to wild animals, including birds. **Wooten's Everglades Airboat Tours** (✉ Wooten's Alligator Farm, 1½ mi east of Rte. 29 on Tamiami Trail, ☎ 941/695–2781 or 800/282–2781) runs airboat and swamp-buggy tours ($12.50) through the Everglades. (Swamp buggies are giant tractorlike vehicles with oversize rubber wheels.) Tours last approximately 30 minutes.

Southwest of Florida City near the entrance to Everglades National Park, **Everglades Alligator Farm** (✉ 40351 S.W. 192nd Ave., ☎ 305/247–2628 or 800/644–9711) runs a 4-mi, 30-minute tour of the River of Grass with departures 20 minutes after the hour. The tour ($12.50) includes a free hourly alligator, snake, or wildlife show, or you can take in the show only ($7).

From the Shark Valley area, **Buffalo Tiger's Florida Everglades Airboat Ride** (✉ 12 mi west of Krome Ave., 20 mi west of Miami city limits on Tamiami Trail, ☎ 305/559–5250) is led by a former chairman of the Miccosukee tribe. The 35- to 40-minute trip includes a stop at an old Native American camp. Tours cost $12 and operate daily 10–5. Reservations are not required. **Coopertown Airboat Ride** (✉ 5 mi west of Krome Ave. on Tamiami Trail, ☎ 305/226–6048) operates the oldest airboat rides in the Everglades (since 1945). The 30- to 35-minute tour visits two hammocks and alligator holes. The charge is $10, with a $24 minimum for the boat. **Everglades Gator Park** (✉ 12 mi west of Florida's Turnpike on Tamiami Trail, ☎ 305/559–2255 or 800/559–2205) offers 45-minute narrated airboat tours ($12). **Everglades Safari Park** (✉ 26700 Tamiami Trail, 9 mi west of Krome Ave., ☎ 305/226–6923 or 305/223–3804) runs 40-minute airboat rides for $15. The price includes a show and gator tour. The **Miccosukee Indian Village**

(⌧ 25 mi west of Florida's Turnpike on Tamiami Trail, ☎ 305/223–8380) offers 30-minute airboat rides ($7) in addition to its other attractions.

Ray Cramer's Everglades Airboat Tours, Inc. (⌧ Coopertown, ☎ 305/852–5339 or 305/221–9888; ⌧ mailing address: Box 651711, Miami 33265) conducts airboat trips accommodating from 6 to 12, for $42.60 per person. Ray Cramer recently sold the business to longtime friend Bill Barlow, who has fished, frogged, and hunted in the Everglades with Cramer since 1949. Though daytime trips are offered, a better option is the tour that departs an hour before sundown so you can see birds and fish in daylight and alligators, raccoons, and other nocturnal animals when night falls.

AIR TOURS

Everglades Air Tours (⌧ Homestead General Aviation Airport, 28790 S.W. 217th Ave., Homestead, ☎ 305/247–7757) gives bird's-eye tours of the Everglades and Florida Bay that last 30 minutes and cost $45 per person, with a two-passenger minimum.

BOAT TOURS

Tours at Biscayne National Park are run by people-friendly **Biscayne National Underwater Park, Inc.** (⌧ Convoy Point, east end of North Canal Dr. [S.W. 328th St.], Box 1270, Homestead 33090, ☎ 305/230–1100). Daily trips (at 10, with a second trip at 1 during high season, according to demand) explore the park's living coral reefs 10 mi offshore on *Reef Rover IV,* a 53-ft glass-bottom boat that carries up to 48 passengers. On days when the weather is unsuitable for reef viewing, an alternative three-hour, ranger-led interpretive tour visits Elliott Key. Reservations are recommended. The cost is $19.95, and you should arrive at least 45 minutes before departure.

Everglades National Park Boat Tours (⌧ Gulf Coast Visitor Center, Everglades City, ☎ 941/695–2591; 800/445–7724 in FL) is the official park concession authorized to operate tours ($13) through the Ten Thousand Islands region and mangrove wilderness. Boats can accommodate large numbers and wheelchairs (not electric), and the two biggest boats have drink concessions. Trips that stop on Sandfly Island include a 30-minute ranger-led tour of the island's flora and fauna. **Flamingo Lodge, Marina & Outpost Resort Boat Tours** (⌧ 1 Flamingo Lodge Hwy., Flamingo, ☎ 941/695–3101, ext. 286 or 180) is the official concession authorized to operate sightseeing tours through Everglades National Park. The two-hour backcountry cruise ($16) is the most popular. The boat winds under a heavy canopy of mangroves, revealing abundant wildlife—from alligators, crocodiles, and turtles to herons, hawks, and egrets. The 90-minute Florida Bay cruise ($10) ventures into the bay to explore shallow nursery areas and encounter plentiful bird life and often dolphins, sea turtles, and sharks. To get really close to nature, adults can take the *Everglades Queen* cruise ($32), a three-hour, small-group backcountry cruise narrated by the captain.

Majestic Everglades Excursions (⌧ Box 241,, Everglades City 34139, ☎ 941/695–2777) are led by exceptionally well-informed guides Frank and Georgia Garrett. The 3½- to 4-hour ecotours, on a 24-ft boat with a covered deck, take in Everglades National Park and the Ten Thousand Islands. Narration focuses on the region's unique flora and fauna and its colorful early residents. Departing from Glades Haven, just shy of a mile south of the circle in Everglades City, tours are limited to six passengers and include brunch or afternoon snacks. The cost is $65.

CANOE AND KAYAK TOURS

North American Canoe Tours (✉ Ivey House, 107 Camellia St., Box 5038, Everglades City 34139, ☎ 941/695–3299) leads one-day to five-night Everglades tours November–April. Highlights include bird and gator sightings, mangrove forests, no-man's-land beaches, relics of the hideouts of infamous and just plain reclusive characters, and spectacular sunsets. Included in the cost of extended tours ($250–$800) are canoes or kayaks, all necessary equipment, a guide, meals, and lodging for the first night at the Ivey House B&B. Day trips by kayak, canoe, or powerboat cost $40–$60.

TRAM TOURS

Starting at the Shark Valley visitor center, **Shark Valley Tram Tours** (✉ Box 1739, Tamiami Station, Miami 33144, ☎ 305/221–8455) follows a 15-mi loop road into the interior, stopping at a 50-ft observation tower especially good for viewing gators. Two-hour narrated tours cost $9 and depart hourly 9–4, except May 1–Christmas, when they run every two hours. Reservations are recommended December–April.

Visitor Information

Big Cypress National Preserve (✉ HCR61, Box 11, Ochopee 34141, ☎ 941/695–4111). **Biscayne National Park** Convoy Point Visitor Center (✉ 9700 S.W. 328th St., Box 1369, Homestead 33090-1369, ☎ 305/230–7275). **Everglades City Chamber of Commerce** (✉ Rte. 29 and Tamiami Trail, Box 130, Everglades City 34139, ☎ 941/695–3941). **Everglades National Park** Ernest F. Coe Visitor Center (✉ 40001 Rte. 9336, Homestead 33034-6733, ☎ 305/242–7700). **Flamingo Visitor Center** (✉ 1 Flamingo Lodge Hwy., Flamingo 33034-6798, ☎ 941/695–2945). Gulf Coast Visitor Center (✉ Rte. 29, Everglades City 34139, ☎ 941/695–3311). **Greater Homestead–Florida City Chamber of Commerce** (✉ 43 N. Krome Ave., Homestead 33030, ☎ 305/247–2332 or 888/352–4891). **Tropical Everglades Visitor Association** (✉ 160 U.S. 1, Florida City 33034, ☎ 305/245–9180 or 800/388–9669).

4 FORT LAUDERDALE AND BROWARD COUNTY

From Hollywood north to Fort Lauderdale and beyond, the county's famous beaches are just one of the attractions. Downtowns are being spruced up, and Fort Lauderdale's Arts and Science District draws the culturally minded.

Updated
by Alan
Macher

A **COLLEGE STUDENT FROM THE 1960S** returning to Fort Lauderdale for a vacation today wouldn't recognize the place. Back then, the Fort Lauderdale beachfront was lined with bars, T-shirt shops, souvenir stores, and fast-food stands, and the downtown area consisted of a single office tower and some government buildings. Now, following an enormous renovation program, the beach is home to upscale shops and restaurants, including the popular Beach Place retail and dining complex, while downtown growth continues at a rapid pace. The long-awaited movie and entertainment complex, Las Olas Riverfront, is complete; several new office towers have been built; and a major airport expansion is finished.

In the years following World War II, sleepy Fort Lauderdale—with miles of inland waterways—promoted itself as the "Venice of America" and the nation's yachting capital. But in 1960 the film *Where the Boys Are* changed everything. The movie described how college students—upward of 20,000—were beginning to swarm to the city for spring break. By 1985 the 20,000 had mushroomed to 350,000. Hotel owners complained of 12 students to a room, the beachfront was littered with tacky bars, and drug trafficking and petty theft were major problems. So city leaders put in place policies and restrictions designed to encourage students to go elsewhere. They did, and no one seems to miss them.

Now the city has been totally transformed into a leading warm-weather vacation destination. This remarkable turnaround has resulted from major investments by both the private and public sectors. Fort Lauderdale has clearly become a city with a mission.

A major beneficiary is Las Olas Boulevard, whose emergence has been credited with creating a whole new identity for Fort Lauderdale. Though it was already famous for its trendy shops, now the sidewalks aren't rolled up when the sun goes down. Nearly two dozen new restaurants have sprung up, and on weekend evenings hundreds of strollers tour the boulevard, taking in the food, the jazz bands, and the scene. On-street parking on weekends has slowed traffic, and the street has a village atmosphere.

Farther west, along New River, is evidence of Fort Lauderdale's cultural renaissance: the arts and entertainment district and its crown jewel, the Broward Center for the Performing Arts. Still farther west the county has entered major-league sports with a new $212 million arena for the National Hockey League's Florida Panthers, in Sunrise.

Of course, what makes Fort Lauderdale and Broward County a major draw for visitors is the beaches. Fort Lauderdale's 2-mi stretch of unobstructed beachfront has been enhanced even further with a sparkling look designed for the pleasure of pedestrians rather than cars.

Tying this all together is a transportation system that is relatively hassle free, unusual in congested South Florida. A new expressway system, including the long-awaited widening of I–95, connects the city and suburbs and even provides a direct route to the airport and Port Everglades. For a slower and more scenic ride to really see this canal-laced city, cruise aboard the water taxi.

None of this was envisioned by Napoleon Bonaparte Broward, Florida's governor from 1905 to 1909, for whom the county was named. His drainage schemes opened much of the marshy Everglades region for farming, ranching, and settling (in retrospect, an environmental disaster). Fort Lauderdale's first-known white settler, Charles Lewis, established a plantation along the New River in 1793. But it was for Major

William Lauderdale, who built a fort at the river's mouth in 1838 during the Seminole Indian wars, that the city was named.

Incorporated in 1911 with just 175 residents, Fort Lauderdale grew rapidly during the Florida boom of the 1920s. Today its population is 160,000, and its suburbs keep growing—1.4 million live in the county. New homes, offices, and shopping centers have filled in the gaps between older communities along the coastal ridge. Now they're marching west along I–75, I–595, and Route 869 (the Sawgrass Expressway). Broward County is blessed with near-ideal weather, with some 3,000 hours of sunshine a year. The average temperature is 66°F–77°F in winter, 84°F in summer. Once a home for retirees, the county today attracts younger, working-age families, many living in such new communities as Weston, southwest of Fort Lauderdale. The area has always been a sane and pleasant place to live. Now it's also becoming one of Florida's most diverse and dynamic places to vacation.

New and Noteworthy

Fort Lauderdale's new **Las Olas Riverfront** offers a variety of shopping, dining, and entertainment choices. Outside are picturesque plazas and sweeping terraces with splashing fountains, making a tranquil spot for relaxing along the New River. Inside is where the action is: 18 restaurants ranging from upscale to casual; the city's first downtown movie complex, with 23 screens and stadium seating; and a two-level spread of video and virtual-reality games.

National Car Rental Center is not where tourists pick up and return rental vehicles. It's Broward County's new 18,000-seat arena and home to the NHL Florida Panthers. The Sunrise facility also gives Broward its first large-capacity indoor venue, drawing big-name performers like Billy Joel and Celine Dion.

Opening its doors in 1999, **World Fishing Center** is an angler's mecca on dry land. The draw is an impressive collection of sportfishing exhibits and demonstrations as well as the World Fishing Hall of Fame.

Pleasures and Pastimes

Beaches

Broward County's beachfront extends for miles without interruption, although the character of the communities behind the beach changes. For example, in Hallandale, the beach is backed by towering condominiums; in Hollywood, by motels and the Broadwalk; and just north of there—blessedly—there's nothing at all.

Dining

Food critics in dining and travel magazines agree that the Greater Fort Lauderdale area offers some of the finest and most varied dining of any U.S. city its size. You can choose from the cuisines of Asia, Europe, or Central and South America—and, of course, good ol' American—and enjoy more than just the food. The ambience, wine, service, and decor can be as varied as the language spoken, and as memorable, too.

Fishing

Four main types of fishing are available in Broward County: bottom or drift-boat fishing from party boats, deep-sea fishing for large sport fish on charters, angling for freshwater game fish, and dropping a line off a pier. For bottom fishing, party boats typically charge between $20 and $22 per person for up to four hours, including rod, reel, and bait. For charters, a half day for as many as six people runs up to $325, six-hour charters up to $495, and full-day charters (eight hours) up to $595.

Skipper and crew plus bait and tackle are included. Split parties can be arranged at a cost of about $85 per person for a full day.

Several Broward towns—Dania, Lauderdale-by-the-Sea, Pompano Beach, and Deerfield Beach—have fishing piers that draw anglers for pompano, amberjack, bluefish, snapper, blue runners, snook, mackerel, and Florida lobster.

Golf

More than 50 courses green the landscape in Greater Fort Lauderdale, including famous championship links. Most area courses are inland, in the suburbs west of the city, and there are some great bargains. Off-season (May–October) greens fees start at $15; peak-season (November–April) charges run from $35 to more than $100. Fees can be trimmed by working through Next Day Golf, a local service, and many hotels offer golf packages.

Scuba Diving

Good diving can be enjoyed within 20 minutes of shore. Among the most popular of the county's 80 dive sites is the 2-mi-wide, 23-mi-long Fort Lauderdale Reef, the product of Florida's most successful artificial reef–building program. More than a dozen houseboats, ships, and oil platforms have been sunk in depths of from 10 to 150 ft to provide a habitat for fish and other marine life, as well as to help stabilize beaches. The most famous sunken ship is the 200-ft German freighter *Mercedes,* which was blown onto Palm Beach socialite Mollie Wilmot's pool terrace in a violent Thanksgiving storm in 1984; the ship is now underwater a mile off Fort Lauderdale beach.

Exploring Fort Lauderdale and Broward County

Though most activity centers on Fort Lauderdale, there's plenty to see in other parts of Broward County, to the north, south, and, increasingly, west.

The metro area is laid out in a basic grid system, and only the hundreds of canals and waterways interrupt the straight-line path of the streets and roads. Nomenclature is important here. Streets, roads, courts, and drives run east–west. Avenues, terraces, and ways run north–south. Boulevards can run any which way. Las Olas Boulevard is one of the most important east–west thoroughfares, whereas Route A1A—referred to as Atlantic Boulevard and Ocean Boulevard along some stretches—runs along the north–south oceanfront. These names can be confusing to visitors, as there are separate streets called Atlantic and Ocean in Hollywood and Pompano Beach.

The boulevards, those that are paved and those made of water, give Fort Lauderdale its distinct character. Honeycombed with more than 260 mi of navigable waterways, the city is home port for about 40,000 privately owned boats. You won't see the gondolas you'd find in Venice, but you will see just about every other type of craft imaginable docked beside the thousands of homes and businesses that each have a little piece of waterfront. Visitors can tour the canals via the city's water-taxi system, made up of small motor launches that provide transportation and quick, narrated tours. Larger, multideck touring vessels and motorboat rentals for self-guided tours are other options. The Intracoastal Waterway, a massive canal that parallels Route A1A, is the nautical equivalent of an interstate highway. It runs north–south through the metro area and provides easy access to neighboring beach communities; Deerfield Beach and Pompano Beach lie to the north and Dania and Hollywood lie to the south. All are within a 15-mi radius of the city center.

Great Itineraries

Since most Broward County sights are relatively close to each other, it's easy to pack a lot into very little time, but you will probably need a car. You can catch a lot of the history, the museums, and the shops and bistros in Fort Lauderdale's downtown area and along Las Olas Boulevard, and then if you feel like hitting the beach, just take a 10-minute drive east to the intersection of Las Olas and A1A and you're there. Many of the neighboring suburbs, with attractions of their own, are just north or south of Fort Lauderdale. As a result, you can hit most of the high points in three days, and with seven to 10 days, you can see virtually all of Broward's mainstream charms.

Numbers in the text correspond to numbers in the margin and on the Broward County and Fort Lauderdale maps.

IF YOU HAVE 3 DAYS

With a bigger concentration of hotels, restaurants, and sights to see than its suburban neighbors, ☆ **Fort Lauderdale** ①–⑪ makes a logical base of operations for any visit. On your first day there see the downtown area, especially Las Olas Boulevard between Southeast 6th and Southeast 11th avenues. After enjoying lunch at a sidewalk café, head for the nearby Arts and Science District and the downtown **Riverwalk** ⑤, which you can see at a leisurely pace in half a day. On your second day spend at least some time at the beach, shopping when the hot sun drives you off the sand. Tour the canals on the third day, either on a rented boat from one of the various marinas along Route A1A, or via the water taxi or a sightseeing boat, both of which can be boarded all along the Intracoastal Waterway.

IF YOU HAVE 5 DAYS

With additional time you can see more of the beach and the arts district and still work in some outdoor sports—and you'll be more able to rearrange your plans depending on the weather. On the first day visit the Arts and Science District and the downtown **Riverwalk** ⑤. Set aside the next day for an offshore adventure, perhaps a deep-sea fishing charter or a dive trip to the Fort Lauderdale Reef. On the third day shop, dine, and relax along the **Fort Lauderdale beachfront** ⑨, and at the end of the day, sneak a peak at the Hillsboro Light, at **Lighthouse Point** ⑱. Another good day can be spent at the **Hugh Taylor Birch State Recreation Area** ⑩. Enjoy your fifth day in **Hollywood** ⑳, perhaps combining time on the Broadwalk with a visit to the Anne Kolb Nature Center, at West Lake Park.

IF YOU HAVE 7 DAYS

With a full week you have time for a wider variety of attractions, fitting in beach time around other activities. In fact, enjoy any of the county's public beach areas on your first day. The second day can be spent in another favorite pastime—shopping, either at chic shops or one of the malls. On the next day tour the canals on a sightseeing boat or water taxi. Then shop and dine along Las Olas Boulevard. The fourth day might be devoted to the many museums in downtown Fort Lauderdale and the fifth to an airboat ride at **Sawgrass Recreation Park** ⑭, at the edge of the Everglades. Fort Lauderdale offers plenty of facilities for outdoor recreation; spend the sixth day fishing and picnicking on one of the area's many piers or playing a round at a top golf course. Set aside the seventh day for **Hollywood** ⑳, where you can stroll along the scenic Broadwalk or walk through the aviary at Flamingo Gardens, in **Davie** ㉒, before relaxing in peaceful Hollywood North Beach Park.

When to Tour Fort Lauderdale and Broward County

Tourists visit the area all year long, choosing to come in winter or summer depending on interests, hobbies, and the climate where they live. The winter season, about Thanksgiving through March, still sees the biggest influx of visitors and "snowbirds"—seasonal residents who show up when the snow starts to fly up north. Concert, art, and show seasons are at their height then, and restaurants and highways all show the stress of crowds, Americans and Europeans alike.

Summer has its own fans. Waits at even the most popular restaurants are likely to be reasonable or even nonexistent, but though few services close in the summer, some may establish slightly shorter hours than during the peak season. Summer is the rainy season; the tropics-style rain arrives about mid-afternoon and is usually gone in an hour. When downpours hit, however, driving can be treacherous.

For golfers, almost anytime is great for playing. Just like everywhere else, waits for tee times are longer on weekends year-round.

Remember that sun can cause real scorching burns all year long, especially at midday, marking the tourist from the experienced resident or vacationer. You might want to plan your beach time for morning and late afternoon and go sightseeing or shopping in between.

FORT LAUDERDALE

Like some southeast Florida neighbors, Fort Lauderdale has been revitalizing itself for several years. What's unusual in a state where gaudy tourist zones stand aloof from workaday downtowns is that the city exhibits consistency at both ends of the 2-mi Las Olas corridor. The sparkling look results from a decision to thoroughly improve both beachfront and downtown, as opposed to focusing design attention in town and letting the beach fall prey to development solely by T-shirt retailers. Matching the downtown's new arts district, cafés, and boutiques is an equally inventive beach area with its own share of cafés and shops facing an undeveloped shoreline.

Downtown

The jewel of the downtown area along the New River is a new arts and entertainment district. Pricey tickets are available for Broadway shows at the riverfront Broward Center for the Performing Arts. Clustered within a five-minute walk are the Museum of Discovery and Science, the expanding Fort Lauderdale Historical Museum, and the Museum of Art. Restaurants, sidewalk cafés, delis, and blues, folk, jazz, reggae, and rock clubs flourish. The latest gem is Las Olas Riverfront, a multistory entertainment, dining, and retail complex along several blocks once owned by pioneers William and Mary Brickell.

Tying this district together is the Riverwalk, which extends 2 mi along the New River's north and south banks. Tropical gardens with benches and interpretive displays fringe the walk on one side, boat landings on the other. East along Riverwalk is Stranahan House, and a block away Las Olas attractions begin. Tropical landscaping and trees separate the traffic lanes in some blocks, setting off fine shops, restaurants, and popular nightspots. From here it's five minutes by car or 30 minutes by water taxi back to the beach.

A Good Tour

Start on Southeast 6th Avenue at Las Olas Boulevard, where you'll find **Stranahan House** ①, a turn-of-the-century structure that's now a museum. Between Southeast 6th and 11th avenues, Las Olas has Spanish Colonial buildings housing high-fashion boutiques, jewelry shops, and art galleries. If you drive east, you'll cross into the Isles, Fort Lauderdale's most prestigious neighborhood, where homes line canals with large yachts beside the seawalls.

Return west on Las Olas to Andrews Avenue, turn right, and park in one of the municipal garages so you can walk around downtown Fort Lauderdale. First stop is the **Museum of Art** ②, which has a major collection of works from the CoBrA (Copenhagen, Brussels, and Amsterdam) movement. Walk one block north to the **Broward County Main Library** ③ to see works from Broward's Art in Public Places program.

Go west on Southeast 2nd Street to Southwest 2nd Avenue, turn left, and stop at the **Fort Lauderdale Historical Museum** ④, which surveys the city's not-so-recent history. Just to the south is the palm-lined **Riverwalk** ⑤, a good place for a leisurely stroll. Head north toward a cluster of new facilities collectively known as the Arts and Science District. The district contains the outdoor Esplanade, whose exhibits include a hands-on display of the science and history of navigation, and the major science attraction, the **Museum of Discovery and Science** ⑥. The adjacent Broward Center for the Performing Arts, a massive glass-and-concrete structure by the river, opened in 1991.

Finally, go west along Las Olas Boulevard to Southwest 7th Avenue and the entrance to **Sailboat Bend** ⑦. You can return to the start of the tour by traveling east along Las Olas Boulevard.

TIMING

Depending on how long you like to linger in museums and how many hours you want to spend in the quaint shops on Las Olas Boulevard, you can spend anything from half a day to an entire day on this tour.

Sights to See

❸ **Broward County Main Library.** This distinctive building was designed by Marcel Breuer. Works on display from Broward's Art in Public Places program include a painting by Yaacov Agam, a wooden construction by Marc Beauregard, an outdoor aluminum-and-steel sculpture by Dale Eldred, and ceramic tile by Ivan Chermayeff. (Art in Public Places displays more than 200 works—painting, sculpture, photographs, weaving—by nationally renowned and Florida artists. Pieces can be found at 13 major sites, including the main bus terminal and the airport.) A community technology center offers personal computers for public use and assistive/adaptive devices for persons with special learning and physical disabilities. Productions from theater to poetry readings are presented in a 300-seat auditorium. ⊠ *100 S. Andrews Ave.,* ☎ *954/357–7444; 954/357–7457 for self-guided Art in Public Places walking tour brochure.* ⌑ *Free.* ☉ *Mon.–Thurs. 9–9, Fri.–Sat. 9–5, Sun. noon–5:30.*

❹ **Fort Lauderdale Historical Museum.** The museum surveys city history from the Seminole era to World War II. A model in the lobby depicts old Fort Lauderdale. In recent years the museum has expanded into several adjacent historic buildings, including the King-Cromartie House and the New River Inn. ⊠ *219 S.W. 2nd Ave.,* ☎ *954/463–4431.* ⌑ *$2.* ☉ *Tues.–Fri. 10–4.*

★ ❷ **Museum of Art.** Housed in an Edward Larrabee Barnes–designed building that's considered an architectural masterpiece, this museum has Florida's largest art exhibition space. The impressive permanent collection features 20th-century European and American art, including works by Picasso, Calder, Moore, Dalí, Rivers, Warhol, and Stella, as

Broward County

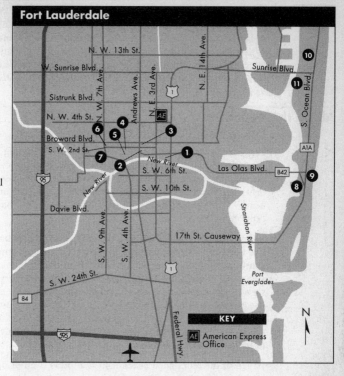

well as a notable collection of works by celebrated Ashcan School artist William Glackens. Opened in 1986, the museum launched a revitalization of the downtown district and nearby Riverwalk area. ⊠ *1 E. Las Olas Blvd.,* ☎ *954/763–6464.* 🔳 *$6.* ☉ *Tues.–Thurs. and Sat. 10–5, Fri. 10–8, Sun. noon–5.*

★ ᕲ ❻ **Museum of Discovery and Science.** Like other similar museums, the aim here is to show children—*and* adults—the wonders of science in an entertaining fashion. And as soon as visitors see the 52-ft-tall Great Gravity Clock in the courtyard entrance, they know they're in for a cool experience. Inside, exhibits include Choose Health, about making healthy lifestyle choices; Kidscience, which encourages youngsters to explore the world around them; and Gizmo City, a look at how gadgets work. Florida Ecoscapes has a living coral reef and also features live bees, bats, frogs, turtles, and alligators. An IMAX theater, part of the complex, shows changing films (some 3-D) on a five-story screen. More than 700,000 visit the museum annually, making it downtown's most popular attraction. ⊠ *401 S.W. 2nd St.,* ☎ *954/467–6637 for museum; 954/463–4629 for IMAX.* 🔳 *Museum $6, IMAX $9, both $12.50.* ☉ *Mon.–Sat. 10–5, Sun. noon–6.*

★ ❺ **Riverwalk.** This lovely, paved promenade on the north bank of the New River is great for entertainment as well as views. On the first Sunday of every month a jazz brunch attracts visitors. The walk has been extended 2 mi on both sides of the beautiful urban stream, connecting the facilities of the Arts and Science District.

❼ **Sailboat Bend.** Between Las Olas and the river, as well as just across the river, lies a neighborhood with much of the character of Old Town in Key West and historic Coconut Grove in Miami. No shops or services are located here.

● **Stranahan House.** The oldest standing structure in the city was once the home of pioneer businessman Frank Stranahan. Stranahan arrived in 1892 and, with his wife, Ivy, befriended the Seminole Indians, traded with them, and taught them "new ways." In 1901 he built a store and later made it his home. Now it's a museum with many of his original furnishings on display. ⊠ *335 S.E. 6th Ave. (at Las Olas Blvd.),* ☎ *954/524–4736.* ☑ *$5.* ⊙ *Wed.–Sat. 10–4, Sun. 1–4.*

Along the Beach

Fort Lauderdale's beachfront offers the best of all possible worlds, with easy access to restaurants and shops. For 2 mi beginning just north of the welcome center and the Bahia Mar yacht basin, strollers and café goers along Route A1A enjoy clear views, typically across rows of colorful beach umbrellas, to the sea and ships passing in and out of nearby Port Everglades. Those on the beach can look back on an exceptionally graceful promenade.

Pedestrians rank ahead of cars in Fort Lauderdale. Broad walkways line both sides of the beach road, and traffic has been trimmed to two gently curving northbound lanes, where in-line skaters dance alongside slow-moving cars. On the beach side, a low masonry wall, which serves as an extended bench, extends the promenade. At night the wall is wrapped in ribbons of fiber-optic color. The most crowded portion of beach is between Las Olas and Sunrise boulevards. This onetime strip—famous from the *Where the Boys Are* era of spring-break madness—is now but a memory.

North of the redesigned beachfront is another 2 mi of open and natural coastal landscape. Much of the way parallels the Hugh Taylor Birch State Recreation Area, which preserves a patch of primeval Florida.

A Good Tour
Go east on Southeast 17th Street across the Brooks Memorial Causeway over the Intracoastal Waterway and bear left onto Seabreeze Boulevard (Route A1A). You will pass through a neighborhood of older homes set in lush vegetation before emerging at the south end of Fort Lauderdale's beachfront strip. On your left is the Radisson Bahia Mar Beach Resort, where novelist John McDonald's fictional hero, Travis McGee, is honored with a plaque at marina slip F-18, where he docked his houseboat. Three blocks north, visit the **International Swimming Hall of Fame Museum and Aquatic Complex** ⑧, which celebrates its 35th anniversary in 2000. As you approach Las Olas Boulevard, you will see the lyrical styling that has given a distinctly European flavor to the **Fort Lauderdale beachfront** ⑨. Plan to break for lunch and perhaps a bit of shopping at Beach Place, the 100,000-square-ft entertainment, retail, and dining complex just north of Las Olas.

Turn left off Route A1A at Sunrise Boulevard, then right into **Hugh Taylor Birch State Recreation Area** ⑩, where many outdoor activities can be enjoyed amid picturesque flora and fauna. Cross Sunrise Boulevard and visit the **Bonnet House** ⑪ to marvel at both the mansion and the surrounding subtropical 35-acre estate.

TIMING
The beach is all about recreation and leisure. To enjoy it as it's meant to be, allow at least a day to loll about, or rent a fishing boat.

Sights to See
★ **⑪** **Bonnet House.** A 35-acre oasis in the heart of the beach area, this subtropical estate is a tribute to the history of old South Florida. The charming mansion was the winter residence of Frederic and Evelyn Bartlett, artists whose personal touches and small surprises are evident through-

out. Whether you're interested in architecture, artwork, or the natural environment, this is a special place. ⊠ *900 N. Birch Rd.,* ☎ *954/563–5393.* 🎫 *$9.* ☉ *Wed.–Fri. 10–1:30, weekends noon–2:30.*

★ ❾ **Fort Lauderdale beachfront.** A wave theme unifies the setting—from the low, white wave wall between the beach and widened beachfront promenade to the widened and bricked inner promenade in front of shops, restaurants, and hotels. Alone among Florida's major beachfront communities, Fort Lauderdale's beach remains open and uncluttered. More than ever, the boulevard is worth promenading.

❿ **Hugh Taylor Birch State Recreation Area.** Amid the tropical greenery of this 180-acre park you can stroll along a nature trail, visit the Birch House Museum, picnic, play volleyball, pitch horseshoes, and paddle a rented canoe. Since parking is limited on A1A, beachgoers can park here and take a walkway underpass to the beach (between 9 and 5). ⊠ *3109 E. Sunrise Blvd.,* ☎ *954/564–4521.* 🎫 *$3.25 per vehicle with up to 8 people.* ☉ *Daily 8–sunset; ranger-guided nature walks Fri. at 10:30.*

★ ❽ **International Swimming Hall of Fame Museum and Aquatic Complex.** This monument to underwater accomplishments has two 10-lane, 50-meter pools and an exhibition building featuring photos, medals, and other souvenirs from major swimming events around the world, as well as a theater that shows films of onetime swimming stars Johnny Weissmuller and Esther Williams. ⊠ *1 Hall of Fame Dr.,* ☎ *954/462–6536 for museum; 954/468–1580 for pool.* 🎫 *$3 museum, $3 pool.* ☉ *Museum and pro shop daily 9–7; pool weekdays 8–4 and 6–8, weekends 8–4; closed late Dec.–mid-Jan.*

Dining

American

$$–$$$ ✕ **Burt & Jack's.** At the far end and most scenic lookout of Port Everglades, this local favorite has been operated by veteran restaurateur Jack Jackson and actor Burt Reynolds since 1984. Behind the heavy mission doors and bougainvillea, guests are presented with Maine lobster, steaks, and chops, and the waitstaff displays the main ingredients in the raw before orders are taken. The two-story gallery of hacienda-like dining rooms surrounded by glass has views of both Port Everglades and John U. Lloyd Beach State Recreation Area. Come for cocktails in early evening on Saturday or Sunday and watch the cruise ships steam out. ⊠ *Berth 23, Port Everglades,* ☎ *954/522–2878 or 954/525–5225. Jacket required. AE, D, DC, MC, V. No lunch.*

$$–$$$ ✕ **Shula's on the Beach.** With all the sports figures attaching their names to restaurants, it's only fitting that Don Shula, a legendary coach in the rough and tough world of pro football, should have a steak house. The good news for steak—and sports—fans is that the staff here turns out winners. The meat is cut thick, grilled over a superhot fire (for quick charring), and served from rare to well done. This is a pure steak house, so don't look for many other menu choices. Appetizers are adequate though unexciting; you'll probably want to go straight to the porterhouse. An outside table gives you a delightful view of sand and ocean. Inside, a spacious bar is decorated with sports memorabilia and large-screen TVs so you can watch your favorite game. ⊠ *Sheraton Yankee Trader, 321 N. Atlantic Blvd.,* ☎ *954/355–4000. AE, D, DC, MC, V.*

Cajun/Creole

$$–$$$ ✕ **Evangeline.** Set inside and out on the ocean drive just south of its sister restaurant Mistral (☞ *below*), Evangeline celebrates Acadian Louisiana in decor and food. The mood is created by paneled wain-

scoting and plank floors—a tankard and tavern look—highlighted by verse from Longfellow's legendary poem inscribed along the turn of the ceiling. Traditional favorites include smoked rabbit gumbo with andouille sausage, a crawfish Caesar salad, jambalaya (clams, mussels, shrimp, and chicken andouille with a creole sauce), sautéed alligator in a meunière sauce topped with flash-fried oysters, and duckling with poached plums and prunelle brandy. There's music nightly, and a Dixieland band plays weekends, including Sunday afternoon. ⊠ *211 S. Atlantic Blvd. (Rte. A1A),* ☎ *954/522–7001. AE, MC, V.*

Contemporary

$$–$$$ ✕ **Mark's Las Olas.** Mark Militello, a star among South Florida chefs,
★   is in command at this popular restaurant, where metallic finishes bounce the hubbub around the room. Militello's loyal following is enchanted with his Florida-style cuisine, which blends flavors from Caribbean, southwestern, and Mediterranean traditions. Entrées change daily, but typical choices include gulf shrimp, dolphinfish, yellowtail snapper, grouper, swordfish, Florida lobster, and callaloo (a West Indian spinach), chayote, ginger, jicama, and plantain, all brilliantly presented and combined in sauces that tend to be low fat. Pastas and full-size dinner pizzas are thoughtful offerings. ⊠ *1032 E. Las Olas Blvd.,* ☎ *954/463–1000. AE, DC, MC, V. No lunch weekends.*

$$ ✕ **Mistral.** This dining room, surrounded by tropical art and pottery,
★   rates high in both taste and looks. The kitchen staff turns out hearty pastas, such as a *primavera* redolent with garlic and herbs and *tagliolini* (an angel-hair pasta) with prosciutto, pine nuts, and tomatoes. Other favorites are grilled shrimp and black-bean cakes as well as pan-seared dolphin. Pizzas, big salads, and a strong selection of affordable wines, available by the bottle and by the glass, are also served. ⊠ *201 S. Atlantic Blvd. (Rte. A1A),* ☎ *954/463–4900. AE, MC, V.*

French

$$ ✕ **French Quarter.** This 1920 building, formerly a Red Cross headquarters, sits on a quiet street, just off bustling Las Olas Boulevard. The French-style architecture has a touch of New Orleans style, and the food captures both creole and traditional French elements. Interior rooms are small and intimate, watched over by the friendly, excellent waitstaff. Among the favorites are shrimp *maison* (large shrimp sautéed with carrots and mushrooms in beurre blanc), bouillabaisse, crab cakes, and escargot appetizers. French baking is done on site, and fresh bread and all pastry desserts are made daily. A fixed-price three-course pretheater dinner ($18.95) is served until 6:30. ⊠ *215 S.E. 8th Ave.,* ☎ *954/463–8000. AE, MC, V. Closed Sun. No lunch Sat.*

$$ ✕ **La Coquille.** Although this French restaurant sits at the edge of busy Sunrise Boulevard, it seems worlds away thanks to a new art deco look, along with paintings of the sea and a tropical garden. The friendly and helpful service comes with a delightful French accent, and the cuisine is equally authentic: Dubonnet and vermouth cassis aperitifs are a prelude to seared sea scallops with spring vegetables, honey-glazed duckling with lingonberry sauce and wild rice, sweetbreads in a morel and truffle sauce, or veal with shallots and sweet bell peppers. There's always a soufflé among the desserts as well as a multicourse dinner special most nights. Chef/owner Jean Bert has been serving up award-winning dishes for 18 years, so he must be doing something right. ⊠ *1619 E. Sunrise Blvd.,* ☎ *954/467–3030. AE, MC, V. Closed Mon. No lunch Sat.–Thurs.*

$$ ✕ **Studio One French Bistro.** More like an art gallery—intimate, black-
★   and-white, mirrored—this restaurant serves up bountiful portions at low prices. About 30 choices are offered as part of the $20 fixed-price dinner. Food is thoughtfully presented, from high-gluten breads through

a dozen or so appetizers, dinner-size salads, and entrées that include a grilled salmon in puff pastry with lobster sauce, Camembert-stuffed chicken breast with French cranberry sauce, and roasted duckling with vanilla sauce. Chef Bernard Asendorf has charge of the kitchen, and his wife, Roberta, carries on the tradition of greeting by name the locals who return time and again. ☒ 2447 E. Sunrise Blvd., ☎ 954/565–2052. AE, DC, MC, V. Closed Mon. mid-May–mid-Dec. No lunch.

Italian

$$–$$$ ✕ **Primavera.** Northern Italian food is the specialty at this lovely find in the middle of an ordinary shopping plaza. Elegant floral arrangements enhance the fine dining experience. In addition to interesting pasta and risotto entrées, there is a wide variety of creative fish, poultry, veal, and beef dinners. One of chef/owner Giacomo Dresseno's favorites is veal chop Boscaiola (with shallots, wild mushrooms, and bordelaise sauce). Primavera is renowned for its spectacular assortment of both appetizers and desserts. ☒ 830 E. Oakland Park Blvd., ☎ 954/564–6363. AE, D, DC, MC, V. No lunch.

Mexican

$$ ✕ **Eduardo de San Angel.** Forget tacos and burritos, which aren't even available here, and try the classic dishes served in true Mexican style. Authentic chilies, spices, and herbs enhance an array of seafood, meat, and poultry dishes. Typical specialties are beef tenderloin tips sautéed with Portobello mushrooms and onions with a chipotle chili sauce, and a marvelous mesquite-grilled red snapper flavored with jalapeños and mango salsa. The gourmet dishes are matched by a sophisticated setting. ☒ 2822 E. Commercial Blvd., ☎ 954/772–4731. AE, MC, V. Closed Sun. No lunch.

Seafood

$$ ✕ **Blue Moon Fish Company.** The setting, on the Intracoastal Water-
★ way, is superb; virtually every table has a lovely water view. But the real magic is in the kitchen, where chefs Baron Skorish and Bryce Statham create some of the region's best seafood dishes. Favorites include pan-seared snapper with asparagus, sea bass fillet crusted with macadamia nuts, and rare-charred tuna. The appetizer selection features choices from the raw bar, including a sushi sampler, plus tasty crab and crawfish cakes and charred portobello mushrooms. On Saturday night, a blues band performs. This is a stunning addition to the waterfront dining scene. ☒ 4405 W. Tradewinds Ave., ☎ 954/267–9888. AE, MC, V.

$–$$ ✕ **Rustic Inn Crabhouse.** Wayne McDonald started with a cozy one-room roadhouse in 1955, when this was a remote service road just west of the little airport. Now, the plain, rustic place is huge. Steamed crabs seasoned with garlic and herbs, spices, and oil are eaten with mallets on tables covered with newspapers; peel-and-eat shrimp are served either with garlic and butter or spiced and steamed with Old Bay seasoning. The big menu includes other seafood items as well. Pies and cheesecakes are offered for dessert. ☒ 4331 Ravenswood Rd., ☎ 954/584–1637. AE, D, DC, MC, V.

$–$$ ✕ **Shirttail Charlie's.** Diners look out on the New River from the outdoor deck or upstairs dining room of this restaurant, named for a yesteryear Seminole Indian who wore his shirttails out. A free 30- to 40-minute after-dinner cruise on *Shirttail Charlie's Express* chugs up-river past an alleged Al Capone speakeasy or across the river to and from the Broward Center for the Performing Arts. Charlie's is built to look old, with a 1920s tile floor that leans toward the water. Florida-style seafood includes conch served four ways, crab balls, blackened tuna with Dijon mustard sauce, crunchy coconut shrimp with a not-too-sweet piña colada sauce, and three fresh catches nightly. A children's menu is available. ⊠ *400 S.W. 3rd Ave.,* ☎ *954/463–3474. AE, MC, V. Closed Mon. June–Sept.*

Southwestern

$–$$ ✕ **Canyon.** Adventurous southwestern cuisine helps you escape the or-
★ dinary at this small but very popular spot. Take, for example, the ostrich skewers, smoked salmon tostada, brie and wild-mushroom quesadilla, and marvelous Chilean sea bass. Free-range chicken and brook trout are served with a tempting crabmeat salsa. Many guests like to start off with Canyon's famous prickly pear margaritas, or choose from a well-rounded wine list or selection of beers, including many microbrews. ⊠ *1818 E. Sunrise Blvd.,* ☎ *954/765–1950. AE, MC, V. No lunch.*

Lodging

On the Beach

$$$$ 🏨 **Marriott's Harbor Beach Resort.** If you look down from the upper stories (14 in all) at night, this 16-acre property south of the big public beach shimmers like a jewel. Spacious guest rooms are done in tropical colors, lively floral prints, rattan, wicker, and wood. Each has a balcony facing the ocean or the Intracoastal Waterway, and there are in-room minibars. Sheffield's is one of the city's top restaurants. No other hotel gives you so many options. ⊠ *3030 Holiday Dr., 33316,* ☎ *954/525–4000 or 800/222–6543,* FAX *954/766–6152. 588 rooms, 36 suites. 5 restaurants, 3 bars, pool, massage, saunas, 5 tennis courts, health club, beach, windsurfing, boating, parasailing, children's program (ages 5–12). AE, DC, MC, V.*

$$$–$$$$ 🏨 **Lago Mar Resort Hotel & Club.** The sprawling Lago Mar has been
★ owned by the Banks family since the early 1950s. In 1999 they added 42 new guest accommodations at a cost of $5 million. The lobby is still luxurious, with fanlight surrounds, a coquina-rock fireplace, and an eye-popping saltwater aquarium behind the registration desk. Allamanda trellises and bougainvillea plantings edge the swimming lagoon, and guests have use of the broadest beach in the city. Lago Mar is less a big resort than a small town—and, in its way, a slice of Old Florida. If price is no object, try one of the two new oceanfront penthouse suites. For $600 a night you get 1,800 square ft of luxury. ⊠ *1700 S. Ocean La., 33316,* ☎ *954/523–6511 or 800/524–6627,* FAX *954/524–6627. 52 rooms, 143 1-bedroom suites, 17 2-bedroom suites. 4 restaurants, 2 pools, miniature golf, 2 tennis courts, shuffleboard, volleyball. AE, DC, MC, V.*

$$–$$$ 🏨 **Bahia Cabana Beach Resort.** *Boating Magazine* ranks the waterfront bar and restaurant here among the world's 10 best, but it's far enough from guest rooms so that nightly entertainment is not disturbing. A video bar yields a sweeping view of the marina. Rooms are spread among five buildings furnished in tropical-casual style. Those in the 500 building are more motel-like and overlook the parking lot, but rates here are lowest. ⊠ *3001 Harbor Dr., 33316,* ☎ *954/524–1555; 800/922–3008; 800/232–2437 in FL;* FAX *954/764–5951. 52 rooms, 10 suites, 37 efficiencies. Restaurant, 2 bars, café, 3 pools, hot tub, saunas, shuffleboard. AE, D, DC, MC, V.*

$$ 🏨 **La Casa Del Mar.** This is a Florida rarity: a true bed-and-breakfast
★ inn located at the beach. Co-owners Larry Ataniso and Lee Prellwitz took the plunge three years ago, and guests have been delighted ever since. Rooms have names like Stolen Kiss, Monet, and Southwest. The full American breakfast might consist of orange-flavored French toast, buttermilk pancakes, poached eggs, and mushroom-sausage casserole, among other treats, and guests can indulge again in the late afternoon

at the poolside wine and cheese party. ⊠ *3003 Grana...* ☎ *954/467–2037,* FAX *954/467–7439. 10 units. Pool. A...*

$–$$ ⊞ **Nina Lee Imperial House.** Recently the Nina Lee ac... adjacent Imperial House. Both now operate as one property, having been extensively refurbished with new carpeting, TVs, furniture, and drapes. The Nina Lee is typical of the modest, affordable 1950s-style lodgings that can be found within a block or two of the ocean along Fort Lauderdale beach. Rooms are homey and clean, but not tiny. Efficiencies have gas kitchens, large closets, and tub-showers. The pool is set in a garden, and the entire property is just removed enough from the beach causeway to be quiet. The Imperial House has apartment-style accommodations consisting of living room, kitchen, and bedroom. Guests may use the facilities at the nearby beachfront Sheraton Yankee Clipper hotel. ⊠ *3048 Harbor Dr., 33316,* ☎ *954/524–1568. 26 units. 2 pools. MC, V.*

Downtown and Beach Causeways

$$$$ ⊞ **Hyatt Regency Pier Sixty-Six.** The trademark of this high-rise resort on the Intracoastal Waterway is its rooftop Pier Top Lounge. ★ Overlooking the resort's marina, it revolves every 66 minutes and is reached by an exterior elevator. The 17-story tower dominates a 22-acre spread that includes the Spa LXVI. Tower and lanai lodgings are tops from the ground up. (In 1999 the resort completed an $8.8 million improvement program, which upgraded all guest rooms and put more lavish touches on the spa.) In the early evening guests try to perch at the Pelican Bar; at 6:06 a cannon is fired, and anybody around the bar gets a drink on the house. When you want to swim in the ocean, hail the water taxi at the resort's dock for a three-minute trip to the beach. ⊠ *2301 S. 17th St., 33316,* ☎ *954/525–6666 or 800/327–3796,* FAX *954/728–3541. 380 rooms, 8 suites. 3 restaurants, 3 bars, pool, hot tub, spa, 2 tennis courts, dock, snorkeling, boating, parasailing, waterskiing, fishing. AE, D, MC, V.*

$$$–$$$$ ⊞ **Riverside Hotel.** This six-story hotel was built in 1936 and has been steadily upgraded. A sidewalk café fronts Bob Jenny's tropical murals, one of which is a New Orleans–style work that stretches across 725 square ft of the hotel's facade. Old Fort Lauderdale photos grace the hallways, and rooms are outfitted distinctively, with antique oak furnishings, framed French prints, and European-style baths. The poolside bar in back offers a great view of the New River, as do the best guest rooms; the least desirable are the 36 series, from which you can hear the elevator. No-smoking rooms are available. An attentive staff includes many who have been with the hotel for two decades or more. ⊠ *620 E. Las Olas Blvd., 33301,* ☎ *954/467–0671 or 800/325–3280,* FAX *954/462–2148. 109 rooms, 7 suites. 2 restaurants, bar, pool, dock. AE, DC, MC, V.*

$$–$$$ ⊞ **Banyan Marina Apartments.** These outstanding waterfront apartments, on a residential island just off Las Olas Boulevard, are set amid ★ imaginative landscaping that includes a walkway through the upper branches of a banyan tree. Featuring leather sofas, springy carpets, real potted plants, sheer curtains, custom drapes, high-quality art, French doors, and jalousies for sweeping the breeze in, the luxurious units are as comfortable as any first-class hotel—but for half the price. Also included are a full kitchen, dining area, beautiful gardens, dockage for eight yachts, and exemplary housekeeping. Recent upgrades include a new phone system and a remodeling of all bathrooms. ⊠ *111 Isle of Venice, 33301,* ☎ *954/524–4430,* FAX *954/764–4870. 10 rooms, 1 efficiency, 4 1-bedroom apartments, 2 2-bedroom apartments. Dining room, pool, dock. MC, V.*

ıghtlife and the Arts

For the most complete weekly listing of events, read the **"Showtime!"** entertainment insert and events calendar in the Friday *Fort Lauderdale News/Sun Sentinel.* **"Weekend,"** in the Friday edition of the *Herald,* the Broward edition of the *Miami Herald,* carries listings of area happenings. The weekly *City Link* is principally an entertainment and dining paper with a relic "underground" look. A 24-hour **Arts & Entertainment Hotline** (☎ 954/357–5700) provides updates on art, attractions, children's events, dance, festivals, films, literature, museums, music, opera, and theater.

Tickets are sold at individual box offices and through **Ticketmaster** (☎ 954/523–3309); there is a service charge.

The Arts

Broward Center for the Performing Arts (✉ 201 S.W. 5th Ave., ☎ 954/462–0222) is the waterfront centerpiece of Fort Lauderdale's cultural arts district. More than 500 events a year are scheduled at the 2,700-seat architectural masterpiece, including Broadway musicals, plays, dance, symphony and opera, rock, film, lectures, comedy, and children's theater.

Nightlife

BARS AND LOUNGES

Baja Beach Club (✉ 3339 N. Federal Hwy., ☎ 954/563–7889), now at a new location, offers the same trendy entertainment: karaoke, lip synching, virtual reality, performing bartenders, temporary tattoos—plus a 40-ft free buffet. At Beach Place, **Cafe Iguana** (✉ 17 S. Atlantic Blvd., ☎ 954/763–7222) has a nightly DJ to keep the dance floor hopping. **Cheers** (✉ 941 E. Cypress Creek Rd., ☎ 954/771–6337) is an action-filled nightspot with a wide variety of rock bands, two bars, and a dance floor. **Chili Pepper** (✉ 200 W. Broward Blvd., ☎ 954/525–0094) brings hot current rock bands to the stage. **O'Hara's Pub & Sidewalk Cafe** (✉ 722 E. Las Olas Blvd., ☎ 954/524–1764) features live jazz and blues nightly. It's packed for TGIF, though usually by the end of each day the trendy crowd spills onto this prettiest of downtown streets. The **Parrot Lounge** (✉ 911 Sunrise La., ☎ 954/563–1493) is a loony feast for the eyes, with a casual, friendly local crowd. Fifteen TVs and frequent sing-alongs add to the fun. A jukebox jams all night. **Squeeze** (✉ 3045 N. Federal Hwy., ☎ 954/564–1074), a favorite of alternative-music fans, continues in a new location at the Culture Room.

COUNTRY AND WESTERN

Desperado (✉ 2520 S. Miami Rd., ☎ 954/463–2855) offers a mechanical bull and free line-dance lessons. The club is open from Wednesday through Sunday.

Outdoor Activities and Sports

Baseball

From mid-February to March the **Baltimore Orioles** (✉ Fort Lauderdale Stadium, N.W. 12th Ave., ☎ 954/776–1921) are in spring training.

Biking

Some of the most popular routes are Route A1A and Bayview Drive, especially early in the morning before traffic builds, and a 7-mi bike path that parallels Route 84 and the New River and leads to Markham Park, which has mountain-bike trails. Most area bike shops also have cycling maps.

Fishing

If you're interested in a saltwater charter, check out the **Radisson Bahia Mar Beach Resort** (⊠ 801 Seabreeze Blvd., ☎ 954/627–6357). Both sportfishing and drift fishing bookings can be arranged.

Scuba Diving and Snorkeling

Lauderdale Diver (⊠ 1334 S.E. 17th St. Causeway, ☎ 954/467–2822 or 800/654–2073), which is PADI affiliated, arranges dive charters throughout the county. Dive trips typically last four hours. Nonpackage reef trips are open to divers for $40; scuba gear is extra.

Pro Dive (⊠ Radisson Bahia Mar Beach Resort, 801 Seabreeze Blvd., ☎ 954/761–3413 or 800/772–3483), a PADI five-star facility, is the area's oldest diving operation and offers packages with Radisson Bahia Mar Beach Resort, from where its 60-ft boat departs. Snorkelers can go out for $24 on a two-hour snorkeling trip, which includes equipment. Scuba divers pay $39 using their own gear or $89 with all rentals included.

Soccer

Major-league soccer has returned to South Florida in the form of the **Fusion** (⊠ 5301 N.W. 12th Ave., ☎ 954/717–2200). Their season, which begins in March, includes 20 home games at 20,000-seat Lockhart Stadium.

Tennis

With 21 courts, 18 of them lighted clay courts, the **Jimmy Evert Tennis Center at Holiday Park** is Fort Lauderdale's largest public tennis facility. Chris Evert, one of the game's greatest players, learned the sport here under the watchful eye of her father, Jimmy, who retired after 37 years as the tennis professional here. ⊠ *701 N.E. 12th Ave., ☎ 954/ 761–5378.* ⌨ *$4.50 per person per hr.* ☉ *Weekdays 8 AM–9:15 PM, weekends 8–7.*

Shopping

Malls

Just north of Las Olas Boulevard on Route A1A is the happening **Beach Place** (⊠ 17 S. Atlantic Blvd.). Here you can browse through such shops as the Gap, Bath & Body Works, and Banana Republic; have lunch or dinner at an array of restaurants, from casual Caribbean to elegant American; or carouse at a selection of nightspots—all open late. By and large, eateries on the lower level are more upscale, whereas on the upper level, the prices are lower and the ocean view is better.

With a convenient in-town location just west of the Intracoastal Waterway, the split-level **Galleria Mall** (⊠ 2414 E. Sunrise Blvd.) contains more than 1 million square ft of space. It's anchored by Neiman-Marcus, Lord & Taylor, Dillards, and Saks Fifth Avenue and features 150 world-class specialty stores with an emphasis on fashion and sporting goods.

Shopping Districts

When you're downtown, check out the new **Las Olas Riverfront** (⊠ 1 block west of Andrews Ave. on the New River) shopping, dining, and entertainment complex. If only for a stroll and some window-shopping, don't miss the **Shops of Las Olas** (⊠ 1 block off New River east of U.S. 1). The city's best boutiques plus top restaurants (many affordable) and art galleries line a beautifully landscaped street.

Side Trips

The Western Suburbs and Beyond

West of Fort Lauderdale is an ever-growing mass of suburbs flowing one into the other. They're home to most of the city's golf courses as well as some attractions and large malls. As you head farther west, the terrain becomes more Everglades-like, and you'll occasionally see an alligator sunning itself on a canal bank. No matter how dedicated developers are to building over this natural resource, the Everglades keeps trying to assert itself. Waterbirds, fish, and other creatures are found in canals and lakes, even man-made ones, throughout the western areas.

☺ ⑫ Thousands of caterpillars representing as many as 150 species pupate and emerge as butterflies in the walk-through laboratory that is **Butterfly World,** on 3 acres inside Tradewinds Park. A screened aviary called North American Butterflies is reserved for native species. The Tropical Rain Forest is a 30-ft-high construction, with observation decks, waterfalls, ponds, and tunnels where colorful butterflies flit and shift about. ✉ *3600 W. Sample Rd., Coconut Creek,* ☎ *954/977–4400.* 🎫 *$11.95.* ☉ *Mon.–Sat. 9–5, Sun. 1–5.*

⑬ The 30-acre **Everglades Holiday Park** provides a good glimpse of the Everglades. Here you can take an airboat tour, look at an 18th-century-style Native American village, or watch an alligator-wrestling show. A souvenir shop, TJ's Grill, a convenience store, and a campground with RV hookups and a tent are all on site. ✉ *21940 Griffin Rd.,* ☎ *954/434–8111.* 🎫 *Free, $12.50 airboat tour.* ☉ *Daily 9–5.*

⑭ To understand and enjoy the Everglades, take an airboat ride at **Sawgrass Recreation Park.** You'll probably see all sorts of plants and wildlife, such as birds, alligators, turtles, snakes, and fish. Included in the entrance fee along with the airboat ride is admission to an Everglades nature exhibit, a native Seminole Indian village, and exhibits about alligators, other reptiles, and birds of prey. A souvenir and gift shop, food service, and an RV park with hookups are also at the park. ✉ *U.S. 27 north of I–595,* ☎ *954/426–2474.* 🎫 *$14.68.* ☉ *Daily 6–6, airboat rides 8–5.*

☺ ⑮ Some distance from Fort Lauderdale's tranquil beaches, but worth the one-hour drive, is the **Big Cypress Seminole Reservation** and its two very different attractions. At the **Billie Swamp Safari,** you can experience the majesty of the Everglades firsthand. Daily tours of the wetlands and hammocks, where wildlife abound, yield sightings of deer, water buffalo, bison, wild hogs, hawks, eagles, alligators, and even the rare Florida panther. Tours are provided aboard swamp buggies—customized motor vehicles specially designed to provide visitors with an elevated view of the frontier. ✉ *Snake Rd., 19 mi north of I–75 Exit 14,* ☎ *941/983–6101 or 800/949–6101.* 🎫 *Free, $38 swamp buggy ecotour/alligator and snake education show/airboat ride package.* ☉ *Daily 8–5.*

Not far away from the Billie Swamp Safari is the **Ah-Tha-Thi-Ki Museum,** whose name means "a place to learn, a place to remember." It is just that. The museum honors the culture and tradition of the Seminoles through artifacts and reenactments of rituals and ceremonies. The site includes a living Seminole village, nature trails, and a boardwalk through a cypress swamp. ✉ *Snake Rd., 17 mi north of I–75 Exit 14,* ☎ *954/792–0745.* 🎫 *$6.* ☉ *Tues.–Sun. 9–5.*

LODGING

$$$$ 🏨 **Wyndham Resort & Spa Fort Lauderdale.** As its name suggests, this resort offers the luxury, amenities, and facilities of a resort with the health-consciousness of a spa. Spacious guest rooms and suites are done in tropical colors with rattan seating and overlook a lake or golf course. Oversize baths have dressing areas. In the morning complimentary caffeine-free herbal teas are offered; in the afternoon it's fresh fruit. The staff nutritionist follows American Heart Association and American Cancer Society guidelines and can accommodate macrobiotic and vegetarian diets. Also on site and open to the public is a full-service beauty salon. The resort offers combination spa-tennis and spa-golf packages. ✉ *250 Racquet Club Rd., 33326,* ☎ *954/389–3300 or 800/ 327–8090,* FAX *954/384–0563. 493 units. 4 restaurants, 2 bars, 5 pools, beauty salon, spa, 2 golf courses, 24 tennis courts, bowling, horseback riding, roller-skating rink, shops. AE, D, MC, V.*

NIGHTLIFE AND THE ARTS

Sunrise Musical Theatre (✉ 5555 N.W. 95th Ave., Sunrise, ☎ 954/741– 7300) is a 4,000-seat theater featuring everything from ballet to top-name pop, rock, and country artists.

OUTDOOR ACTIVITIES AND SPORTS

Fishing. The marina at **Everglades Holiday Park** (✉ 21940 Griffin Rd., ☎ 954/434–8111) caters to freshwater fishing. For $52.50 for five hours, you can rent a 14-ft johnboat (with a 9.9-horsepower Yamaha outboard) that carries up to four people. A rod and reel rent for $9 a day, and bait is extra. For two people, a fishing guide for a half day (four hours) is $140; for a full day (eight hours), $190. A third person adds $35 for a half day, $70 for a full day. You can also buy a freshwater fishing license (mandatory) here; a seven-day nonresident license is $17. Freshwater fishing with a guide out of **Sawgrass Recreation Park** (✉ U.S. 27 north of I–595, ☎ 954/426–2474) costs $175 for two people for a half day, $225 for a full day. Resident and nonresident fishing licenses and live bait are available.

Golf. Next Day Golf (☎ 954/772–2582) provides access at no extra fee to private courses normally limited to members and arranges bookings up to 12 months in advance—a big advantage for golfers planning trips during the busy winter months. And they also offer last-minute discount tee times (call 12 hours in advance). **Bonaventure Country Club** (✉ 200 Bonaventure Blvd., ☎ 954/389–2100) has 36 holes. **Broken Woods Country Club** (✉ 9000 Sample Rd., Coral Springs, ☎ 954/752– 2140) has 18 holes. **Colony West Country Club** (✉ 6800 N.W. 88th Ave., Tamarac, ☎ 954/726–8430) offers play on 36 holes. Just west of Florida's Turnpike, the **Inverrary Country Club** (✉ 3840 Inverrary Blvd., Lauderhill, ☎ 954/733–7550) has three 18-hole courses. **Jacaranda Golf Club** (✉ 9200 W. Broward Blvd., Plantation, ☎ 954/ 472–5855) has 18 holes to play. **Sabal Palms Golf Course** (✉ 5101 W. Commercial Blvd., Tamarac, ☎ 954/731–2600) has 18 holes. **Sunrise Country Club** (✉ 7400 N.W. 24th Pl., Sunrise, ☎ 954/742–4333) provides 18 holes.

Ice Hockey. National Car Rental Center, Broward's new arena, is the home of the National Hockey League's **Florida Panthers** (✉ 2555 N.W. 137th Way, Sunrise, ☎ 954/523–3309).

SHOPPING

Broward's shopping extravaganza, **Fashion Mall at Plantation** (✉ University Dr. north of Broward Blvd., Plantation) is a jewel of a mall. The three-level complex includes such department stores as Macy's, Lord & Taylor, and Burdines; a Sheraton Suites Hotel; and more than 100 specialty shops. In addition to a diverse food court, the Brasserie Max restaurant offers gourmet dining.

Containing more than 270 stores, the huge (2 million square ft) **Sawgrass Mills Mall** (✉ 12801 W. Sunrise Blvd., at Flamingo Rd., Sunrise),

THE MALL

TRAVEL INDUSTRY SURVEYS reveal that shopping is vacationers' number one activity. With 25 million visitors annually, Sawgrass Mills proves the point, ranking as the second-biggest tourist attraction in Florida, behind Disney. This so-called world's largest retail outlet mall is one of the first places visitors ask about. And they come from all over; in 1999, 48% were international, primarily from Latin America, Germany, and the United Kingdom.

Sawgrass Mills: the adventure. This is not your average mall. Tour buses hum near entrances with names like Pink Flamingo, Red Snapper, and White Seahorse. The complex itself is alligator shaped, and walking every nook and cranny is about 2 mi. (If the 800-member Mall Walkers Club—mostly seniors—can do it, so can you.) Mall sections are called halls; for example, the Designer Hall contains women's designer clothing. At the Oasis, a Hard Rock Cafe and 24-screen movieplex are being joined by Wolfgang Puck's first South Florida eatery. And then there are the prices—as much as 80% below retail according to management, but buyers should compare.

Sawgrass Mills: the growth magnet. Western Broward, especially Sunrise, has seen huge growth. In addition to the nearby National Car Rental Center, a number of companies, other retail and restaurant operations, and even residential communities have located nearby, and with the mall has come sprawl.

9 mi west of downtown Fort Lauderdale, is a destination in itself. Travelers and locals alike come for shopping, restaurants, food courts, and entertainment, and the place teems on weekends and holidays. Shops, many of them manufacturer's outlets, retail outlets, and name-brand discounters, include Neiman-Marcus, Loehmann's, JCPenney, Ann Taylor, Alfred Angelo Bridal, Levi's, TJ Maxx, Donna Karan, Saks Fifth Avenue, and Kenneth Cole. The mall is also accessible from Miami-Dade and the Palm Beaches via the Sawgrass Expressway.

NORTH ON SCENIC A1A

North of Fort Lauderdale's Birch Recreation Area, Route A1A edges back from the beach through the section known as the Galt Ocean Mile, and a succession of ocean-side communities line up against the sea. Traffic can line up, too, as it passes through a changing pattern of beach-blocking high-rises and modest family vacation towns and back again. Here and there a scenic lighthouse or park punctuates the landscape, while other attractions and recreational opportunities are found inland.

Lauderdale-by-the-Sea

16 *5 mi north of Fort Lauderdale.*

Tucked just north of Fort Lauderdale's northern boundary, this low-rise family resort town bans construction of more than three stories. You can drive along lawn-divided El Mar Drive, lined with garden-style motels a block east of Route A1A. However, you don't actually need a car in Lauderdale-by-the-Sea. Dozens of good restaurants and shops are in close proximity to hotels and the beach.

Where Commercial Boulevard meets the ocean, you can walk out onto **Anglin's Fishing Pier,** stretching 875 ft into the Atlantic. Here you can fish, stop in at any of the popular restaurants clustered around the seafront plaza, or just soak up the scene.

Dining and Lodging

$$ ✕ **Sea Watch.** It's set back from the road and easy to miss, but after 25 years, this nautical-theme restaurant right on Lauderdale-by-the-Sea's beach stays packed during lunch and dinner. Waits can be as long as 30 minutes, but time passes quickly in the sumptuous upstairs lounge with comfy sofas and high-back rattan chairs. The menu has all the right appetizers: oysters Rockefeller, gulf shrimp, clams casino, and Bahamian conch fritters. Typical daily specials might be sautéed yellowtail snapper, oat-crusted with roasted red bell pepper sauce and basil, or a charbroiled dolphin fillet marinated with soy sauce, garlic, black pepper, and lemon juice. Desserts include a cappuccino brownie and strawberries Romanoff. Good early bird specials are offered off-season. ✉ *6002 N. Ocean Blvd. (Rte. A1A), Fort Lauderdale,* ☎ *954/ 781–2200. AE, MC, V.*

$ ✕ **Aruba Beach Cafe.** This is your best bet at the pier. A big beachside barn of a place—very casual, always crowded, always fun—it serves large portions of Caribbean conch chowder, Cuban black-bean soup, fresh tropical salads, burgers, sandwiches, and seafood. A reggae/jazz band performs Friday and Sunday 2–6. ✉ *1 E. Commercial Blvd.,* ☎ *954/776–0001. AE, D, DC, MC, V.*

$$–$$$ 🏠 **A Little Inn by the Sea.** French, German, and English are spoken at this inn, which caters to a very international clientele. Innkeeper Uli Brandt and his family maintain tropical charm and bed-and-breakfast style. Since taking over the property in 1994, they have continued to make upgrades, including remodeled kitchens in efficiencies and one- and two-bedroom suites, and new bamboo and rattan furniture throughout. Adding to the flavor are fountains and classical background music at breakfast. The inn is directly on the ocean, and rooms have nice views from private balconies. ✉ *4546 El Mar Dr., 33308,* ☎ *954/772–2450 or 800/492–0311,* FAX *954/938–9354. 10 rooms, 7 suites, 12 efficiencies. Pool, beach, bicycles. AE, D, DC, MC, V.*

$$ 🏠 **Tropic Seas Resort Inn.** It's only a block off A1A, but it's a million-dollar location—directly on the beach and two blocks from municipal tennis courts. Built in the 1950s, units are plain but clean and comfortable, with tropical rattan furniture and ceiling fans. Managers Sandy and Larry Lynch tend to the largely repeat, family-oriented clientele. The complimentary Sunday brunch and weekly wiener roast and rum swizzle party are good opportunities to mingle with other guests. ✉ *4616 El Mar Dr., 33308,* ☎ *954/772–2555 or 800/952–9581,* FAX *954/771–5711. 16 rooms, 6 efficiencies, 7 apartments. Pool, beach. AE, D, DC, MC, V.*

$–$$ 🏠 **Blue Seas Courtyard.** Bubbly innkeeper Cristie Furth runs this one- and two-story motel with her husband, Marc, and small as it is, they keep investing their future in it. Lattice fencing and gardens of cactus and impatiens were added in front for more privacy around the brick patio and garden-set pool. Guest quarters feature kitchenettes, terracotta tiles, bright Haitian and Peruvian art, and generally Tex-Mex and Danish furnishings, whose woody textures work well together. Handmade painted shutters and indoor plants add to the look. This remains an excellent buy in a quiet resort area just a block from the beach. ✉ *4525 El Mar Dr., 33308,* ☎ *954/772–3336 or 877/225–8373,* FAX *954/772–6337. 12 units. Pool, coin laundry. MC, V.*

Outdoor Activities and Sports

Anglin's Fishing Pier (☎ 954/491–9403) is open for fishing 24 hours a day. Fishing costs $3 for adults and $2 for children up to 12, tackle rental is an additional $5 (plus $10 deposit), and bait averages $2.

Pompano Beach

⑰ *3 mi north of Lauderdale-by-the-Sea.*

As Route A1A enters this town directly north of Lauderdale-by-the-Sea, the high-rise procession begins again. Sportfishing is big in Pompano Beach, as its name implies, but there's more to beachside attractions than the popular Fisherman's Wharf. Behind a low coral-rock wall, Alsdorf Park extends north and south of the wharf along the road and beach.

Dining and Lodging

$$$ ✕ **Cafe Maxx.** New-wave epicurean dining had its South Florida start
★ here in the early 1980s, and Cafe Maxx remains popular among regional food lovers. The setting is ordinary, in a little strip of stores, but inside there's a holiday glow year-round. Chef Oliver Saucy demonstrates ritual devotion to the preparation of fine cuisine. The menu changes nightly but always showcases foods from the tropics: jumbo stone-crab claws with honey-lime mustard sauce and black-bean and banana pepper chili with Florida avocado. Appetizer favorites include duck and smoked mozzarella ravioli with brown butter, basil, and sundried tomatoes—a pure delight. Desserts also reflect a tropical theme, from praline macadamia mousse over chocolate cake with butterscotch sauce to candied ginger with pears poached in muscatel and sundried cherry ice cream. More than 200 wines are offered by the bottle, another 20 by the glass. ⌂ *2601 E. Atlantic Blvd.,* ☎ *954/782–0606. AE, D, DC, MC, V. No lunch.*

$$$–$$$$ ⌂ **Palm-Aire Spa Resort.** This 750-acre health, fitness, and stress-reduction spa offers exercise activities, personal treatments, and calorie-controlled meals. Separate men's and women's pavilions have private sunken Roman baths, Swiss showers, and some of the most experienced hands in the massage business. There are 166 spacious rooms and 18 golf villas with private terraces. All have separate dressing rooms, and some have two baths. You can have use of the spa for $96 for a half day or $220 for the whole day, including lunch, massage, facial, and fitness classes. ⌂ *2601 Palm-Aire Dr. N, 33069,* ☎ *954/972–3300 or 800/272–5624. 184 units. Restaurant, pools, hot tubs, massage, saunas, spa, steam rooms, 94 holes of golf, 37 tennis courts, aerobics, exercise room, racquetball, squash. AE, D, MC, V.*

$$$ ⌂ **Beachcomber.** This Best Western property's beach location is central to most Broward County attractions. Ocean views are everywhere, from the oversize guest room balconies to the dining rooms. Though there are also villas and penthouse suites atop the eight-story structure, standard rooms are spacious. The multilingual staff seems attentive to guest requests. ⌂ *1200 S. Ocean Blvd., 33062,* ☎ *954/941–7830 or 800/231–2423. 134 rooms, 9 villas, 4 suites. Restaurant, bar, 2 pools, beach. AE, D, MC, V.*

Outdoor Activities and Sports

FISHING

Pompano Pier (☎ 954/943–1488) extends 1,080 ft into the Atlantic. The cost is $2.65 for adults, $1.06 for children under 10; rod-and-reel rental is $10.18 (including admission and initial bait).

For drift fishing try **Fish City Pride** (⌂ Fish City Marina, 2621 N. Riverside Dr., ☎ 954/781–1211). Morning, afternoon, and evening trips cost $25 and include fishing gear. You can arrange for a saltwater charter

In case you want to see the world.

At American Express, we're here to make your journey a smooth one. So we have over 1,700 travel service locations in over 130 countries ready to help. What else would you expect from the world's largest travel agency?

do more

Travel

Call 1 800 AXP-3429 or visit
www.americanexpress.com/travel

In case you want to be welcomed there.

We're here to see that you're always welcomed at establishments everywhere. That's why millions of people carry the American Express® Card – for peace of mind, confidence, and security, around the world or just around the corner.

do more

Cards

To apply, call 1 800 THE-CARD
or visit www.americanexpress.com

In case you're running low.

We're here to help with more than 190,000 Express Cash locations around the world. In order to enroll, just call American Express at 1 800 CASH-NOW before you start your vacation.

do more® **AMERICAN EXPRESS**

Express Cash

And in case you'd rather be safe than sorry.

We're here with American Express® Travelers Cheques. They're the safe way to carry money on your vacation, because if they're ever lost or stolen you can get a refund, practically anywhere or anytime. To find the nearest place to buy Travelers Cheques, call 1 800 495-1153. Another way we help you do more.

do more

Travelers Cheques

boat through the **Hillsboro Inlet Marina** (✉ 2629 N. Riverside Dr., ☎ 954/943–8222). The 10-boat fleet offers half-day charters for $325, including gear, for up to six people.

GOLF

Crystal Lake South Course (✉ 3800 Crystal Lake Dr., ☎ 954/943–2902) has 18 holes. **Palm-Aire Country Club & Resort** (✉ 3701 Oaks Clubhouse Dr., ☎ 954/978–1737; 954/975–6244 for tee line), part of the Palm-Aire Spa Resort, has 94 holes of golf, including a course with an extra four holes.

HORSE RACING

Pompano Harness Track, Florida's only harness track, features world-class trotters and pacers during its October–August meet. The Top o' the Park restaurant overlooks the finish line. ✉ 1800 S.W. 3rd St., ☎ 954/972–2000. ✉ Grandstand free, clubhouse $2. ☉ Racing Mon., Wed., Fri., and Sat. 7:30.

ICE-SKATING

Visitors from the North who miss ice and cold can skate at the **Gold Coast Ice Arena** during morning, afternoon, or evening sessions. You can also watch the NHL Florida Panthers practice mornings during the hockey season. ✉ 4601 N. Federal Hwy., ☎ 954/943–1437. ✉ Sessions $5 ($5.50 weekend evenings), skate rental $2. ☉ Sun.–Thurs. 8:30–4 plus Tues. 8:15 PM–10 PM, Fri.–Sat. 8:15 AM–11 PM.

Shopping

Bargain hunters head to the **Festival Flea Market** (✉ 2900 W. Sample Rd.), where more than 600 vendors sell merchandise in a 400,000-square-ft building. There are also a games section for youngsters and an 18-screen cinema. The old Pompano Fashion Square has been reborn as **Pompano Square** (✉ 2001 N. Federal Hwy.) and now features a tropical motif. This comfortably sized city mall has 60 shops, three department stores, and a few places for food.

Lighthouse Point

⑱ *2 mi north of Pompano Beach.*

A big attraction here is the view across Hillsboro Inlet to **Hillsboro Light,** the brightest lighthouse in the Southeast. Mariners have used this landmark for decades. From the ocean you can see the light almost halfway to the Bahamas. Although the lighthouse is on private property and is inaccessible to the public, it's well worth a peek.

Dining

$$–$$$ ★ **✕ Cafe Arugula.** Chef Dick Cingolani draws upon the culinary traditions of warm climates from Italy to the American Southwest. The decor, too, blends southwestern with Mediterranean looks—a row of mauve-velvet booths beneath steamboat-wheel windows surrounds an entire wall of chili peppers, corn, cactus, and garlic cloves. A frequently changing menu may include succulent fresh hogfish with capers and shaved almonds over fettuccine or a free-range loin of venison with juniper–wild mushroom sauce, quesadilla, and stir-fried vegetables. ✉ 3110 N. Federal Hwy., ☎ 954/785–7732. AE, D, DC, MC, V. No lunch.

$$ ★ **✕ Cap's Place.** On an island that was once a bootlegger's haunt, this seafood restaurant is reached by launch and has served such luminaries as Winston Churchill, FDR, and John F. Kennedy. Cap was Captain Theodore Knight, born in 1871, who, with partner-in-crime Al Hasis, floated a derelict barge to the area in the 1920s. Today the rustic restaurant, built on the barge, is run by descendants of Hasis. Baked wahoo steaks are lightly glazed and meaty, the long-cut french fries

arouse gluttony, hot and flaky rolls are baked fresh several times a night, and tangy lime pie is a great finishing touch. Turn east off Federal Highway onto Northeast 24th Street (two blocks north of Pompano Square); follow the double yellow line to the launch. ⊠ *Cap's Dock, 2765 N.E. 28th Ct.,* ☎ *954/941–0418. AE, MC, V. No lunch.*

En Route   To the north, Route A1A traverses the so-called Hillsboro Mile (actually more than 2 mi), a millionaire's row of some of the most beautiful and expensive homes in Broward County. The road runs along a narrow strip of land between the Intracoastal Waterway and the ocean, with bougainvillea and oleanders edging the way and yachts docked along both banks. In winter the traffic often creeps at a snail's pace, as vacationers and retirees gawk at the views.

Deerfield Beach

⓳   *3½ mi north of Lighthouse Point.*

☃   The name **Quiet Waters Park** belies what's in store for kids here. Splash Adventure is a high-tech water-play system with swings, slides, and tunnels, among other activities. There's also cable waterskiing and boating on the park's lake. ⊠ *401 S. Powerline Rd.,* ☎ *954/360–1315.* ☞ *$1 weekends, free weekdays; Splash Adventure $2.* ☉ *Daily 8–6.*

Deerfield Island Park, an 8½-acre island that can only be reached by boat, is a paradise of coastal hammock, or tree islands. Officially designated an urban wilderness area along the Intracoastal Waterway, it contains mangrove swamp that provides critical habitat for gopher tortoises, gray foxes, raccoons, and armadillos. ⊠ *1 Deerfield Island; boat landing at Riverview Restaurant, Riverview Rd.,* ☎ *954/360–1320.* ☞ *Free.* ☉ *Boat shuttles run on the hr Wed. 10–noon and Sun. 10–3; call for special events and tours.*

Dining and Lodging

$$ ✕ **Brooks.** This is one of the city's better restaurants, thanks to a
★   French perfectionist, Bernard Perron. Meals are served in a series of rooms filled with replicas of old masters, cut glass, antiques, and tapestrylike floral wallpapers, though the shedlike dining room still feels very Florida. Fresh ingredients go into distinctly Floridian cuisine. Main courses include red snapper in papillote, broiled fillet of pompano with seasoned root vegetables, and a sweet lemongrass linguine with bok choy and julienned crisp vegetables. ⊠ *500 S. Federal Hwy.,* ☎ *954/427–9302. AE, D, MC, V.*

$ ✕ **Whale's Rib.** If you're looking for a casual, almost funky, nautical
★   setting near the beach, look no farther. For nearly 20 years the Williams family has been serving up excellent seafood and good cheer. Fish specials are offered daily, along with Whale Fries—thinly sliced potatoes that look like hot potato chips. Those with smaller appetites can choose from a good selection of salads and fish sandwiches. Other favorites are specials from the raw bar and a popular fish dip for starters. The place is crowded on weekends, and parking is limited. ⊠ *2031 N.E. 2nd St.,* ☎ *954/421–8880. AE, MC, V.*

$$–$$$$ ⊡ **Ocean Terrace Suites.** This four-story motel is in one of the quieter sections of north Broward, just south of the Palm Beach county line, across the narrow shore road from the beach. Large units—efficiencies and one- and three-bedroom apartments—all have big balconies overlooking the sea. Colors vary from shore washed to bright; pink and green pastels tint the bedrooms. The furniture is rattan, and units are clean and neat. Art is throwaway, flowers are artificial, and materials are bargain quality. Still, for size, location, and price this is a good buy. An outdoor barbecue grill is available. ⊠ *2080 E. Hillsboro Blvd., 33441,* ☎ *954/427–8400,* ℻ *954/427–0555. 30 units. Pool. AE, D, DC, MC, V.*

$$–$$$ ⊞ **Royal Flamingo Villas.** This small community of hou~~~~
built in the 1970s, reaches from the Intracoastal Wate~~~~
ocean. The roomy and comfortable one- and two-bedro~~~~ ...llas are
all condominium owned, so they're fully furnished the way owners want
them. All are so quiet that you hear only the soft click of ceiling fans
and kitchen clocks. The development is wisely set back a bit from the
beach, which is scheduled to be restored. If you don't need lavish public facilities, this is your upscale choice at a reasonable price. ⊠ *1225
Hillsboro Mile (Rte. A1A), Hillsboro Beach 33062,* ☎ *954/427–0669,
954/427–0660, or 800/241–2477,* FAX *954/427–6110. 41 villas. Pool,
putting green, shuffleboard, beach, dock, boating, coin laundry. D, MC,
V.*

$–$$ ⊞ **Carriage House Resort Motel.** This clean and tidy motel sits one block
from the ocean. Run by a French-German couple, the white, two-story
Colonial-style motel with black shutters is actually two buildings connected by a second-story sundeck. Steady improvements have been made
to the facility, including the addition of Bahama beds that feel and look
like sofas. Kitchenettes are equipped with good-quality utensils. Rooms
are self-contained and quiet and have walk-in closets and room safes.
⊠ *250 S. Ocean Blvd., 33441,* ☎ *954/427–7670,* FAX *954/428–4790.
6 rooms, 14 efficiencies, 10 apartments. Pool, shuffleboard, coin laundry. AE, MC, V.*

Outdoor Activities and Sports

FISHING

The **Cove Marina** (⊠ Hillsboro Blvd. and the Intracoastal Waterway,
☎ 954/360–9343) is home to a deep-sea charter fleet. During the winter season there are excellent runs of sailfish, kingfish, dolphinfish, and
tuna. A half-day charter costs about $325 for six people. Enter the ma-
rina through the Cove Shopping Center.

GOLF

Off Hillsboro Boulevard west of I–95, **Deer Creek Golf Club** (⊠ 2801
Country Club Blvd., ☎ 954/421–5550) has 18 holes.

SCUBA DIVING

One of the area's most popular dive boats, the 43-ft *Get Down* (⊠ Cove
Marina, Hillsboro Blvd. and the Intracoastal Waterway, ☎ 954/421–
2601) goes on morning and afternoon dives, plus evening dives on weekends. Divers can explore the marine life of nearby reefs and shipwrecks. The cost is $39 for a two-tank dive, and riders are welcome
for $18.

SOUTH BROWARD

From Hollywood's Broadwalk, a 27-ft-wide thoroughfare paralleling
2 mi of palm-fringed beach, to the western reaches of Old West–flavored Davie, this region has a personality all its own. South Broward's
roots are in early Florida settlements. Thus far it has avoided some of
the glitz and glamour of its neighbors to the north and south, and folks
here like it that way. Still, there's plenty to see and do—excellent
restaurants in every price range, world-class pari-mutuels, and a new
focus on the arts.

Hollywood

②⓪ *7 mi south of Fort Lauderdale.*

Hollywood is a city undergoing a revival. New shops, restaurants, and
art galleries are opening at a rate that rivals that of Miami's South Beach.
The city recently spiffed up its Broadwalk, a wide pedestrian walkway

along the beach, where Rollerbladers are as common as visitors from the North. Trendy sidewalk cafés have opened, vying for space with mom-and-pop T-shirt shops. Downtown, along Harrison Street, jazz clubs and still more fashionable restaurants are drawing young professionals to the scene.

In 1921 Joseph W. Young, a California real estate developer, began developing the community of Hollywood from the woody flatlands. It quickly became a major tourist magnet, home to casino gambling and everything else that made Florida hot. Reminders of the glory days of the Young era remain in places like Young Circle (the junction of U.S. 1 and Hollywood Boulevard) and the stately old homes that line east Hollywood streets.

The **Art and Culture Center of Hollywood** is a visual and performing arts center with an art reference library, outdoor sculpture garden, arts school, and museum store. It's just east of Young Circle. ⊠ *1650 Harrison St.,* ☎ *954/921–3274.* ▨ *Wed.–Sat. $3, Sun. $8 (including classical or jazz concert); donation welcome Tues.* ☉ *Tues.–Sat. 10–4, Sun. 1–4.*

With the Intracoastal Waterway to its west and the beach and ocean to the east, the 2.2-mi paved promenade known as the **Broadwalk** has been popular with pedestrians and cyclists since 1924. Expect to hear French spoken along this scenic stretch, especially during the winter; Hollywood Beach has been a favorite winter getaway for Québecois ever since Joseph Young hired French-Canadians to work here in the 1920s.

Hollywood North Beach Park is at the north end of the Broadwalk. No high-rises overpower the scene, nothing hip or chic, just a laid-back old-fashioned place for enjoying the sun, sand, and sea. ⊠ *Rte. A1A and Sheridan St.,* ☎ *954/926–2444.* ▨ *Free; parking $4 until 2, $2 after.* ☉ *Daily 8–6.*

Comprising 1,500 acres at the Intracoastal Waterway, **West Lake Park** is one of Florida's largest urban nature facilities, providing a wide range of recreational activities. You can rent a canoe, kayak, or boat with an electric motor (no fossil fuels are allowed in the park) or take the 40-minute environmental boat tour. Extensive boardwalks traverse a mangrove community, where endangered and threatened species abound. A 65-ft observation tower allows views of the entire park. More than $1 million in exhibits are on display at the **Anne Kolb Nature Center,** named after the late county commissioner who was a leading environmental advocate. A great place to take youngsters, the center's exhibit hall features 27 interactive displays, an ecology room, and a trilevel aquarium. ⊠ *1200 Sheridan St.,* ☎ *954/926–2410.* ▨ *Weekends $1, weekdays free; exhibit hall $3.* ☉ *Daily 8–6.*

At the edge of Hollywood lies **Seminole Native Village,** a reservation where you can pet a cougar, hold a baby alligator, and watch other wildlife demonstrations. The Seminole Indians also sell their arts and crafts. ⊠ *3551 N. Rte. 7,* ☎ *954/961–4519.* ▨ *Self-guided tour $5, guided tour including alligator wrestling and snake demonstrations $10.* ☉ *Daily 9–5.*

Across the street from the Seminole Native Village, **Hollywood Seminole Gaming** features high-stakes bingo, low-stakes poker, and more than 500 gaming machines. ⊠ *4150 N. Rte. 7,* ☎ *954/961–3220.* ▨ *Free.* ☉ *Daily 24 hrs.*

In addition to displaying a collection of artifacts from the Seminoles and other tribes, Joe Dan and Virginia Osceola sell contemporary Native American arts and crafts at the **Anhinga Indian Museum and Art Gallery.** It's also across the street from the Seminole Native Village, though that technically puts it over the Fort Lauderdale border. ⊠ *5791 S. Rte. 7, Fort Lauderdale,* ☎ *954/581–0416.* ⊙ *Daily 9–5.*

Dining and Lodging

$$$ ╳ **Martha's.** Guests have two choices of dining location, both providing impressive views of the Intracoastal Waterway. Martha's Tropical Grille, on the upper deck, is more informal. Martha's Supper Club, on the lower level, is dressier—tables adorned with orchid buds, fanned napery, etched-glass dividers, brass, rosewood, and an outdoor patio surrounded by a floral mural. Piano music accompanies dinner downstairs, and later a band plays for dancing, setting a supper-club mood. Both floors offer similar menus, however—chiefly Florida seafood: flaky dolphinfish in a court bouillon; shrimp dipped in a piña colada batter, rolled in coconut, and panfried with orange mustard sauce; and snapper prepared 17 ways. For dessert try sorbet and vanilla and chocolate ice cream topped with meringue and hot fudge brandy sauce. Complimentary dock space is provided for those arriving by boat. ⊠ *6024 N. Ocean Dr.,* ☎ *954/923–5444. Reservations essential. AE, D, DC, MC, V.*

$$ ╳ **Las Brisas.** There's a wonderful bistro atmosphere at this small and cozy restaurant with Mexican tiles and blue-and-white-checked tablecloths beneath paddle fans. Right next to the beach, Las Brisas offers eating inside or out, and the food is Argentine with an Italian flair. Antipasto salads are prepared for two; the roasted vegetables are crunchy and flavorful. A small pot sits on each table filled with *chimichurri* (a paste made of oregano, parsley, olive oil, salt, garlic, and crushed pepper), for spreading on steaks. Grilled or deep-fried fish are favorites, as are pork chops, chicken, and pasta entrées. Desserts include a rum cake, a flan like *mamacita* used to make, and a *dulce con leche* (a sweet milk pudding). The wine list is predominantly Argentine. ⊠ *600 N. Surf Rd.,* ☎ *954/923–1500. AE, MC, V. Closed Mon. No lunch.*

$–$$ ╳ **Revolution 2029.** Chef David Sloane and partner William Kassner have created a restaurant that pleases both the eye and the palate. Revolution 2029 takes its name from a combination of the address and its role in revolutionizing (i.e., reviving) the area. The kitchen is topflight, the young staff experienced, and the atmosphere decidedly trendy. On offer is creative Pacific Rim cuisine, including such appetizers as saffron-herb-seared tuna and jumbo lump crab cake. Entrées feature ginger-plum-seared Atlantic salmon, pasta with mesquite chicken, and bourbon-glazed beef tenderloin. ⊠ *2029 Harrison St.,* ☎ *954/920–4748. AE, MC, V. Closed Mon. No lunch weekends.*

$–$$ ╳ **Sushi Blues Cafe.** First-class Japanese food is served up in a cubicle setting that's so jammed you wonder where this hip group goes by day. Japanese chefs prepare conventional and macrobiotic-influenced dishes that range from a variety of sushi and rolls (California, tuna, and the Yozo roll, with snapper, flying-fish eggs, asparagus, and Japanese mayonnaise) to steamed veggies with tofu and steamed snapper with miso sauce. Also available are a few wines by the glass or bottle, a selection of Japanese beers, and some very un-Japanese desserts—fried banana and Swiss chocolate mousse cake. The house band, the Sushi Blues Band, performs on Friday and Saturday; guest musicians often sit in. ⊠ *1836 S. Young Circle,* ☎ *954/929–9560. No credit cards. Closed Sun. No lunch.*

$ ╳ **Istanbul.** The owners of this Turkish delight take pride in preparing everything from scratch: hummus, tabbouleh, *adana* kebab (partially grilled, chopped lamb on skewers on a bed of yogurt-soaked pita squares, oven-finished with hot butter sauce), pizza, salads, soups, and phyllo-pie fingers filled with spinach, chicken, or meat. At lunch blue-suited attorney types dine alongside beachgoers. You should also consider getting takeout. After all, how often can you lounge on the beach with a reasonably priced Turkish picnic? ⊠ *707 N. Broadwalk,* ☎ *954/ 921–1263. No credit cards.*

$ ✕ **Le Tub.** Formerly a Sunoco gas station, this place is now a quirky waterside saloon with a seeming affection for claw-foot bathtubs. Hand-painted tubs are everywhere—under ficus, sea grape, and palm trees. The eatery is highly favored by locals for affordable food: mostly shrimp, burgers, and barbecue. ⊠ *1100 N. Ocean Dr.,* ☎ *954/921– 9425. No credit cards.*

$$–$$$ ⊞ **Greenbriar Beach Club.** In a neighborhood of Hollywood Beach known for its flowered streets, this oceanfront all-suites hotel retains its 1950s style outside, but inside the rooms have been upgraded and feature full kitchens. The staff is multilingual, and the TVs even feature four Spanish and two French channels. Fronting on a 200-ft stretch of beach, the hotel bills itself as "Florida's best-kept secret," and it just could be. ⊠ *1900 S. Surf Rd., 33019,* ☎ *954/922–2606,* ℻ *954/923–0897. 47 suites. Pool, volleyball, beach, coin laundry. AE, MC, V.*

$$ ⊞ **Manta Ray Inn.** Canadians Donna and Dwayne Boucher run this
★ exemplary two-story lodging on the beach and have kept the place immaculate and the rates affordable. Dating from the 1940s, the inn offers the casual, comfortable beachfront for which vacations in Hollywood are famous. Nothing's fussy—white spaces with burgundy trim and rattan furniture—and everything's included. Kitchens are equipped with pots, pans, and mini-appliances that make housekeeping convenient. All apartments have full closets, and all except for two-bedroom units with stalls have tub-showers. Grills are available. ⊠ *1715 S. Surf Rd., 33019,* ☎ *954/921–9666,* ℻ *954/929–8220. 12 units. Beach. No credit cards.*

$–$$ ⊞ **Sea Downs.** This three-story lodging directly on the Broadwalk is a good choice for efficiency or apartment living (one-bedroom apartments can be joined to make two-bedroom units). All but two units have ocean views, and all are comfortably done in chintz, but with blinds, not drapes. Kitchens are fully equipped, and most units have tub-showers and closets. Housekeeping is provided once a week. In between, guests receive fresh towels daily and sheets on request, but they make their own beds. Sea Downs's sister property, Bougainvillea, is a few paces off the beach, so rates are slightly lower. However, Bougainvillea's guests can use the Sea Downs pool, while those at Sea Downs can enjoy Bougainvillea's gardens. ⊠ *2900 N. Surf Rd., 33019-3704,* ☎ *954/923–4968,* ℻ *954/923–8747. 5 efficiencies, 8 1-bedroom apartments. Pool. No credit cards.*

$ ⊞ **Driftwood on the Ocean.** This attractive late-'50s-era resort motel faces the beach at the secluded south end of Surf Road. The setting is what draws guests, but attention to maintenance and frequent refurbishing are what make it a value. Accommodations range from a standard hotel room to a deluxe two-bedroom, two-bath suite. Most units have a kitchen, one-bedroom apartments have a daybed, and standard rooms have a queen-size Murphy bed. All have balconies. ⊠ *2101 S. Surf Rd., 33019,* ☎ *954/923–9528,* ℻ *954/922–1062. 6 rooms, 4 suites, 39 efficiencies. Pool, shuffleboard, beach, bicycles, coin laundry. AE, MC, V.*

Outdoor Activities and Sports

BIKING

The 2-mi **Broadwalk,** which has its own bike path, is popular with cyclists.

DOG RACING

Hollywood Greyhound Track has dog-racing action during its December–May season. There is a clubhouse dining room. ⊠ *831 N. Federal Hwy., Hallandale,* ☎ *954/454–9400.* 🎟 *Grandstand $1, clubhouse $3; parking free.* ☻ *Racing Tues., Thurs., and Sat. 12:30 and 7:30; Sun.– Mon., Wed., and Fri. 7:30.*

FISHING

Sea Leg's III (⊠ 5400 N. Ocean Dr., ☎ 954/923–2109) runs drift-fishing trips from 8 to 12:30 and 1:30 to 6 and bottom-fishing trips from 7 PM to midnight. All trips cost $25 and include fishing gear.

GOLF

The **Diplomat Country Club** (⊠ 501 Diplomat Pkwy., Hallandale, ☎ 954/457–2000), with 18 holes, is south of town. The course at **Emerald Hills** (⊠ 4100 Hills Dr., ☎ 954/961–4000) has 18 holes.

HORSE RACING

Gulfstream Park Race Track is the winter home of some of the nation's top Thoroughbreds. The park greatly improved its facilities during the past few years: Admission costs have been lowered, time between races shortened, and the paddock ring elevated for better viewing by fans. The season is capped by the $500,000 Florida Derby, which always features Kentucky Derby hopefuls. Racing is held from January through mid-March. ⊠ *901 S. Federal Hwy., Hallandale,* ☎ *954/454–7000.* 🎟 *$3, including parking and program; clubhouse $5 plus $2 for reserved seat or $1.75 for grandstand.* ☻ *Racing Wed.–Mon. 1.*

Dania

㉑ *3 mi north of Hollywood, 4 mi south of Fort Lauderdale.*

This town at the south edge of Fort Lauderdale is probably best known for its antiques dealers, but there are other attractions as well.

The **Graves Museum of Archaeology & Natural History,** a little-known treasure, has the goal of becoming the "Smithsonian of the South." Its wide-ranging collections feature everything from pre-Columbian art and Greco-Roman materials to underwater artifacts from the St. Thomas harbor and a 9,000-square-ft dinosaur hall. Also on display are a 3-ton quartz crystal and dioramas on Tequesta Indian life and jaguar habitat. Monthly lectures, conferences, field trips, and a summer archaeological camp are offered. The museum bookstore is one of the best in Florida. ⊠ *481 S. Federal Hwy.,* ☎ *954/925–7770.* 🎟 *$6.* ☻ *Tues.–Sat. 10–6, Sun. 1–5.*

★ The **John U. Lloyd Beach State Recreation Area** is a pleasant plot of land with a pine-shaded beach, a jetty pier where you can fish, a marina, nature trails, and canoeing on Whiskey Creek. This is a great spot to watch cruise ships entering and departing Port Everglades, to the west across the waterway. ⊠ *6503 N. Ocean Dr.,* ☎ *954/923–2833.* 🎟 *$4 per vehicle with up to 8 people.* ☻ *Daily 8–sunset.*

The new **World Fishing Center,** which opened in 1999, is a shrine to the sport of fishing. Near the Fort Lauderdale airport, the center is the creation of the International Game Fishing Association, which spent $32 million to develop the campus at 51-acre Sportsman's Park. In addition to checking out the World Fishing Hall of Fame, a marina, and an extensive museum and research library, you can visit seven galleries with virtual-reality fishing and other interactive displays. For example, in the Catch Gallery, you can cast off via virtual reality and try to reel in a marlin, sailfish, or bass. ⊠ *I–95 and Griffin Rd., Fort Lauderdale,* ☎ *954/924–4310.* 🎟 *$9.* ☻ *Daily 10–5.*

Outdoor Activities and Sports

FISHING

The 920-ft **Dania Pier** (☎ 954/927–0640) is open around the clock. Fishing is $3 for adults (including parking), tackle rental is $6, bait is about $2, and spectators pay $1.

JAI ALAI

Dania Jai-Alai Palace has one of the fastest games on the planet, scheduled year-round. ⊠ *301 E. Dania Beach Blvd.,* ☎ *954/428–7766.* ⊠ *$1.50; reserved seats $2–$7, including parking and program.* ☉ *Games Tues. and Sat. noon and 7:15, Wed.–Fri. 7:15, Sun. 1; closed Wed. in June.*

Shopping

More than 75 **antiques** dealers line Federal Highway (U.S. 1), ½ mi south of the Fort Lauderdale airport and ½ mi north of Hollywood. Take the Stirling Road or Griffin Road East exit off I–95.

Davie

㉒ *4 mi west of Dania.*

This town's horse farms and estates are the closest thing to the Old West in South Florida. Folks in western wear ride their fine horses through downtown and order up takeout at "ride-through" windows. A weekly rodeo is Davie's most famous activity.

Gators, crocodiles, river otters, and birds of prey can be seen at **Flamingo Gardens,** as can a 23,000-square-ft walk-through aviary, a plant house, and an Everglades museum in the pioneer Wray Home. A half-hour guided tram ride winds through a citrus grove and wetlands area. ⊠ *3750 Flamingo Rd.,* ☎ *954/473–2955.* ⊠ *$10, tram ride $2.* ☉ *Daily 9:30–5:30.*

At the **Young at Art Children's Museum,** kids can work in paint, graphics, sculpture, and crafts according to themes that change three times a year. Then they take their masterpieces home with them. ⊠ *11584 Rte. 84, in the Plaza,* ☎ *954/424–0085.* ⊠ *$4.* ☉ *Mon.–Sat. 10–5, Sun. noon–5.*

Dining

$$ ✕ **Armadillo Cafe.** Eve Montella and Kevin McCarthy have created a
★ restaurant whose southwestern theme, casual decor, and award-wining food make it worth the drive from anywhere in Broward County. It has been named to best-restaurant lists in local and national publications, and visitors from around the world have feasted on its southwestern-style South Florida seafood. In addition to fish dishes, other specialties include boneless duck and marinated leg of lamb. Though some exotic dishes are prepared, everything is served in a creative and fun atmosphere. ⊠ *4630 S.W. 64th Ave.,* ☎ *954/791–5104. AE, D, DC, MC, V.*

Nightlife and the Arts

THE ARTS

Bailey Concert Hall (⊠ Central Campus of Broward Community College, 3501 S.W. Davie Rd., ☎ 954/475–6884) is a popular place for classical music concerts, dance, drama, and other performing arts activities, especially October–April.

NIGHTLIFE

Uncle Funny's Comedy Club (⊠ 9160 Rte. 84, ☎ 954/474–5653) showcases national and local comics Wednesday–Sunday at 8:30 plus Friday and Saturday at 11.

Outdoor Activities and Sports

BIKING

Bicycle enthusiasts can ride at the **Brian Piccolo Park velodrome** (✉ Sheridan St. and N.W. 101st Ave., Cooper City), south of Davie.

GOLF

Rolling Hills (✉ 3501 Rolling Hills Circle, ☎ 954/475–3010) has 18 holes.

RODEO

The local **rodeo** (✉ 6591 S.W. 45th St., ☎ 954/475–9787) is held every Wednesday night. Special national rodeos come to town some weekends.

FORT LAUDERDALE AND BROWARD COUNTY A TO Z

Arriving and Departing

By Bus

Greyhound Lines (☎ 800/231–2222) buses stop in Fort Lauderdale (✉ 515 N.E. 3rd St., ☎ 954/764–6551).

By Car

Access to Broward County from north or south is via Florida's Turnpike, I–95, U.S. 1, or U.S. 441. I–75 (Alligator Alley) connects Broward with Florida's west coast and runs parallel to Route 84 within the county.

By Plane

Fort Lauderdale–Hollywood International Airport (☎ 954/359–6100), 4 mi south of downtown Fort Lauderdale and just off U.S. 1, is one of Florida's busiest, serving more than 12 million passengers a year. A major airport expansion added 5,000 parking spaces, and new access roads are due in 2000. Scheduled airlines include **Air Canada** (☎ 800/776–3000), **Air Jamaica** (☎ 800/523–5585), **AirTran** (☎ 800/825–8538), **American** (☎ 800/433–7300), **America West** (☎ 800/235–9282), **Comair** (☎ 800/354–9822), **Continental** (☎ 800/525–0280), **Delta** (☎ 800/221–1212), **Icelandair** (☎ 954/359–2735), **Island Express** (☎ 954/359–0380), **Laker** (☎ 888/525–3724), **Midway** (☎ 800/446–4392), **Northwest** (☎ 800/225–2525), **Southwest** (☎ 800/435–9792), **TWA** (☎ 800/221–2000), **United** (☎ 800/241–6522), and **US Airways** (☎ 800/428–4322).

BETWEEN THE AIRPORT AND CENTER CITY

Broward Transit (☎ 954/357–8400) operates bus route Number 1 between the airport and its main terminal at Broward Boulevard and Northwest 1st Avenue, in the center of Fort Lauderdale. Service from the airport begins daily at 5:30 AM; the last bus from the downtown terminal to the airport leaves at 9:50 PM. The fare is $1 (50¢ for senior citizens). **Airport Express** (☎ 954/561–8886) provides limousine service to all parts of Broward County. Fares to most Fort Lauderdale beach hotels are in the $8–$10 range.

By Train

Amtrak (☎ 800/872–7245) provides daily service to the Fort Lauderdale station (✉ 200 S.W. 21st Terr., ☎ 954/463–8251) as well as other Broward County stops at Hollywood and Deerfield Beach.

Tri-Rail (☎ 954/728–8445) operates train service daily 5 AM–11 PM (more limited on weekends) through Broward, Miami-Dade, and Palm Beach counties. There are six Broward stations west of I–95: Hillsboro Boulevard in Deerfield Beach, Cypress Creek, Fort Lauderdale, Fort Lauderdale Airport, Sheridan Street in Hollywood, and Hollywood Boulevard.

Getting Around

By Boat

Water Taxi (☎ 954/467–6677) provides service along the Intracoastal Waterway in Fort Lauderdale between the 17th Street Causeway and Commercial Boulevard 10 AM–1 AM. Boats stop at more than 30 restaurants, hotels, shops, and nightclubs; the fare is $7 one-way, $13 round-trip, and $15 for an all-day pass. Children under 12 accompanied by an adult pay half fare.

By Bus

Broward County Mass Transit (☎ 954/357–8400) bus service covers the entire county. The fare is $1 plus 15¢ for a transfer. Service on all beach routes starts before 6 AM and continues past 10 PM except on Sunday. Call for route information. Special seven-day tourist passes, which cost $9, are good for unlimited use on all county buses. These are available at some hotels, at Broward County libraries, and at the main bus terminal (✉ Broward Blvd. at N.W. 1st Ave., Fort Lauderdale).

Fort Lauderdale has replaced its motorized trolley service with expanded, free **TMAX** (☎ 954/761–3543) bus service. Routes cover both the downtown loop and the beach area, with the Las Olas/Beach Line connecting major tourist sites in both places. Buses run every 30 minutes, weekdays 11:15–3:15 and Friday and Saturday nights 7–2.

By Car

Except during rush hour, Broward County is a fairly easy place in which to drive. East–west I–595 runs from westernmost Broward County and links I–75 with I–95 and U.S. 1, providing handy access to the airport. The scenic but slow Route A1A generally parallels the beach. Another road less traveled is the Sawgrass Expressway (Route 869), a toll road that's a handy link to Sawgrass Mills shopping and the new ice-hockey arena, both in Sunrise.

By Taxi

It's difficult to hail a cab on the street. Sometimes you can pick one up at a major hotel. Otherwise, phone ahead. Fares are not cheap; meters run at a rate of $2.45 for the first mile and $1.75 for each additional mile; waiting time is 25¢ per minute. The major company serving the area is **Yellow Cab** (☎ 954/565–5400).

Contacts and Resources

Car Rentals

Agencies in the airport include **Avis** (☎ 954/359–3255), **Budget** (☎ 954/359–4700), **Dollar** (☎ 954/359–7800), **Hertz** (☎ 954/359–5281), and **National** (☎ 954/359–8303). In addition, **Alamo** (☎ 954/525–4713) and **Enterprise** (☎ 954/760–9888) offer shuttle service to nearby rental centers.

Emergencies

Dial **911** for police or ambulance.

Florida Poison Information Center (☎ 800/282–3171).

HOSPITALS

The following hospitals have a 24-hour emergency room: **Broward General Medical Center** (✉ 1600 S. Andrews Ave., Fort Lauderdale, ☎ 954/355–4400; 954/355–4888 physician referral), **Columbia Plantation**

General Hospital (⊠ 401 N.W. 42nd Ave., Plantation, ☎ 954/797–6470; 954/587–5010 physician referral), **Coral Springs Medical Center** (⊠ 3999 Coral Hills Dr., Coral Springs, ☎ 954/344–3000; 954/355–4888 physician referral), **Florida Medical Center** (⊠ 5000 W. Oakland Park Blvd., Fort Lauderdale, ☎ 954/735–6000; 954/730–2700 physician referral), **Hollywood Medical Center** (⊠ 3600 Washington St., Hollywood, ☎ 954/966–4500; 800/237–8701 physician referral), **Holy Cross Hospital** (⊠ 4725 N. Federal Hwy., Fort Lauderdale, ☎ 954/771–8000; 954/771–9082 physician referral), **Imperial Point Medical Center** (⊠ 6401 N. Federal Hwy., Fort Lauderdale, ☎ 954/776–8500; 954/355–4888 physician referral), and **North Broward Medical Center** (⊠ 201 E. Sample Rd., Pompano Beach, ☎ 954/786–6400; 954/355–4888 physician referral).

LATE-NIGHT PHARMACIES

The following are open 24 hours: **Eckerd Drug** (⊠ 1385 S.E. 17th St., Fort Lauderdale, ☎ 954/525–8173; ⊠ 1701 E. Commercial Blvd., Fort Lauderdale, ☎ 954/771–0660; ⊠ 154 University Dr., Pembroke Pines, ☎ 954/432–5510) and **Walgreens** (⊠ 2855 Stirling Rd., Fort Lauderdale, ☎ 954/981–1104; ⊠ 5001 N. Dixie Hwy., Oakland Park, ☎ 954/772–4206; ⊠ 289 S. Federal Hwy., Deerfield Beach, ☎ 954/481–2993).

Guided Tours

BOAT TOURS

Carrie B. (⊠ Riverwalk at S.E. 5th Ave., Fort Lauderdale, ☎ 954/768–9920), a 300-passenger day cruiser, gives 90-minute tours up the New River and Intracoastal Waterway. Cruises depart at 11, 1, and 3 each day and cost $10.50.

Jungle Queen III and IV (⊠ Radisson Bahia Mar Beach Resort, 801 Seabreeze Blvd., Fort Lauderdale, ☎ 954/462–5596) are 175-passenger and 527-passenger tour boats that take day and night cruises up the New River through the heart of Fort Lauderdale. The sightseeing cruises at 10 and 2 cost $11.50, while the evening dinner cruise costs $24.50. You can also take a daylong trip to Miami's Bayside Marketplace ($14.95), on Biscayne Bay, for shopping and sightseeing.

Patriot (⊠ Cove Shopping Center, Hillsboro Blvd. at Intracoastal Waterway, Deerfield Beach, ☎ 954/428–4026) offers leisurely narrated tours along the Intracoastal Waterway. There are two options: cruise only ($9.50), which departs at 12:30, and a cruise/meal combination ($28.50), which leaves at 10 and features lunch at the dockside Charley's Crab restaurant.

Professional Diving Charters (⊠ Radisson Bahia Mar Beach Resort, 801 Seabreeze Blvd., Fort Lauderdale, ☎ 954/761–3413) operates the 60-ft glass-bottom boat *Pro Diver II*. On Tuesday through Saturday mornings and Sunday afternoon, two-hour sightseeing trips take in offshore reefs, and snorkeling can be arranged.

ECOTOURS

National Audubon Society Education Dept. (⊠ 444 Brickell Ave., Suite 850, Miami 33131, ☎ 305/371–6399 or 800/498–8129), a not-for-profit organization, conducts dry-land field trips throughout South Florida and one-day, overnight, and longer boat tours as part of its program. Call in advance for availability.

WALKING TOURS

Cosponsored by the Fort Lauderdale Historical Society, **Walking Tours** (⊠ 219 S.W. 2nd Ave., Fort Lauderdale, ☎ 954/463–4431) traces the New River by foot during the winter and spring.

Visitor Information

Chamber of Commerce of Greater Fort Lauderdale (⊠ 512 N.E. 3rd Ave., Fort Lauderdale 33301, ☎ 954/462–6000). **Davie/Cooper City Chamber of Commerce** (⊠ 4185 S.W. 64th Ave., Davie 33314, ☎ 954/581–0790). **Greater Deerfield Beach Chamber of Commerce** (⊠ 1601 E. Hillsboro Blvd., Deerfield Beach 33441, ☎ 954/427–1050). **Greater Fort Lauderdale Convention & Visitors Bureau** (⊠ 1850 Eller Dr., Suite 303, Fort Lauderdale 33301, ☎ 954/765–4466). **Hollywood Chamber of Commerce** (⊠ 330 N. Federal Hwy., Hollywood 33019, ☎ 954/923–4000). **Lauderdale-by-the-Sea Chamber of Commerce** (⊠ 4201 N. Ocean Dr., Lauderdale-by-the-Sea 33308, ☎ 954/776–1000). **Pompano Beach Chamber of Commerce** (⊠ 2200 E. Atlantic Blvd., Pompano Beach 33062, ☎ 954/941–2940).

5 PALM BEACH AND THE TREASURE COAST

Long stretches of golden beaches are the unifying theme along this part of the Florida coast. The southern end is anchored by the sophisticated beach towns of Boca Raton and Delray Beach. Just north is wealthy and glitzy Palm Beach, internationally known for power shopping and pricey dining. Then comes the Treasure Coast, a collection of quaint, rustic, and uncrowded beach towns and peaceful nature preserves.

Updated by
Pamela
Acheson

THIS SECTION OF ATLANTIC COAST defies categorization. Though it's easy to affix labels—the stretch from Palm Beach to Boca Raton is considered the northern reaches of the Gold Coast (which in its entirety extends all the way to Miami), while north of Palm Beach is called the Treasure Coast—the individual communities along this section of the Florida coastline all have their own personalities. Here you'll find the center-stage glitziness of Palm Beach and the low-key quiet of Hutchinson Island. The unifying attraction is compelling—golden beaches bordered by luxuriant palms. The arts also flourish here. In town after town you will find a profusion of museums, galleries, theaters, and groups committed to historic preservation.

The focus of the region is indisputably Palm Beach. Although tourists may go to Delray Beach or Jupiter Island or scores of other towns to catch some rays and feel sand between their toes, most stop in Palm Beach for a completely different pastime: gawking. The gold on this stretch of coast is the kind you put in a vault, and for a century now the island town has been a hotbed of conspicuous consumption. Palm Beach is the richest city in Florida and would easily compete for honors with places like Monaco and Malibu as the most affluent community in the world. It has long been the winter address for families with names such as Rockefeller, Vanderbilt, Kennedy, and Trump.

It all started with Henry Morrison Flagler, cofounder of Standard Oil, who, in addition to bringing the railroad to Florida in the 1890s, brought his own view of civilization. The poor and middle-class fishermen and laborers who inhabited the place in the pre-Flagler era were moved a mile west or so to West Palm Beach. Still a proletarian cousin, West Palm is home to those who serve Flagler's successors on the island.

The town of Palm Beach represents only 1% of the land area in Palm Beach County, however. The rest is given over to sprawling West Palm Beach, classic Florida beach towns, malls, and to the west, citrus farms, the Arthur R. Marshall–Loxahatchee National Wildlife Refuge, and Lake Okeechobee, the largest lake in Florida and one of the country's hot spots for bass-fishing devotees.

Also worth exploring is the Treasure Coast, which encompasses the northernmost part of Palm Beach County plus Martin, St. Lucie, and Indian River counties. Although late to develop, the Treasure Coast now has its share of malls and beachfront condominiums, and yet much of its shoreline is laid-back and peaceful. Inland is largely devoted to citrus and sugar production and cattle ranching in rangelands of pine and palmetto scrub.

Along the coast the broad tidal lagoon called the Indian River separates the barrier islands from the mainland. In addition to sheltering boaters on the Intracoastal Waterway and playing nursery for many saltwater game fish, it's a natural radiator, keeping frost away from the tender orange and grapefruit trees that grow near its banks. Sea turtles come ashore at night from late April to September to lay their eggs on the beaches.

Pleasures and Pastimes

Beaches

Half the towns in the area include the word *beach* in their name, and for good reason. Here are miles of golden strands—some relatively remote and uncrowded, some buzzing with activity, and all blessed with the kind of blue-green waters you just won't find farther north. Among the least crowded are those at Hobe Sound National Wildlife Refuge and Fort Pierce Inlet State Recreation Area. Boca Raton's three beaches and Delray Beach's broad stretch of sand are among the most popular.

Dining

Not surprisingly, numerous elegant establishments offer Continental and contemporary cuisine that stacks up well among foodies, but the area also has many good, casual waterfront watering holes that serve up a mean fried or blackened grouper. Just an hour west, on Lake Okeechobee, you can dine on panfried catfish a few hundred yards from where it was caught. Most restaurants have early bird menus, a Florida hallmark, which usually offer most or all dinner entrées at a reduced price if ordered during certain hours.

Fishing

Within a 50-mi radius of Palm Beach, you'll find virtually every form of fishing except, of course, ice fishing. If it involves a hook and a line, you can do it here—year-round. Charter a boat for deep-sea fishing out of towns from Boca Raton to Sebastian Inlet. West of Vero Beach, there's tremendous marsh fishing for catfish, bass, and perch. Lake Okeechobee is one of the world's bass-fishing capitals.

Golf

Palm Beach County is to golf what Saudi Arabia is to oil. For openers, there's the Professional Golfing Association (PGA) headquarters at the PGA National Resort & Spa in Palm Beach Gardens (a mere five golf courses). In all, there are approximately 150 public, private, and semiprivate golf courses in Palm Beach County. A Golf-A-Round program, in which more than 100 hotels participate, lets you play at one of 10 courses each day, with no greens fees.

Shopping

Some of the most expensive stores in the United States cluster on Worth Avenue, which is comparable to Rodeo Drive in Beverly Hills as an upscale shopper's nirvana. But there's also plenty of middle-American shopping nearby, including the likes of the Palm Beach Mall and the Manufacturers Outlet Center. You can browse in art galleries and antiques shops in Vero Beach, Delray Beach, and Boca Raton's Mizner Park.

Exploring Palm Beach and the Treasure Coast

The center of most any visit to the area is Palm Beach proper (and it certainly is!). Not only is it within an hour's drive of most of the region, but its Gatsby-era architecture, stunning mansions, and highbrow shopping make it unlike any other place in Florida. From there you can head in any of three directions: south along the Gold Coast toward Boca Raton, back to the mainland and north to the barrier-island treasures of the Treasure Coast, or west for some inland delights.

Great Itineraries

Tucked into an island 12 mi long and about ¼ mi wide, Palm Beach is easy to cover thoroughly in just a day or two. If you have several days, you can take in a lot of varied sights, exploring everything from galleries to subtropical wildlife preserves, and with a week you'll easily be able to see the whole area. Of course you could just do what a lot of visitors prefer—laze around soaking up the rays and the atmosphere.

Numbers in the text correspond to numbers in the margin and on the Gold Coast and Treasure Coast and the Palm Beach and West Palm Beach maps.

IF YOU HAVE 3 DAYS

With a short amount of time, make ⊞ **Palm Beach** ①–⑪ your base. On the first day start in the middle of downtown, **Worth Avenue** ⑦, to do some window-shopping and gallery browsing. After you've refreshed yourself with a *très* chic bistro lunch, head for that other must-see on even the shortest itinerary: the **Henry Morrison Flagler Museum** ②. Your second day is for the beach; two good options are Lantana Public Beach, which has great food concessions, and Oceanfront Park, in **Boynton Beach** ㉔. Spend the better part of your last day exploring attractions you wouldn't expect to find in South Florida, such as the Morikami Museum and Japanese Gardens in nearby **Delray Beach** ㉖. Trite as it may sound, it's like a one-day visit to Japan.

IF YOU HAVE 5 DAYS

With five days you can be more contemplative at the galleries and museums, more leisurely at the beaches, and have time for more serendipitous exploring. Stay in ⊞ **Palm Beach** ①–⑪ for two nights. The first day visit the **Henry Morrison Flagler Museum** ② and the luxury hotel known as **The Breakers** ④, another Flagler legacy. Then head to **Worth Avenue** ⑦ for a leisurely lunch and an afternoon of window-shopping. On the second day drive over to **West Palm Beach** ⑫–㉑ and the **Norton Museum of Art** ⑬, which has an extensive collection of 19th-century French Impressionists. On day three, choose between making an overnight visit to ⊞ **Lake Okeechobee,** the bass-fishing capital of the world, and staying in Palm Beach another night and driving a half hour to explore the Arthur R. Marshall–Loxahatchee National Wildlife Refuge. Head south to ⊞ **Boca Raton** ㉗ on the fourth day, and check into a beachfront hotel before spending the rest of the afternoon wandering through Mizner Park's shops. On your fifth day meander through the Boca Raton Museum of Art in the morning and get some sun at South Beach Park after lunch.

IF YOU HAVE 7 DAYS

With an entire week you can see the Gold and Treasure coasts thoroughly, with time left to fit in such recreational pursuits as taking sailboard or croquet lessons, catching a polo match, or going deep-sea fishing or jet skiing. Stay two nights in ⊞ **Palm Beach** ①–⑪, spending your first day taking in its best sights, mentioned above. On day two, rent a bicycle and follow the 10-mi path along Lake Worth, providing a great look at the backyards of many of Palm Beach's big mansions. Drive north on day three, going first to the mainland and then across Jerry Thomas Bridge to Singer Island and John D. MacArthur Beach State Park. Spend the third night farther north, on ⊞ **Hutchinson Island** �33, and relax the next morning on the beach in front of your hotel. On your way back south, explore **Stuart** ㉜ and its tiny but interesting historic downtown area, and pause at the Arthur R. Marshall–Loxahatchee National Wildlife Refuge before ending up in ⊞ **Boca Raton** ㉗, for three nights at a beachfront hotel. Split day five between shopping at Mizner Park and beaching it at South Beach Park. Day six is for cultural attractions: the Boca Raton Museum of Art followed by the galleries and interesting Japanese museum in **Delray Beach** ㉖. If you have time on your last day, take in one of Boca Raton's other two beaches, Spanish River and Red Reef parks.

When to Tour Palm Beach and the Treasure Coast

The weather is optimum November–May, but the trade-off is that facilities are more crowded and prices somewhat higher. In summer you'll need a tolerance for heat and humidity if you want to spend time outside; also watch for frequent afternoon downpours. If you're set on watching the sea turtles come ashore to nest, make sure to visit between mid-May and early August, which is when most of the turtles lay their eggs, and remember that nesting occurs at night. No matter when you visit, bring insect repellent if you plan outdoor outings.

PALM BEACH

78 mi north of Miami.

Setting the tone in this incredibly wealthy town is the ornate architecture of developer Addison Mizner, who began building homes, stores, and public buildings here in the 1920s and whose Moorish-Gothic style has influenced virtually all the landmarks of the community. Thanks to Mizner and those influenced by him, Palm Beach looks like a kind of neo-Camelot, the perfect backdrop for a playground of the rich and famous.

Exploring Palm Beach

You can get a taste of what this town is all about when you squeeze into a parking place on Worth Avenue, among the Mercedes and Bentleys, and head to its boutiques to rub Versace-covered shoulders with shoppers whose credit card limits likely exceed the gross national product of Liechtenstein. Away from downtown, along County Road and Ocean Boulevard (the shore road, also designated as Route A1A), are Palm Beach's other defining landmarks: mansions. In some parts they're fronted by thick 20-ft hedgerows and topped by the seemingly de rigueur barrel-tile roofs. The low wall that separates the dune-top shore road from the sea hides a badly eroded beach in many places. Here and there, where the strand deepens a bit, homes are built directly on the beach.

A Good Tour

Start on the north end of the island with a quick look at the sandstone and limestone minicanyon that is the **Canyon of Palm Beach** ①, on Lake Way Road. Drive south, across Royal Poinciana Way, to the **Henry Morrison Flagler Museum** ②, in a 73-room palace that was once Flagler's home. From here backtrack to Royal Poinciana Way, turn right, and follow the road until it ends at North County Road and the Spanish-style **Palm Beach Post Office** ③. Here County Road changes from north to south designations. Take it southbound and look for the long, stately driveway on the left that leads to **The Breakers** ④, a famous hotel built in the style of an Italian Renaissance palace. Continue south on South County Road about ¼ mi farther to **Bethesda-by-the-Sea** ⑤, a Spanish Gothic Episcopal church. Keep driving south on South County Road until you reach Royal Palm Way; turn right, then right again on Cocoanut Row. In just a few blocks you'll see the gardens of the **Society of the Four Arts** ⑥.

Head south on Cocoanut Row until you reach famed **Worth Avenue** ⑦, where you can park and walk around—that is, if the prices in the art galleries and designer shops haven't knocked your socks off. After taking in the sights, drive south on South County Road for a peek at some magnificent estates, including **El Solano** ⑧, built by Addison Mizner, and **Mar-A-Lago** ⑨, now owned by Donald Trump. At this point you might want to get out of the car for some sun and fresh air, so continue south on South County Road until you reach **Phipps Ocean**

Park ⑩ and its stretch of sandy beach, or head back toward town along South Ocean Boulevard to the popular **Mid-Town Beach** ⑪.

You'll need half a day minimum to see these sights. A few of the destinations are closed Sunday or Monday, so be sure to do your sightseeing during daytime business hours. In the winter, traffic can be very heavy and usually gets worse as the day wears on. Consider doing your exploring in the morning, when sights are less crowded and roads are less congested.

Sights to See

❺ **Bethesda-by-the-Sea.** This Spanish Gothic Episcopal church was built in 1927 by the first Protestant congregation in southeast Florida. Next to it are the formal, ornamental **Cluett Memorial Gardens.** ✉ *141 S. County Rd.,* ☎ *561/655–4554.* ☉ *Church and gardens daily 8–5; services Sept.–May, Sun. 8, 9, and 11; June–Aug., Sun. 8 and 10; call for weekday schedule.*

★ ❹ **The Breakers.** Originally built by Henry Flagler in 1895 and rebuilt by his descendants after a fire in 1925, this luxury hotel was one of the starting points of Florida tourism. It resembles an ornate Italian Renaissance palace and was renovated to the tune of $150 million not long ago. Walk into the lobby and take a look at the painted arched ceilings hung with crystal chandeliers, and peek into the ornate Florentine Dining Room with its 15th-century Flemish tapestries. ✉ *1 S. County Rd.,* ☎ *561/655–6611.*

❶ **Canyon of Palm Beach.** A road cut about 25 ft deep through a ridge of reddish-brown sandstone and oolite limestone gives you a brief feeling of being in the desert Southwest. ✉ *Lake Way Rd.*

❽ **El Solano.** Perhaps no Palm Beach mansion represents the town's ongoing generations of flashbulb fame better than this one. The Spanish-style home was built by Addison Mizner as his personal residence in 1925. Mizner then sold it to Harold Vanderbilt, and the property made the rounds of socialites, photo shoots, and expansions until it was bought by John Lennon and Yoko Ono 10 months before Lennon's death. Now owned by a banking executive, El Solano is not open to the public. ✉ *721 S. County Rd.*

★ ❷ **Henry Morrison Flagler Museum.** The opulence of Florida's Gilded Age is still apparent at Whitehall, the palatial 73-room mansion Henry Flagler had built in 1901 for his third wife, Mary Lily Kenan, and that is now home to a museum. Then-famous architects John Carrère and Thomas Hastings were instructed to spare no expense in creating the finest home they could imagine. They did as they were told, and Whitehall rivals some of the fine palaces of Europe. In 1960 Flagler's granddaughter, Jean Flagler Matthews, bought the building and made it a museum. On display are many of the original furnishings, an art collection, a 1,200-pipe organ, and exhibits on the history of the Florida East Coast Railway. Flagler's personal railroad car, the *Rambler,* is parked behind the building. A tour by well-informed guides takes about an hour. ✉ *1 Whitehall Way,* ☎ *561/655–2833.* 🎫 *$7.* ☉ *Tues.–Sat. 10–5, Sun. noon–5.*

❾ **Mar-A-Lago.** Still one of the grandest of homes along Ocean Boulevard, the former estate of breakfast-food heiress Marjorie Meriweather Post has Italianate towers silhouetted against the sky. It's currently owned by real estate magnate Donald Trump, who first turned it into a membership club and is continuing with plans (despite local opposition) to

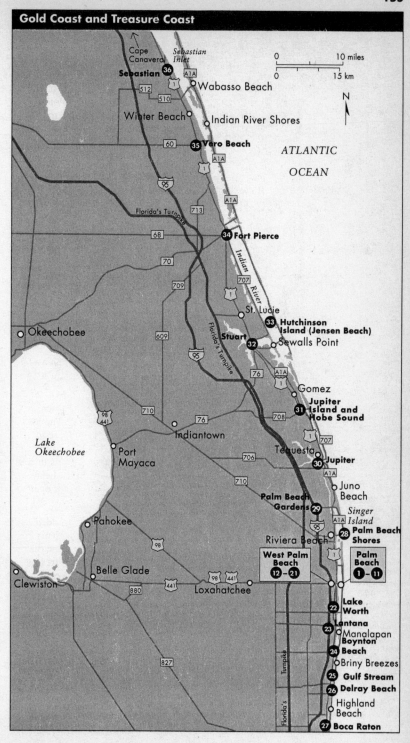

156

Palm Beach and West Palm Beach

Ann Norton Sculpture Gardens, **14**

Armory Arts Center, **15**

Bethesda-by-the-Sea, **5**

The Breakers, **4**

Canyon of Palm Beach, **1**

Dreher Park Zoo, **16**

El Solano, **8**

Henry Morrison Flagler Museum, **2**

Lion Country Safari, **20**

Mar-A-Lago, **9**

Mid-Town Beach, **11**

Mounts Horticultural Learning Center, **21**

Norton Museum of Art, **13**

Okeeheelee Nature Center, **19**

Old Northwood Historic District, **12**

Palm Beach Post Office, **3**

Phipps Ocean Park, **10**

Pine Jog Environmental Education Center, **18**

Society of the Four Arts, **6**

South Florida Science Museum, Planetarium, and Aquarium, **17**

Worth Avenue, **7**

subdivide the property, which curves for ⅓ mi along the road. ⊠ *1100 S. Ocean Blvd.*

⑪ Mid-Town Beach. This small beach directly east of Worth Avenue is especially popular because it's so close to town. But be warned: The only parking meters along Ocean Boulevard—ergo, the only convenient public beach access—are found between Worth Avenue and Royal Palm Way. ⊠ *400 S. Ocean Blvd.,* ☎ *no phone.* ⊟ *Parking 25¢ for 15 mins.* ☉ *Daily 8–8.*

❸ Palm Beach Post Office. Spanish-style architecture defines the exterior, while inside murals depict Seminole Indians in the Everglades and stately royal and coconut palms. ⊠ *95 N. County Rd.,* ☎ *561/832–1867.*

⑩ Phipps Ocean Park. Besides the ubiquitous beautiful beach, some picnic tables, and grills, this park contains a Palm Beach County landmark in the **Little Red Schoolhouse.** Dating from 1886, it was the first schoolhouse in what was then Dade County and is open Monday–Saturday 8–8. ⊠ *2145 S. Ocean Blvd.,* ☎ *no phone.* ⊟ *Parking 25¢ for 20 mins.*

❻ Society of the Four Arts. In addition to presenting cultural events, this privately endowed arts and educational institution incorporates an exhibition hall, library, 13 distinct gardens, and the Philip Hulitar Sculpture Garden. ⊠ *Four Arts Plaza,* ☎ *561/655–7226.* ⊟ *$3.* ☉ *Galleries Dec.–mid-Apr., Mon.–Sat. 10–5, Sun. 2–5; library, children's library, and gardens Nov.–May, weekdays 10–5, Sat. 9–1.*

★ ❼ Worth Avenue. This ¼-mi-long street is synonymous with posh, pricey shopping. A stroll amid the Moorish architecture of its scores of top-drawer shops—Cartier, Charles Jourdan, and Giorgio Armani, to name a few—gives you a taste of what the good life must be like. ⊠ *Between Cocoanut Row and S. Ocean Blvd.*

Dining and Lodging

$$$–$$$$
★ ✕ **Café L'Europe.** This is one of the most popular and elegant restaurants in Palm Beach. Sumptuous oak paneling, dim lighting, and elaborate flower bouquets set the mood. Ladies-who-lunch can enjoy spa cuisine, whereas evening guests dine expensively on specialty pastas such as *orecchiette* with broccoli rapini, Italian sausage, tomato, and ricotta; seafood dishes like sautéed pompano with herbal mustard crust; or a traditional Wiener schnitzel with spinach spaetzle and red cabbage. Veal chops and steaks are on the menu, too. Apple pancake with lingonberries is the signature dessert, and a caviar bar has a wide assortment of the delicacy, with prices to match. ⊠ *331 S. County Rd.,* ☎ *561/655–4020. Reservations essential. Jacket required. AE, DC, MC, V. No lunch Sun.–Mon.*

$$$–$$$$
★ ✕ **Janeiro.** Versace-designed Rosenthal china and Riedel crystal on black-on-black tablecloths provide the setting for a spectacularly elegant contemporary French dining experience. Wild mushrooms sautéed with garlic, scallopini of goose liver with shredded turnips and port wine, and baked goat cheese with tomatoes in a pastry shell are some of the appetizers. Entrées, brought to the table under silver domes, include Mediterranean bouillabaisse, lemon sole fillets with tomato and black squid and spinach lasagna, boneless rack of lamb stuffed with spinach and wild mushrooms wrapped in puff pastry, and a beef fillet with green peppercorn sauce. Save room for the chocolate soufflé dessert. It's topped with edible 24-carat gold leaf! ⊠ *191 Bradley Pl.,* ☎ *561/659–5223. Reservations essential. Jacket required. AE, DC, MC, V. No lunch.*

$$$ ✕ **Bice Ristorante.** This dining establishment is so thoroughly Italian that it's easy to be disappointed when the parking attendant speaks to you in English. Brilliant flower arrangements and lots of brass accent a dark beige-and-yellow color scheme. Aromas of basil, chives, and oregano fill the air as waiters bring out the divine home-baked focaccia accompanying such house favorites as *Robespierre alla moda della Bice* (sliced steak topped with arugula salad) and *costoletta di vitello impanata alla milanese* (breaded veal cutlet with a tomato salad). The name is short for Beatrice, mother of Roberto Ruggeri, who founded the original in Milan in 1926 and has opened branches here and in other smart places since then. ✉ 313¼ *Worth Ave.*, ☎ *561/835–1600. Jacket required. AE, DC, MC, V.*

$$–$$$$ ✕ **Amici.** Night after night a steady stream of six-figure automobiles
★ pulls into the valet parking spot of this trendy eatery. Inside, the lighting is dim, and tables are close together but never empty. The northern Italian menu features such house specialties as antipasti of cold marinated and grilled vegetables, rigatoni with spicy tomato sauce and roasted eggplant, potato gnocchi with grilled chicken and roasted peppers, grilled veal chops, risottos, and a long list of pizzas cooked in the wood-burning oven. There are nightly pasta and fresh-fish specials as well. If you want to avoid the crowds, stop by for a late lunch. ✉ *228 S. County Rd.*, ☎ *561/832–0201. Reservations essential. AE, D, DC, MC, V. No lunch Sun.*

$$–$$$$ ✕ **Chuck & Harold's.** Ivana Trump, Larry Holmes, Brooke Shields, and Michael Bolton are among the celebrities who have eaten at this combination power-lunch bar, sidewalk café, and jazz–big band garden, which is popular day and night, as well as for breakfast. Locals who want to be part of the scenery and tourists hot to people-watch catch a seat and linger in the outdoor café, next to pots of red and white begonias mounted on the sidewalk rail. Specialties include conch chowder, terrific hamburgers, an onion-crunchy gazpacho, grilled steaks, and tangy key lime pie. A big blackboard lists daily specials and celebrity birthdays. ✉ *207 Royal Poinciana Way*, ☎ *561/659–1440. AE, DC, MC, V.*

$$–$$$ ✕ **Ta-boó.** Dressed in gorgeous pinks, greens, and florals, the spaces
★ of this Worth Avenue landmark are divided into discreet salons: One resembles a courtyard, another an elegant living room with a fireplace, and a third a skylighted gazebo. The Tiki Tiki bar makes an elegant salon for the neighborhood crowd. Appetizers range from a very proletarian nachos grande with chili to Beluga caviar; dinners include chicken and arugula from the grill, prime rib, steaks, frogs' legs, and main course salads. White pizza with goat and mozzarella cheeses, pesto, and sweet roasted red peppers is a favorite. Drop in late at night during the season, and you're bound to spot a famous face or two. ✉ *221 Worth Ave.*, ☎ *561/835–3500. AE, MC, V.*

$$ ✕ **Aquaterra.** Chef Charlie Palmer, of New York City's famed Aureole, brings his culinary talents south to this popular 150-seat eatery. Decor is artistic but spare and the atmosphere more electric than romantic, but the cuisine, billed as progressive American, is definitely star quality. Choices abound. There's a long list of hors d'oeuvres, almost as many side dishes, and a dozen entrées from land and sea (Aquaterra—get it?), such as fresh Florida grouper, large gulf shrimp, or filet mignon roasted, grilled, or sautéed. ✉ *230 Sunrise Ave.*, ☎ *561/366–9693. AE, MC, V. Closed Mon. No lunch.*

$ ✕ **TooJay's.** New York deli food served in a bright California-style setting—what could be more Florida? The menu at this spot, one of nine TooJay's in the Sunshine State, includes matzo ball soup, corned beef on rye, and a killer cake made with five kinds of chocolate and topped with whipped cream. A salami-on-rye sandwich layered with onions,

Muenster cheese, coleslaw, and Russian dressing is a house favorite. On the High Holidays look for carrot tzimmes (a sweet vegetable compote), brisket, and roast chicken. Wisecracking waitresses keep the pace fast. ⊠ *313 Royal Poinciana Plaza,* ☎ *561/659–7232. AE, DC, MC, V. Beer and wine only.*

$$$$ 🏨 **Brazilian Court.** Spread out over half a block, the yellow-stucco Span-
★ ish-style facade with a red-tile roof reminds you of this hotel's Roar-
ing '20s origins. Rooms and spacious suites are decorated in soft, muted tones, and original art hangs on the walls. Remodeled bathrooms are marble and completely modernized. The closets, however, are still big enough for people who once brought trunks for the entire season (some still do). Outside, stone fountains and private courtyards (one with a wishing well) offer peaceful oases. Not only are pets welcome, there's a pet room-service menu, with items like Chancellor Chow and Chicken Meow Mein. ⊠ *301 Australian Ave., 33480,* ☎ *561/655–7740; 800/552–0335; 800/228–6852 in Canada;* FAX *561/655–0801. 63 rooms, 40 suites. Restaurant, bar, pool, beauty salon, exercise room, library. AE, D, DC, MC, V.*

$$$$ 🏨 **The Breakers.** Dating from 1926 and enlarged in 1969, this opu-
★ lent seven-story Italian Renaissance–style resort sprawls over 140 splendidly manicured acres. Cupids frolic in the Florentine fountain at the main entrance, while majestic ceiling vaults and frescoes grace the lobby and the long hallways that lead to restaurants and ballrooms. A recent $100 million renovation included the construction of a fab-
ulous spa and beach club plus a complete modernization of the rooms and bathrooms. Though the resort's elegance has been enhanced, a new relaxed atmosphere has replaced the old-world formality that pre-
vailed for three-quarters of a century. For example, men are no longer *required* to wear jackets and ties everywhere after 7 PM. ⊠ *1 S. County Rd., 33480,* ☎ *561/655–6611 or 800/833–3141,* FAX *561/659–8403. 572 rooms, 48 suites. 5 restaurants, 2 bars, 5 pools, saunas, spa, 2 18-hole golf courses, putting green, 14 tennis courts, croquet, health club, jogging, shuffleboard, beach, boating, children's programs. AE, D, DC, MC, V.*

$$$$ 🏨 **The Chesterfield.** Just two blocks north of famous Worth Avenue,
★ you'll find this four-story, white stucco, European-style hotel. Inviting rooms are on the small side but are individually and richly decorated with print bedspreads and draperies, plush upholstered chairs, an-
tique desks, paintings, and marble bathrooms. Service is exceptional. Settle into a leather couch in front of the cozy library's fireplace with the latest newspapers from around the world or with a book selected from the floor-to-ceiling shelves. A quiet courtyard surrounds a large pool. ⊠ *363 Cocoanut Row, 33480,* ☎ *561/659–5800 or 800/243–7871,* FAX *561/659–6707. 44 rooms, 11 suites. Restaurant, bar, pool, library. AE, D, DC, MC, V.*

$$$$ 🏨 **The Colony.** What distinguishes this legendary pale, pale yellow
★ Georgian-style hotel only steps from Worth Avenue is its attentive staff; youthful yet experienced, they demonstrate a buzz of competence and a true desire to please. Cool and classical guest rooms have fluted blond cabinetry and matching draperies and bedcovers in deep floral prints. As in many older hotels, bathrooms are small. The "scene" for glitterati after charity balls at the Breakers, this is where Roxanne Pulitzer retreated after her infamous seven-week marriage in 1992. ⊠ *155 Hammon Ave., 33480,* ☎ *561/655–5430 or 800/521–5525,* FAX *561/832–7318. 63 rooms, 39 suites and apartments, 7 villas. Restaurant, bar, pool, spa. AE, D, DC, MC, V.*

$$$$ 🏨 **Four Seasons Ocean Grand.** This 6-acre property at the south end
★ of town is coolly elegant but warm in detail. Marble, art, fanlight windows, swagged drapes, chintz, and palms create a serene atmosphere.

Rooms are spacious, with a separate seating area and private balcony, and many have gorgeous ocean views. On weekend evenings year-round, piano music accompanies cocktails in the Living Room lounge. On some weekend nights in season, jazz groups perform, and there are classical recitals on Sunday afternoon. Although its name suggests grandeur, this four-story hotel with a long beach is more like a small jewel. ⊠ *2800 S. Ocean Blvd., 33480, ☎ 561/582–2800 or 800/432–2335, FAX 561/547–1557. 203 rooms, 7 suites. 2 restaurants, bar, pool, saunas, 3 tennis courts, health club, beach. AE, D, DC, MC, V.*

$$$ 🏨 **Plaza Inn.** This three-story hotel, Deco-designed from the 1930s,
★   operates B&B style; a full breakfast is included. The pool, gardens, and piano bar have the intimate charm of a trysting place for the likes of Cary Grant and Katharine Hepburn. Inn owner Ajit Asrani is a retired Indian army officer who raises show horses and polo ponies. The courteous staff and location in the heart of Palm Beach are pluses, and the uncluttered, individually decorated rooms with phone and refrigerator provide a welcome change from other B&Bs. So, too, does the appealing courtyard with waterfalls and a pool. ⊠ *215 Brazilian Ave., 33480, ☎ 561/832–8666 or 800/233–2632, FAX 561/835–8776. 50 rooms and suites. Bar, pool, hot tub. AE, MC, V.*

$$–$$$$ 🏨 **Palm Beach Historic Inn.** Longtime hoteliers Harry and Barbara Kehr manage this delightfully unexpected inn in the heart of downtown. The setting, tucked between Town Hall and a seaside residential block, combines town and vacationland. B&B touches include flowers, wine and fruit, snacks, seasonal turndown, tea and cookies in rooms, and a generous Continental breakfast. Guest rooms tend to the frilly with lots of lace, ribbons, and scalloped edges. Most are furnished with Victorian antiques and reproductions (some out of old mansions, others more secondhand than authentic) and chiffon wall drapings above the bed. A 1944 Coke machine still supplies an 8-ounce bottle for a dime. Bath towels are as thick as parkas. ⊠ *365 S. County Rd., 33480, ☎ 561/ 832–4009, FAX 561/832–6255. 9 rooms, 4 suites. Library. AE, D, DC, MC, V.*

$$–$$$ 🏨 **Palm Beach Sea Lord Hotel.** If you don't need glamour or brand names, and you're not the B&B type, this garden-style hideaway is for you. Choose from accommodations that overlook Lake Worth, the pool, or the ocean; the reasonably priced café adds to the at-home, comfy feeling and attracts repeat customers. Units are plain but not cheap in season and come with carpet, at least one comfortable chair, small or large refrigerator, and tropical print fabrics. ⊠ *2315 S. Ocean Blvd., 33480, ☎ FAX 561/582–1461. 23 rooms, 11 apartments, 6 efficiencies. Restaurant, pool, beach. D, MC, V.*

Nightlife and the Arts

The Arts

The **Royal Poinciana Playhouse** (⊠ 70 Royal Poinciana Plaza, ☎ 561/ 659–3310) presents seven productions each year between December and April. **Society of the Four Arts** (⊠ Four Arts Plaza, ☎ 561/655– 7226) offers concerts, lectures, and Friday films December–March. Movie tickets can be purchased at time of showing; other tickets may be obtained a week in advance.

Nightlife

Cheek-to-cheek dancers head to the **Colony** (⊠ 155 Hammon Ave., ☎ 561/655–5430) for a spin around the dance floor. A trio plays Thursday, Friday, and Saturday nights. Young professionals gather at **E. R. Bradley's Saloon** (⊠ 111 Bradley Pl., ☎ 561/833–3520) to trade stories of the day and to try their hand at 3-D video golf. As the weekend dinner crowd thins out, late-night party seekers fill up **Ta-boó** (⊠

221 Worth Ave., ☎ 561/835–3500), where a DJ keeps everyone on their feet.

Outdoor Activities and Sports

Biking

Bicycling is an excellent way to get a good look at Palm Beach, which is as small and flat as the top of a billiard table (and just as green). The wonderful 10-mi, palm-fringed **Palm Beach Bicycle Trail** (⊠ Parallel to Lake Way) skirts the backyards of many palatial mansions and the edge of Lake Worth. Just a block from the bike trail, the **Palm Beach Trail Bicycle Shop** (⊠ 223 Sunrise Ave., ☎ 561/659–4583) rents bikes by the hour or day.

Dog Racing

Since 1932 the hounds have been racing year-round at the 4,300-seat **Palm Beach Kennel Club.** There are also simulcasts of jai alai and horse racing, as well as wagering on live and televised sports. ⊠ 1111 N. Congress Ave., ☎ 561/683–2222. 🖅 50¢, terrace level $1, parking free. ☉ Racing Mon. 12:30, Wed.–Thurs. and Sat. 12:30 and 7:30, Fri. 7:30, Sun. 1; simulcasts Mon. and Fri. noon, Tues. 12:30.

Golf

Breakers Hotel Golf Club (⊠ 1 S. County Rd., ☎ 561/655–6611 or 800/833–3141) features 36 holes. The **Palm Beach Par 3** (⊠ 2345 S. Ocean Blvd., ☎ 561/547–0598) has 18 holes, including four on the Atlantic and three on the inland waterway.

Shopping

One of the world's showcases for high-quality shopping, **Worth Avenue** runs ¼-mi east–west across Palm Beach, from the beach to Lake Worth. The street has more than 250 shops, and many upscale stores (Cartier, Gucci, Hermès, Pierre Deux, Saks Fifth Avenue, and Van Cleef & Arpels) are represented, their merchandise appealing to the discerning tastes of Palm Beach clientele. The six blocks of **South County Road** north of Worth Avenue have appealing (and somewhat less expensive) stores. For specialty items (out-of-town newspapers, health foods, and books), try the shops along the north side of **Royal Poinciana Way.**

WEST PALM BEACH

2 mi west of Palm Beach.

Long considered Palm Beach's impoverished cousin, West Palm is now economically vibrant in its own right. Far larger in area than its upper-crust neighbor to the east, it has become the cultural, entertainment, and business center of the county and of the region to the north. Sparkling government buildings like the mammoth $124 million Palm Beach County Judicial Center and Courthouse and the State Administrative Building exemplify the health of the city's corporate life, and facilities such as the $60 million Kravis Center for the Performing Arts attest to the strength of the arts and entertainment community.

Downtown

The heart of revived West Palm Beach is a small but attractive downtown area, which has been spurred on by an active historic preservation movement. Along beautifully landscaped Clematis Street, you'll find boutiques and restaurants in charmingly restored buildings and exuberant nightlife that mimics that of South Beach. Even at the downtown's fringes, you'll encounter sights of cultural interest. There's a free downtown shuttle by day and free on-street parking at night and on weekends.

A Good Tour

From a geographical perspective, the best place to start is at the north end of the city with a walk through the **Old Northwood Historic District** ⑫, on the National Register of Historic Places. Drive south on U.S. 1, take a left onto 12th Street, and then a right onto South Olive Avenue to view the exceptional art collection at the **Norton Museum of Art** ⑬. From here it is just a few blocks farther south to the peaceful **Ann Norton Sculpture Gardens** ⑭. Finally, drive west across Barcelona Road to the **Armory Arts Center** ⑮ and check out the current exhibit.

TIMING

Late morning is a good time to start this tour, so you can walk through the historic neighborhood before having lunch on Clematis Street. In the afternoon you'll need about three hours at the various arts-oriented sights. It's important to take this tour during daytime business hours.

Sights to See

⑭ **Ann Norton Sculpture Gardens.** This monument to the late American sculptor Ann Weaver Norton, second wife of Norton Museum founder Ralph H. Norton, consists of charming 3-acre grounds displaying seven granite figures and six brick megaliths. The plantings were designed by Norton, an environmentalist, to attract native bird life. ⊠ *253 Barcelona Rd.,* ☎ *561/832–5328.* ⊡ *$3.* ☉ *Tues.–Sat. 10–4 (call ahead; schedule is not always observed) or by appointment.*

⑮ **Armory Arts Center.** Built by the WPA in 1939, the facility is now a complete visual arts center. Its gallery hosts rotating exhibitions, and classes are held throughout the year. ⊠ *1703 S. Lake Ave.,* ☎ *561/ 832–1776.* ⊡ *Free.* ☉ *Weekdays 9–5, Sun. 10–2.*

★ ⑬ **Norton Museum of Art.** Constructed in 1941 by steel magnate Ralph H. Norton, this museum boasts an extensive permanent collection of 19th- and 20th-century American and European paintings with special emphasis on 19th-century French Impressionists. There are also Chinese bronze and jade sculptures, a sublime outdoor patio with sculptures on display in a tropical garden, and a library housing more than 3,000 art books and periodicals. Nine galleries showcase traveling exhibits as well as art from the permanent collection. ⊠ *1451 S. Olive Ave.,* ☎ *561/832–5194.* ⊡ *$5.* ☉ *Tues.–Sat. 10–5, Sun. 1–5.*

⑫ **Old Northwood Historic District.** This 1920s-era neighborhood, on the National Register of Historic Places, hosts special events and Sunday walking tours (☞ *Guided Tours in* Palm Beach and the Treasure Coast A to Z, *below*). ⊠ *West of Flagler Dr. between 26th and 35th Sts.*

Away from Downtown

At its outskirts, West Palm Beach sprawls. Flat, straight stretches lined with fast-food outlets and car dealerships may not be pretty to drive past, but it's worth it to reach some of the interesting attractions scattered around the southern and western reaches of the city. Several are especially rewarding for children and other animal- and nature-lovers.

A Good Tour

Head south from downtown and turn right on Southern Boulevard, left onto Parker Avenue, and right onto Summit Boulevard to reach the **Dreher Park Zoo** ⑯. In the same area (just turn right onto Dreher

Trail) and also appealing to kids, the **South Florida Science Museum, Planetarium, and Aquarium** ⑰ is full of hands-on exhibits.

Backtrack to Summit Avenue and go west to the 150-acre **Pine Jog Environmental Education Center** ⑱. For more natural adventure, head farther west on Summit until you reach Forest Hills Boulevard, where you turn right to reach the **Okeeheelee Nature Center** ⑲ and its miles of wooded trails.

Now retrace your steps to Summit Boulevard, drive east until you reach Military Trail, and take a left. Drive north to Southern Boulevard and turn west to reach **Lion Country Safari** ⑳, a 500-acre cageless zoo. For the last stop on this tour, backtrack to Military Trail and travel north to the gardens of the **Mounts Horticultural Learning Center** ㉑.

TIMING

You could easily spend most of a day at some of these sights, so you'll want to pick and choose based on your interests, creating your own subtour. During morning and afternoon rush hours and in the winter, be prepared for heavy traffic; sightseeing in the morning (not *too* early) will help somewhat.

Sights to See

⑯ Dreher Park Zoo. This wild kingdom is a 22-acre complex with more than 500 animals representing more than 100 species, including Florida panthers, red kangaroos, and Bengal tigers. Also of note are a nature trail, an Australian Outback exhibit, and a children's zoo. ⊠ *1301 Summit Blvd.,* ☎ *561/533–0887 or 561/547–9453.* ⌨ *$6, boat rides $1.* ☉ *Daily 9–5 (until 7 on spring and summer weekends), boat rides every 15 mins.*

⑳ Lion Country Safari. Drive (with car windows closed, please) on 8 mi of paved roads through a 500-acre cageless zoo where 1,300 wild animals roam. Lions, elephants, white rhinoceroses, giraffes, zebras, antelopes, chimpanzees, and ostriches are among those in residence. Special exhibits include the Kalahari Bushvelt, designed after a South African plateau and featuring water buffalo and Nilgai (the largest type of Asian antelope), and the Gir Forest, modeled after a game forest in India and showcasing a pride of lions. Stop by the petting zoo, or take a ride on the *Safari Queen* cruise. ⊠ *Southern Blvd. W,* ☎ *561/793–1084.* ⌨ *$15.50, van rental $6 per hr.* ☉ *Daily 9:30–5:30.*

㉑ Mounts Horticultural Learning Center. Take advantage of balmy weather by walking among the tropical and subtropical plants here. Free tours are given. ⊠ *531 N. Military Trail,* ☎ *561/233–1749.* ⌨ *Free.* ☉ *Mon.–Sat. 8:30–5, Sun. 1–5; tours Sat. 11, Sun. 2:30.*

⑲ Okeeheelee Nature Center. At this popular spot, you can explore 5 mi of trails through 90 acres of native pine flat woods and wetlands. A spacious visitor center/gift shop features hands-on exhibits. ⊠ *7715 Forest Hill Blvd.,* ☎ *561/233–1400.* ⌨ *Free.* ☉ *Visitor center Tues.–Fri. 1–4:45, Sat. 8:15–4:45; trails open daily.*

⑱ Pine Jog Environmental Education Center. The draw here is 150 acres of mostly undisturbed Florida pine flat woods with two self-guided ½-mi trails. Formal landscaping around the five one-story buildings features an array of native plants, and dioramas and displays show native ecosystems. Trails are reserved for the classes that are given here during the week but are open to the public on Sunday. ⊠ *6301 Summit Blvd.,* ☎ *561/686–6600.* ⌨ *Free.* ☉ *Sun. 2–5.*

⑰ South Florida Science Museum, Planetarium, and Aquarium. Here you'll find hands-on exhibits, aquarium displays with touch tanks, planetarium shows, and a chance to observe the heavens Friday nights through the most powerful telescope in South Florida (weather permitting). ⊠ *4801 Dreher Trail N,* ☎ *561/832–1988.* ⬧ *$5, planetarium $2 extra, laser show $4 extra.* ☉ *Sat.–Thurs. 10–5, Fri. 10–10.*

Dining and Lodging

$$–$$$ ✕ **Café Protégé.** The restaurant of the Florida Culinary Institute, this is the place to come to sample superb cuisine at less than astronomical prices. The contemporary Continental menu changes frequently, and patrons can watch students at work slicing, dicing, and sautéing in the unique observation kitchen. ⊠ *2400 Metrocentre Blvd.,* ☎ *561/687–2433. AE, MC, V. No lunch weekends; no dinner Sun.–Mon.*

$$ ✕ **Rain Dancer Steak House.** Since 1975 steak lovers have been stopping by this dark and cozy establishment to indulge in thick and juicy filet mignons, giant 24-ounce porterhouse steaks, sizzling sirloins for two, and grilled lean flank steaks. But if beef isn't your entrée of choice, there are lobster, shrimp scampi, baked scallops, stuffed shrimp, and a bountiful salad bar. ⊠ *2300 Palm Beach Lakes Blvd.,* ☎ *561/ 684–2811. AE, MC, V. No lunch.*

$–$$ ✕ **Aleyda's Tex-Mex Restaurant.** Since 1981 this casual family-friendly eatery has been showing up as a favorite on local popularity polls. Fajitas, the house specialty, are brought to the table sizzling in the pan, and enchilidas, chili con queso, and quesadillas are just a few more examples of the classic Mexican offerings. The bar claims to make the best margaritas in town. ⊠ *1890 Okeechobee Blvd.,* ☎ *561/688–9033. AE, DC, MC, V. No lunch Sun.*

$–$$ ✕ **Pescatore Seafood and Oyster Bar.** When you want to rest your feet after wandering around Clematis Street, slip through the handsome French doors of this trendy spot for a light lunch, an afternoon snack, or a leisurely dinner. Tables are close together, and there's a sophisticated bustle. Naturally, fresh oysters and clams are on the menu, but you'll also find a variety of grilled fish, including mahimahi, tuna, and salmon; steamed Maine lobster; grilled shrimp; assorted pasta dishes; and a grilled Black Angus burger. ⊠ *200 Clematis St.,* ☎ *561/837– 6633. AE, DC, MC, V.*

$$–$$$ ⊡ **Hibiscus House.** Few Florida B&B hosts work harder at hospital-
★ ity and at looking after their neighborhood than Raleigh Hill and Colin Rayner. As proof, since the inn opened in the late 1980s, 11 sets of guests have bought houses in Old Northwood, which is listed on the National Register of Historic Places thanks to Hill and Rayner's efforts. Their Cape Cod–style B&B is full of the antiques Hill has collected during decades of in-demand interior designing: a 150-year-old four-square piano, a gorgeous green cane planter chair, and Louis XV pieces in the living room. Outstanding, too, is the landscaped, tropical pool-patio area. Both Hill and Rayner are informed about the best—and most affordable—dining in the area. ⊠ *501 30th St., 33407,* ☎ *561/863–5633 or 800/203–4927. 8 rooms. Pool. AE, DC, MC, V.*

$–$$ ⊡ **Tropical Bed & Breakfast.** More informal and Key West–like than most of Old Northwood, this tiny cottage-style B&B has a clump of rare paroutis palms out front. The three cozy rooms are individually decorated, but the splashy poolside carriage house and the brightly striped cottage with the fruity fabrics and Peter Max–style posters are where you want to be. ⊠ *419 32nd St., 33407,* ☎ *561/848–4064 or 800/ 736–4064,* FAX *561/842–1688. 3 rooms, carriage house, cottage. Pool, bicycles. AE, MC, V.*

Nightlife and the Arts

The Arts

Part of the treasury of arts attractions is the **Raymond F. Kravis Center for the Performing Arts** (✉ 701 Okeechobee Blvd., ☎ 561/832–7469), a $60 million, 2,200-seat glass, copper, and marble showcase occupying the highest ground in West Palm Beach. Its 250-seat Rinker Playhouse includes a space for children's programming, family productions, and other special events. Some 300 performances of drama, dance, and music—everything from gospel and bluegrass to jazz and classical—are scheduled each year.

Palm Beach Opera (✉ 415 S. Olive Ave., ☎ 561/833–7888) stages four productions each winter at the Kravis Center. The **Carefree Theatre** (✉ 2000 S. Dixie Hwy., ☎ 561/833–7305) is Palm Beach County's premier showcase of foreign and art films.

Nightlife

The **Jamestown Cigar Bar** (✉ 330 Clematis St., ☎ 561/659–7273) not only carries the best selection of cigars in Palm Beach County; it also features live jazz and blues. The **Respectable Street Cafe** (✉ 518 Clematis St., ☎ 561/832–9999) explodes in high energy like an indoor Woodstock. It's open until 4 AM Tuesday–Saturday (Thursday night features the best in underground alternative sound) and for special concerts on other days. **Underground Coffeeworks** (✉ 105 S. Narcissus Ave., ☎ 561/835–4792), a retro '60s spot, has "something different going on" (but always live music) Tuesday–Saturday. The cover charge varies, depending on the performers.

Outdoor Activities and Sports

Picturesque **Binks Forest Golf Club** (✉ 400 Binks Forest Dr., Wellington, ☎ 561/795–0595) has an 18-hole layout. The plush **Emerald Dunes** (✉ 2100 Emerald Dunes Dr., ☎ 561/684–4653) sports 18 holes of golf. **Palm Beach Polo and Country Club** (✉ 13198 Forest Hill Blvd., Wellington, ☎ 561/798–7000 or 800/327–4204) features 45 holes with an excellent overall layout. The **West Palm Beach Country Club** (✉ 7001 Parker Ave., ☎ 561/582–2019) offers 18 holes with no water hazards, unusual for Florida.

Shopping

As good as the malls are, they're sterile compared to the in-the-midst-of-things excitement—the mix of food, art, performance, landscaping, and retailing—that has renewed downtown West Palm around **Clematis Street.** Water-view parks, outdoor performing areas, and attractive plantings and lighting—including fanciful palm tree sculptures—add to the pleasure of browsing, window-shopping, and resting at an outdoor café. For those single-mindedly bent on mall shopping, the **Palm Beach Mall** (✉ Palm Beach Lakes Blvd. at I–95) has a Burdines, JCPenney, Lord & Taylor, and Sears.

Side Trip

Lake Okeechobee

40 mi west of West Palm Beach.

Rimming the western shore of Palm Beach and Martin counties, this second-largest freshwater lake in the United States is girdled by 120 mi of roads; yet for almost its entire circumference, it remains hidden from sight. The Seminole's Big Water and the heart of the great Everglades watershed, Lake Okeechobee measures 730 square mi—roughly

33 mi north–south and 30 mi east–west—with an average natural depth of only 10 ft (flood control brings the figure up to 12 ft and deeper). Six major lock systems and 32 separate water-control structures manage the water.

Encircling the lake is a 30-ft-high grassy levee, known locally as the "wall," and the Lake Okeechobee Scenic Trail, a coarse track that has been integrated into the Florida National Scenic Trail. Inside the wall, on the big lake itself, fisherfolk come from everywhere for reputedly the best bass fishing in North America.

Small towns dot the lakeshore in an area that's still largely agricultural. To the southeast is Belle Glade, whose motto—"Her soil is her fortune"—results from the town's role as the eastern hub of the 700,000-acre Everglades Agricultural Area, the crescent of farmlands lying south and east of the lake. To the southwest lies Clewiston, the most prosperous lake town. It's known as "the sweetest town in America" thanks to the resident headquarters of the United States Sugar Corporation. At the north end of the lake, around Okeechobee, citrus production has outgrown cattle ranching as the principal economy, while dairying, though still important, is diminishing as the state acquires land in its efforts to reduce water pollution. Somewhat set back from the lake, Indiantown is the western hub of Martin County, noteworthy for citrus production, cattle ranching, and timbering. The town reached its apex in 1927, when the Seaboard Airline Railroad briefly established its southern headquarters and a model town here.

Grouped together in Belle Glade's **Municipal Complex** are the public library and the **Lawrence E. Will Museum**, both with materials on the town's history. On the front lawn is a Ferenc Verga sculpture of a family fleeing the wall of water that rose from the lake during the catastrophic hurricane of 1928. More than 2,000 people lost their lives and 15,000 families were left homeless by the torrential flood. ⊠ *530 Main St., Belle Glade,* ☎ *561/996–3453.* 🎟 *Free.* ☉ *Mon.–Tues. and Fri. 9–4, Wed. and Sat. 9–1, Thurs. 9–8.*

The **Clewiston Museum** details the history of the city, with stories not only of sugar and of the Herbert Hoover Dike construction, but also of a ramie crop grown here to make rayon, of World War II RAF pilots who trained at the Clewiston airfield, and of a German POW camp. ⊠ *112 S. Commercio St., Clewiston,* ☎ *941/983–2870.* 🎟 *Free.* ☉ *Tues.–Fri. 10–4.*

The Florida Power and Light Company's Martin Power Plant maintains the **Barley Barber Swamp,** a 400-acre freshwater cypress swamp preserve. A 5,800-ft-long boardwalk enables you to walk through this vestige of what near-coastal Florida was largely like before vast water-control efforts began in the 19th century. Dozens of birds, reptiles, and mammals inhabit these wetlands and lowlands, with an outstanding reserve of bald cypress trees, land and swamp growth, and slow-flowing coffee-color water. Reservations are required at least one week in advance for tours. During certain times of the year there are manatee and turtle walks. Call for schedules. ⊠ *Rte. 710, Indiantown,* ☎ *800/ 552–8440.* 🎟 *Free.* ☉ *Tours Fri.–Wed. 8:30 and 12:30.*

DINING AND LODGING

$–$$ ✕ **Colonial Dining Room.** The Clewiston Inn's restaurant has ladder-back chairs, chandeliers, and fanlight windows, and though the food is good, the attitude's not fancy. Southern regional and Continental dishes—chicken, pork, steak, and the ubiquitous catfish—are served. ⊠ *108 Royal Palm Ave., at U.S. 27, Clewiston,* ☎ *941/983–8151. MC, V.*

$–$$ ✕ **Lightsey's.** The pick of the lake, this beautiful lodgelike restaurant at the Okee-Tantie Recreation Area started closer to town as a fish company with four tables in a corner. Now everybody comes out here. You can get most items fried, steamed, broiled, or grilled. The freshest are the catfish, cooter (freshwater turtle), frogs' legs, and gator. ⊠ *10430 Rte. 78W, Okeechobee,* ☎ *941/763–4276. MC, V. Beer and wine only.*

$–$$ 🏨 **Seminole Country Inn.** This two-story, Mediterranean Revival inn, ★ once the southern headquarters of the Seaboard Airline Railroad, was restored by longtime Indiantown patriarch the late Holman Wall. It's now being run for the second time (other innkeepers didn't get it right) by his daughter, Jonnie Wall Williams, a fifth-generation native, who is devoted to the inn's restoration. Rooms are done in country ruffles and prints, with full carpeting and comfy beds. There are rocking chairs on the porch, Indiantown memorabilia in the lobby, a sitting area on the second floor, and good local art throughout. ⊠ *15885 S.W. Warfield Blvd., Indiantown 34956,* ☎ *561/597–3777. 21 rooms. 2 restaurants, pool. AE, D, MC, V.*

$ 🏨 **Clewiston Inn.** This classic antebellum-style country hotel in the heart of town was built in 1938. Its cypress-panel lobby, wood-burning fireplace, Colonial Dining Room, and Everglades Lounge with a wraparound Everglades mural are standouts. Rooms are pleasant but basic, with reproduction furniture. Still it's worth a stay to soak up the lore and take advantage of the excellent value (full breakfast included). A pool is across the street in the park. ⊠ *108 Royal Palm Ave., at U.S. 27, Clewiston 33440,* ☎ *941/983–8151 or 800/749–4466,* 𝙵𝙰𝚇 *941/983– 4602. 48 rooms, 5 suites. Restaurant, bar, 6 tennis courts, jogging. AE, MC, V.*

$ 🏨 **Okeechobee Days Inn Pier II.** This modern two-story motel on the ★ rim canal has a five-story observation tower for looking over the levee to the lake. Large, clean, motel-plain rooms are well maintained. Out back there are a 600-ft fishing pier and the Oyster Bar, one of the best hangouts on the lake for shooting a game of pool or watching a game on TV. It attracts a good mix of locals and out-of-towners. ⊠ *2200 S.E. U.S. 441, Okeechobee 34974,* ☎ *941/763–8003 or 800/874–3744,* 𝙵𝙰𝚇 *941/763–2245. 89 rooms. Bar, fishing. AE, D, DC, MC, V.*

$ 🏨 **Okeechobee Inn.** Rooms in this simple, two-story L-shape motel, 2 mi west of Belle Glade, are furnished in green floral prints. Large windows let in plenty of light. All rooms have balconies that overlook the pool, and fishing and boat ramps are just a mile away. ⊠ *265 N. U.S. 27, South Bay 33493,* ☎ *561/996–6517. 115 rooms. Pool, playground. MC, V.*

$ ⛺ **Belle Glade Marina Campground.** A few miles north of downtown Belle Glade, just offshore in Lake Okeechobee, is Torry Island. Campsites have water and electrical hookups; some have sewer hookups and docking facilities. ⊠ *Torry Island 33493,* ☎ *561/996–6322. 350 campsites. Picnic area, horseshoes, shuffleboard, dock, boating, fishing. MC, V.*

$ ⛺ **Okee-Tantie Recreation Area.** In addition to its recreational facilities, the park offers 215 RV sites, 38 tent sites, picnic spots, rest rooms, showers, Lightsey's restaurant, and a shop at which you can buy groceries and sandwiches. ⊠ *10430 Rte. 78W, Okeechobee 34974,* ☎ *941/ 763–2622. Restaurant, grocery, picnic area, dock, boating, fishing, playground. MC, V.*

OUTDOOR ACTIVITIES AND SPORTS

Biking. Okeechobee Cycling & Fitness (⊠ 50 S.E. U.S. 441, Okeechobee, ☎ 941/357–0458) is the only source for bicycle rentals and repairs on the lake.

Fishing. In addition to operating the bridge to Torry Island (the last remaining swing bridge in Florida, it is cranked open and closed by hand, swinging at right angles to the road), brothers Charles and Gordon Corbin run **Slim's Fish Camp** (⊠ Torry Island, ☎ 561/996–3844). Here you'll find a complete tackle shop, guides, camping facilities, fully equipped bass boats, and even the name of a good taxidermist to mount your trophy. **J-Mark Fish Camp** (⊠ Torry Island, ☎ 561/996–5357) provides fully equipped bass boats, fishing guides, tackle, bait, and licenses. Since the **Okee-Tantie Recreation Area** (⊠ 10430 Rte. 78W, Okeechobee, ☎ 941/763–2622) has direct access to the lake, it's a popular place for fishing. There are two public boat ramps, fish-cleaning stations, a marina, picnic areas and a restaurant, a playground, rest rooms, showers, and a **bait shop** (☎ 941/763–9645) that stocks groceries.

Golf. Belle Glade Municipal Country Club (⊠ Torry Island Rd., Belle Glade, ☎ 561/996–6605) features an 18-hole golf course and restaurant open to the public.

SOUTH TO BOCA RATON

Strung together by Route A1A, the towns between Palm Beach and Boca Raton are notable for their variety. Though the glamour of Palm Beach has rubbed off on many towns, there are pockets of modesty and unpretentiousness alongside the well-established high and mighty. In one town you might find a cluster of sophisticated art galleries and fancy eateries, while the very next town could have a few hamburger stands and mom-and-pop "everything" stores.

Lake Worth

㉒ *2 mi south of West Palm Beach.*

Tourists are mainly interested in this mainland town for its inexpensive lodging in close proximity to Palm Beach, which is accessible via a nearby bridge.

Lake Worth Municipal Park, also known as Casino Park, has a beach, Olympic-size swimming pool, fishing pier, picnic areas, shuffleboard, restaurants, and shops. ⊠ *Rte. A1A at end of Lake Worth Bridge,* ☎ *561/533–7367.* ☞ *Pool $2, parking 25¢ for 15 mins.* ☉ *Daily 9–4:45.*

The Arts
Klein Dance Company (⊠ 3208 2nd Ave. N, No. 10, 33461, ☎ 561/586–1889) is a nationally acclaimed, world-touring professional troupe that also gives local performances.

Dining and Lodging
$ ✕ **John G's.** About the only time the line lets up is when the restaurant closes at 3 PM. The menu is as big as the crowd: big fruit platters, sandwich-board superstars, grilled burgers, seafood, and eggs every which way, including a United Nations of omelets. Breakfast is served until 11. ⊠ *Lake Worth Casino,* ☎ *561/585–9860. No credit cards. No dinner.*

$ 🏨 **New Sun Gate Motel.** Each room is dedicated to a famous movie star of a bygone era—Cary Grant, Rita Hayworth, James Dean—in this simple establishment near downtown. Units are decorated in Art Deco style, and some have microwaves. ⊠ *901 S. Federal Hwy., 33460,* ☎ *561/588–8110,* 🆙 *561/588–8041. 31 rooms. Restaurant, pool, coin laundry. AE, MC, V.*

Outdoor Activities and Sports

The **Gulfstream Polo Club,** the oldest club in the Palm Beach area, began in the 1920s and plays medium-goal polo (for teams with handicaps of 8–16 goals). There are six polo fields. ⊠ *4550 Polo Rd.,* ☎ *561/965–2057.* ☞ *Free.* ◷ *Games Dec.–Apr.*

Lantana

㉓ *2 mi south of Lake Worth.*

Like Lake Worth, Lantana has inexpensive lodging and a bridge connecting the town to Palm Beach's barrier island. It's just a bit farther away from Palm Beach. A closer island neighbor is **Manalapan,** a tiny residential community with a luxury beach resort.

Lantana Public Beach has one of the best food concessions around. You'll find fresh fish on weekends and breakfast and lunch specials every day outdoors under beach umbrellas. ⊠ *100 N. Ocean Ave.,* ☎ *no phone.* ☞ *Parking 25¢ for 15 mins.* ◷ *Daily 9–4:45.*

Dining and Lodging

$$ ✕ **Old House.** Overlooking the Intracoastal Waterway, the 1889 Lyman House has grown in spurts over the years and is now a patchwork of shedlike spaces. Partners Wayne Cordero and Captain Bob Hoddinott have turned it into an informal Old Florida seafood house that serves not only local seafood but also, incongruously, Baltimore steamed crab—the specialty. Although there's air-conditioning, dining is still open-air most evenings and in cooler weather. ⊠ *300 E. Ocean Ave.,* ☎ *561/533–5220. AE, MC, V.*

$$$$ 🏨 **Ritz-Carlton, Palm Beach.** Despite its name, this hotel is actually in
★ Manalapan, halfway between Palm Beach and Delray. The bisque-color, triple-tower landmark may look like the work of Addison Mizner, but in fact it was built in 1991. Dominating the lobby is a huge double-sided marble fireplace, foreshadowing the luxury of the guest rooms' marble tubs and upholstered furniture. Most rooms have ocean views, and oceanfront rooms have balconies. Not to be outdone by the fabulous beaches, a large pool and courtyard area has more than 100 coconut palms. Bikes and scuba and snorkeling equipment can be rented. ⊠ *100 S. Ocean Blvd., Manalapan 33462,* ☎ *561/533–6000 or 800/241–3333,* ☒ *561/588–4555. 257 rooms, 13 suites. 4 restaurants, 2 bars, pool, beauty salon, massage, sauna, spa, steam room, 7 tennis courts, beach, bicycles. AE, D, DC, MC, V.*

$ 🏨 **Super 8 Motel.** There's nothing special about this sprawling one-story motel except the price—a real bargain, considering the proximity to Palm Beach. Efficiencies and rooms (some with refrigerators) are clean but basically furnished. ⊠ *1255 Hypoluxo Rd., 33462,* ☎ *561/585–3970,* ☒ *561/586–3028. 129 rooms, 11 efficiencies. Pool, coin laundry. AE, DC, MC, V.*

Outdoor Activities and Sports

B-Love Fleet (⊠ 314 E. Ocean Ave., ☎ 561/588–7612) offers three deep-sea fishing excursions daily: 8–noon, 1–5, and 7–11. No reservations are needed; just show up 30 minutes before the boat is scheduled to leave. The cost is $24 per person.

Boynton Beach

㉔ *3 mi south of Lantana.*

This town is far enough from Palm Beach to have kept its laid-back, low-key atmosphere. Its two parts, on the mainland and the barrier island, are connected by a causeway.

Knollwood Groves dates from the 1930s, when it was planted by the partners of the *Amos & Andy* radio show. You can take a 30-minute, 30-acre tram tour through the orange groves and a processing plant and visit the **Hallpatee Seminole Indian Village,** where there are an alligator exhibit and crafts shop. During the busy season, special guest Martin Twofeather gives a weekly one-hour alligator-handling show. ⊠ *8053 Lawrence Rd.,* ☎ *561/734–4800.* ⊡ *Tour $1, show $5.* ☉ *Daily 8:30–5:30, show Sat. 2.*

The **Puppetry Arts Center** provides shows and educational programs from the home of the Gold Coast Puppet Guild. ⊠ *3633 S. Federal Hwy.,* ☎ *561/687–3280.* ⊡ *Shows $2.50.* ☉ *Call for schedule.*

Oceanfront Park has a beach, boardwalk, concessions, grills, a jogging trail, and playground. Parking is expensive if you're not a Boynton resident. ⊠ *Ocean Ave. at Rte. A1A,* ☎ *no phone.* ⊡ *Parking $10 per day in winter, $5 per day rest of year.* ☉ *Daily 9 AM–midnight.*

OFF THE
BEATEN PATH

ARTHUR R. MARSHALL–LOXAHATCHEE NATIONAL WILDLIFE REFUGE – The most robust part of the Everglades, this 221-square-mi refuge is one of three huge water-retention areas that account for much of the Everglades outside the national park. These areas are managed less to protect natural resources, however, than to prevent flooding to the south. Start from the visitor center, where there are two walking trails: a boardwalk through a dense cypress swamp and a marsh trail to a 20-ft-high observation tower overlooking a pond. There is also a 5½-mi canoe trail, recommended for more experienced canoeists because it's rather overgrown. Wildlife viewing is good year-round, and you can fish for bass and panfish. ⊠ *10119 Lee Rd., off U.S. 441 between Boynton Beach Blvd. (Rte. 804) and Atlantic Ave. (Rte. 806), west of Boynton Beach,* ☎ *561/734–8303.* ⊡ *$5 per vehicle, $1 per pedestrian.* ☉ *Daily 6 AM–sunset; visitor center weekdays 9–4, weekends 9–4:30.*

Dining

$–$$ ✕ **Mama Jennie's.** Tucked at the end of a strip mall, this inviting, casual Italian restaurant attracts families, who come here to share large, traditional pizza pies topped with mozzarella, mushrooms, and anchovies. Spaghetti with meatballs, eggplant parmigiana, and stuffed shells are also fine choices, and all dishes are homemade. ⊠ *706 W. Boynton Beach Blvd.,* ☎ *561/737–2407. AE, MC, V. No lunch.*

Outdoor Activities and Sports

FISHING

You can fish the canal at the **Arthur R. Marshall–Loxahatchee National Wildlife Refuge** (☎ 561/734–8303). There's a boat ramp, and the waters are decently productive, but bring your own equipment.

GOLF

Boynton Beach Municipal Golf Course (⊠ 8020 Jog Rd., ☎ 561/742–6500) offers 27 holes.

Gulf Stream

㉕ *2 mi south of Boynton Beach.*

This beautiful little beachfront community was also touched by Mizner. As you pass the bougainvillea-topped walls of the Gulf Stream Club, a private police officer may stop traffic for a golfer to cross.

Lodging

$ ⊞ **Riviera Palms Motel.** Hans and Herter Grannemann have owned this small two-story motel dating from the 1950s since 1978. It has two primary virtues: It's clean, and it's well located. Across Route A1A from mid-rise apartment houses on the water, it has three wings surrounding a grassy front yard and heated pool. Rooms are done in Danish modern and a blue, brown, and tan color scheme; all have at least a refrigerator but no phone. ⊠ *3960 N. Ocean Blvd., 33483,* ☎ *561/ 276–3032. 17 rooms, suites, and efficiencies. Pool. No credit cards.*

Delray Beach

26 *2 mi south of Gulf Stream.*

What began as an artists' retreat and a small settlement of Japanese farmers is now a sophisticated beach town with a successful local historic-preservation movement. Atlantic Avenue, the main drag, has been transformed into a 1-mi stretch of palm-dotted brick sidewalks, almost entirely lined with stores, art galleries, and dining establishments. Running east–west and ending at the beach, it's a pleasant place for a stroll day or night. Another lovely pedestrian way begins at the edge of town, across Northeast 8th Street (George Bush Boulevard), along the big broad swimming beach that extends north and south of Atlantic Avenue.

Municipal Beach (⊠ Atlantic Ave. at Rte. A1A) has a boat ramp and volleyball court.

The chief landmark along Atlantic Avenue is the Mediterranean Revival **Colony Hotel** (⊠ 525 E. Atlantic Ave., ☎ 561/276–4123), still open only for the winter season as it has been almost every year since 1926.

Cason Cottage, a restored Victorian-style home that dates from about 1915, now serves as offices of the Delray Beach Historical Society. The house is filled with relics of the Victorian era, including an old pipe organ donated by descendants of one of the original families to settle Delray Beach. Periodic displays celebrate the town's architectural evolution. The cottage is a block north of the cultural center. ⊠ *5 N.E. 1st St.,* ☎ *561/243–0223.* ▨ *Free.* ⊗ *Tues.–Fri. 11–4.*

The **Old School Square Cultural Arts Center,** just off Atlantic Avenue, houses several museums in restored school buildings dating from 1913 and 1926. The **Cornell Museum of Art & History** offers an ever-changing array of art exhibits. ⊠ *51 N. Swinton Ave.,* ☎ *561/243– 7922.* ▨ *Donation welcome.* ⊗ *Tues.–Sat. 11–4, Sun. 1–4.*

Florida seems an odd place for the ★**Morikami Museum and Japanese Gardens.** At this 200-acre cultural and recreational facility, a display in a building modeled after a Japanese imperial villa recalls the Yamato Colony, an agricultural community of Japanese settlers who came to Florida in 1905. Gardens include the only known collection of bonsai Florida plants. There are also programs and exhibits in a lakeside museum and theater, as well as a nature trail, picnic pavilions, a library and audiovisual center, and snack bar. The on-site Cornell Cafe is a pleasant retreat serving light Asian fare. ⊠ *4000 Morikami Park Rd.,* ☎ *561/495–0233.* ▨ *Park free; museum $4.25, free Sun. 10–noon.* ⊗ *Park daily sunrise–sunset; museum Tues.–Sun. 10–5; café Tues.–Sun. 11–3.*

Dining and Lodging

$$–$$$ ✕ **Damiano's at the Tarrimore Home.** Dinner is an intimate affair at this sophisticated restaurant in an Old Florida home. Nothing on the menu is ordinary. The eclectic cuisine from around the world often incorporates local ingredients and always with a twist. Consider the escargots tossed in mint and garlic oil and served in a nest of phyllo dough or the sweet Vidalia and green onion soup; or try the lobster potpie with nuggets of Florida lobster plus peas and carrots in a light cream sauce or oven-roasted yellowtail snapper served with thin slices of Florida lemon, capers, and a chardonnay sauce. ⊠ *52 N. Swinton Ave.,* ☎ *561/ 272–4706. AE, MC, V.*

$–$$ ✕ **Blue Anchor.** Unbelievably, this pub was actually shipped from En-
★ gland, where it stood for 150 years as the old Blue Anchor Pub, in London's historic Chancery Lane. There it was a regular watering hole for many famous Englishmen, including Winston Churchill. The Delray Beach incarnation still cooks up authentic British pub fare: ploughman's lunch (a chunk of cheddar or Stilton cheese, a chunk of bread, and English pickled onions), steak-and-kidney pie, fish-and-chips, and bangers (sausage) and mash, to name just a few. You can also get delicious hamburgers, sandwiches, and salads. The dessert menu includes an English sherry trifle and a Bailey's Irish Cream pie. English beers and ales are available on tap and in the bottle. ⊠ *804 E. Atlantic Ave.,* ☎ *561/272– 7272. AE, MC, V.*

$–$$ ✕ **Boston's on the Beach.** Often a restaurant that's facing a beach re-
★ lies on its location to fill the place up and doesn't worry enough about the food. Not so with Boston's, which is just across the street from the public beach. As you might expect from the name, you'll find good New England clam chowder and several lobster dishes, as well as fresh fish grilled, fried, or prepared just about any other way. All this is presented in an ultra-informal setting. Tables are old and wooden, and walls are decorated with traffic signs and other conversation stoppers, most notably paraphernalia from the Boston Bruins, New England Patriots, and Boston Red Sox, including a veritable shrine to Ted Williams. An outdoor deck upstairs is a terrific place to catch ocean breezes. After dark the place becomes a casual club with live music. ⊠ *40 S. Ocean Blvd. (Rte. A1A),* ☎ *561/278–3364. AE, MC, V.*

$$$–$$$$ 🏨 **Seagate Hotel & Beach Club.** One of the best garden hotels in Palm Beach County, this property offers value, comfort, style, and personal attention. The one-bedroom suite is all chintz and rattan, with many upholstered pieces. All units have at least kitchenettes. The less expensive studios have compact facilities behind foldaway doors, while more expensive units have a separate living room and a larger kitchen. You can dress up and dine in a smart little mahogany- and lattice-trimmed beachfront salon or have the same Continental fare in casual attire in the equally stylish bar. Guests enjoy privileges at the private beach club. ⊠ *400 S. Ocean Blvd., 33483,* ☎ *561/276–2421 or 800/233–3581. 70 1- and 2-bedroom suites. Restaurant, bar, freshwater and saltwater pools, beach. AE, DC, MC, V.*

$$ 🏨 **Harbor House Inn.** These white, two-story 1950s buildings have a privileged location in a quiet residential enclave three blocks east of U.S. 1 and across from the Delray Marina. In addition to two tiny motel rooms, there are 23 efficiencies and one- and two-bedroom apartments with kitchens and a mix of seating generally done in white, beige, tan, and blue. Everything retains a 1950s look, but carpets and upholstery are replaced before they look tired. In a nice touch, matching fabrics are changed by the season: solid blue in summer, blue florals in winter. ⊠ *124 Marine Way, 33483,* ☎ *561/276–4221. 2 rooms, 23 suites. Pool, shuffleboard, coin laundry. MC, V.*

Nightlife and the Arts

THE ARTS

The **Crest Theater** (✉ 51 N. Swinton Ave., ☎ 561/243–7922), in the Old School Square Cultural Arts Center, presents productions in dance, music, and theater.

NIGHTLIFE

The **Back Room Blues Lounge** (✉ 909 W. Atlantic Ave., ☎ 561/243–9110), behind Westside Liquors, has comedy night on Wednesday and live bands Thursday–Saturday. **Boston's on the Beach** (✉ 40 S. Ocean Blvd., ☎ 561/278–3364) presents live reggae music Monday and rock and roll Tuesday–Sunday.

Outdoor Activities and Sports

BIKING

There is a bicycle path in Barwick Park and a special oceanfront lane along Route A1A. **Rich Wagen's Bicycle Shop** (✉ 217 E. Atlantic Ave., ☎ 561/276–4234) rents bikes by the hour or day.

SCUBA DIVING AND SNORKELING

Scuba and snorkeling equipment can be rented from longtime family-owned **Force E** (✉ 660 Linton Blvd., ☎ 561/276–0666). It has PADI affiliation, provides instruction at all levels, and offers charters.

TENNIS

Each winter the **Delray Beach Tennis Center** (✉ 201 W. Atlantic Ave., ☎ 561/243–7380) hosts a professional women's tournament that attracts players like Steffi Graf. The center is also a great place to practice or learn; it has 14 clay courts and five hard courts and offers individual lessons and clinics.

WATERSKIING

Lake Ida Park (✉ 2929 Lake Ida Rd., ☎ 561/964–4420) is an excellent place to water-ski, whether you're a beginner or a veteran. The park has a boat ramp, slalom course, and trick ski course.

Shopping

Street-scaped **Atlantic Avenue** is a showcase for art galleries, shops, and restaurants. In addition to serving lunch and a traditional afternoon tea, the charmingly old-fashioned **Sundy House** (✉ 106 S. Swinton Ave., ☎ 561/272–5678) sells antiques and gifts in the former home of one-time Flagler foreman and first Delray mayor John Shaw Sundy. The structure's beautiful gardens and five gingerbread gables complement Delray's finest wraparound porch.

Boca Raton

㉗ *6 mi south of Delray Beach.*

This upscale town at the south end of Palm Beach County, 30 minutes south of Palm Beach, has a lot in common with its ritzy cousin. For one thing, both reflect the unmistakable architectural presence of Addison Mizner, their principal developer in the mid-1920s. Mizner Park, an important Boca Raton shopping district, bears his name.

Built in 1925 as the headquarters of the Mizner Development Corporation, the structure at **2 East El Camino Real** is a good example of Mizner's characteristic Spanish Revival architectural style, with its wrought-iron grills and handmade tiles.

☪ Championed by *Beetle Bailey* cartoonist Mort Walker, the **International Museum of Cartoon Art** is the only museum of its kind in the world. It showcases more than 160,000 pieces of art created over two centuries by more than 1,000 artists from more than 50 countries—everything from turn-of-the-century Buster Brown cartoons to the *Road Runner* to Charles Schulz's *Peanuts.* ✉ *201 Plaza Real,* ☎ *561/391–2200.* ✉ *$6.* ☉ *Tues.–Sat. 10–6, Sun. noon–6.*

Containing whimsical metal sculptures on the lawn, the **Boca Raton Museum of Art** is a must. The permanent collection includes works by Picasso, Degas, Matisse, Klee, and Modigliani as well as notable pre-Columbian art. ✉ *801 W. Palmetto Park Rd.,* ☎ *561/392–2500.* ✉ *$3.*☉ *Weekdays 10–4, weekends noon–4.*

The residential area behind the Boca Raton Museum of Art is known as **Old Floresta.** Developed by Addison Mizner starting in 1925 and landscaped with many varieties of palms and cycads, it includes houses that are mainly in a Mediterranean style, many with upper balconies supported by exposed wood columns.

☾ Hands-on interactive exhibits make the new **Children's Science Explorium** a definite kid pleaser. Children can create their own laser-light shows, explore a 3-D kiosk that illustrates wave motion, and try all kinds of electrifying experiments. There are also wind tunnels, microscopes, and microwave and radiation experiment stations. ✉ *300 S. Military Trail,* ☎ *561/395–8401.* ✉ *Free.* ☉ *Weekdays 8 AM–10:30 PM, Sat. 8–5, Sun. 10–5.*

☾ A big draw for kids, the **Gumbo Limbo Nature Center** has four huge saltwater sea tanks and a long boardwalk through dense forest with a 50-ft tower you can climb to overlook the tree canopy. In the spring and early summer, staff members lead nighttime turtle walks to see nesting females come ashore and lay their eggs. ✉ *1801 N. Ocean Blvd.,* ☎ *561/338–1473.* ✉ *Donation welcome; turtle tours $3 (tickets must be obtained in advance).* ☉ *Mon.–Sat. 9–4, Sun. noon–4; turtle tours late May–mid-July, Mon.–Thurs. 9 PM–midnight.*

Red Reef Park (✉ 1400 N. Rte. A1A) offers a beach and playground plus picnic tables and grills. In addition to its beach, **Spanish River Park** (✉ 3001 N. Rte. A1A) has picnic tables, grills, and a large playground. Popular **South Beach Park** (✉ 400 N. Rte. A1A) has a concession stand along with its sand and ocean.

The Arts
Caldwell Theatre Company (✉ 7873 N. Federal Hwy., ☎ 561/241–7432), an Equity regional theater, hosts the multimedia Mizner Festival each April and May and stages four productions each winter. **Jan McArt's Royal Palm Dinner Theatre** (✉ 303 S.E. Mizner Blvd., Royal Palm Plaza, ☎ 561/392–3755 or 800/841–6765), an Equity theater, presents five or six musicals a year.

Dining and Lodging
$$–$$$$ ✗ **La Vieille Maison.** This French restaurant remains one of the temples of haute cuisine along the Gold Coast. Featuring a stunning courtyard, it occupies a 1920s-era dwelling believed to be an Addison Mizner design. Closets and cubbyholes have been transformed into intimate private dining rooms. Fixed-price, à la carte, Temptations, and Grand menus are available, and all feature Provençal dishes, including *soupe au pistou* (vegetable soup with basil and Parmesan cheese) and venison chop with red currant–pepper sauce and roasted chestnuts. Health-conscious selections are available on all menus. Dessert choices include French sponge cake with lemon cream and strawberries, French apple tart, and a chocolate lover's delight called *L'Indulgence de Chocolat.* ✉ *770 E. Palmetto Park Rd.,* ☎ *561/391–6701 or 561/737–5677. AE, D, DC, MC, V. Closed early July–Aug.*

FLORIDA'S SEA TURTLES:
THE NESTING SEASON

FROM MAY TO OCTOBER it's turtle nesting season all along the Florida coast. During the night female Loggerhead, Kemp's Ridley, and other species of turtles that live way out in the Atlantic or Gulf of Mexico swim to shore. They drag their 100- to 400-pound bodies up the beach, arduously dig a hole with their flippers, drop in about 100 eggs, cover up the hole, and return to sea.

About 60 days later, generally in the middle of the night, the baby turtles hatch. It can take them several days just to make it up to the surface. However, once they burst out of the ground, the little hatchlings must get to the sea as fast as possible, or they will be caught by crabs or birds or become dehydrated by the morning sun.

Instinctively the baby turtles head to the brightest light. It's believed they do this because for millions of years starlight or moonlight reflected on the waves was the brightest light around, and it guided the hatchlings right to water. These days, however, light from buildings along the beach can disorient the baby turtles and cause them to go in the wrong direction. To prevent this, many coastal towns have lighting restrictions during nesting months. These are seriously enforced, and more than one homeowner has been surprised by a police officer at the door requesting that lights be dimmed.

At night volunteers walk the beaches, searching for signs of turtle nests. When they find the telltale scratches in the sand, they cordon off the site, so daytime beach-goers will leave the spots undisturbed. These same volunteers keep an eye on the nests when babies are about to hatch and provide assistance if the hatchlings do get disoriented.

It's a hazardous world for baby turtles. They can die after eating tar balls or plastic garbage or can get eaten by sharks, large fish, or circling birds. Only about one in 1,000 survives to adulthood. Once the baby turtles reach the water, they make their way to warm currents. East coast hatchlings drift into the Gulf Stream and spend several years floating around the Atlantic.

MALES NEVER, EVER return to land, but when females attain maturity, which takes 15–50 years, they come back to shore to lay their eggs. Remarkably, even though they migrate hundreds and even thousands of miles out at sea, most return to the very beach where they were born to deposit their eggs. Sea turtles nest at least twice a season—sometimes as many as 10 times—and then skip a year or two. Each time they nest, they come back to the same tiny stretch of beach. In fact, the more they nest, the more accurate they get, until eventually they return time and again to within a few feet of where they last laid their eggs. Though scientists have studied these incredible navigation skills for some time, they remain a complete mystery. If you want to find out more about sea turtles, check out the website at www.cccturtle.org.

$$–$$$$ ✕ **Ristorante La Finestra.** Belle Epoque lithographs decorate the walls,
★ and though the formal interior is just this side of austere, the cuisine
itself is an extravaganza of taste treats. Start with the Portobello mush-
room with garlic or the roasted red peppers and anchovies. For a main
course try a pasta dish, such as ricotta ravioli with vodka or rigatoni
Bolognese (with ground veal, marinara sauce, and Parmesan). Or
order the scallopini of veal stuffed with crabmeat, lobster, and Gor-
gonzola; the Tuscan fish stew; or the baked jumbo shrimp wrapped in
bacon and stuffed with Swiss cheese. ⊠ *171 E. Palmetto Rd.,* ☎ *561/
392–1838. AE, DC, MC, V. No lunch.*

$$–$$$ ✕ **Crab House Seafood Restaurant.** Crowds come here day and night
to dine on fresh Florida seafood and the restaurant's well-known crab
specials. Landlubbers will find chicken, steaks, and salads to satisfy
their fancies. There's a nautical theme to the decor, a wide deck for
outside dining, a raw bar, and a cocktail lounge. ⊠ *6909 S.W. 18th
St.,* ☎ *561/750–0498. AE, D, MC, V.*

$$–$$$ ✕ **Mark's at the Park.** Exotic cars pour into valet parking at this lat-
est Mark Militello creation, where eating is only half the fun. Decor
constitutes a whimsical 21st-century interpretation of retro and art deco.
On the outside terrace, furnishings are metal, but wood and fabric reign
indoors, where asymmetrical columns and banquettes with immense
backs and fabric inserts create cozy but noisy dining spaces. If you can
tear your eyes away to focus on the dazzling menu, consider the
chopped Sicilian salad, calamari cakes, or pizza with Maine lobster or
onion, bacon, gorgonzola, and walnuts. For an entrée, try the fusilli
with a roasted eggplant and tomato ragout or the braised lamb shank
with almond and raisin couscous. Desserts are deliciously old-fashioned.
⊠ *344 Plaza Real, Mizner Park,* ☎ *561/395–0770. AE, D, MC, V.*

$$–$$$ ✕ **Uncle Tai's.** People flock here for some of the best Szechuan cuisine
on Florida's east coast. House specialties include sliced duck with
snow peas and water chestnuts in a tangy plum sauce, sliced fillet of
snapper stir-fried and sautéed in a rice-wine sauce, and Uncle Tai's fa-
mous Orange Beef Delight—flank steak stir-fried until crispy and then
sautéed with pepper sauce, garlic, and orange peel. Szechuan-style
cooking is extremely hot and spicy, so remember to specify if you want
the chef to go easy on you. ⊠ *5250 Town Center Circle,* ☎ *561/368–
8806. AE, MC, V. No lunch.*

$ ✕ **Tom's Place.** "This place is a blessing from God," says the sign over
★ the fireplace, and after braving the long lines and sampling the superb
menu, you will add, "Amen!" That's in between mouthfuls of Tom
Wright's soul food—sauce-slathered ribs, pork chop sandwiches,
chicken cooked in peppery mustard sauce over hickory and oak, sweet
potato pie. Buy a bottle or two of Tom's barbecue sauce ($2.25 a pint)
just as Lou Rawls, Ben Vereen, Sugar Ray Leonard, and a rush of NFL
players have before you. ⊠ *7251 N. Federal Hwy.,* ☎ *561/997–0920.
MC, V. Closed Sun., also Mon. May–mid-Nov.*

$$$$ ☷ **Boca Raton Resort & Club.** Addison Mizner built the Mediterranean-
★ style Cloister Inn here in 1926; it has been added to several times since
to create this sprawling resort with a beach accessible by shuttle.
Rooms in the Cloister are small and warmly traditional; those in the
27-story Tower are in a similar style but larger, while rooms in the Beach
Club are light, airy, and contemporary. Golf villas are, naturally, near
the golf course. The concierge staff speaks at least 12 languages. Win-
ter rates don't include meals, but you can pay extra for MAP (includ-
ing breakfast and dinner). Rooms have been recently refurbished, the
main golf course has been redesigned, and there's a new $10 million
Tennis & Fitness Center. ⊠ *501 E. Camino Real, 33431-0825,* ☎ *561/
395–3000 or 800/327–0101,* ℻ *561/447–5888. 840 rooms, 63 suites,
60 golf villas. 7 restaurants, 3 bars, 5 pools, 36 holes of golf, 40 ten-*

nis courts, basketball, 3 health clubs, beach, boating, fishing. AE, DC, MC, V.

$$ 🏨 **Inn at Boca Teeca.** If golf is your game, this is an excellent place to stay. Inn guests can play the outstanding golf course at the adjoining Boca Teeca Country Club, otherwise available only to club members. Guest rooms are in a three-story building, and most have a patio or balcony. Although the inn is nearly 30 years old, the interior was recently refurbished, and rooms are small but comfortable and contemporary. ✉ *5800 N.W. 2nd Ave., 33487,* ☎ *561/994–0400,* FAX *561/998–8279. 46 rooms. Restaurant, 27 holes of golf, 6 tennis courts. AE, DC, MC, V.*

$$ 🏨 **Ocean Lodge.** The price is right at this small motel because instead of being right on the beach, it's just across the street. Rooms are in a simple two-story building, and all have refrigerators. Eleven rooms also have small kitchenettes with a two-burner stove top. Restaurants are within easy walking distance. ✉ *531 N. Ocean Blvd., 33432,* ☎ *561/395–7772,* FAX *561/395–0554. 18 rooms. Pool, coin laundry. AE, DC, MC, V.*

Outdoor Activities and Sports

BIKING

Plenty of bike trails and quiet streets make for pleasant pedaling in the area; for current information contact the city of Boca Raton's **Bicycle Coordinator** (☎ 561/393–7910).

BOATING

If you ever wanted the thrill of blasting across the water at up to 80 mph, check out **Air and Sea Charters** (✉ 490 E. Palmetto Park Rd., Suite 330, ☎ 561/368–3566). For $80 per person (four-person minimum), you can spend a wild-eyed hour holding on to your life vest aboard an 800-horsepower offshore racing boat. For a more leisurely trip go for Air and Sea's 55-ft catamaran or 45-ft sailboat.

GOLF

Two championship courses and golf programs run by Dave Pelz and Nicklaus/Flick are available at **Boca Raton Resort & Club** (✉ 501 E. Camino Real, ☎ 561/395–3000 or 800/327–0101).

POLO

Royal Palm Polo Sports Club, founded in 1959 by Oklahoma oilman John T. Oxley and now home to the $100,000 International Gold Cup Tournament, has seven polo fields within two stadiums. ✉ *6300 Old Clint Moore Rd.,* ☎ *561/994–1876.* 🎟 *$6, box seats $10–$25.* ☉ *Games Jan.–Apr., Sun. 1 and 3.*

SCUBA DIVING AND SNORKELING

Information about dive trips, as well as rental scuba and snorkeling equipment, can be obtained at **Force E** (✉ 877 E. Palmetto Park Rd., ☎ 561/368–0555).

Shopping

Mizner Park (✉ Federal Hwy. between Palmetto Park Rd. and Glades Rd.) is a distinctive 30-acre shopping village with apartments and town houses among its gardenlike spaces. Some three dozen retail stores include the excellent Liberties Fine Books & Music, a Jacobson's specialty department store, seven restaurants with sidewalk cafés, and 12 movie screens. **Town Center** (✉ 6000 W. Glades Rd.) combines a business park with ritzy shopping and great dining. Major retailers include Bloomingdale's, Burdines, Lord & Taylor, Saks Fifth Avenue, and Sears—201 stores and restaurants in all.

THE TREASURE COAST

From south to north, the Treasure Coast encompasses the top end of Palm Beach County plus Martin, St. Lucie, and Indian River counties. Though dotted with towns, this section of coastline is one of Florida's quietest. Most towns are small and laid-back, and there's lots of undeveloped land between them. Vero is the region's most sophisticated town and the one place you'll find clusters of fine-dining establishments and upscale shops. The beaches along here are sought out by nesting sea turtles; you can join locally organized watches, which go out to view the turtles laying their eggs in the sand between late April and August. Remember that you mustn't touch or disturb the turtles or their nests in any way.

Palm Beach Shores

28 *7 mi north of Palm Beach.*

This residential town rimmed by mom-and-pop motels is at the southern tip of Singer Island, across Lake Worth Inlet from Palm Beach. To get between the two, however, you must cross over to the mainland before returning to the beach. The main attraction of this unpretentious middle-class community is its affordable beachfront lodging and its proximity to several nature parks.

Peanut Island, a 79-acre island in the Intracoastal Waterway between Palm Beach Shores and Riviera Beach, is a brand-new recreational park, opened in 1999. The $2.75 million project includes a 20-ft-wide walking path surrounding the entire island, a 19-slip boat dock, a 170-ft T-shape fishing pier, six picnic pavilions, a visitor center, and 20 overnight campsites. To get to the island, you'll have to drive your own boat or catch a water taxi (call for schedules and pickup locations). ✉ *6500 Peanut Island Rd., Riviera Beach,* ☎ *561/966–6600.* ☒ *Free.* ☉ *Sunrise–sunset for noncampers.*

OFF THE
BEATEN PATH

JOHN D. MACARTHUR BEACH STATE PARK – Here you will find almost 2 mi of beach, good fishing and shelling, and one of the finest examples of subtropical coastal habitat remaining in southeast Florida. To learn about what you see, take an interpretive walk to a mangrove estuary along the upper reaches of Lake Worth. Or visit the **William T. Kirby Nature Center** (☎ 561/624–6952), open Wednesday–Monday from 9 to 5, which has exhibits on the coastal environment. ✉ *10900 Rte. A1A, North Palm Beach,* ☎ *561/624–6950.* ☒ *$3.25 per vehicle with up to 8 people.* ☉ *8–sunset.*

LOGGERHEAD PARK MARINE LIFE CENTER OF JUNO BEACH – Established by Eleanor N. Fletcher, "the turtle lady of Juno Beach," the center focuses on the natural history of sea turtles. Also on view are displays of coastal natural history, sharks, whales, and shells. ✉ *1200 U.S. 1 (entrance on west side of park), Juno Beach,* ☎ *561/627–8280.* ☒ *Donation welcome.* ☉ *Tues.–Sat. 10–4, Sun. noon–3.*

Dining and Lodging

$$ ✕ **The Galley.** Don't overlook this open-air waterfront restaurant. After a hot day of mansion gawking or beach bumming, there's no better place to chill out. The blender seems to run nonstop, churning out tropical drinks like piña coladas and Goombay Smashes. Old Florida favorites like grouper and conch chowder are mainstays, but there are also a few highbrow entrées (this is Palm Beach County, after all), such as lobster tail or baby sea scallops sautéed in garlic and lemon butter.

This is also a good spot for breakfast. ✉ *98 Lake Dr.,* ☎ *561/848–1492. MC, V. No dinner Mon.–Tues.*

$$ 🏨 **Sailfish Marina.** This long-established one-story motel has a marina
★ with 94 deep-water slips and 15 rooms and efficiencies that open to
landscaped grounds. None is directly on the water, but Units 9–11 have
ocean views across the blacktop drive. Rooms have peaked ceilings,
carpeting, king-size or twin beds, and stall showers; many have ceil-
ing fans. From the seawall you can see fish through the clear inlet water.
The motel's staff is informed and helpful, and the proprietors are as
promotional as they are friendly. ✉ *98 Lake Dr., 33404,* ☎ *561/844–
1724 or 800/446–4577,* 🖷 *561/848–9684. 15 units. Restaurant, bar,
grocery, pool, dock. AE, MC, V.*

Palm Beach Gardens

㉙ *5 mi north of West Palm Beach.*

About 15 minutes northwest of Palm Beach is this relaxed, upscale res-
idential community widely known for its high-profile golf complex,
the PGA National Resort & Spa. Although the town is not on the beach,
the ocean is just a 15-minute drive away.

Dining and Lodging

$$–$$$ ✕ **Arezzo.** The pungent smell of fresh garlic tips you off that the food's
★ the thing at this outstanding Tuscan grill at the PGA National Resort
& Spa. In this unusually relaxed, upscale resort setting, you can dine
in shorts or in jacket and tie. Families are attracted by the affordable
prices (as well as the food), so romantics might be tempted to pass Arezzo
up. Their loss. Dishes include the usual variety of chicken, veal, fish,
and steaks, but there are a dozen pastas, including rigatoni Bolognese
(a specialty), and almost as many pizzas. The decor, too, has the right
idea: an herb garden in the center of the room, slate floors, upholstered
banquettes to satisfy the upscale mood, and butcher paper over yel-
low table covers to establish the light side. ✉ *400 Ave. of the Cham-
pions,* ☎ *561/627–2000. AE, MC, V. Closed Mon. No lunch.*

$$ ✕ **River House.** People keep returning to this waterfront restaurant for
the large portions of straightforward American fare; the big salad bar
and fresh, slice-it-yourself breads; the competent service; and, thanks
to the animated buzz of a rewarded local clientele, the feeling that you've
come to the right place. Choices include seafood (always with a daily
catch), steaks, chops, and seafood-steak combo platters. Booths and
freestanding tables are surrounded by lots of blond wood, high ceilings, and nautical art under glass. The wait on Saturday night in season can be 45 minutes. Reserve one of the 20 upstairs tables, available
weekends only; the upstairs is a little more formal and doesn't have a
salad bar (bread comes from below), but it does possess a cathedral
ceiling. ✉ *2373 PGA Blvd.,* ☎ *561/694–1188. AE, MC, V. No lunch.*

$$$$ 🏨 **PGA National Resort & Spa.** Outstanding mission-style rooms are
decorated in deep, almost somber florals, and the rest of the resort is
equally richly detailed, from lavish landscaping to limitless sports facilities to excellent dining. The spa is housed in a building styled after
a Mediterranean fishing village. Its six outdoor therapy pools, dubbed
"Waters of the World," are joined by a collection of imported mineral
salt pools; there are 22 private treatments. Golf courses and croquet
courts are adorned with 25,000 flowering plants amid a 240-acre nature preserve. Two-bedroom, two-bath cottages with fully equipped
kitchens and no-smoking rooms are available, too. ✉ *400 Ave. of the
Champions, 33418,* ☎ *561/627–2000 or 800/633–9150. 279 rooms,
60 suites, 80 cottages. 4 restaurants, 2 bars, lake, pool, hot tubs,*

saunas, spa, 90 holes of golf, 19 tennis courts, croquet, racquetball, boating. AE, D, DC, MC, V.

Nightlife

Irish Times (✉ 9920 Alternate A1A, Promenade Shopping Plaza, ☎ 561/624–1504) is a four-leaf-clover find, featuring a microbrewery. There are live music and live Irish acts Wednesday–Saturday.

Outdoor Activities and Sports

AUTO RACING

Weekly ¼-mi drag racing; monthly 2¼-mi, 10-turn road racing; and monthly AMA motorcycle road racing take place year-round at the **Moroso Motorsports Park** (✉ 17047 Beeline Hwy., ☎ 561/622–1400).

GOLF

PGA National Resort & Spa (✉ 1000 Ave. of the Champions, ☎ 561/627–1800) offers a reputedly tough 90 holes.

Shopping

The Gardens mall (✉ 3101 PGA Blvd.) contains the standards if you want to make sure you're not missing out on anything at home: Bloomingdale's, Burdines, Macy's, Saks Fifth Avenue, and Sears.

Jupiter

③⓪ *12 mi north of Palm Beach Shores.*

This little town is on one of the few parts of the east coast of Florida that do not have an island in front of them. Beaches here are part of the mainland, and Route A1A runs for almost 4 mi along the beachfront dunes.

Take a look at how life once was in the **Dubois Home,** a modest pioneer home dating from 1898. Sitting atop an ancient Jeaga Indian mound 20 ft high and looking onto Jupiter Inlet, it features Cape Cod as well as Cracker design. Even if you arrive when the house is closed, surrounding **Dubois Park** is worth the visit for its lovely beaches and swimming lagoons. ✉ *Dubois Rd.,* ☎ *no phone.* 🎫 *Donation welcome.* ☉ *Wed. 1–4.*

Permanent exhibits at the **Florida History Center and Museum** review not only modern-day development along the Loxahatchee River but also shipwrecks, railroads, and Seminole, steamboat-era, and pioneer history. ✉ *805 N. U.S. 1, Burt Reynolds Park,* ☎ *561/747–6639.* 🎫 *$5.* ☉ *Tues.–Fri. 10–4, weekends noon–5.*

The **Jupiter Inlet Lighthouse,** a redbrick Coast Guard navigational beacon designed by Civil War hero General George Meade, has operated here since 1860. Tours of the 105-ft-tall local landmark are given every half hour, and there is also a small museum. Those familiar with the lighthouse may notice a significant change, courtesy of an $858,000 federal grant: the lighthouse is being transformed from bright red to natural brick, which is how it looked from 1860 to 1918. ✉ *Off U.S. 1,* ☎ *561/747–8380.* 🎫 *Tour $5.* ☉ *Sun.–Wed. 10–4, last tour 3:15.*

Carlin Park (✉ 400 Rte. A1A) provides beachfront picnic pavilions, hiking trails, a baseball diamond, playground, six tennis courts, fishing sites, and, naturally, a beach. The Park Galley, serving snacks and burgers, is usually open daily 9–5.

Dining and Lodging

$$–$$$$ ✗ **Charley's Crab.** The grand view across the Jupiter River complements
    ★   the soaring ceiling and striking interior architecture of this marina-side restaurant. You'll have great water views whether you choose to dine

inside or out, and if you eat after dark, you can watch the searching beam of the historic Jupiter Inlet Lighthouse. Come here for expertly prepared seafood, including outstanding pasta choices: *pagliara* with scallops, fish, shrimp, mussels, spinach, garlic, and olive oil; fettuccine *verde* with lobster, sun-dried tomatoes, fresh basil, and goat cheese; and shrimp and tortellini Boursin with cream sauce and tomatoes. Consider also such fresh fish as black grouper, Florida pompano, red snapper, or Gulf Stream yellowfin tuna. Other branches of Charley's are in Boca Raton, Deerfield Beach, Fort Lauderdale, Palm Beach, and Stuart. ⊠ *1000 N. U.S. 1,* ☎ *561/744–4710. AE, D, DC, MC, V.*

$$–$$$ ✕ **Sinclairs Ocean Grill & Rotisserie.** This popular spot in the Jupiter Beach Resort has tall French doors that look out to the pool and tropical greenery. The menu features a daily selection of fresh locally caught fish, such as cashew-encrusted Florida grouper, Cajun-spiced tuna, and mahimahi with pistachio sauce. Landlubbers can choose thick juicy steaks (filet mignon is the house specialty) and a variety of chicken and veal dishes. Sunday brunch is a big draw. ⊠ *5 N. Rte. A1A,* ☎ *561/ 746–2551. AE, MC, V.*

$ ✕ **Lighthouse Restaurant.** Low prices match the plain decor in this coffee shop–style building, but the menu and cuisine are a delightful surprise. You can get chicken breast stuffed with sausage and fresh vegetables, burgundy beef stew, and king crab cakes, and a full-time pastry chef is at work, too. The same people-pleasing formula has been employed since 1936: round-the-clock service (except 10 PM Sunday– 6 AM Monday) and a menu that changes daily to take advantage of the best market buys. Those looking for something less stick-to-the-ribs can order one of the affordable "lite dinners." ⊠ *1510 U.S. 1,* ☎ *561/746–4811. D, DC, MC, V.*

$$$$ ▨ **Jupiter Beach Resort.** This unpretentious resort is popular with families thanks to plentiful activities and a casual atmosphere. Rooms, which are painted in pastel colors and decorated in floral prints and rattan, are in an eight-story tower. Most rooms have balconies, and higher rooms have excellent ocean views. Taking further advantage of its location, the resort offers turtle watches in season, during which you can see newly hatched turtles make their way to the water for the first time. Snorkeling and scuba equipment and Jet Skis are available for rent, and the restaurant is worth staying in for. ⊠ *5 N. Rte. A1A, 33477,* ☎ *561/746–2511 or 800/228–8810,* ℻ *561/747–3304. 187 rooms, 28 suites. Restaurant, 2 bars, pool, tennis court, beach, dive shop, recreation room, children's programs, coin laundry, business services. AE, D, MC, V.*

Outdoor Activities and Sports

BASEBALL

Both the **St. Louis Cardinals and Montreal Expos** (⊠ 4751 Main St., ☎ 561/684–6801) train at the $28 million Roger Dean Stadium, which has seating for 7,000 fans and 12 practice fields.

CANOEING

Canoe Outfitters of Florida (⊠ 4100 W. Indiantown Rd., ☎ 561/746– 7053) runs trips along 8 mi of the Loxahatchee River, Florida's only designated Wild and Scenic River. Canoe rental for two people, with drop-off and pickup, costs $30 plus tax. You can also just paddle around for an hour.

GOLF

The **Golf Club of Jupiter at Indian Creek** (⊠ 1800 Central Blvd., ☎ 561/747–6262) offers 18 holes of varying difficulty. **Jupiter Dunes Golf Club** (⊠ 401 Rte. A1A, ☎ 561/746–6654) features 18 holes and a putting green.

Jupiter Island and Hobe Sound

③① *5 mi north of Jupiter.*

Northeast across the Jupiter Inlet from Jupiter is the southern tip of Jupiter Island, which includes a carefully planned community of the same name. Here estates often retreat from the road behind screens of vegetation, while at the north end of the island, turtles come to nest in a wildlife refuge. To the west, on the mainland, is the little community of Hobe Sound.

Within **Blowing Rocks Preserve,** a 73-acre Nature Conservancy holding, you'll find plant communities native to beachfront dune, coastal strand (the landward side of the dunes), mangrove, and hammock (tropical hardwood forests). The best time to visit is when high tides and strong offshore winds coincide, causing the sea to blow spectacularly through holes in the eroded outcropping. Park in the lot; police ticket cars parked along the road. ⊠ *Rte. 707, Jupiter Island,* ☎ *561/744–6668.* ☞ *$3 donation.* ☼ *Daily 6–5.*

The **Hobe Sound National Wildlife Refuge** actually consists of two tracts: 232 acres of sand pine and scrub oak forest in Hobe Sound and 735 acres of coastal sand dune and mangrove swamp on Jupiter Island. Trails are open to the public in both places. Turtles nest and shells wash ashore on the 3½-mi beach, which has been severely eroded by winter high tides and strong winds. ⊠ *13640 S.E. Federal Hwy., Hobe Sound,* ☎ *561/546–6141;* ⊠ *Beach Rd. off Rte. 707, Jupiter Island.* ☞ *$5 per vehicle.* ☼ *Daily sunrise–sunset.*

Though on the Hobe Sound National Wildlife Refuge, the appealing ☺ **Hobe Sound Nature Center** is an independent organization. Its museum, which has baby alligators, baby crocodiles, and a scary-looking tarantula, is a child's delight. Interpretive exhibits focus on the environment, and a ½-mi trail winds through a forest of sand pine and scrub oak—one of Florida's most unusual and endangered plant communities. A classroom program on environmental issues is for preschool-age children to adults. ⊠ *13640 S.E. Federal Hwy., Hobe Sound,* ☎ *561/546–2067.* ☞ *Free.* ☼ *Trail daily sunrise–sunset; nature center weekdays 9–11 and 1–3, call for Sat. hrs, group tours by appointment.*

Once you've gotten to the **Jonathan Dickinson State Park,** follow signs to Hobe Mountain. An ancient dune topped with a tower, it yields a panoramic view across the park's 10,285 acres of varied terrain, as well as the Intracoastal Waterway. The Loxahatchee River, part of the federal government's Wild and Scenic Rivers program, cuts through the park and harbors manatees in winter and alligators year-round. Two-hour boat tours of the river leave four times daily. Among amenities here are bicycle and hiking trails, a campground, and a snack bar. ⊠ *16450 S.E. Federal Hwy., Hobe Sound,* ☎ *561/546–2771.* ☞ *$3.25 per vehicle with up to 8 people, boat tours $10.* ☼ *Daily 8–sunset.*

Outdoor Activities and Sports

Jonathan Dickinson's River Tours (⊠ Jonathan Dickinson State Park, ☎ 561/746–1466) rents canoes for use around the park.

Stuart

③② *7 mi north of Hobe Sound.*

This compact little town on a peninsula that juts out into the St. Lucie River has a remarkable amount of river shoreline for its size as well as a charming historic district. The ocean is about 5 mi east.

★ Strict architectural and zoning standards guide civic renewal projects in **historic downtown Stuart,** which now claims eight antiques shops, six restaurants, and more than 50 specialty shops within a two-block area. The old courthouse has become the **Cultural Court House Center** (⊠ 80 E. Ocean Blvd., ☎ 561/288–2542), which features art exhibits. The George W. Parks General Store is now the **Stuart Heritage Museum** (⊠ 101 S.W. Flagler Ave., ☎ 561/220–4600). On the National Register of Historic Places, the **Lyric Theatre** (⊠ 59 S.W. Flagler Ave., ☎ 561/220–1942) has been revived for performing and community events; a gazebo features free music performances. For information on downtown, contact the **Stuart Main Street Office** (⊠ 151 S.W. Flagler Ave., 34994, ☎ 561/286–2848).

Dining and Lodging

$$ ★ ✕ **The Ashley.** Although plants hang from the ceiling and art decorates the walls, this restaurant still has elements of the old bank that was robbed three times early in the century by the Ashley Gang (hence the name). The big outdoor mural in the French Impressionist style was paid for by downtown revivalists, whose names are duly inscribed on wall plaques inside. The Continental menu appeals, with lots of salads, fresh fish, and pastas. Crowds head to the lounge for a popular happy hour. ⊠ 61 S.W. Osceola St., ☎ 561/221–9476. AE, MC, V. Closed Mon. in off-season.

$$ ✕ **Jolly Sailor Pub.** In an old historic-district bank building, this eatery is owned by a 27-year British Merchant Navy veteran, which may account for the endless ship paraphernalia. A veritable Cunard museum, it has a model of the Britannia, prints of 19th-century side-wheelers, and a big bar painting of the QE2. There are a wonderful brass-railed wood bar, a dartboard, and such pub grub as fish-and-chips, cottage pie, and bangers and mash, with Guinness and Double Diamond ales on tap. You can also get hamburgers and salads. ⊠ 1 S.W. Osceola St., ☎ 561/221–1111. AE, MC, V.

$$ ▦ **The Homeplace.** The house was built in 1913 by pioneer Sam Matthews, who contracted much of the early town construction for railroad developer Henry Flagler. Hardwood floors have been restored, and rooms are individually and quaintly decorated with antiques. The fern-filled dining room and Victorian parlor, full of cushioned wicker, overlook a pool, heated spa, and patio. A full breakfast is included. ⊠ 501 Akron Ave., 34994, ☎ 561/220–9148. 4 rooms. Pool, hot tub. MC, V.

$–$$$ ▦ **HarborFront.** On a quiet site that slopes to the St. Lucie River, this ★ B&B combines an unusual mix of accommodations and imaginative extras, including picnic baskets and conciergelike custom planning. Units are cozy and eclectic, ranging from a spacious chintz-covered suite to a cozy apartment with full kitchen, from rooms that are tweedy and dark to those that are airy and bright with a private deck. Furnishings mix wicker and antiques. From hammocks in the yard you can watch pelicans and herons, or take a full- or half-day sail on the 33-ft sailboat that's tied up to the dock. ⊠ 310 Atlanta Ave., 34994, ☎ 561/ 288–7289. 6 rooms, 2 suites, 1 cottage, 2 apartments. Hot tub, dock, boating. MC, V.

Outdoor Activities and Sports

Deep-sea charters are available at the **Sailfish Marina** (⊠ 3565 S.E. St. Lucie Blvd., ☎ 561/283–1122).

Shopping

More than 60 restaurants and shops featuring antiques, art, and fashions have opened along **Osceola Street** in the restored downtown area, with hardly a vacancy.

Hutchinson Island (Jensen Beach)

③ *5 mi northeast of Stuart.*

Unusual care limits development here and prevents the commercial crowding found to the north and south, although there are some high-rises here and there along the shore. The small town of Jensen Beach, part of which is in the central part of the island, actually stretches across both sides of the Indian River. Citrus farmers and fishermen still play a big role in the community, giving the area a down-to-earth feel. Its most notable population is that of the sea turtles; between late April and August more than 600 turtles come to nest along the town's Atlantic beach.

Built in 1875, the **House of Refuge Museum** is the only remaining building of nine such structures erected by the U.S. Life Saving Service (a predecessor of the Coast Guard) to aid stranded sailors. Exhibits include antique lifesaving equipment, maps, artifacts from nearby wrecks, and boat-making tools. ⊠ *301 S.E. Mac Blvd.,* ☎ *561/225–1875.* ⊠ *$2.* ☉ *Tues.–Sun. 11–4.*

Run by the Florida Oceanographic Society, the **Coastal Science Center** consists of a coastal hardwood hammock and mangrove forest. Expansion has yielded a visitor center, a science center with interpretive exhibits on coastal science and environmental issues, and a ½-mi interpretive boardwalk. Guided nature walks are offered. ⊠ *890 N.E. Ocean Blvd.,* ☎ *561/225–0505.* ⊠ *$3.50.* ☉ *Mon.–Sat. 10–5, nature walks Mon.–Sat. 10:30 and by request.*

The pastel-pink **Elliott Museum** was built in 1961 in honor of Sterling Elliott, inventor of an early automated addressing machine and a four-wheel cycle. The museum features antique automobiles, dolls and toys, and fixtures from an early general store, blacksmith shop, and apothecary shop. ⊠ *825 N.E. Ocean Blvd.,* ☎ *561/225–1961.* ⊠ *$6.* ☉ *Daily 10–4.*

Bathtub Beach (⊠ MacArthur Blvd. off Rte. A1A), at the north end of the Indian River Plantation, is ideal for children because the waters are shallow for about 300 ft offshore and usually calm. At low tide bathers can walk to the reef. Facilities include rest rooms and showers.

Dining and Lodging

$$–$$$ ✕ **11 Maple Street.** This 16-table restaurant is as good as it gets on
★   the Treasure Coast. Run by Margee and Mike Perrin, it offers a Continental menu that changes nightly. The soft recorded jazz and the earnest, friendly staff satisfy as fully as the brilliant food served in ample portions. Appetizers might include walnut bread with melted fontina cheese or sautéed conch with balsamic vinegar; among entrées are salmon with leeks, lobster, and blue-crab cake, and porcini mushroom risotto. For dessert look out for cherry *clafouti* (like a bread pudding) and white-chocolate custard with blackberry sauce. ⊠ *3224 Maple Ave.,* ☎ *561/334–7714. Reservations essential. MC, V. Closed Mon.–Tues. No lunch.*

$$–$$$ ✕ **Scalawags.** The look is plantation tropical—coach lanterns, gingerbread, wicker, slow-motion paddle fans—but the top-notch buffets are aimed at today's resort guests. Standouts are the all-you-can-eat Wednesday evening Seafood Extravaganza, with jumbo shrimp, Alaskan crab legs, clams on the half shell, marinated salmon, and fresh catch. A regular menu with a big selection of fish, shellfish, and grills plus a big salad bar is also offered. The main dining room in this second-floor restaurant at the Indian River Plantation Marriott Beach Resort over-

looks the Indian River; there is also a private 20-seat wine room and a terrace that looks out on the marina. ✉ *555 N.E. Ocean Blvd.,* ☎ *561/225–6818. AE, DC, MC, V.*

$$ ✕ **Conchy Joe's.** This classic Florida stilt house full of antique fish mounts, gator hides, and snakeskins dates from the late 1920s—but Conchy Joe's, like a hermit crab sliding into a new shell, only moved up from West Palm Beach in 1983. Under a huge Seminole-built *chickee* (raised wood platform) with a palm through the roof, you find a supercasual atmosphere and the freshest Florida seafood from a menu that changes daily. Staples, however, are the grouper marsala, broiled sea scallop, and fried cracked conch. Try the rum drinks with names like Goombay Smash and Bahama Mama, while listening to steelband calypso or reggae Wednesday–Sunday. Happy hour is 3–6 daily and during all NFL games. ✉ *3945 N. Indian River Dr.,* ☎ *561/334–1130. AE, D, MC, V.*

$ ✕ **The Emporium.** Indian River Plantation Marriott Beach Resort's coffee shop is an old-fashioned soda fountain and grill that also serves hearty breakfasts. Specialties include eggs Benedict, omelets, deli sandwiches, and salads. ✉ *555 N.E. Ocean Blvd.,* ☎ *561/225–3700. AE, DC, MC, V.*

$$$–$$$$ 🏨 **Indian River Plantation Marriott Beach Resort.** With a wealth of recreational activities and facilities as well as many restaurants and bars, this 200-acre sprawling yet self-contained resort is an excellent choice for families. Reception, some of the restaurants, and many rooms are in three yellow four-story buildings that form an open courtyard with a large swimming pool. Additional rooms and apartments with kitchens are in numerous other buildings spread around the property. Some overlook the Intracoastal Waterway and the resort's 77-slip marina, while other rooms look out to the ocean or onto tropical gardens. Complimentary tram service runs to key points around the property day and night. ✉ *555 N.E. Ocean Blvd., Hutchinson Island, Stuart 34996,* ☎ *561/225–3700 or 800/775–5936. 299 rooms, 27 suites, 150 condominiums. 5 restaurants, 4 bars, 4 pools, spa, 18-hole golf course, 13 tennis courts, beach, docks, boating, children's program. AE, DC, MC, V.*

$$–$$$ 🏨 **Hutchinson Inn.** Sandwiched among the high-rises, this modest and affordable two-story motel from the mid-1970s has the feel of a B&B thanks to pretty canopies at the entrance and management's friendly attitude. An expanded Continental breakfast is served in the well-appointed lobby or on little tables outside, and you can borrow a book or a stack of magazines to take to your room, where homemade cookies are delivered in the evenings. On Saturday there's a noon barbecue. Motel-style rooms range from small but comfortable to fully equipped efficiencies and seafront suites with private balconies. ✉ *9750 S. Ocean Dr., 34957,* ☎ *561/229–2000,* 𝖥𝖠𝖷 *561/229–8875. 19 rooms, 2 suites. Pool, tennis court, beach. MC, V.*

Outdoor Activities and Sports

BASEBALL
The **New York Mets** (✉ 525 N.W. Peacock Blvd., Port St. Lucie, ☎ 561/871–2115) train at the St. Lucie County Sport Complex.

GOLF
Indian River Plantation Marriott Beach Resort (✉ 555 N.E. Ocean Blvd., ☎ 561/225–3700 or 800/444–3389) sports 18 holes. The PGA-operated **PGA Golf Club at the Reserve** (✉ 1916 Perfect Dr., Port St. Lucie, ☎ 407/467–1300 or 800/800–4653) is a public facility scheduled to open its third 18-hole course by early 2000.

Fort Pierce

 11 mi north of Stuart.

This community, about an hour north of Palm Beach, has a distinctive rural feel, focusing on ranching and citrus farming rather than tourism. It has several worthwhile stops for visitors, including those easily seen while following Route 707.

Once a reservoir, 550-acre **Savannahs Recreation Area** has been returned to its natural state. Today the semiwilderness has campsites, a petting zoo, botanical garden, boat ramps, and trails. ✉ *1400 E. Midway Rd.,* ☎ *561/464–7855.* ✉ *$1 per vehicle.* ☉ *Daily 8–6.*

At the **Heathcote Botanical Gardens,** a self-guided tour takes in a palm walk, Japanese garden, and subtropical foliage. ✉ *210 Savannah Rd.,* ☎ *561/464–4672.* ✉ *$2.50.* ☉ *Tues.–Sat. 9–5, also Sun. 1–5 Nov.–Apr.*

As the home of the Treasure Coast Art Association, the **A. E. "Bean" Backus Gallery** displays the works of one of Florida's foremost landscape artists. The gallery also mounts changing exhibits and offers exceptional buys on work by local artists. ✉ *500 N. Indian River Dr.,* ☎ *561/465–0630.* ✉ *Donation welcome.* ☉ *Tues.–Sun. 1–5.*

Highlights at the **St. Lucie County Historical Museum** include historic photos, early 20th-century memorabilia, vintage farm tools, a restored 1919 American La France fire engine, replicas of a general store and the old Fort Pierce railroad station, and the restored 1905 Gardner House. ✉ *414 Seaway Dr.,* ☎ *561/462–1795.* ✉ *$3.* ☉ *Tues.–Sat. 10–4, Sun. noon–4.*

The 340-acre **Fort Pierce Inlet State Recreation Area** contains sand dunes and a coastal hammock. The park offers swimming, surfing, picnicking, hiking, and walking along a self-guided nature trail. ✉ *905 Shorewinds Dr.,* ☎ *561/468–3985.* ✉ *$3.25 per vehicle with up to 8 people.* ☉ *Daily 8–sunset.*

The **UDT-Seal Museum** commemorates the site where more than 3,000 navy frogmen trained during World War II. Weapons and equipment are on view, and exhibits depict the history of the UDTs (Underwater Demolition Teams). Numerous patrol boats and vehicles are displayed outdoors. ✉ *3300 N. Rte. A1A,* ☎ *561/595–5845.* ✉ *$3.25.* ☉ *Mon.–Sat. 10–4, Sun. noon–4.*

Accessible only by footbridge, the **Jack Island Wildlife Refuge** contains 4⅓ mi of trails. The 1½-mi Marsh Rabbit Trail across the island traverses a mangrove swamp to a 30-ft observation tower overlooking the Indian River. ✉ *Rte. A1A,* ☎ *561/468–3985.* ✉ *Free.* ☉ *Daily 8–sunset.*

The **Harbor Branch Oceanographic Institution** is an internationally recognized diversified research and teaching facility that offers a glimpse into the high-tech world of marine research. Its fleet of research vessels—particularly its two submersibles—operates around the world for NASA, NOAA, and NATO, among other contractors. Visitors can take a 90-minute tour of the 500-acre facility, including aquariums of sea life indigenous to the Indian River Lagoon, exhibits of marine technology, and other learning facilities. There are also lifelike and whimsical bronze sculptures created by founder J. Seward Johnson, Jr., and a gift shop with imaginative sea-related items. ✉ *5600 Old Dixie Hwy.,* ☎ *561/465–2400.* ✉ *$6.* ☉ *Tours Mon.–Sat. 10, noon, and 2.*

Dining and Lodging

$–$$ ✕ **Mangrove Mattie's.** Since its opening in the late 1980s, this upscale but rustic spot on Fort Pierce Inlet has provided dazzling waterfront views and imaginative nautical decor with delicious seafood. Dine outdoors on the terrace or inside in the cool air-conditioning, and try the coconut-fried shrimp or the chicken and scampi. Or come by during happy hour (weekdays 5–8) for a free buffet of snacks. ✉ *1640 Seaway Dr.,* ☎ *561/466–1044. AE, D, DC, MC, V.*

$–$$ ✕ **Theo Thudpucker's Raw Bar.** Businesspeople dressed for work mingle here with people fresh from the beach wearing shorts. On squally days everyone piles in off the jetty. Specialties include oyster stew, smoked fish spread, conch salad and conch fritters, fresh catfish, and alligator tail. ✉ *2025 Seaway Dr. (South Jetty),* ☎ *561/465–1078. No credit cards.*

$$ 🏠 **Mellon Patch Inn.** This tiny B&B has an excellent location—across the shore road from a beach park, at the end of a canal leading to the Indian River Lagoon. One side of the canal has a bank of attractive new homes; the other has the Jack Island Wildlife Refuge. Images of split-open melons permeate the house—on pillows, crafts, and candies on night tables. Each of the guest rooms has imaginative accessories, art, and upholstery appropriate to its individual theme. The cathedral-ceiling living room features a wood-burning fireplace, and full breakfast is included. ✉ *3601 N. Rte. A1A, North Hutchinson Island 34949,* ☎ *561/461–5231. 4 rooms. Dock, fishing. MC, V.*

$–$$ 🏠 **Harbor Light Inn.** The pick of the pack of lodgings lining the Fort Pierce Inlet along Seaway Drive is this modern nautical-style, blue-trimmed motel. Spacious units on two floors feature kitchen or wet bar and routine but well-cared-for furnishings. Half the rooms have a waterfront porch or balcony. In addition to the motel units there is a set of four apartments across the street (off the water), where in-season weekly rates are $360. ✉ *1156–1160 Seaway Dr., 34949,* ☎ *561/ 468–3555 or 800/433–0004. 17 rooms, 4 apartments. Pool, fishing, coin laundry. AE, D, DC, MC, V.*

Outdoor Activities and Sports

FISHING

For charter boats and fishing guides, try the **Dockside Inn** (✉ 1152 Seaway Dr., ☎ 561/461–4824).

JAI ALAI

Fort Pierce Jai Alai operates seasonally for live jai alai and year-round for off-track betting on horse-racing simulcasts. ✉ *1750 S. Kings Hwy., off Okeechobee Rd.,* ☎ *561/464–7500 or 800/524–2524.* 💳 *$1.* ☉ *Games Jan.–Apr., Wed. and Sat. 12:30 and 7, Thurs.–Fri. 7, Sun. 1; call to double-check schedule; simulcasts Wed.–Mon. noon and 7.*

SCUBA DIVING

Some 200 yards from shore and ¼ mi north of the UDT-Seal Museum on North Hutchinson Island, the **Urca de Lima Underwater Archaeological Preserve** features the remains of a flat-bottom, round-bellied storeship. Once part of a treasure fleet bound for Spain, it was destroyed by a hurricane. Dive boats can be chartered through the **Dockside Inn** (✉ 1152 Seaway Dr., ☎ 561/461–4824).

Shopping

One of Florida's best discount malls, the **Manufacturer's Outlet Center** (✉ Rte. 70, off I–95 at Exit 65) contains 41 stores offering such brand names as American Tourister, Jonathan Logan, Aileen, Polly Flinders, Van Heusen, London Fog, Levi Strauss, and Geoffrey Beene.

En Route To reach Vero Beach, you have two options—Route A1A, along the coast, or Route 605 (often called Old Dixie Highway), on the mainland. As you approach Vero on the latter, you'll pass through an ungussied landscape of small farms and residential areas. On the beach route, part of the drive is through an unusually undeveloped section of the Florida coast. Both trips are very relaxing.

Vero Beach

  12 mi north of Fort Pierce.

There's a tranquility to this Indian River County seat, an affluent town with a strong commitment to the environment and the arts. Retirees make up about half the winter population. In the exclusive Riomar Bay area of town, "canopy roads" are shaded by massive live oaks, and a popular cluster of restaurants and shops is just off the beach.

At the **Indian River Citrus Museum,** photos, farm tools, and videos tell about a time when oxen hauled the citrus crop to the railroads, when family fruit stands dotted the roadsides, and when gorgeous packing labels made every crate arriving up north an enticement to visit the Sunshine State. You can also book free citrus tours of actual groves. ⊠ *2140 14th Ave.,* ☎ *561/770–2263.* 🖼 *Donation welcome.* ☉ *Tues.– Sat. 10–4, Sun. 1–4.*

In Riverside Park's Civic Arts Center, the **Center for the Arts** presents a full schedule of exhibitions, art movies, lectures, workshops, and other events, with a focus on Florida artists. ⊠ *3001 Riverside Park Dr.,* ☎ *561/231–0707.* 🖼 *Free.* ☉ *Fri.–Wed. 10–4:30, Thurs. 10–8.*

In addition to a wet lab containing aquariums filled with Indian River Lagoon life, the outstanding 51-acre **Environmental Learning Center** has a 600-ft boardwalk through mangrove shoreline and a 1-mi canoe trail. The center is on the north edge of Vero Beach, on Wabasso Island, but it's a pretty drive and worth the trip. ⊠ *255 Live Oak Dr.,* ☎ *561/589–5050.* 🖼 *Free.* ☉ *Weekdays 9–5, weekends 1–4.*

Humiston Park is just one of the beach-access parks along the east edge of town that have boardwalks and steps bridging the foredune. It has a large children's play area and picnic tables and is across the street from shops. ⊠ *Ocean Dr. below Beachland Blvd.,* ☎ *no phone.* 🖼 *Free.* ☉ *Daily 7 AM–10 PM.*

The Arts
The **Civic Arts Center** (⊠ Riverside Park), a cluster of cultural facilities, includes the Riverside Theatre (⊠ 3250 Riverside Park Dr., ☎ 561/ 231–6990), which stages six productions each season in its 633-seat performance hall; the Agnes Wahlstrom Youth Playhouse (⊠ 3280 Riverside Park Dr., ☎ 561/234–8052), which mounts children's productions; and the Center for the Arts (⊠ 3001 Riverside Park Dr., ☎ 561/231– 0707), which presents art movies and lectures in addition to its other offerings. **Riverside Children's Theatre** (⊠ 3280 Riverside Park Dr., ☎ 561/234–8052) offers a series of professional touring and local productions, as well as acting workshops at the Agnes Wahlstrom Youth Playhouse.

Dining and Lodging
$$–$$$ ✕ **Black Pearl.** This intimate and sophisticated restaurant, one of Vero's trendiest dining picks, has moved to a new riverfront location, and now water views accompany the superb cuisine. The menu emphasizes fresh local ingredients. Specialties include chilled leek-and-asparagus soup, fresh oysters, local fish in parchment paper with fresh vegetable chutney, and panfried veal with local shrimp and vermouth.

⊠ *4455 N. Rte. A1A,* ☎ *561/234–4426. AE, MC, V. No lunch weekends.*

$$–$$$ ✕ **Ocean Grill.** Opened by Waldo Sexton as a hamburger shack in 1938,
★ the oceanfront Ocean Grill is now furnished with Tiffany lamps,
wrought-iron chandeliers, and Beanie Backus paintings of pirates and
Seminole Indians. The menu includes black-bean soup, jumbo lump-
crabmeat salad, and at least three kinds of fish every day. The house
drink, the Leaping Limey, a curious blend of vodka, blue curaçao, and
lemon, commemorates the 1894 wreck of the *Breconshire,* which occurred just offshore and from which 34 British sailors escaped. The
bar and some tables look over the water. ⊠ *1050 Sexton Plaza (Beachland Blvd. east of Ocean Dr.),* ☎ *561/231–5409. AE, D, DC, MC, V.
Closed 2 wks following Labor Day. No lunch weekends.*

$–$$ ✕ **Pearl's Bistro.** Island-style cuisine is the draw at this laid-back and
less expensive sister restaurant to the Black Pearl (☞ *above*). For
starters try the pasta Rasta, the seafood chowder, or the Jamaican jerk
shrimp. Then move on to grilled Yucatán-spiced local fish, barbecued
ribs, Bahamian shrimp and grouper pepper pot, or blackened New York
strip with peppery rum sauce. ⊠ *56 Royal Palm Blvd.,* ☎ *561/778–
2950. AE, MC, V. No lunch Sun.*

$$$–$$$$ ▦ **Disney's Vero Beach Resort.** Built on 71 oceanfront acres, this
sprawling vacation getaway, which operates both as a time-share and
a hotel, is the classiest resort in Vero Beach. The main four-story build-
ing, three freestanding villas, and six beach cottages are nestled among
tropical greenery. Buildings are painted in pale pastels and sport steeply
pitched gables, and many units have balconies. Bright interiors feature
rattan furniture and tile floors. ⊠ *9235 Rte. A1A, 32963,* ☎ *561/234–
2000. 161 rooms, 14 suites, 6 cottages. 2 restaurants, bar, pool, wad-
ing pool, 6 tennis courts, basketball, bicycles, video games. AE, D, DC,
MC, V.*

$$$–$$$$ ▦ **DoubleTree Guest Suites.** This five-story rose-color stucco hotel is
conveniently located—right on the beach and near restaurants, specialty
shops, and boutiques. One- and two-bedroom suites have patios open-
ing onto a pool or balconies and excellent ocean views. ⊠ *3500 Ocean
Dr., 32963,* ☎ *561/231–5666. 55 suites. Bar, 2 pools, wading pool,
hot tub. AE, D, DC, MC, V.*

$$ ▦ **Captain Hiram's Islander Motel.** Across from the beach, the aqua-
and-white-trim Islander has a snoozy Key West style that contrasts
stylishly with the smart shops it's tucked between. Jigsaw-cut brack-
ets and balusters and beach umbrellas dress up the pool. All rooms feature white wicker, paddle fans hung from vaulted ceilings, and fresh
flowers. It's just right for beachside Vero. ⊠ *3101 Ocean Dr., 32963,*
☎ *561/231–4431 or 800/952–5886. 16 rooms, 1 efficiency. Pool. AE,
DC, MC, V.*

Outdoor Activities and Sports

The **Los Angeles Dodgers** (⊠ 4101 26th St., ☎ 561/569–4900) train
at Dodgertown, actually in Vero Beach.

Shopping

Along **Ocean Drive** near Beachland Boulevard, a specialty shopping area
includes art galleries, antiques shops, and upscale clothing stores.

Sebastian

③⑥ *7 mi north of Vero Beach.*

One of only a few sparsely populated areas on Florida's east coast, this
little fishing village has as remote a feeling as you'll find anywhere between Jacksonville and Miami Beach. That remoteness adds to the ap-

peal of the recreation area around Sebastian Inlet, where you can walk for miles along quiet beaches.

The **McLarty Treasure Museum,** designated a National Historical Landmark, features displays dedicated to the 1715 hurricane that sank a fleet of Spanish treasure ships. ⊠ *13180 N. Rte. A1A,* ☎ *561/589–2147.* ☜ *$1.* ☉ *Daily 10–4:30.*

You've really come upon hidden loot when you step into **Mel Fisher's Treasure Museum.** Here you can view some of what was recovered from the Spanish treasure ship *Atocha* and its sister ships of the 1715 fleet. Fisher operates a similar museum in Key West. ⊠ *1322 U.S. 1,* ☎ *561/589–9875.* ☜ *$5.* ☉ *Mon.–Sat. 10–5, Sun. noon–5.*

Because of the highly productive fishing waters of Sebastian Inlet, at the north end of Orchid Island, the 578-acre **Sebastian Inlet State Recreation Area** is one of the best-attended parks in the Florida state system. On both sides of the high bridge that spans the inlet—from which the views are spectacular—the recreation area attracts plenty of anglers as well as those eager to enjoy the fine sandy beaches (both within the recreation area and outside it), which are known for having the best waves in the state. A concession stand on the north side of the inlet sells short-order food, rents various craft, and has an apparel and surf shop. A boat ramp is available. Not far away along the sea is a dune area that's part of the **Archie Carr National Wildlife Refuge,** a haven for sea turtles and other protected Florida wildlife. ⊠ *9700 S. Rte. A1A, Melbourne Beach,* ☎ *407/984–4852;* ⊠ *1300 Rte. A1A, Melbourne Beach,* ☎ *561/589–9659.* ☜ *$3.25.* ☉ *Daily 24 hrs, bait and tackle shop daily 7:30–6, concession stand daily 8–5.*

Dining and Lodging

$–$$ ✕ **Capt. Hiram's.** This family-friendly restaurant on the Indian River Lagoon is easygoing, fanciful, and fun—definitely not purposefully hip. As the sign says, NECKTIES ARE PROHIBITED. The place is "real"—full of wooden booths, stained glass, umbrellas on the open deck, and ceiling fans. Don't miss Capt. Hiram's Sandbar, where kids can play while parents enjoy a drink at stools set in an outdoor shower or a beached boat. Choose among seafood brochette, New York strip steak, the fresh catch, and lots of other seafood dishes as well as raw-bar items. The full bar has a weekday happy hour and free hot hors d'oeuvres Friday 5–6. There's nightly entertainment in season. ⊠ *1606 N. Indian River Dr.,* ☎ *561/589–4345. AE, D, MC, V.*

$–$$ ✕ **Hurricane Harbor.** Built in 1927 as a garage and used during Prohibition as a smugglers' den, Hurricane Harbor now draws a year-round crowd of retirees and locals. Guests love the waterfront window seats on stormy nights, when sizable waves break outside in the Indian River Lagoon. The menu features seafood, steaks, and grills, along with lighter fare. On Friday and Saturday nights the Antique Dining Room is opened, with linen, stained glass, and a huge antique breakfront. There's also live music nightly. ⊠ *1540 Indian River Dr.,* ☎ *561/589–1773. AE, D, MC, V. Closed Mon.*

$–$$ 🏠 **Captain's Quarters Riverfront Motel.** Five units—four overlooking the Indian River Lagoon and the marina at Capt. Hiram's restaurant and one two-room suite—are all Key West cute. Painted in bright colors with matching fabrics, the rooms have pine and white-wicker furniture and pine plank floors with grass rugs. The adequate bathrooms have large stall showers. Glass doors open to a plank porch, but the porches are all within sight of each other. ⊠ *1606 Indian River Dr., 32958,* ☎ *561/589–4345. 4 rooms, 1 suite. Restaurant. AE, D, MC, V.*

$-$$ ☑ **Davis House Inn.** Vero native Steve Wild modeled his two-story inn after the clubhouse at Augusta National, and, perhaps surprisingly, it fits right in with Sebastian's fishing-town look. Wide overhung roofs shade wraparound porches. In a companion house that Steve calls the Gathering Room, he serves a complimentary expanded Continental breakfast. Rooms are huge—virtual suites, with large sitting areas—though somewhat underfurnished. Overall, it's a terrific value. ☒ *607 Davis St., 32958,* ☎ *561/589–4114. 12 rooms. Bicycles. MC, V.*

Outdoor Activities and Sports

CANOEING AND KAYAKING

Bill Rogers Outdoor Adventures (☒ 1541 DeWitt La., ☎ 561/564–9600) outfits canoe trips down the Sebastian River, along Indian River Lagoon, and through Pelican Island Wildlife Refuge, as well as more distant locations. The concession stand at **Sebastian Inlet State Recreation Area** (☒ 9700 S. Rte. A1A, Melbourne Beach, ☎ 561/984–4852) rents canoes, kayaks, and paddleboats.

FISHING

The best inlet fishing in the region is at **Sebastian Inlet State Recreation Area** (☒ 9700 S. Rte. A1A, Melbourne Beach), where the catch includes bluefish, flounder, jack, redfish, sea trout, snapper, snook, and Spanish mackerel. For deep-sea fishing try *Miss Sebastian* (☒ Sembler Dock, ½ block north of Capt. Hiram's restaurant, ☎ 561/589–3275); $25 for a half day covers rod, reel, and bait. **Sebastian Inlet Marina at Capt. Hiram's** (☒ 1606 Indian River Dr., ☎ 561/589–4345) offers half- and full-day fishing charters.

WINDSURFING

The **Sailboard School** (☒ 9125 U.S. 1, ☎ 561/589–2671 or 800/253–6573) provides year-round one-day, weekend, and five-day programs of windsurfing instruction, including boards, for $120 a day, $575 for five days.

PALM BEACH AND THE TREASURE COAST A TO Z

Arriving and Departing

By Bus

Greyhound Lines (☎ 800/231–2222) buses arrive at the station in West Palm Beach (☒ 100 Banyan Blvd., ☎ 561/833–8534).

By Car

I–95 runs north–south, linking West Palm Beach with Miami and Fort Lauderdale to the south and with Daytona, Jacksonville, and the rest of the Atlantic coast to the north. To get to central Palm Beach, exit at Belvedere Road or Okeechobee Boulevard. Florida's Turnpike runs up from Miami through West Palm Beach before angling northwest to reach Orlando.

By Plane

Palm Beach International Airport (PBIA) (☒ Congress Ave. and Belvedere Rd., West Palm Beach, ☎ 561/471–7400) is served by **Air Canada** (☎ 800/776–3000), **American/American Eagle** (☎ 800/433–7300), **American Trans-Air** (☎ 800/225–2995), **Canadian Holidays** (☎ 800/661–8881), **Carnival Airlines** (☎ 800/824–7386), **Comair** (☎ 800/354–9822), **Continental** (☎ 800/525–0280), **Delta** (☎ 800/221–1212), **KIWI International Airlines** (☎ 800/538–5494), **Northwest** (☎ 800/225–2525), **Paradise Island** (☎ 800/432–8807), **Republic Air Travel** (☎ 800/233–

0225), **Spirit Airlines** (☎ 561/471–7467), **TWA** (☎ 800/221–2000), **United** (☎ 800/241–6522), and **US Airways/US Airways Express** (☎ 800/428–4322).

BETWEEN THE AIRPORT AND THE TOWNS

Route 10 of **Tri-Rail Commuter Bus Service** (☎ 800/874–7245) runs from the airport to Tri-Rail's nearby Palm Beach airport station daily. **CoTran** (☞ Getting Around by Bus, *below*) Route 4-S operates from the airport to downtown West Palm Beach every two hours at 35 minutes after the hour from 7:35 until 5:35. The fare is $1.

Palm Beach Transportation (☎ 561/689–4222) provides taxi and limousine service from PBIA. Reserve at least a day in advance for a limousine. The lowest fares are $1.50 per mile, with the meter starting at $1.25. Depending on your destination, a flat rate (from PBIA only) may save money. Wheelchair-accessible vehicles are available.

By Train

Amtrak (☎ 800/872–7245) connects West Palm Beach (✉ 201 S. Tamarind Ave., ☎ 561/832–6169) with cities along Florida's east coast and the Northeast daily and via the *Sunset Limited* to New Orleans and Los Angeles three times weekly. Included in Amtrak's service is transport from West Palm Beach to Okeechobee (✉ 801 N. Parrott Ave.); the station is unmanned.

Getting Around

The **Downtown Transfer Facility** (✉ Banyan Blvd. and Clearlake Dr., West Palm Beach), off Australian Avenue at the west entrance to downtown, links the downtown shuttle, Amtrak, Tri-Rail (the commuter line of Miami-Dade, Broward, and Palm Beach counties), CoTran (the county bus system), Greyhound, and taxis.

By Bus

CoTran (Palm Beach County Transportation Authority) buses require exact change. The cost is $1.50, $1 for students, senior citizens, and people with disabilities (with reduced-fare ID); transfers are 20¢. Service operates 5 AM–8:30 PM, though pickups on most routes are 5:30 AM–7 PM. For details call CoTran (☎ 561/233–1111 for Palm Beach; 561/930–5123 for Boca Raton–Delray Beach).

Palmtran (☎ 561/833–8873) is a shuttle system that provides free transportation around downtown West Palm Beach, weekdays 6:30 AM–7:30 PM.

By Car

U.S. 1 threads north–south along the coast, connecting most coastal communities, while the more scenic Route A1A ventures out onto the barrier islands. The interstate, I–95, runs parallel to U.S. 1 but a bit farther inland.

A nonstop four-lane route, Okeechobee Boulevard carries traffic from west of downtown West Palm Beach, near the Amtrak station in the airport district, directly to the Flagler Memorial Bridge and into Palm Beach. Plans are in the works to turn Flagler Drive over for pedestrian use sometime in the next several years.

The best way to get to Lake Okeechobee from West Palm is to drive west on Southern Boulevard from I–95 past the cutoff road to Lion Country Safari. From there the boulevard is designated U.S. 98/441.

By Taxi

Palm Beach Transportation (☎ 561/689–4222) has a single number serving several cab companies. Meters start at $1.25, and the charge is $1.25

per mile within West Palm Beach city limits; if the trip at any point leaves the city limits, the fare is $1.50 per mile. Some cabs may charge more. Waiting time is 25¢ per 75 seconds.

By Train

Tri-Rail (☎ 800/874–7245), the commuter rail system, has six stations in Palm Beach County (13 stops altogether between West Palm Beach and Miami). The round-trip fare is $5, $2.50 for students and senior citizens.

Contacts and Resources

Emergencies

Dial **911** for police or ambulance.

HOSPITALS

The following hospitals have 24-hour emergency rooms: **Good Samaritan Hospital** (⊠ Flagler Dr. and Palm Beach Lakes Blvd., West Palm Beach, ☎ 561/655–5511; 561/650–6240 physician referral), **JFK Medical Center** (⊠ 5301 S. Congress Ave., Atlantis, ☎ 561/965–7300; 561/642–3628 physician referral), **Palm Beaches Medical Center** (⊠ 2201 45th St., West Palm Beach, ☎ 561/694–7124; 561/881–2661 physician referral), **Palm Beach Regional Hospital** (⊠ 2829 10th Ave. N, Lake Worth, ☎ 561/967–7800), and **St. Mary's Hospital** (⊠ 901 45th St., West Palm Beach, ☎ 561/844–6300; 561/881–2929 physician referral).

LATE-NIGHT PHARMACIES

Eckerd Drug (⊠ 3343 S. Congress Ave., Palm Springs, ☎ 561/965–3367) and **Walgreens** (⊠ 1688 S. Congress Ave., Palm Springs, ☎ 561/968–8211; ⊠ 7561 N. Federal Hwy., Boca Raton, ☎ 561/241–9802; ⊠ 1634 S. Federal Hwy., Boynton Beach, ☎ 561/737–1260; ⊠ 1208 Royal Palm Beach Blvd., Royal Palm Beach, ☎ 561/798–9048; ⊠ 6370 Indiantown Rd., Jupiter, ☎ 561/744–6822; ⊠ 20 E. 30th St., Riviera Beach, ☎ 561/848–6464).

Guided Tours

BOAT TOURS

Capt. Doug's (⊠ Sebastian Marina, Sebastian, ☎ 561/589–2329) offers three-hour lunch and dinner cruises along the Indian River on board a 35-ft sloop. Cost is $100 per couple, including meal, tips, beer, and wine. **J-Mark Fish Camp** (⊠ Torry Island, ☎ 561/996–5357) has 45- to 60-minute airboat rides for $20 per person, with a minimum of two people and a maximum of six; 90- to 120-minute rides for $30 per person include a look at an active eagle's nest. **Jonathan Dickinson's River Tours** (⊠ Jonathan Dickinson State Park, 16450 S.E. Federal Hwy., Hobe Sound, ☎ 561/746–1466) runs two-hour guided riverboat cruises daily at 9, 11, 1, and 3 and once a month, at the full moon, at 7. The cost is $12. **Loxahatchee Everglades Tours** (⊠ 10400 Loxahatchee Rd., ☎ 561/482–6107) operates airboat tours year-round from west of Boca Raton through the marshes between the built-up coast and Lake Okeechobee. The *Manatee Queen* (⊠ Jonathan Dickinson State Park, 16450 S.E. Federal Hwy., Hobe Sound, ☎ 561/744–2191), a 49-passenger catamaran, offers day and evening cruises November–May on the Intracoastal Waterway and into the park's cypress swamps.

Ramblin' Rose Riverboat (⊠ 1 N.E. 1st St., Delray Beach, ☎ 561/243–0686) operates luncheon, dinner-dance, and Sunday brunch cruises along the Intracoastal Waterway. The *Spirit of St. Joseph* (⊠ 109 Myrtle St., Fort Pierce, ☎ 561/467–2628) offers seven lunch and dinner cruises weekly on the Indian River, leaving from alongside the St. Lucie County Historical Museum. Atlantic Cruises' *Star of Palm Beach* (⊠ Phil Foster Park, 900 E. Blue Heron Rd., Palm Beach, ☎ 561/842–0882) runs year-round from Singer Island, each day offering one dinner-dance and three sightseeing cruises on the Intracoastal Waterway. **Water Taxi Scenic Cruises** (✉ Sailfish Marina and Riviera Beach Marina, Palm Beach, ☎ 561/775–2628) offers several different daily sightseeing tours in a 16-person launch. Two are designed to let you get a close-up look at the mansions of the rich and famous. The southern tour features the mansions of Palm Beach, while the northern tour follows the North Palm Beach Canal. There are also a one-hour BYOB sunset cruise and a 2½-hour environmental tour to Munyon Island, which usually includes many dolphin sightings.

ECOTOURS

Contact the **Audubon Society of the Everglades** (✉ Box 16914, West Palm Beach 33461, ☎ 561/588–6908) for field trips and nature walks. **Swampland Tours** (✉ 103 75th Hwy. 78W, Okeechobee 34974, ☎ 941/467–4411), on Lake Okeechobee, operates interpretive boat tours through the National Audubon Society Wildlife Sanctuary.

HISTORICAL TOURS

The **Boca Raton Historical Society** (✉ 71 N. Federal Hwy., Boca Raton, ☎ 561/395–6766) offers afternoon tours of the Boca Raton Resort & Club on Tuesday year-round and to other South Florida sites. The **Fort Pierce Historical Society** (✉ 131 Main St., Fort Pierce, ☎ 561/466–3880) gives walking tours of the town's historic section, past buildings built by early settlers. The **Indian River County Historical Society** (✉ 2336 14th Ave., Vero Beach, ☎ 561/778–3435) conducts walking tours of downtown Vero on Wednesday at 11 and 1 (by reservation). **Old Northwood Historic District Tours** (✉ 501 30th St., West Palm Beach, ☎ 561/863–5633) leads two-hour walking tours that include visits to historic home interiors. They leave Sunday at 2, and a $5 donation is requested. Tours for groups of six or more can be scheduled almost any day.

Visitor Information

Belle Glade Chamber of Commerce (✉ 540 S. Main St., Belle Glade 33430, ☎ 561/996–2745). **Chamber of Commerce of the Palm Beaches** (✉ 401 N. Flagler Dr., West Palm Beach 33401, ☎ 561/833–3711). **Clewiston Chamber of Commerce** (✉ 544 W. Sugarland Hwy., Clewiston 33440, ☎ 941/983–7979). **Glades County Chamber of Commerce** (✉ U.S. 27 and 10th St., Moore Haven 33471, ☎ 941/946–0440). **Indian River County Tourist Council** (✉ 1216 21st St., Box 2947, Vero Beach 32961, ☎ 561/567–3491). **Indiantown and Western Martin County Chamber of Commerce** (✉ 15518 S.W. Osceola St., Indiantown 34956, ☎ 561/597–2184). **Okeechobee County Chamber of Commerce** (✉ 55 S. Parrott Ave., Okeechobee 34974, ☎ 941/763–6464). **Pahokee Chamber of Commerce** (✉ 115 E. Main St., Pahokee 33476, ☎ 561/924–5579). **Palm Beach Chamber of Commerce** (✉ 45 Cocoanut Row, Palm Beach 33480, ☎ 561/655–3282). **Palm Beach County Convention & Visitors Bureau** (✉ 1555 Palm Beach Lakes Blvd., Suite 204, West Palm Beach 33401, ☎ 561/471–3995). **St. Lucie County Tourist Development Council** (✉ 2300 Virginia Ave., Fort Pierce 34982, ☎ 561/462–1535). **Stuart/Martin County Chamber of Commerce** (✉ 1650 S. Kanner Hwy., Stuart 34994, ☎ 561/287–1088). For more information on the Okeechobee area, contact the **U.S. Army Corps of Engineers** (✉ South Florida Operations Office, 525 Ridgelawn Rd., Clewiston 33440-5399, ☎ 941/983–8101).

6 THE FLORIDA KEYS

The Keys are one of America's last frontiers. Here both humans and nature seek refuge in a verdant island chain that stretches raggedly west-southwest across a deep blue-green seascape at the base of the Florida peninsula.

Updated by
Diane P.
Marshall

THE FLORIDA KEYS ARE A WILDERNESS of flowering jungles and shimmering seas, a jade necklace of mangrove-fringed islands dangling toward the tropics. The Florida Keys are also a 110-mi traffic jam lined with garish billboards, hamburger stands, shopping centers, motels, and trailer courts. Unfortunately, in the Keys you can't have one without the other. A river of tourist traffic gushes along U.S. 1 (also called the Overseas Highway), the main artery between Key Largo and Key West. Residents of Monroe County live by diverting that river's flow of green dollars to their own pockets. In the process, the fragile beauty of the Keys—or at least the 45 that are inhabited and linked to the mainland by 43 bridges—has paid an environmental price.

Despite designation as "an area of critical state concern" in 1975 and a subsequent state-mandated development slowdown, rapid growth has continued, and the Keys' natural resources are still in peril. In 1990 Congress established the Florida Keys National Marine Sanctuary, covering 2,800 square nautical mi of coastal waters. Adjacent to the Keys landmass are spectacular, unique, and nationally significant marine environments, including sea-grass meadows, mangrove islands, and extensive living coral reefs. These fragile environments support rich and diverse biological communities possessing extensive conservation, recreational, commercial, ecological, historical, research, educational, and aesthetic values.

The Florida Keys National Marine Sanctuary and Protection Act is intended to protect the coral reefs and restore worsening water quality. But problems continue. Increased salinity in Florida Bay causes large areas of sea grass to die and drift in mats out of the bay. These mats then block sunlight from reaching the reefs, stifling their growth and threatening both the Keys' recreational diving economy and tourism in general.

Other threats to the Keys' charm also loom. As government officials with one hand sign the national marine sanctuary into effect, with the other they bring about the four-laning of U.S. 1 to the mainland, opening the floodgates to increased traffic, population, and tourism. Observers wonder if the four-laning of the rest of U.S. 1 throughout the Keys can be far away and if a trip to paradise will then be worth it.

For now, however, take pleasure as you drive down U.S. 1 along the islands. Most days you can gaze over the silvery blue and green Atlantic and its still-living reef, with Florida Bay, the Gulf of Mexico, and the backcountry on your right (the Keys extend east–west from the mainland). At a few points the ocean and gulf are as much as 10 mi apart. In most places, however, they are within 1–4 mi, and on the narrowest landfill islands, they are separated only by the road.

Things to do and see are everywhere, but first you have to remind yourself to get off the highway. Once you do, rent a boat and find a secluded anchorage and fish, swim, or marvel at the sun, sea, and sky. In the Atlantic you can dive to spectacular coral reefs or pursue dolphin, blue marlin, and other deep-water game fish. Along the Florida Bay coastline you can seek out the bonefish, snapper, snook, and tarpon that lurk in the grass flats and in the shallow, winding channels of the backcountry.

Along the reefs and among the islands are more than 600 kinds of fish. Diminutive deer and pale raccoons, related to but distinct from their mainland cousins, inhabit the Lower Keys. And throughout the islands you'll find such exotic West Indian plants as Jamaica dogwood, pigeon plum, poisonwood, satin leaf, and silver and thatch palms, as well as tropical birds, including the great white heron, mangrove cuckoo, roseate spoonbill, and white-crowned pigeon. Mangroves, with their gracefully bowed prop roots, appear to march out to sea. Day by day they busily add more keys to the archipelago.

With virtually no distracting air pollution or obstructive high-rises, sunsets are a pure, unadulterated spectacle that each evening attracts thousands of tourists and locals to waterfront parks, piers, restaurants, bars, and resorts throughout the Keys.

Another attraction is the weather: In the winter it's typically 10°F warmer than on the mainland; in the summer it's usually 10°F cooler. The Keys also get substantially less rain, around 30 inches annually, compared to an average 55–60 inches in Miami and the Everglades. Most rain falls in quick downpours on summer afternoons, except in June, September, and October, when tropical storms can dump rain for two to four days straight. In winter continental cold fronts occasionally stall over the Keys, dragging overnight temperatures down to the 40s.

The Keys were only sparsely populated until the early 20th century. In 1905, however, railroad magnate Henry Flagler began building the extension of his Florida railroad south from Homestead to Key West. His goal was to establish a rail link to the steamships that sailed between Key West and Havana, just 90 mi across the Straits of Florida. The railroad arrived at Key West in 1912 and remained a lifeline of commerce until the Labor Day hurricane of 1935 washed out much of its roadbed. For three years thereafter, the only way in and out of Key West was by boat. The Overseas Highway, built over the railroad's old roadbeds and bridges, was completed in 1938, and many sections and bridges have recently been widened or replaced.

New and Noteworthy

Hurricane Georges roared through the Florida Keys in September 1998, flooding and ripping apart waterfront hotels, businesses, and parks in Key West and the Middle and Lower keys. In most cases, recovery was swift, with all but a few properties reopening within a few days or weeks. The most long-term visible effects are in the landscaping, once lush with mature trees, sea oats, and palms, but now thin or nonexistent. In one way, visitors will benefit from the storm: Many properties took the opportunity to renovate and upgrade.

Florida State Parks opened two new facilities. After nearly a six-month closing, Windley Key Fossil Reef State Geologic Site, in Islamorada, reopened with the new Alison Fahrer Environmental Education Center and improved trails. In the Middle Keys, Curry Hammock State Park, considered one of the best kayaking areas in the Keys, opened with a wide beach, bathhouse, and picnic tables.

In Key West, the **Historic Seaport at Key West Bight** officially debuted after a $30 million renovation of the 8.5-acre waterfront area. More than 100 land- and sea-based businesses are now open.

Pleasures and Pastimes

Biking

Cyclists are now able to ride all but a tiny portion of the bike path that runs along the Overseas Highway from MM 106 south to the Seven Mile Bridge. The state plans to extend the route throughout the Keys. Some areas have lots of cross traffic, however, so ride with care.

Boating

If it floats, local marinas rent it. For up-close exploration of the mangroves and near-shore islands in Florida Bay, nothing beats a kayak or canoe. You can paddle within a few feet of a flock of birds without disturbing them. Visiting the backcountry islands and inlets of Everglades National Park requires a shallow-draft boat: A 14- to 17-ft skiff with a 40- to 50-horsepower outboard is sufficient. For diving the reef or fishing on the open ocean, you'll need a larger boat with greater horsepower. Houseboats are ideal for cruising the Keys.

Only experienced sailors should attempt to navigate the shallow waters surrounding the Keys with deep-keeled sailboats. On the other hand, small shallow-draft, single-hulled sailboats and catamarans are ideal. Personal water vehicles, such as Wave Runners and Jet Skis, rent by the half hour or hour but are banned in many areas. Flat, stable pontoon boats are a good choice for anyone with seasickness. Those interested in experiencing the reef without getting wet can take a glass-bottom boat trip.

Dining

A number of talented young chefs have settled in the Keys—especially Key West—contributing to the area's image as one of the nation's points of culinary interest. Restaurants' menus, rum-based fruit beverages, and music reflect the Keys' tropical climate and their proximity to Cuba and other Caribbean islands. Better restaurants serve imaginative and tantalizing fusion cuisine that draws on traditions from all over the world.

Florida citrus, seafood, and tropical fruits figure prominently, and Florida lobster and stone crab should be local and fresh from August to March. Also keep an eye out for authentic key lime pie. The real McCoy has a yellow custard in a graham-cracker crust and tastes like nothing else.

Restaurants may close for a two- to four-week vacation during the slow season—between mid-September and mid-November. Check local newspapers or call ahead, especially if driving any distance.

Fishing

These sun-bathed waters are home to 100 species of game fish as well as lobster, shrimp, and crabs. Flats fishing and backcountry fishing are Keys specialties. In flats fishing, a guide poles a shallow-draft outboard boat through the shallow, sandy-bottomed waters while sighting for bonefish and snook to be caught on light tackle, spin, and fly. Backcountry fishing may include flats fishing or fishing in the channels and basins around islands in Florida Bay. Charter boats fish the reef and Gulf Stream for deep-sea fish. Party boats, which can be crowded, carry up to 50 people to fish the reefs for grouper, kingfish, and snapper. Some operators boast a guarantee, or "no fish, no pay" policy.

Scuba Diving and Snorkeling

Diving in the Keys is spectacular. In shallow and deep water with visibility up to 120 ft, you can explore sea canyons and mountains covered with waving sea plumes, brain and star coral, historic shipwrecks, and sunken submarines. The colors of the coral are surpassed only by the brilliance of the fish that live around it. There's no best season for diving, but occasional storms in June, September, and October cloud the waters and make seas rough.

You can dive the reefs with scuba, snuba, or snorkeling gear, using your own boat, renting a boat, or booking a tour with a dive shop. Tours depart two or three times a day, stopping at two sites on each trip. The first trip of the day is usually the best. It's less crowded—vacationers like to sleep in—and visibility is better before the wind picks up in the afternoon. There's also night diving.

If you want to scuba dive but are not certified, take an introductory resort course. Though it doesn't result in certification, it allows you to scuba with an instructor in the afternoon following morning classroom and pool instruction.

Nearly all the waters surrounding the Keys are part of the Florida Keys National Marine Sanctuary and thus are protected. Signs, brochures, tour guides, and marine enforcement agents remind visitors that the reef is fragile and shouldn't be touched.

Exploring the Florida Keys

Finding your way around the Keys isn't hard once you understand the unique address system. Many addresses are simply given as a mile marker (MM) number. The markers themselves are small, green rectangular signs along the side of the Overseas Highway (U.S. 1). They begin with MM 126 a mile south of Florida City and end with MM 0, in Key West. Keys residents use the abbreviation BS for the bay side of U.S. 1 and OS for the ocean side. From Marathon to Key West, residents may refer to the bay side as the gulf side.

The Keys are divided into four areas: the Upper Keys, from Key Largo to the Long Key Channel (MM 106–65) and Ocean Reef and North Key Largo, off Card Sound Road and Route 905, respectively; the Middle Keys, from Conch (pronounced *konk*) Key through Marathon to the south side of the Seven Mile Bridge, including Pigeon Key (MM 65–40); the Lower Keys, from Little Duck Key south through Big Coppitt Key (MM 40–9); and Key West, from Stock Island through Key West (MM 9–0). The Keys don't end with the highway, however; they stretch another 70 mi west of Key West to the Dry Tortugas.

Numbers in the text correspond to numbers in the margin and on the Florida Keys and Key West maps.

Great Itineraries

IF YOU HAVE 3 DAYS

You can fly and then dive; but if you dive, you can't fly for 24 hours, so spend your first morning diving or snorkeling at John Pennekamp Coral Reef State Park in ⊞ **Key Largo** ②. If you aren't certified, take a resort course, and you'll be exploring the reefs by afternoon. Afterward, breeze through the park's visitor center. The rest of the afternoon can be whiled away either lounging around a pool or beach or visiting the Maritime Museum of the Florida Keys. Dinner or cocktails at a bay-side restaurant or bar will give you your first look at a fabulous Keys sunset. On day two, get an early start to savor the breathtaking views on the two-hour drive to Key West. Along the way make stops at the natural history museum that's part of the Museums of Crane Point Hammock, in **Marathon** ⑧, and Bahia Honda State Park, on **Bahia Honda Key** ⑨, where you can stretch your legs on a forest trail or snorkel on an offshore reef. Once in ⊞ **Key West** ⑫–㉜, you can watch the sunset before dining at one of the island's first-class restaurants. Spend the next morning exploring beaches, visiting any of the myriad museums, or taking a walking or trolley tour of Old Town before driving back to the mainland.

IF YOU HAVE 4 DAYS

Spend the first day as you would above, overnighting in ⊞ **Key Largo** ②. Start the second day by renting a kayak and exploring the mangroves and small islands of Florida Bay or take an ecotour of the islands in Everglades National Park. In the afternoon stop by the Florida Keys Wild Bird Rehabilitation Center before driving down to ⚅ **Islamorada** ④. Pause to read the inscription on the Hurricane Monument, and before day's end, make plans for the next day's fishing. After a late lunch on day three—perhaps at one of the many restaurants that will prepare your catch for you—set off for ⚅ **Key West** ⑫–㉜. Catch the sunset celebration at Mallory Square, and spend the last day as you would above.

IF YOU HAVE 7 DAYS

Spend your first three days as you would in the four-day itinerary, but stay the third night in ⚅ **Islamorada** ④. In the morning catch a boat to Lignumvitae Key State Botanical Site, before making the one-hour drive to ⚅ **Marathon** ⑧, where you can visit the natural history museum that's part of the Museums of Crane Point Hammock and walk or take a train across the Old Seven Mile Bridge to Pigeon Key. The next stop is just 10 mi away at Bahia Honda State Park, on ⚅ **Bahia Honda Key** ⑨. Take a walk on a wilderness trail, go snorkeling on an offshore reef, wriggle your toes in the beach's soft sand, and spend the night in a waterfront cabin, letting the waves lull you to sleep. Your sixth day starts with either a half day of fabulous snorkeling or diving at Looe Key National Marine Sanctuary or a visit to the National Key Deer Refuge, on **Big Pine Key** ⑩. Then continue on to ⚅ **Key West** ⑫–㉜, and get in a little sightseeing before watching the sunset. The next morning take a walking, bicycling, or trolley tour of town or catch a ferry or seaplane to Dry Tortugas National Park before heading home.

When to Tour the Florida Keys

High season in the Keys is mid-December through March, and traffic on the Overseas Highway is inevitably heavy. From November to the middle of December, crowds are thinner, the weather is superlative, and hotels and shops drastically reduce their prices. Summer, which is hot and humid, is becoming a second high season, especially among families and Europeans. Key West's annual Fantasy Fest is the last week in October; if you plan to attend this popular event, reserve at least six months in advance. Rooms are also scarce the first few weekends of lobster season, which starts in August.

THE UPPER KEYS

The tropical coral reef tract that runs a few miles off the seaward coast accounts for most of the Upper Keys' reputation. This is a diving heaven, thanks to scores of diving options, accessible islands and dive sites, and an established tourism infrastructure.

Yet although diving is king here, fishing, kayaking, and nature touring draw an enviable number of tourists. Within 1½ mi of the bay coast lie the islands of Everglades National Park; here naturalists lead ecotours to see one of the world's only saltwater forests, endangered manatees, dolphins, roseate spoonbills, and tropical bird rookeries. Though the number of birds has dwindled since John James Audubon captured their beauty on a visit to the Keys, bird-watchers won't be disappointed. At sunset flocks take to the skies, and in spring and autumn migrating birds add their numbers. Tarpon and bonefish teem in the shallow waters surrounding the islands, providing food for birds and a challenge to light-tackle fishermen. These same crystal-clear waters attract windsurfers, sailors, and powerboaters.

Dining in the Upper Keys used to be, with one or two exceptions, ho hum. However, within the last five years, half a dozen fine restaurants have opened and are thriving on repeat local customers and word-of-mouth tourist business.

Accommodations are as varied as they are plentiful. The majority are in small waterfront resorts, whose efficiency and one- or two-bedroom units are decorated in tropical colors. They offer dockage and either provide or will arrange boating, diving, and fishing excursions. Depending on which way the wind blows and how close the property is to the highway, noise from U.S. 1 can be bothersome. In high season, expect to pay $65–$165 for an efficiency (in low season, $45–$145). Campground and RV park rates with electricity and water run $22–$48. Some properties require two- or three-day minimum stays during holidays and on weekends in high season. Conversely, discounts are given for midweek, weekly, and monthly stays, and rates can drop 20%–40% April–June and October–mid-December. Keep in mind that salty winds and soil play havoc with anything man-made, and constant maintenance is a must; inspect your accommodations before checking in.

Key Largo

56 mi south of Miami International Airport.

The first Key reachable by car, 30-mi-long Key Largo—named Cayo Largo (long key) by the Spanish—is also the largest island in the chain. Comprising three areas—North Key Largo, Key Largo, and Tavernier—it runs northeast–southwest between Lake Surprise and Tavernier Creek, at MM 95. Most businesses are on the four-lane divided highway (U.S. 1) that runs down the middle, but away from the overdevelopment and generally suburban landscape you can find many areas of pristine wilderness.

❶ One such area is **North Key Largo,** which still contains a wide tract of virgin hardwood hammock and mangrove as well as a crocodile sanctuary (not open to the public). To reach North Key Largo, take Card Sound Road just south of Florida City, or from within the Keys, take Route 905 north.

The 2,005-acre **Key Largo Hammocks State Botanical Site** is the largest remaining stand of the vast West Indian tropical hardwood hammock and mangrove wetland that once covered most of the Keys' upland areas. Among the site's 84 species of protected plants and animals are the endangered American crocodile and the Key Largo wood rat. Concrete skeletons of defunct developments remain but are slowly disappearing under vegetation. To protect the land from further development, state and federal governments are acquiring as much of the hammock as they can. You can take a self-guided tour by picking up a brochure at the park entrance. Better still are the biweekly tours led by Ranger Joseph Nemec, who points out rare species, tells humorous nature stories, and encourages visitors to taste the fruits of native plants. Pets are welcome if on a 6-ft leash. ⊠ *1 mi north of U.S. 1 on Rte. 905, OS, North Key Largo,* ☎ *305/451–1202.* ⊡ *Free.* ☉ *Daily 8–5, tours Thurs. and Sun. 10.*

❷ Taking the Overseas Highway from the mainland lands you closer to **Key Largo** proper, abounding with shopping centers, chain restaurants, and, of course, dive shops.

The small but earnest not-for-profit **Maritime Museum of the Florida Keys** depicts the local history of shipwrecks and salvage efforts through

The Florida Keys

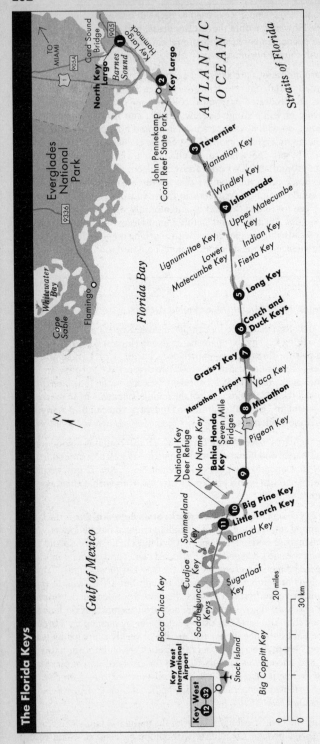

TO MIAMI

Card Sound Bridge

905

905A

1

North Key Largo

Barnes Sound

Key Largo Hammock

1

2 **Key Largo**

A T L A N T I C

O C E A N

Straits of Florida

John Pennekamp Coral Reef State Park

3 **Tavernier**

Plantation Key

Windley Key

4 **Islamorada**

Upper Matecumbe Key

Indian Key

Lignumvitae Key

Lower Matecumbe Key

Fiesta Key

5 **Long Key**

6 **Conch and Duck Keys**

Florida Bay

Everglades National Park

9336

Whitewater Bay

Flamingo

Cape Sable

7 **Grassy Key**

Vaca Key

Marathon Airport

8 **Marathon**

Pigeon Key

National Key Deer Refuge

No Name Key

Bahia Honda Key

Seven Mile Bridges

9

Big Pine Key

10 **Big Pine Key**

11 **Little Torch Key**

Ramrod Key

Summerland Key

Cudjoe Key

Gulf of Mexico

Boca Chica Key

Saddlebunch Keys

Sugarloaf Key

Big Coppitt Key

Stock Island

Key West International Airport

Key West **12** **32**

N

20 miles

30 km

0

0

retrieved treasures, reconstructed wreck sites, and artifacts in various stages of preservation. Some of the more notable exhibits have come from a fleet of treasure ships wrecked by a hurricane in 1715. A bottle exhibit tells Keys history through more than 200 salvaged bottles, dating from as early as the 1600s. The museum is a labor of love, and its primary purpose is preservation. ⊠ *MM 102.5, BS,* ☎ *305/451–6444.* ⌨ *$5.* ☼ *Mon.–Sat. 10–4.*

★ **John Pennekamp Coral Reef State Park** encompasses 78 square mi of coral reefs, sea-grass beds, and mangrove swamps. Its reefs contain 40 of the 52 species of coral in the Atlantic Reef System and more than 650 varieties of fish, and the diving and snorkeling here are famous. A concessioner rents canoes and sailboats and offers boat trips to the reef. Even a landlubber can appreciate the superb interpretive aquarium, exhibits, and video in the visitor center. The park also includes a nature trail through a mangrove forest, two man-made beaches, picnic shelters, a snack bar, and a campground. ⊠ *MM 102.5, OS, Box 487, 33037,* ☎ *305/451–1202.* ⌨ *$4 per vehicle plus 50¢ per person, $1.50 per pedestrian or bicyclist.* ☼ *Daily 8–sunset.*

You can see the *African Queen*—the steam-powered workboat on which Katharine Hepburn and Humphrey Bogart rode in the movie of the same name—moored at the **Key Largo Harbor Marina,** next to the Holiday Inn Key Largo Resort. You can even arrange to take an hour-long ride on the classic vessel. Also on display is the *Thayer IV,* a 22-ft mahogany Chris Craft used by Hepburn and Henry Fonda in *On Golden Pond.* Both vessels are in demand at boat shows and occasionally vacate their moorings. ⊠ *MM 99.7, OS,* ☎ *305/451–4655.* ⌨ *Boat ride $15.* ☼ *Boat ride by appointment.*

❸ The southernmost part of Key Largo is **Tavernier.** Wood-carver and teacher Laura Quinn brought the **Florida Keys Wild Bird Rehabilitation Center** here in 1991, and nowhere else in the Keys can you see birds so close up. Many are kept for life because of injuries that can't be healed, while others are brought for rehabilitation and then set free. At any time the residents can include ospreys, hawks, pelicans, cormorants, terns, and herons of various types. A short nature trail runs into the mangrove forest (bring bug spray May–October), and a video explains the center's mission. ⊠ *MM 93.6, BS, Tavernier,* ☎ *305/852–4486.* ⌨ *Donation welcome.* ☼ *Daily sunrise–sunset.*

Harry Harris County Park (⊠ MM 93, OS, Burton Dr., Tavernier, ☎ 305/852–7161 or 888/227–8136) has play equipment, a small swimming lagoon, a boat ramp, ball fields, barbecue grills, and rest rooms. Though the turnoff is clearly marked on the Overseas Highway, the road to the ocean is circuitous.

Dining and Lodging

$–$$$ ✕ **The Fish House.** Behind the screened, diner-style facade are display
★ cases filled with the freshest catches, which are then baked, blackened, broiled, fried, sautéed, steamed, or stewed as if every night were the finals of a seafood competition (in fact, the Fish House wins many such competitions). The dining room—festooned with nets and fishy Christmas ornaments—is as redolent of the Keys as a Bogart movie. Generous portions come with corn on the cob, new potatoes or rice, and coleslaw; the key lime pie is homemade. You can't beat the fast service and great eats. ⊠ *MM 102.4, OS,* ☎ *305/451–4665. AE, D, MC, V. Closed early Sept.–early Oct.*

$–$$$ ✕ **Frank Keys Cafe.** This contemporary restaurant is hidden in a nat-
★ ural hardwood hammock except at night, when little white lights in the branches mark the spot. The wooden Victorian-style house has a

deep porch for dining alfresco, and the kitchen is skillfully staffed by chef-owner Frank Graves III and returning executive chef Ralph Salvatore. Their fresh-fish dishes remain local favorites. Try the pan-sautéed catch washed in egg, lightly coated, then given a kiss of sherry, or opt for delicate pasta entrées like seafood Mediterranean (sautéed fresh seafood over pesto linguine with a marinara cream sauce). Salvatore enthusiastically welcomes special requests. If he has the ingredients, he'll make it, whatever it is. ⊠ *MM 100, OS,* ☎ *305/453–0310. AE, MC, V. Closed Tues., plus Mon. Easter–Christmas.*

$–$$ ✕ **Anthony's Italian Restaurant & Lounge.** The portly proprietor greets guests at the door or their tables, making sure they are enjoying his hospitality. There's little to be concerned about; the food, faithful to Italian tradition, speaks for itself. The solid kitchen serves veal, chicken, and home-style pasta dishes in a comfortable setting. Spicy mussels marinara are so good you'll want an order to go. Friday and Saturday nights bring live music. ⊠ *MM 97.6, in the median,* ☎ *305/853–1177. AE, D, MC, V.*

$–$$ ✕ **Cafe Largo.** Soothing jazz plays in this intimate bistro-style Italian
★ restaurant. Dinner starts with a basket of focaccia bread and garlic rolls. Next choose one of the chef's specials; they won't disappoint. The chicken garlic—two thin breast cutlets lightly coated and sautéed, then covered in a light sauce of garlic and rosemary—is divine. The penne with shrimp and broccoli has tender shrimp, al dente broccoli, and a hint of garlic. A more than ample wine list, international beers, Italian bottled waters, and, of course, espresso and cappuccino are offered, and the dessert list is short but sweet. ⊠ *MM 99.5, BS,* ☎ *305/451–4885. AE, MC, V. No lunch.*

$–$$ ✕ **Calypso's.** Hidden away on the waterfront at Ocean Bay Marina is one of the best-kept secrets in the Upper Keys. The self-taught cook Todd Lollis consistently takes away a pan full of prizes at local cook-offs thanks to innovative seafood dishes. One example is seafood burritos, a multitaste dish of grilled shrimp, onion, garlic, and green and red peppers mixed with well-seasoned black beans, tomatoes, and cilantro served on a flour tortilla. A select wine list shows he knows his wines, too, but there are no desserts. The setting is Keys casual; plastic outdoor furniture is complemented by paper napkins and plastic cutlery. ⊠ *MM 99.5, OS, 1 Seagate Blvd.,* ☎ *305/451–0600. D, MC, V. Closed Tues.*

$–$$ ✕ **Mrs. Mac's Kitchen.** Hundreds of beer cans, beer bottles, and expired license plates from all over the world decorate the walls of this wood-paneled, screened, open-air restaurant, which offers traditional American sandwiches, burgers, barbecue, and seafood. At breakfast and lunch, the counter and booths fill up early with locals. Regular nightly specials are worth the stop: meat loaf on Monday, Italian on Wednesday, and seafood Thursday–Saturday. The chili is always good, and the beer of the month is $1.50 a bottle. ⊠ *MM 99.4, BS,* ☎ *305/451–3722. No credit cards. Closed Sun.*

$ ✕ **Alabama Jack's.** In 1953 Alabama Jack Stratham opened his open-air seafood restaurant on two barges in an old fishing community 13 mi southeast of Homestead. The spot, something of a no-man's-land, belongs to the Keys in spirit thanks to Card Sound Road. Regular customers include Keys fixtures, Sunday cyclists, local retirees, and boaters, who come to admire tropical birds in nearby mangroves, the occasional crocodile in the canal, the live band on weekends, or simply the food. Favorites include peppery crab cakes, crispy-chewy conch fritters, crunchy breaded shrimp, and homemade tartar sauce. The place closes by 7 or 7:30, when the skeeters come out. ⊠ *58000 Card Sound Rd., Card Sound,* ☎ *305/248–8741. MC, V.*

$ ✕ **Chad's Deli & Bakery.** Each morning Chad, the owner, bakes eight kinds of breads, which he uses to make sandwiches ($5–$6) large enough to feed two hungry adults. Residents recently voted them the best sandwiches in the Upper Keys. If you're not in the mood for one of the regular sandwiches, ranging from certified Angus roast beef to veggie, try the daily special. The menu also features salads, sides, soft drinks, and a choice of two cookies—white-chocolate macadamia nut and chocolate chip—with a whopping 8-inch diameter (75¢–$1). Most orders in this four-table establishment are takeout. ⊠ *MM 92.3, BS,* ☎ *305/853–5566. No credit cards. No dinner.*

$ ✕ **Harriette's Restaurant.** If you're looking for a traditional American eatery, this is it. Little has changed here over the years other than a new mural and a new, bright, island-style paint job. Owner Harriette Mattson still welcomes her guests, and the same wisecracking but efficient waitresses make breakfast and lunch entertaining. Harriette's is famous for breakfast: steak and eggs with hash browns or grits and toast and jelly for $6.95, or old-fashioned hotcakes with butter and syrup and sausage or bacon for $3.75. The comfy, Keys-y eatery is a local institution. ⊠ *MM 95.7, BS,* ☎ *305/852–8689. No credit cards. No dinner.*

$$$$ ⛱ **Jules' Undersea Lodge.** In the "not for everyone" category, this novel accommodation caters to well-finned visitors who want a total Keys diving experience. The hotel, a former underwater research lab, is 5 fathoms (30 ft) below the surface. Hence, to be one of the six guests, you have to be a certified diver or take the hotel's three-hour introductory course (an additional $75). Rooms have a shower, telephone, VCR and stereo (no TV), and galley. The lodge is popular with honeymooners. Rates include breakfast, dinner, snacks, beverages, and diving gear. Because of the length of stay underwater, once back on terra firma, you can't fly or make deep dives for 24 hours. ⊠ *MM 103.2, OS, 51 Shoreland Dr., 33037,* ☎ *305/451–2353,* FAX *305/451–4789. 2 bedrooms, sleeps up to 6. Dining room. AE, D, MC, V.*

$$$$ ⛱ **Marriott's Key Largo Bay Beach Resort.** This 17-acre bay-side resort's five lemon-yellow, grill-balconied, and spire-topped stories are sliced between highway and bay and give off an air of warm, indolent days. The facilities are as good as the guest rooms, which feature rattan, paddle fans, and balconies. From some you can watch the sunset sweep across the bay. ⊠ *MM 103.8, BS, 103800 Overseas Hwy., 33037,* ☎ *305/453–0000 or 800/932–9332,* FAX *305/453–0093. 153 rooms, 20 2-bedroom suites, 6 3-bedroom suites, 1 penthouse suite. Restaurant, 3 bars, pool, beauty salon, hot tub, massage, beach, dive shop, fishing, meeting rooms. AE, D, DC, MC, V.*

$$$–$$$$ ⛱ **Westin Beach Resort, Key Largo.** This large resort with lush land-
★ scaping is tucked away in a hardwood hammock. Fourth-floor bay-side rooms afford marvelous water views. Units on the first three floors overlook the woods, except the 230, 330, and 430 series, which face the landscaped parking lot. The spacious, comfortable rooms have tropical decor. Lighted nature trails and boardwalks wind through the woods to a small beach. Two pools, one for adults only, are separated by a coral rock wall and waterfall. Both restaurants overlook the water. ⊠ *MM 96.9, BS, 97000 Overseas Hwy., 33037,* ☎ *305/852–5553 or 800/826–1006,* FAX *305/852–8669. 190 rooms, 10 suites. 2 restaurants, 2 bars, 2 pools, hot tub, 2 tennis courts, beach, dock, windsurfing, boating, fishing. AE, D, DC, MC, V.*

$$$ ⛱ **Kona Kai Resort.** A sidewalk winds between beautifully landscaped
★ cottages to a small beach and marina at this stylish laid-back resort. The garden alone makes it worth staying here, as do rooms with tropical furnishings, toiletries made from fruits and flowers, and Noritake china. This is not your typical first-class resort with staff everywhere

you turn. Privacy is paramount: There are no room phones, and maid service is every fourth morning. Guests trade in their fluffy towels at a linen cabinet as they please. Studios and one- and two-bedroom suites—with full kitchens and original art—are spacious and light filled. Beachfront hammocks and a toasty pool make it easy to while away the day, but there's also plenty to do. Try a paddleboat or kayak, or visit the art gallery, with works by major South Florida artists. Smoking is not permitted, nor are guests under 16. ⊠ *MM 97.8, BS, 97802 Overseas Hwy., 33037,* ☎ *305/852–7200 or 800/365–7829. 11 units. Pool, lighted tennis court, basketball, volleyball, boating, beach, dock. AE, D, MC, V.*

$$–$$$ ⊞ **Marina Del Mar Resort and Marina.** This two- to four-story resort on a deep-water marina caters to sailors and divers. Units have original watercolors by Keys artist Mary Boggs, as well as refrigerators. Suites 502–504 have kitchens (as do studios) and plenty of room for groups. There's a free Continental breakfast in the lobby; live entertainment nightly in Coconuts, a popular restaurant and bar; and spectacular sunrise and sunset views from the fourth-floor observation deck. ⊠ *MM 100, OS, 527 Caribbean Dr., 33037,* ☎ *305/451–4107 or 800/451–3483,* ℻ *305/451–1891. 52 rooms, 8 suites, 16 studios. Restaurant, bar, pool, 2 tennis courts, exercise room, dock, boating, fishing. AE, D, DC, MC, V.*

$$ ⊞ **Frank's Key Haven Resort.** In a quiet neighborhood under a canopy of graceful, towering gumbo-limbo trees, this lodge, made of beams from Flagler's railroad tracks and imported German concrete, was built in the 1930s to withstand hurricane-force winds. The original owner ran bird-watching tours, and though the enlarged property still offers ecotours, it now caters to divers. The resort has its own dive boat, waterfront, and training pool and offers diving certification as well as diving-lodging packages that include night dives. Screened porches have racks for dive equipment. Rooms vary from one-room efficiencies to one- and two-bedroom apartments and family units. A public area has a TV, half kitchen, and comfy seating. ⊠ *MM 92, BS, 198 Harborview Dr., Tavernier 33070,* ☎ *305/852–3017 or 800/765–5397,* ℻ *305/852–3880. 14 units. Pool, docks. MC, V.*

$$ ⊞ **Largo Lodge.** No two rooms are the same in this 1950s-vintage adults-
★ only resort, but all are cozy and fully equipped with kitchens, rattan furniture, and screened porches but no phones. The prettiest palm alley you've ever seen sets the mood, while tropical gardens with more palms, sea grapes, and orchids surround the guest cottages. There's 200 ft of bay frontage. Late in the day, wild ducks, pelicans, herons, and other birds come looking for a handout from longtime owner Harriet "Hat" Stokes. If you want a laid-back, top-value tropical hideaway not too far down the Keys, this is it. ⊠ *MM 101.5, BS, 101740 Overseas Hwy., 33037,* ☎ *305/451–0424 or 800/468–4378. 6 apartments, 1 efficiency. Beach, dock. MC, V.*

$ ⊞ **Popp's Motel.** Since 1951 and for four generations, Popp family members have welcomed guests to this small and private motel. Rooms are just yards from a sandy beach, and you can take part in activities galore or relax in a hammock while the kids play on swings. All bedroom units and efficiencies have a kitchen. Though the place is clean and has been updated several times, dark wood paneling and terrazzo floors in some rooms reveal their age. Other than that, it's a gem of a resort. ⊠ *MM 95.5, BS, 95500 Overseas Hwy., 33037,* ☎ *305/852–5201,* ℻ *305/852–5200. 9 units. Picnic area, beach, dock, playground. AE, MC, V.*

$ ⚠ **America Outdoors.** Reserve early to camp here, especially around holidays and from January to mid-March. A waterfront location and woodsy setting, security, boat ramps and rentals, a sandy beach, store, bait shop, bathhouse, and an adult recreation center make it popular with snowbirds and South Floridians, who come back year after year and weekend after weekend. It's also very clean, orderly, and well managed. Rates for tents are $20–$40, for RVs $33–$55, depending on season, day of week, and services. ✉ *MM 97.5, BS, 97450 Overseas Hwy., 33037,* ☎ *305/852–8054. 154 sites. Grocery, beach, dock, boating, fishing, coin laundry, recreation room. AE, D, MC, V.*

Nightlife

The semiweekly *Keynoter* (Wednesday and Saturday), weekly *Reporter* (Thursday), and Friday to Sunday editions of the *Miami Herald* are the best sources of information on entertainment and nightlife.

Breezers Tiki Bar (✉ MM 103.8, BS, ☎ 305/453–0000), in Marriott's Key Largo Bay Beach Resort (☞ Dining and Lodging, *above*), is popular with the smartly coiffed crowd. Office workers join guests for cocktails to toast the sun going down. Walls plastered with Bogart memorabilia remind customers that the classic 1948 Bogart-Bacall flick *Key Largo* was shot in the **Caribbean Club** (✉ MM 104, BS, ☎ 305/451–9970). An archetype of a laid-back Keys bar, it draws a hairy-faced, down-home group to shoot the breeze while shooting pool but is friendlier than you might imagine. It also has postcard-perfect sunsets. **Coconuts** (✉ MM 100, OS, 528 Caribbean Dr., ☎ 305/453–9794), in Marina Del Mar Resort (☞ Dining and Lodging, *above*), has blues on Tuesday and nightly entertainment year-round, except Sunday and Monday during football season. The crowd is primarily thirty- and fortysomething. The new **Zappie's Bar and Tackle** (✉ MM 99.2, BS, ☎ 305/451–0531) goes by the slogan "Live Bait & Live Music." Sorry, this isn't the ultimate pickup spot. The bait refers to fishing bait that's sold in the adjoining shop, Bill's Bait, which has been here for years. There's good, live music on weekends ($3 cover) and on other nights in high season.

Outdoor Activities and Sports

BIKING

Equipment Locker Sport & Cycle (✉ Tradewinds Plaza, MM 101, OS, ☎ 305/453–0140) rents single-speed adult and children's bikes. Cruisers go for $10 a day, $50 a week. No helmets are available.

FISHING

Sailors Choice (✉ MM 99.7, OS, ☎ 305/451–1802 or 305/451–0041) runs a party boat daily plus a night trip on Friday and Saturday. The ultramodern 60-ft, 49-passenger boat with air-conditioned cabin leaves from the Holiday Inn docks.

SCUBA DIVING AND SNORKELING

American Diving Headquarters (✉ MM 105.5, BS, ☎ 305/451–0037) offers certification and dive tours on request, not a schedule, and a Water-Tight Guarantee ensures you'll get your money's worth. The staff is concerned about guests and the environment, the latter demonstrated by a reef ecology and fish identification course. Before getting their toes wet, divers attend lectures and slide presentations to help them get more out of the dive experience. The cost is $55 for a two-tank dive with tank and weight rental, $80 if you need everything; $92 includes a wet suit, suggested in winter.

Amy Slate's Amoray Dive Resort (✉ MM 104.2, BS, ☎ 305/451–3595 or 800/426-6729) is a full-service dive shop (NAUI, PADI, YMCA, and British BSAC certified) that has accommodations packages and also performs underwater weddings. **Coral Reef Park Co.** (✉ John Pennekamp Coral Reef State Park, MM 102.5, OS, ☎ 305/451–1621) offers scuba and snorkeling tours of the park. **Quiescence Diving Service, Inc.** (✉

MM 103.5, BS, ☎ 305/451–2440) sets itself apart in two ways: It limits groups to six to ensure personal attention and offers day, night, and twilight dives an hour before sundown, the time when sea creatures are most active.

WATER SPORTS

Coral Reef Park Co. (✉ John Pennekamp Coral Reef State Park, MM 102.5, OS, ☎ 305/451–1621) rents boats and equipment for sailing, canoeing, and windsurfing. You can rent a canoe or a one- or two-person sea kayak, even camping equipment, from **Florida Bay Outfitters** (✉ MM 104, BS, ☎ 305/451–3018). Real pros, they match the right equipment to the right skill level, so even novices feel confident paddling off. Rentals are by the hour, half day, or full day. They also sell lots of accessories.

Islamorada

❹ *MM 90.5–70.*

Early settlers named Islamorada after their schooner, the *Island Home,* but to make the name more romantic, they translated it into Spanish— *isla morada.* The local chamber of commerce prefers to say it means "the purple isles." Early maps show Islamorada as only Upper Matecumbe Key. Historians refer to it as the group of islands between Tavernier Creek at MM 90 and Fiesta Key at MM 70, including Plantation Key, Windley Key, Upper Matecumbe Key, Lower Matecumbe Key, Craig Key, and Fiesta Key. In addition, two islands—Indian Key, in the Atlantic Ocean, and Lignumvitae Key, in Florida Bay—belong to the group.

Claiming they were fed up with a county government more interested in the needs of Key West than the Upper Keys, residents voted for self-incorporation in a controversial election in 1997. Though it's now officially the Village of Isles, some things haven't changed. The area remains a great place to fish. For nearly 100 years, seasoned anglers have recognized these sun-bathed waters as home to a huge variety of game fish as well as lobster, shrimp, and crabs. The rich, the famous, the powerful have all fished here, including Lou Gehrig, Ted Williams, Zane Grey, and presidents Hoover, Truman, Carter, and Bush. More than 150 backcountry guides and 400 offshore captains operate out of this 20-mi stretch.

Activities range from fishing tournaments to historic reenactments. During September and October, Heritage Days feature free lectures on Islamorada history, a golf tournament, and the Indian Key Festival. Holiday Isle Resort sponsors boating, fishing, car, and golf tournaments, as well as bikini and body-building contests.

Between 1885 and 1915 settlers earned good livings growing pineapples on **Plantation Key** (✉ MM 90.5–86), using black Bahamian workers to plant and harvest their crops. The plantations are gone, replaced by a dense concentration of homes and businesses.

At 16 ft above sea level, **Windley Key** (✉ MM 86–84) is the highest point in the Keys. Originally two islets, the area was first inhabited by Native Americans, who left middens and other remains, and then by settlers, who farmed and fished in the mid-1800s and called the islets the Umbrella Keys. The Florida East Coast Railway bought the land from homesteaders in 1908, filled in the inlet between the two islands, and changed the name. They quarried rock for the rail bed and bridge approaches in the Keys—the same rock used in many historic South Florida structures, including Miami's Vizcaya and the Hurricane Monument on Upper Matecumbe. Though the Quarry Station stop was destroyed by the 1935 hurricane, quarrying continued until the 1960s. Today a few resorts and attractions occupy the island.

When the Florida East Coast Railway drilled, dynamited, and carved Windley Key's limestone bed, it exposed the once-living fossilized coral reef that was laid down about 125,000 years ago, now visible at the **Windley Key Fossil Reef State Geologic Site.** Five trails lead to old quarrying equipment and cutting pits, where you can stand within a petrified reef and take rubbings of beautifully fossilized brain coral and sea ferns. The new Alison Fahrer Environmental Education Center contains historic, biological, and geological displays. For information contact the Long Key State Recreation Area (☞ Long Key, *below*). ⊠ *MM 85.5, BS,* ☎ *305/664–4815.* ☜ *Education center free, quarry trails $1.50.* ⊙ *Education center Thurs.–Mon. 8–5; inquire about quarry tour schedule.*

At **Theater of the Sea,** dolphins, sea lions, stingrays, and tropical fish swim in the 1907 Windley Key railroad quarry, whose huge blasted holes are now filled with seawater. The park features marine-mammal shows, sea-life interaction programs, snorkel ecotours, and cruises. Allow at least two hours to attend the dolphin and sea-lion shows and visit all the exhibits, which include an injured birds of prey display, a "bottomless" boat ride, a shell-life touch tank, a pool where sharks are fed by a trainer, and several small-fish aquariums. For an additional fee, you can even swim with dolphins, sea lions, or stingrays for 30 minutes, after a 15- or 30-minute orientation, and arrange for video or still photos of your experience. ⊠ *MM 84.5, OS, Box 407, 33036,* ☎ *305/664–2431.* ☜ *$15.75; snorkel ecotours $50; swim with dolphins $85, with sea lions $65, with stingrays $50; reservations required with 50% deposit.* ⊙ *Daily 9:30–4.*

Upper Matecumbe Key (⊠ MM 84–79) was one of the earliest in the Upper Keys to be permanently settled. Homesteaders were so successful at growing pineapples and limes in the rocky soil that at one time the island had the largest U.S. pineapple crop; however, Cuban pineapples and the hurricane of 1935 killed the industry. Today life centers on fishing and tourism, and the island is lively with homes, charter fishing boats, bait shops, restaurants, stores, nightclubs, marinas, nurseries, and offices.

Somewhere in Time is a small, unlikely combination museum and antiques and jewelry shop crowded with hundreds of interesting artifacts. Nearly every inch of wall and counter space is filled with objects salvaged from merchant and slave ships that used to ply Florida's waters. There are coins from the *Atocha*, rare ceramic containers, original 18th-century maps, cannon, solid silver bars, slave artifacts, religious medallions, rare bottles, and a corny diorama of two infamous English women who were pirates. The owner tells marvelous stories about the objects' provenance. ⊠ *MM 82.7, OS,* ☎ *305/664–9699.* ☜ *Free.* ⊙ *Daily 9–5.*

Home to the local chamber of commerce, a **red train caboose** sits at the site where the Florida East Coast Railway had a station and living quarters, before they washed away with the hurricane of 1935. Artifacts ranging from dishes and flatware to uniform buttons and medicine bottles were excavated and are on display. ⊠ *MM 82.5, BS.* ☜ *Free.* ⊙ *Weekdays 9–5, Sat. 9–4.*

Beside the highway, the **Hurricane Monument** (⊠ MM 81.6, OS) marks the mass grave of 423 victims of the 1935 Labor Day hurricane. Many of those who perished were World War I veterans who had been working on the Overseas Highway and died when a tidal surge overturned a train sent to evacuate them. The 65-ft by 20-ft Art Deco–style monument, built of Keys coral limestone with a ceramic map of the Keys, depicts wind-driven waves and palms bowing before the storm's fury. Note that the trees bend in the wrong direction.

Tucked away behind the Islamorada library is a small beach on a creek at **Islamorada County Park** (⊠ MM 81.5, BS, ☎ 305/852–7161 or 888/ 227–8136). The water isn't very deep, but it is crystal clear. Currents are swift, making swimming unsuitable for young children, but they can enjoy the playground as well as picnic tables, grassy areas, and rest rooms.

OFF THE
BEATEN PATH

INDIAN KEY STATE HISTORIC SITE – On the ocean side of the Matecumbe islands, 10½-acre Indian Key was inhabited by Native Americans for several thousand years before Europeans arrived, as archaeological excavations here show. The islet was a county seat and base for early 19th-century shipwreck salvagers until an Indian attack wiped out the settlement in 1840. Dr. Henry Perrine, a noted botanist, was killed in the raid. Today his plants overgrow the town's ruins. On the first weekend in October the Indian Key Festival celebrates the Key's heritage. Guided tours are available most days, but even when they're not, you can roam among the marked trails and sites. The island is reachable only by boat—either your own, a rental, or a ferry. Robbie's Marina (☞ *below*), the official concessioner, rents kayaks and boats and operates twice-daily ferry service coordinated with the tours. To arrange for a ranger-led tour if you're using your own or a rental boat, contact Long Key State Recreation Area (☞ Long Key, *below*). Locals like to kayak out from **Indian Key Fill** (⊠ MM 78.5, BS). ⊠ *MM 78.5, OS, ☎ 305/ 664–9814 for ferry service; 305/664–4815 for Long Key State Recreation Area. ☎ Free, tour $1, ferry (includes tour) $15, $25 with Lignumvitae Key. ☉ Tours Thurs.–Mon. 9 and 1.*

LIGNUMVITAE KEY STATE BOTANICAL SITE – A virgin hardwood forest still cloaks this 280-acre bay-side island, punctuated by the home and gardens that chemical magnate William Matheson built as a private retreat in 1919. Access is only by boat—either your own, a rental, or a ferry operated by the official concessioner, Robbie's Marina (☞ *below*), which also rents kayaks and boats. (Kayaking out from Indian Key Fill, at MM 78.5, is popular with locals.) Once on the key you can take a tour with the resident ranger, from whom you can request a list of native and well-naturalized plants. As a courtesy, you should arrange for a tour in advance with Long Key State Recreation Area (☞ Long Key, *below*) if you're using your own or a rental boat. ⊠ *MM 78.5, BS, ☎ 305/664– 9814 for ferry service; 305/664–4815 for Long Key State Recreation Area. ☎ Free, tour $1, ferry (includes tour) $15, $25 with Indian Key. ☉ Tours Thurs.–Mon. 10 and 2.*

Though tarpon are known for the exciting fight they put up when hooked, you'd never know it judging by the 50 or so prehistoric-looking specimens that gather around the docks at **Robbie's Marina,** on Lower Matecumbe Key. These fish—some as long as 5 ft—literally eat out of the hands of children who buy a $2 bucket of bait fish. Both kids and adults enjoy watching them. ⊠ *MM 77.5, BS, ☎ 305/664–9814 or 877/664–8498. ☎ Dock access $1. ☉ Daily 8–5:30.*

Anne's Beach (⊠ MM 73.5, OS, ☎ 305/852–7161 or 888/227–8136), on Lower Matecumbe Key, has a ½-mi elevated wooden boardwalk that meanders through a natural wetland hammock. Covered picnic areas along the boardwalk provide a place to rest and enjoy the view. Rest rooms are at the north end.

Dining and Lodging

$$–$$$$ **✕ Morada Bay.** The owners of the tony Moorings resort opened this
★ restaurant, which has a bay-front location perfect for sunset watching. Conch architecture is enhanced by the black-and-white Everglades photos of Clyde Butcher, which line the walls. The contemporary menu features a died-and-gone-to-heaven shrimp bisque, Portobello burger, and cumin-seared snapper with roasted red peppers and a spinach quesadilla. It's a small place (there's often a wait to be seated), with half a dozen tables inside and a dozen on the porch overlooking a sandy beach dotted with Adirondack chairs. The melodic tunes of a guitar player waft out to sea on the breezes Friday to Sunday nights. Another restaurant with the same name but with fine dining is opening next door. ⊠ MM 81, BS, ☎ 305/664–0604. AE, MC, V.

$–$$ **✕ Islamorada Fish Company.** In one of the prettiest spots in the Keys, this very casual seafood restaurant has undertaken a major expansion of its indoor seating area by moving its fish market and retail section into a new building. Charm will be retained, however, with small umbrella-covered tables and family-style awning-covered picnic benches overlooking several islets and the calm waters of Florida Bay. At the fish market's dock, boats unload the fresh catch, which minutes later is served fried, grilled, blackened, or broiled. The kitchen staff prepares good, satisfying, and simple food. Wine, beer, soda, and pink lemonade are served icy cold. ⊠ MM 81.5, BS, ☎ 305/664–9271. MC, V.

$–$$ **✕ Manny & Isa's.** Fewer than a dozen tables are squeezed into the simple room, where the namesake owners serve always perfect Cuban and Spanish cuisine. The regular menu is split between traditional Cuban dishes and local seafood, and there are several fish, chicken, and pork chop specials, all served with salad and Cuban bread. Succulent fish fingers served with black beans and rice will set you back only $9.95. Manny's key lime pies are legendary. On any evening a parade of customers comes through to get them takeout, and speaking of takeout, many people call ahead for meals to go, to avoid lines on weekends and in high season. ⊠ MM 81.6, OS, 81610 Old Hwy., ☎ 305/664–5019. AE, D, MC, V. Closed Tues. and mid-Oct.–mid.-Nov.

$–$$ **✕ Squid Row.** This affable roadside seafood eatery serves the freshest
★ fish possible, courtesy of the seafood wholesalers who own it. Grouper comes grilled, divinely flaky, or in bread crumbs and sautéed, served with citrus butter, and the nightly special bouillabaisse ($23.95) is simply wonderful. If you finish it by yourself—no cheating—you get a free slice of key lime pie. The waitstaff will brew a fresh pot of coffee and volunteer to wrap what's left of the flavorful, airy banana bread that comes at the start of the meal but is best as dessert. There's also a bar with happy hour 4–7. ⊠ MM 81.9, OS, ☎ 305/664–9865. AE, D, DC, MC, V.

$$$$ **▥ Cheeca Lodge.** This 27-acre low-rise resort sits amid tranquil fish-filled lagoons and gardens. Decorated with high-grade fabrics, carpets, and furniture, units are washed in oh-so-tropical blue and rich sand. Suites have kitchens and screened balconies; fourth-floor rooms in the main lodge have ocean or bay views. The resort is the local leader in green activism with everything from recycling efforts to ecotours. Camp Cheeca for kids is fun and educational. ⊠ MM 82, OS, Box 527, 33036, ☎ 305/664–4651 or 800/327–2888, FAX 305/664–2893. 139 rooms, 64 suites. 2 restaurants, lobby lounge, 2 pools, saltwater tidal pool, 9-hole golf course, 6 lighted tennis courts, boating, parasailing, fishing, children's programs, playground. AE, D, DC, MC, V.

$$$–$$$$ **▥ The Moorings.** This onetime coconut plantation on 18 acres is one
★ of the finest places to stay in the Keys. Tucked in a tropical forest, one-, two-, and three-bedroom cottages and two-story houses are furnished with wicker and artistic African fabrics and have pristine white kitchens.

Peaked roofs rise behind French doors, lighting is soft, and there are many exquisite touches, from thick towels to extra-deep, cushiony bedcovers. The beach has a scattering of Adirondack chairs and hammocks, complimentary windsurfing and kayaking, and a swimming dock. There's a two-night minimum on one-bedrooms and a one-week minimum on other lodgings. ✉ MM 81.6, OS, 123 Beach Rd., 33036, ☎ 305/664–4708, FAX 305/664–4242. 18 cottages and houses. Pool, tennis court, beach, windsurfing. MC, V.

$$ 🏠 **White Gate Court.** Far from the madding crowds of Islamorada's business district, this recently restored resort consists of five wooden cottages laid out on 3 pretty landscaped acres along 200 ft of white-sand beach. Susanne Orias de Cargnelli spent two years restoring and decorating the cottages, which date from the 1940s. The result is a simple, intimate escape, where everyone in the family, including the dog, is welcome. All the units, which sleep either two or four, have a full kitchen, cable TV, direct phone lines, and air-conditioning. Barbecue grills and umbrella-shaded tables, big old palm and native trees create a relaxing mood. ✉ MM 76, BS, 76010 Overseas Hwy., 33036, ☎ 305/664–4136. 7 units. Picnic area, beach, dock, coin laundry. MC, V.

$ 🏠 **Ragged Edge Resort.** People come to the Keys to get away. The fortunate ones find the Ragged Edge, a come-as-you-are, be-who-you-are kind of place. There are lots of regulars, some of whom have been coming for 20 years. Clean rooms feature pine paneling, chintz, and a tile bath suite, and most have kitchens with irons. Most downstairs units have screened porches, while upper units have large decks, more windows, and beam ceilings. Though the place feels expensive, it's affordable due to a lack of staff and things like in-room phones. Amenities take the form of a thatch-roof observation tower, picnic areas, barbecue pits, and free bikes. There's not much of a beach, but you can swim off the remodeled dock—a virtual rookery when boats don't disturb the pelicans, herons, anhingas, and terns. ✉ MM 86.5, OS, 243 Treasure Harbor Rd., 33036, ☎ 305/852–5389. 10 units. Picnic area, pool, shuffleboard, dock, bicycles. MC, V.

Nightlife

Holiday Isle Beach Resorts & Marina (✉ MM 84, OS, ☎ 305/664–2321) is the liveliest spot in the Upper Keys. On weekends, especially during spring break and holidays, the resort's three entertainment areas are mobbed, primarily with the under-30 set, whose IDs are carefully scrutinized. Live bands play everything from reggae to heavy metal. Behind the larger-than-life mermaid is the Keys-easy, over-the-water cabana bar the **Lorelei** (✉ MM 82, BS, ☎ 305/664–4656). Live nightly sounds are mostly reggae and light rock.

Outdoor Activities and Sports

BOATING

To experience the Keys as they were before the highway intruded, rent a houseboat from **Houseboat Vacations of the Florida Keys** (✉ MM 85.9, BS, 85944 Overseas Hwy., 33036, ☎ 305/664–4009). The new fleet of 40- to 44-ft boats accommodate from six to eight people and come fully outfitted with safety equipment and necessities—except food—as well as an AM/FM cassette stereo. The three-day minimum runs $595–$890; a week costs $1,025–$1,575. Kayaks, canoes, and 16-ft skiffs are also for hire. **Robbie's Boat Rentals & Charters** (✉ MM 77.5, BS, 77520 Overseas Hwy., 33036, ☎ 305/664–9814) rents a 15-ft skiff with a 25-horsepower outboard (the smallest you can charter) for $20 an hour, $70 for four hours, and $90 for the day. Boats up to 27 ft are also available, but there's a two-hour minimum. Other than clothes and food, Captains Pam and Pete Anderson of **Treasure Har-**

bor Marine (⊠ MM 86.5, OS, 200 Treasure Harbor Dr., 33036, ☎ 305/852–2458 or 800/352–2628) provide everything you'll need for a vacation at sea—linens, safety gear, and, best of all, advice on where to find the best beaches, marinas, and lobster sites. You can rent a vessel bareboat or crewed, with sail or with power. Boats include a 19-ft Cape Dory, 41-ft custom-built ketch, 35-ft Mainship, and 35-ft Chenhwa trawler, as well as Morgans, Watkins, and Hunters. A new 47-ft Tradewind comes with a captain. Rates start at $95 a day, $395 a week. Most business is repeat customers. Marina facilities are basic—water, electric, ice machine, laundry, picnic tables, and shower/rest rooms—and dockage is only $1 a foot.

FISHING

Sandy Moret is one of the most respected and recognizable names in Keys fly-fishing. He operates **Florida Keys Outfitters** (⊠ MM 82, BS, ☎ 305/664–5423), home to a store and the Florida Keys Fly Fishing School, which attracts anglers from around the world. Two-day weekend fly-fishing classes, which include classroom instruction, equipment, arrival cocktails, and daily breakfast and lunch, cost $795. Add another $800 for two days of fishing. Guided fishing trips cost $275 for a half day, $400 for a full day. Fishing and accommodations packages (at Cheeca Lodge) are available. The 65-ft party boat *Gulf Lady* (⊠ Bud 'n' Mary's Marina, MM 79.8, OS, ☎ 305/664–2628 or 305/664–2461) has a new look, having been rebuilt after being destroyed by a Tropical Storm Mitch tornado. If you take full-day and night trips, the boat can be crowded, so call about loads in advance. Since 1957 Captain Ken Knudsen of the *Hubba Hubba* (⊠ Bud 'n' Mary's Marina, MM 79.8, OS, ☎ 305/664–9281) has fished the waters around Islamorada, first taking out guests at his family's hotel when he was 12, later as a licensed backcountry guide. His expertise earned him ranking as one of the top 10 guides in Florida by national fishing magazines, and he fishes what he knows best: bonefish, permit, snook, redfish, trout, and tarpon. Unlike most guides, he offers four-hour sunset trips for tarpon ($300) and two-hour sunset trips for bonefish ($175), as well as half- ($275) and full-day ($375) outings. Prices are for one or two anglers, and tackle and bait are included.

SCUBA DIVING AND SNORKELING

Florida Keys Dive Center (⊠ MM 90.5, OS, Box 391, Tavernier 33070, ☎ 305/852–4599 or 800/433–8946) organizes dives from John Pennekamp Coral Reef State Park to Alligator Light. The center has two Coast Guard–approved dive boats, offers scuba training, and is one of the few Keys dive centers to offer Nitrox (mixed gas) diving. Since 1980 **Lady Cyana Divers** (⊠ MM 85.9, BS, Box 1157, 33036, ☎ 305/664–8717 or 800/221–8717), a PADI five-star training resort, has operated dives on deep and shallow wrecks and reefs between Molasses and Alligator reefs. The 40- and 55-ft boats provide everything a diver needs, including full bathrooms.

TENNIS

New owners of the four clay and two hard courts at **Islamorada Tennis Club** (⊠ MM 76.8, BS, ☎ 305/664–5340) keep the center buzzing year-round. It's popular partly because it's inexpensive (from $12 an hour) and partly because it's well run. Amenities include racket stringing, ball machines, private lessons, a full-service pro shop, night games, and partner pairing.

Shopping

Two former Miami teachers knocked down walls, added a coffee bar, and turned the once tiny **Cover to Cover Books** (⊠ MM 90.1, OS, 90130 Old Hwy., ☎ 305/852–1415) into one of the best bookstores in the

Keys. They also sell gifts and jewelry and hold book signings and readings for kids. There is an extensive selection of books, cards, and maps on Florida and the Keys. There's chic shopping at the **Gallery at Morada Bay** (⊠ MM 81.6, BS, ☎ 305/664–3650), stocked with blown glass and glassware, furniture and home furnishings, original paintings and lithographs, sculptures, and hand-painted scarves and earrings by top South Florida artists. At **Island Silver & Spice** (⊠ MM 82, OS, ☎ 305/664–2714), the first floor is devoted to women's and men's resort wear, a large jewelry section with high-end Swiss watches and marine-theme jewelry, tropical housewares, cards, and toys and games. Climb the wooden stairway to the second floor to browse through tropical bedding and bath goods and a sale section.

A circa-1977 crafts village set in a tropical garden of native plants and orchids, **Rain Barrel** (⊠ MM 86.7, BS, ☎ 305/852–3084) represents works by numerous local and national artists and has eight resident artists in separate studios. On the third weekend in March, the largest arts show in the Keys takes place here; some 20,000 visitors view the work of 100 artists and listen to live jazz. A new café offers a primarily vegetarian menu. Such nationally and internationally recognized outdoor artists as sculptor Kendall Van Sant; watercolorists Chet Reneson, Jeanne Dobie, and Kathleen Denis; and painters C. D. Clarke and Tim Borski are represented at the **Redbone Gallery** (⊠ MM 81, OS, 200 Industrial Dr., ☎ 305/664–2002). At **Treasure Village** (⊠ MM 86.7, OS, 86729 Old Hwy., ☎ 305/852–0511), salvage master Art McKee ran McKee's Treasure Museum in the 1950s. An enormous fabricated lobster by artist Richard Blaes stands in front of the center, where a dozen crafts and specialty shops plus the excellent little Made to Order eat-in and carryout restaurant operate. **World Wide Sportsman** (⊠ MM 82.5, BS, ☎ 305/664–4615) is a two-level attraction, lounge, and retail center selling very upscale fishing equipment. It has a pricey art gallery, marina, and departments for clothing and gifts. Black-and-white photos of former U.S. presidents, celebs, and record holders beaming alongside their catches adorn the walls.

Long Key

❺   *MM 70–65.5.*

This island is best known for the **Long Key State Recreation Area.** On the main, ocean side, the Golden Orb Trail leads onto a boardwalk through a mangrove swamp alongside a lagoon, where waterbirds congregate. The park has a campground, picnic area, rest rooms and showers, a canoe trail through a tidal lagoon, and a not-very-sandy beach fronting a broad expanse of shallow grass flats. Bring a mask and snorkel to observe the marine life in this rich nursery area. In 1998 Hurricane Georges flooded the park's ocean side and killed almost all the vegetation. Although the park is open, all repairs and replantings may not be completed by the time you visit. Across the road, near a historical marker partially obscured by foliage, is the **Layton Nature Trail** (⊠ MM 67.7, BS), which takes 20–30 minutes to walk and leads through tropical hardwood forest to a rocky Florida Bay shoreline overlooking shallow grass flats. A marker relates the history of the Long Key Viaduct, the first major bridge on the rail line, and the exclusive Long Key Fishing Camp, which Henry Flagler established nearby in 1906 and which attracted sportsman Zane Grey, the noted western novelist and conservationist, who served as its first president. The camp was washed away in the 1935 hurricane and never rebuilt. For Grey's efforts, the creek running near the recreation area was named for him. ⊠ *MM 67.5, OS, Box 776, 33001,* ☎ *305/664–4815.* ⛨ *$3.25 for 1* *person, plus 50¢ each additional person; canoe rental $4 per hr, $10 per day; Layton Nature Trail free. ☉ Daily 8–sunset.*

Dining and Lodging

$–$$ ✕ **Little Italy.** The hearty Italian and seafood dishes here are a great value. Food is consistently good, and prices are consistently low. Recent lunch menu changes added Caesar salads, chicken marsala, stone crabs, and stuffed snapper priced at $3.95–$7.95, including salad, french fries, and bread. Dinner selections are equally tasty and well priced—pasta, chicken, seafood, veal, and steak for $8.50–$13.95. Don't miss the rich, dreamy hot chocolate pecan pie. Breakfast, too, is served, and a light-bites menu features smaller portions. ✉ *MM 68.5, BS,* ☎ *305/664–4472. AE, D, MC, V.*

$$ ⌂ **Lime Tree Bay Resort Motel.** This popular 2½-acre hideaway has attractive wicker- and rattan-furnished guest rooms, tropical art, and cottages with kitchens along with a little beach, nice landscaping, a beautiful pool deck, hammocks, a gazebo, and a covered walkway. The best units are the cottages out back (no bay views) and four deluxe rooms upstairs, which have cathedral ceilings and skylights. The upstairs Tree House, the best bet for two couples traveling together, has a palm tree growing through its private deck. You can swim and snorkel in the shallow grass flats offshore. An on-site concessioner offers water sports, available separately or with an accommodation package. ✉ *MM 68.5, BS, Box 839, Layton 33001,* ☎ *305/664–4740 or 800/723–4519,* ⬛ *305/664–0750. 30 rooms. Restaurant, picnic area, pool, hot tub, tennis court, horseshoes, shuffleboard, beach, dive shop, snorkeling, windsurfing, boating, jet skiing. AE, D, DC, MC, V.*

$ ⚠ **Long Key State Recreation Area.** Situated along the park's narrow, semi-sandy beach are tent and RV sites under tall, shady trees. Fishing in the near-shore flats is superb, yielding bonefish, permit, and tarpon. A new reservation system went into effect in 1998 (you can reserve up to 11 months in advance by phone or in person) along with major upgrades. All sites now have water and electricity, signage has been improved, and campground hostesses are available to answer questions and help out. Sites cost $17, plus $2 for electricity. ✉ *MM 67.5, OS, Box 776, 33001,* ☎ *305/664–4815. 60 sites. Picnic area, hiking, beach, fishing. D, MC, V.*

Outdoor Activities and Sports

Based at Lime Tree Bay Resort, Captain Elizabeth Jolin's **Lime Tree Water Sports** (✉ MM 68.5, BS, ☎ 305/664–0052) provides a wide variety of recreational opportunities, including sunset cruises; sailboat, powerboat, kayak, sailboard, and Wave Runner rentals; backcountry fishing trips; and snorkeling and scuba. She also offers PADI diving certification and windsurfing and sailing lessons.

En Route As you cross Long Key Channel, look beside you at the old **Long Key Viaduct.** The second-longest bridge on the former rail line, this 2-mi-long structure has 222 reinforced-concrete arches.

THE MIDDLE KEYS

Stretching from Conch Key to the far side of the Seven Mile Bridge, the Middle Keys contain U.S. 1's most impressive stretch, MM 65–40, bracketed by the Keys' two longest bridges—Long Key Bridge and Seven Mile Bridge, both historic landmarks. Activity centers on the town of Marathon, the Keys' third-largest metropolitan area.

Fishing and diving are the main attractions. In both bay and ocean, the deep-water fishing is superb at places like the Marathon West

Hump, whose depth ranges from 500 to more than 1,000 ft. Anglers successfully fish from a half-dozen bridges, including Long Key Bridge, the old Seven Mile Bridge, and both ends of Toms Harbor. There are also many beaches and natural areas to enjoy in the Middle Keys.

Conch and Duck Keys

❻ *MM 63–61.*

This stretch of islands is rustic. Fishing dominates the economy, and many residents are descendants of immigrants from the mainland South. Across a causeway from Conch Key, a tiny fishing and retirement village, lies Duck Key, an upscale community and resort.

Dining and Lodging

$–$$$ ✕ **Watersedge.** A collection of historic photos on the walls depicts the railroad era, the development of Duck Key, and many of the notables who have visited this eatery at the Hawk's Cay Resort (☞ *below*). Dine in the newly renovated indoor dining room or under the dockside canopy. Soup and a 40-item salad bar are included with dinners. The menu emphasizes seafood, and specialties range from spicy conch chowder, chicken Key West (stuffed with crab and shrimp), and Florida stone-crab claws (in season) to mud pie and coconut ice cream. ⊠ *MM 61, OS, Duck Key,* ☎ *305/743–7000. AE, D, DC, MC, V. No lunch mid-Dec.–mid-Apr.*

$$$$ ⊡ **Hawk's Cay Resort.** This rambling Caribbean-style resort, which opened in 1959, has entertained film stars and politicians. Today it's big with families and businesspeople, who enjoy golf on a nearby course, dive trips, volleyball on a sand court overlooking the Atlantic, swimming in the smooth saltwater lagoon or pool, a new fitness center with state-of-the-art equipment, new basketball courts, and a new whirlpool spa. There are programs for kids and teens as well as an interactive, in-the-water educational program called Dolphin Discovery. The light, casual decor comprises lots of wicker and earthy colors. Rooms facing the water are getting makeovers, and construction continues on additional two-bedroom villas. ⊠ *MM 61, OS, 33050,* ☎ *305/743–7000 or 800/432–2242,* ℻ *305/743–5215. 160 rooms, 16 suites, 130 two-bedroom villas. 4 restaurants, 2 bars, 2 pools, golf privileges, 8 tennis courts, basketball, health club, volleyball, boating, fishing, video games, children's programs. AE, D, DC, MC, V.*

$$ ⊡ **Conch Key Cottages.** This happy hideout on its own island bridged by a pebbly causeway has a castaway, live-and-let-live mood. Allamanda, bougainvillea, and hibiscus jiggle colorfully, and the beach curves around a mangrove-edged cove. Lattice-trimmed cottages with kitchens, some with two bedrooms, rise up on pilings, old-fashioned in Dade County pine. Cool tile floors, hammocks, and furnishings of reed, rattan, and wicker create an island look. Three cottages face the beach. Though not on the water, the small honeymoon cottage is very charming. If you need a coffee fix, bring your own to prepare, as the closest source is 1½ mi away. Highway noise can be distracting. ⊠ *MM 62.3, OS, R.R. 1, Box 424, Marathon 33050,* ☎ *305/289–1377 or 800/330–1577,* ℻ *305/743–8207. 12 units. Pool, beach. D, MC, V.*

Grassy Key

❼ *MM 60–57.*

Local lore has it that this sleepy little key was named not for its vegetation—mostly native trees and shrubs—but for an early settler. It's primarily inhabited by a few families who operate small fishing camps and motels.

The former home of Milton Santini, creator of the original *Flipper* movie, the **Dolphin Research Center** is now home to a colony of about 15 dolphins. A not-for-profit organization offers a half-day program called Dolph*Insight*, which teaches dolphin biology and human–dolphin communications and allows you to touch the dolphins out of the water. A 2½-hour instruction-education program aptly called Dolphin Encounter enables you to do just that in the water for 20 minutes. ⊠ *MM 59, BS, Box 522875, Marathon Shores 33052,* ☎ *305/289–1121.* ⊠ *$12.50, DolphInsight $75, Dolphin Encounter $110.* ☉ *Daily 9–4, walking tours daily 10, 11, 12:30, 2, and 3:30. Children 5–12 must swim with accompanying, paying adult. Reserve 30 days in advance for all programs.*

<table>
<tr><td>OFF THE
BEATEN PATH</td><td>CURRY HAMMOCK STATE PARK – Comprising upland hammock, wetlands, and mangroves, the state's latest land acquisition open for public use is a jewel. The park covers 260 acres—the largest uninhabited parcel between Key Largo and Big Pine—and is bordered by a sandy beach. There are a new bathhouse and picnic tables, but plans for a campground and entrance fees are still undecided. Locals consider this one of the best areas for kayaking in the Keys. Trails meander under canopies of arching mangroves. Manatees frequent the area, and it's a birding paradise. For now, information is provided by Long Key State Recreation Area (☞ Long Key, above). ⊠ MM 57, OS, Crawl Key, ☎ 305/664–4815. ⊠ Free. ☉ Daily 8–sunset.</td></tr>
</table>

Dining and Lodging

$–$$ ✕ **Grassy Key Dairy Bar.** This little seafood and steak landmark dates from 1959. Locals and construction workers stop here for quick lunches and good company. Despite the name, the only ice cream served is an ice cream pie. To reflect that—and cut down on confusion—the new sign outside says simply GRASSY KEY DB. What they do serve is a popular broiled dolphin with black beans and rice and cheese sauce. Owner-chefs George and Johnny Eigner are also proud of their broiled or grilled fish with wasabi, as well as the fresh-daily homemade bread and fresh-cut beef. On Tuesday night they add Mexican dishes to the menu, and in fall their OctoberFest features German foods, beers, and live entertainment. ⊠ *MM 58.5, OS,* ☎ *305/743–3816. MC, V. Closed Sun.–Mon. No lunch Sat. Apr.–Dec.*

$ ▥ **Curry Hammock Resort & Marina.** Since the early '60s people have come to the Valhalla Beach Resort Motel, an unpretentious Crawl Key lodging with the waterfront location of a posh resort. In the late '90s the property was split into two resorts, Valhalla Beach Motel (☞ *below*) and Curry Hammock Resort & Marina, with a fence dividing the property. This half has the feel of a friend's beach house. There are a very good beach with hammocks and chaises, a dock from which manatees are frequently sighted, picnic tables, barbecue grills, and kayaks and canoes, a nice touch since the property borders the state's new park, Curry Hammock (☞ *above*), which locals say has one of the Keys' best kayak trails. Family-oriented snorkeling trips to the reefs are offered. There are no phones in rooms. ⊠ *MM 57.5, OS, 56223 Ocean Dr., Crawl Key 33050,* ☎ *305/289–0614. 1 room, 4 efficiencies. Picnic area, beach, dock, boating. MC, V.*

$ ▥ **Valhalla Beach Motel.** Bruce Schofield runs this motel, which has a few more units than his brother's next door (☞ *above*). Rooms have small refrigerators, while efficiencies have kitchens. The property features a small beach, boat ramp, dock, barbecue grills, canoes and rental fishing boats, and Adirondack chairs. Some things haven't changed, like the palm trees rustling in the wind, clean and simple rooms with TVs but no telephones, and peace and quiet. ⊠ *MM 57.5, OS,*

56243 Ocean Dr., Crawl Key 33050, ☎ 305/289–0616. 4 rooms, 1 suite, 5 efficiencies. Beach, dock, boating. No credit cards.

Marathon

⑧ *MM 53–47.5.*

This community is the commercial hub of the Middle Keys. Commercial fishing—still a big local industry—began here in the early 1800s. Pirates, salvors, fishermen, spongers, and later farmers eked out a living, traveling by boat between islands. About half the population were blacks, who burned charcoal for a living. According to local lore, Marathon was renamed after a 1906 hurricane, when a worker commented that it was a marathon task to rebuild the railway across the 6-mi island.

The railroad brought businesses and a hotel, and today Marathon is a bustling town by Keys standards. Yet the town remains laid-back. Fishing, diving, and boating are the primary attractions.

The small **Museums of Tropical Crane Point Hammock**—part of a 63-acre tract that includes the last-known undisturbed thatch-palm hammock—is owned by the Florida Keys Land Trust, a private, nonprofit conservation group. In the **Museum of Natural History of the Florida Keys,** behind a stunning bronze-and-copper door crafted by Roy Butler of Plantation, are a few dioramas, a shell exhibit, and displays on Keys geology, wildlife, and cultural history. Also here is the **Florida Keys Children's Museum,** which has iguanas, fish, and a pirate dress-up room. Outside, on the 1-mi indigenous loop trail, you can visit the remnants of a Bahamian village, site of the restored **George Adderly House,** the oldest surviving example of Conch-style architecture outside Key West. From November to Easter, docent-led tours, included in the price, are available; bring good walking shoes and bug repellent. ⊠ *MM 50.5, BS, 5550 Overseas Hwy., Box 536, 33050, ☎ 305/743–9100.* 🖃 *$7.50. ☉ Mon.–Sat. 9–5, Sun. noon–5; tours conducted when docents available.*

Sombrero Beach has separate areas for swimmers, jet boats, and windsurfers, as well as a grassy park with barbecue grills, picnic kiosks, showers, rest rooms, a baseball diamond, large playground, and volleyball court. The park is accessible for travelers with disabilities and allows leashed pets. Turn left at the traffic light in Marathon and follow signs to the end. There's a wide bike path from U.S. 1 to the entrance. ⊠ *MM 50, OS, Sombrero Rd., ☎ 305/289–6077 or 888/227–8136.* 🖃 *Free. ☉ Daily 7:30–sunset.*

OFF THE BEATEN PATH

PIGEON KEY – This 5-acre island under the Seven Mile Bridge was once the site of a railroad work camp and, later, a fish camp, park, and government administration building. Today the focus is on Florida Keys culture, environmental education, and marine research. You can tour on your own, using a free printed walking guide that highlights the restored railroad work-camp buildings, the earliest of which dates from 1908, or take a trolley tour on the hour. Museum exhibits recall the history of the railroad and the Keys, and a 28-minute video captures railroad baron Henry M. Flagler's life. To reach the island, you can either take the shuttle, which departs from the depot on Knight's Key (⊠ MM 47), or walk across a 2.2-mi stretch of the Old Seven Mile Bridge. Bring a picnic and stay the day. ⊠ MM 45, OS, Box 500130, Pigeon Key 33050, ☎ 305/289–0025. 🖃 $7.50. ☉ Daily 10–5.

Dining and Lodging

$$–$$$ ✕ **Kelsey's.** This steak and seafood eatery at the Faro Blanco Marine Resort (☞ *below*) is hung with boat paddles inscribed by charter-boat captains and other frequent diners. Entrées like Maryland-style crab cakes and horseradish-encrusted grouper over mashed potatoes are served with fresh-toasted baguettes prepared here daily. You can bring your own cleaned and filleted catch for the chef to prepare. Desserts may include banana pecan delight, white-chocolate mousse, macadamia pie, and key lime cheesecake. ⊠ *MM 48.5, BS,* ☎ *305/743–9018. AE, MC, V. Closed Mon. No lunch.*

$–$$$$ ✕ **Barracuda Grill.** It's right there on the menu: "The owners are cooking for you; pop your head in the kitchen if you'd like to say hello." Guests who do will find Lance and Jan Hill busily preparing an eclectic menu that capitalizes on the local bounty—fresh fish—but is equally represented by tender, juicy aged Angus beef; rack of lamb; and even meat loaf. The latter, Mama's Meatloaf, will not make you think of your childhood. Innovation is in everything but not at the expense of good, solid cooking. Thai Money Bags, a delicate pastry pouch filled with shrimp and veggies, suggests an Asian influence. Ribbiting Frog's Legs, with butter, garlic, and a touch of tomato sauce, screams South Florida. You can't miss on either. The well-thought-out wine list is heavily Californian. ⊠ *MM 49.5, BS,* ☎ *305/743–3314. AE, MC, V. Closed Sun. No lunch.*

$–$$ ✕ **Hurricane Grille.** The same folks who bring you the good food at Key Colony Inn and Little Italy have taken over this restaurant. The menu is packed with good value—rib-sticking seafood, chicken, and steaks—but the best is the shellfish, which comes steamed (clams, crabs, oysters, shrimp, lobster) or raw (clams only) from the moment the doors open until the bar closes, as late as 4 AM. The owners plan to bring in jazz, blues, and rock bands several nights a week. Satellite TV broadcasts sports games, keeping the bar, which takes up half the building, humming. There's indoor and outdoor seating, but the decor, a mishmash of tropical kitsch, is distracting. ⊠ *MM 49.5, BS, 4650 Overseas Hwy.,* ☎ *305/743–2220. AE, MC, V.*

$–$$ ✕ **Island Tiki Bar & Restaurant.** Location, location, location. The new owners of this eatery are taking advantage of its best asset: prime waterfront. The tables and tiki bar overlook the gulf and sunsets. Diners can arrive by boat and tie up at the dock, while those without boats can take a pre- or postprandial sunset cruise. The staff is sharp, and the food—predominantly seafood—is well prepared. She-crab soup ($3.95) has become a local favorite, and jumbo Key West shrimp come four ways, from grilled to *fra diavolo.* ⊠ *MM 54, BS, 12648 Overseas Hwy.,* ☎ *305/743–4191. AE, D, MC, V.*

$–$$ ✕ **Key Colony Inn.** This local institution features chicken, steak, pasta, and veal dishes with an Italian accent. Food is well prepared, and service is friendly and attentive. For lunch there are well-priced fish and steak entrées ($4.50–$6.95) served with fries, salad, and bread. At dinner you can't miss with the seafood Italiano, a light dish of scallops and shrimp sautéed in garlic butter over a bed of linguine with a hint of marinara sauce. ⊠ *MM 54, OS, 700 W. Ocean Dr., Key Colony Beach,* ☎ *305/743–0100. AE, MC, V.*

$ ★ ✕ **7 Mile Grill.** The walls of this open-air diner built in 1954 at the Marathon end of Seven Mile Bridge are lined with beer cans, mounted fish, sponges, and signs describing individual menu items. The prompt, friendly service rivals the great food at breakfast, lunch, and dinner. Favorites on the mostly seafood menu include fresh-squeezed orange juice, creamy shrimp bisque, and fresh grouper and dolphin grilled, broiled, or fried. Don't pass up the authentic key lime pie, which won the local paper's "Best in the Keys" award three years in a row. A wine license was recently added. ⊠ *MM 47, BS,* ☎ *305/743–4481. No credit cards. Closed Wed., plus Thurs. mid-Apr.–mid-Nov. and at owner's discretion Aug.–Sept.*

$$–$$$$ 🏨 **Faro Blanco Marine Resort.** One of the oldest resorts in the Keys, Faro Blanco has built up a loyal following of repeat guests, thanks to service that's first-rate without being fussy. Before Hurricane Georges, the property stretched on both sides of the highway with guest rooms (most with kitchens); cottages; houseboats; three-bedroom, two-bath condominiums; and two lighthouse apartments. Houseboat accommodations on the ocean side that were heavily damaged by the storm are gradually being replaced. Bay-side properties weathered the storm just fine. A full-service marina and marine repair shop meet boaters' needs, and diving and fishing charters can be arranged. Pets are allowed in all units except condominiums. ⊠ *MM 48.2, BS and OS, 1996 Overseas Hwy., 33050,* ☎ *305/743–9018 or 800/759–3276,* 🖷 *305/743–2918. 100 units. 3 restaurants, pool, docks, boating, bicycles. AE, MC, V.*

$$–$$$ 🏨 **Seascape Ocean Resort.** If you're looking for an exclusive but un-
★ pretentious hotel in the Middle Keys, look no farther. Nine rooms, three with kitchen, occupy what was once a large, two-story bay-front house that, thanks to a faux stone exterior, wrought-iron grills, and adjacent barn, seems like a villa in Provence. Owned by Sara and Bill Stites, a nationally recognized painter and a magazine photographer, respectively, the 5-acre property has wicker, soothing sea colors, and artistic touches throughout. Rooms are decorated with original artwork and hand-painted headboards and come with fresh fruit, flowers, and specialty soaps. Guests can while away the time at the pool, on the beach, under a shade tree, in a kayak, or in the barn–turned–art studio, where Sara paints. Continental breakfast and afternoon cocktails and hors d'oeuvres are set out for guests to indulge in at leisure. Rooms are nonsmoking and have no phones. ⊠ *MM 50.5, OS, 1075 75th St., 33050,* ☎ *305/743–6455 or 800/332–7327,* 🖷 *305/743–8469. 9 rooms. Pool, beach, dock. AE, MC, V.*

$$ 🏨 **Coral Lagoon.** Surrounded by lush landscaping on a short, deep-water canal, these charming pastel-color duplex cottages each have a hammock on a private sundeck, a kitchen, and king or twin beds and a sofa bed. Units also have central air, ceiling fans, videocassette players ($1 tape rental), wall safes, and hair dryers, and you can take advantage of complimentary morning coffee, tennis rackets, fishing equipment, dockage, and barbecues. For a fee you can also enjoy admission to a private beach club, charter fishing, and scuba and snorkel trips arranged through the Diving Site, a dive shop that also offers certification. ⊠ *MM 53.5, OS, 12399 Overseas Hwy., 33050,* ☎ *305/289–0121,* 🖷 *305/289–0195. 18 units. Pool, tennis court, dive shop, dock, library. AE, D, MC, V.*

Outdoor Activities and Sports

BIKING

Some of the best paths in the area include those along Aviation Boulevard on the bay side of Marathon Airport, the four-lane section of the Overseas Highway through Marathon, Sadowski Causeway to Key Colony Beach, Sombrero Beach Road to the public beach, and the roads on Boot Key (across a bridge on 20th Street, OS). There's easy cycling at the south end of Marathon, where a 1-mi off-road path connects to the 2 mi of the Old Seven Mile Bridge that go to Pigeon Key.

Equipment Locker Sport & Cycle (⊠ MM 53, BS, ☎ 305/289–1670) rents cruisers for $10 per day, $50 per week and mountain bikes for adults and children.

BOATING

Fish 'n' Fun (⊠ MM 53.5, OS, ☎ 305/743–2275), next to the Boat House Marina, rents 18- to 25-ft boats starting at $85 for a half day, $125 for a full day. It also supplies bait, tackle, licenses, and snorkel gear.

FISHING

A pair of 65-ft party boats, **Marathon Lady** and **Marathon Lady III** (⊠ MM 53.5, OS, at 117th St., 33050, ☎ 305/743–5580), go on two half-day ($25) trips from the Vaca Cut Bridge, north of Marathon. Those who don't want to pay $200–$350 for a half-day charter or share a party boat with 30 or more other anglers are turning to **Sea Dog Charters** (⊠ MM 47.5, BS, ☎ 305/743–8255), next to the 7 Mile Grill. Captain Jim Purcell, a deep-sea specialist for ESPN's *The Outdoorsman,* offers personalized half- and full-day offshore, reef and wreck, tarpon, and backcountry fishing trips as well as combination fishing and snorkeling trips on the 32-ft *Bad Dog* for up to six people. The cost is $59.99 per person for a half day, regardless of whether your group fills the boat, and includes bait, light tackle, licensing, ice, and coolers.

GOLF

Key Colony Beach Par 3 (⊠ MM 53.5, OS, 8th St., Key Colony Beach, ☎ 305/289–1533), a nine-hole course near Marathon, charges $7.50 for nine holes, $2 per person for club rental, and $1 for a pull cart. The beauty of this course is that there are no tee times and no rush. Play from 7:30 to dusk. A little golf shop meets basic golf needs.

SCUBA DIVING AND SNORKELING

Hall's Diving Center and Career Institute (⊠ MM 48.5, BS, 1994 Overseas Hwy., 33050, ☎ 305/743–5929 or 800/331–4255), next to Faro Blanco Resort, runs two trips a day to Looe Key, Sombrero Reef, Delta Shoal, Content Key, Coffins Patch, the 110-ft wreck *Thunderbolt,* and the new wreck *Adolphus Busch.*

En Route   To cross the broad expanse of water separating the Middle and Lower keys, you'll travel over the **Seven Mile Bridge,** actually 6.79 mi long. Believed to be the world's longest segmental bridge, it has 39 expansion joints separating its cement sections. Each April runners gather in Marathon for the annual Seven Mile Bridge Run. You can look across at what remains of the **Old Seven Mile Bridge,** an engineering marvel in its day that's now on the National Register of Historic Places. It rested on a record 546 concrete piers. No private cars are allowed on the bridge today, but locals like to ride bikes on it to watch the sunset and to reach Pigeon Key.

THE LOWER KEYS

In truth, the Lower Keys include Key West, but since it's covered in its own section and is as different from the rest of the Lower Keys as peanut butter is from jelly, this section comprises just the limestone keys between MM 37 and MM 9. From Bahia Honda Key south, islands are clustered, smaller, and more numerous, a result of ancient tidal waters flowing between the Florida Straits and the gulf. Here you're likely to see more birds and mangroves than other tourists, and more refuges, beaches, and campgrounds than museums, restaurants, and hotels.

The islands are made up of two types of limestone, both more dense than the highly permeable Key Largo limestone of the Upper Keys. As a result, freshwater forms pools rather than percolating, creating watering holes that support Key deer, alligators, fish, snakes, Lower Keys rabbits, raccoons, migratory ducks, Key cotton and silver rice rats, pines, saw palmettos, silver palms, grasses, and ferns. (Many of these animals and plants can be seen in the National Key Deer Refuge on Big Pine Key ☞ *below.*)

Nature was generous with her beauty in the Lower Keys. They're home to both Looe Key National Marine Sanctuary, arguably the most beautiful coral reef tract in the Keys, and Bahia Honda State Park, considered by many one of the best beaches in the world.

Bahia Honda Key

❾ *MM 38–36.*

★ Bahia Honda translates from Spanish as "deep bay," a good description of local waters. The government owns most of the island, which is devoted to 524-acre **Bahia Honda State Park.** The park was devastated by Hurricane Georges in September 1998 and was closed for three months. Rangers expect to have everything back to normal by late 1999. The Silver Palm Trail leads through a dense—though slightly less dense following the hurricane—tropical forest where you can see rare West Indian plants and several species found nowhere else in the Keys. The park also contains the Keys' only natural sandy beach of notable size; it extends on both gulf and ocean sides and has deep water close to shore. Plenty of year-round activities are available, and there are cabins, a campground, a snack bar, marina, and dive shop. You can get a panoramic view of the island from what's left of the railroad—the Bahia Honda Bridge. ✉ *MM 37, OS, 36850 Overseas Hwy., 33043,* ☎ *305/ 872–2353.* ▣ *$2 for 1 person, $4 per vehicle for 2–8 people plus 50¢ per person county surcharge; $2 per vehicle an hour before closing.* ☉ *Daily 8–sunset.*

Lodging

$$ ⊞ **Bahia Honda State Park.** Views from the six bay-front cabin units on stilts are spectacular. Each is completely furnished (no TV or radio); has two bedrooms, full kitchen, and bath; and sleeps six. The park also has 80 popular campsites, suitable for motor homes and tents. Cabins and campsites are very popular, so reserve up to 11 months before your planned visit. ✉ *MM 37, OS, 36850 Overseas Hwy., 33043,* ☎ *305/872–2353. 3 duplex cabins. Picnic area, beach, boating, fishing. MC, V.*

Outdoor Activities and Sports

Bahia Honda Dive Shop (✉ MM 37, OS, ☎ 305/872–3210), the concessioner at Bahia Honda State Park, operates offshore-reef snorkel trips and boat rentals. Snorkel trips ($22) run almost three hours (with an hour on the reef) and leave daily at 10 and 2 (also at 1, October–November). Rental craft range from a 20-ft pontoon boat and 22-ft center console fishing-dive boat to kayaks.

Big Pine Key

❿ *MM 32–30.*

Known for its concentration of Key deer, this island is the site of the 2,300-acre **National Key Deer Refuge,** established in 1954 to protect the dwindling population of Key deer, a subspecies of the Virginia white-tailed deer. These deer once ranged throughout the Lower and Middle keys, but hunting, habitat destruction, and a growing human population have caused their numbers to decline to around 250. The best place to see Key deer in the refuge is at the end of Key Deer Boulevard (Route 940), along U.S. 1, and on No Name Key, a sparsely populated island just east of Big Pine Key. Deer may turn up along the road at any time of day—especially in early morning and late afternoon. Admire their beauty, but feeding them is against the law. The **Blue Hole,** a quarry left over from railroad days, is the largest body of freshwater in the Keys. From the observation platform and walking trail, you might see alligators, birds, turtles, Key deer, and other wildlife. There are two well-marked trails: the Jack Watson Nature Trail (⅔ mi), named after Jack Watson, an environmentalist and the refuge's first warden; and the Fred Mannillo Nature Trail, one of the most accessible places to see an unspoiled hardwood hammock and subtropical foliage. The latter has a hard surface for wheelchair access. ✉ *Headquarters, Big Pine Shopping Center, MM 30.5, BS,* ☎ *305/872–2239.* ☜ *Free.* ☉ *Daily sunrise–sunset; headquarters weekdays 8–5.*

Dining and Lodging

$ ✕ **No Name Pub.** The Upper Keys has Alabama Jack's and the Caribbean Club. The Lower Keys has this ramshackle American-casual establishment, in existence since 1936, or so the staff's shirts read. As long as anyone can remember, locals have come for the cold beer, excellent pizza, and sometimes questionable companionship. In 1998 the pub introduced a full menu, featuring pastas, chicken wings, and, of course, pizza. Inside is poorly lighted, with rough furnishings, a jukebox, and pool table; outside is a garden area. The pub is hard to find but worth the search if you want to experience the Keys as old-timers say they once were; turn north at the Big Pine Key traffic light, right at the fork, left at the four-way stop, and then over a humpback bridge. It's on the left, before the No Name Bridge. ✉ *MM 30, BS, N. Watson Blvd.,* ☎ *305/872–9115. MC, V.*

$$–$$$ 🏠 **Deer Run.** The most casual of three local B&Bs, this lodging set on 2 wooded beachfront acres is populated by cats, caged tropical birds, and a herd of Key deer, which forage along the beach. Like her fellow innkeepers, longtime Big Pine resident Sue Abbott is caring and informed, well settled and hospitable. Two large oceanfront rooms are furnished with whitewashed wicker and king-size beds. An upstairs unit looks out on the sea through trees. Guests have use of a living room, a 52-ft veranda cooled by paddle fans, hammocks, a large barbecue grill, a hot tub on a deck overlooking the ocean, and water toys. Smokers and children are not welcome. ✉ *MM 33, OS, 1985 Long Beach Dr., Box 431, 33043,* ☎ *305/872–2015,* 🖷 *305/872–2842. 3 rooms. Hot tub, beach, bicycles. No credit cards.*

$$ 🏠 **The Barnacle.** Hurricane Georges soaked furnishings upstairs and
★ swept away everything on the ground that wasn't bolted down, including the beach, the lush landscaping, and the fences. But B&B owners Tim and Jane Marquis turned the storm into an opportunity. They busily replanted and improved upon what was already the perfect getaway, comprising two rooms in the main house, both on the second floor; one in a cottage with a kitchen; and another, below the house, that opens to the beach. Guest rooms are large, and those in the main house adjoin an atrium, where a hot tub sits in a beautiful garden overlooking sea and sky. Full breakfast is included, as is use of paddleboats and kayaks. As former owners of a diving business, Tim and Jane offer personalized snorkel and dive charters and certifications, as well as fishing excursions. ✉ *MM 33, OS, 1557 Long Beach Dr., 33043,* ☎ *305/ 872–3298 or 800/465–9100,* 🖷 *305/872–3863. 4 rooms. Hot tub, beach, dock, boating, bicycles. D, MC, V.*

$$ 🏠 **Casa Grande.** Owner Kathleen Threlkeld took advantage of the dam-
★ age done by Hurricane Georges to upgrade everything from the Berber carpeting to the screened porch. The service remains the same at this

popular bed-and-breakfast, whose guests like to sun themselves on the white-sand beach abutting the rocky, shallow shoreline. The lodging is markedly Mediterranean, with a massive Spanish door and mainly contemporary furnishings. Spacious guest rooms have new color TVs, small refrigerators, new air-conditioning, and high open-beam ceilings with paddle fans, and there is a screened, second-story atrium facing the sea. Guests cozy up to the sitting-room fireplace and get to know one another on cool nights. ⊠ *MM 33, OS, 1619 Long Beach Dr., Box 378, 33043,* ☎ *305/872–2878. 3 rooms. Hot tub, beach, dock, boating, bicycles. No credit cards.*

$–$$ 🏠 **Big Pine Key Fishing Lodge.** The five lodge rooms at this family-owned
★ and family-oriented lodge and campground ($24–$31 per site) are one of the Keys' best buys. They feature tile floors, wicker furniture, louvered and screened windows, doors that allow sea breezes to blow through, queen-size beds, a second-bedroom loft, vaulted ceilings, and mini-kitchens. A skywalk joins them with a pool and deck. Over the next few years, the other units in this almost-30-year-old business— either spic-and-span mobile homes or efficiencies—will slowly be replaced with more modern facilities. Immaculately clean tile lines the spacious bathhouse for campers. Separate game and recreation rooms house TVs, organized family-oriented activities, and other amusements, and there is dockage along a 735-ft canal. A three-day minimum is required. ⊠ *MM 33, OS, Box 430513, 33043,* ☎ *305/872–2351,* 𝐅𝐀𝐗 *305/872–3868. 16 rooms, 158 campsites. Pool, Ping-Pong, shuffleboard, dock, billiards, recreation room, video games. D, MC, V.*

Outdoor Activities and Sports

BIKING

A good 10 mi of paved and unpaved roads run from MM 30.3, BS, along Wilder Road, across the bridge to No Name Key, and along Key Deer Boulevard into the National Key Deer Refuge. You might see some Key deer. Stay off the trails that lead into wetlands, where fat tires can do damage.

In addition to selling and repairing bikes, **Big Pine Bicycle Center** (⊠ MM 30, OS, ☎ 305/872–0130) rents old-fashioned single-speed, fat-tired cruisers for adults ($6 per half day, $9 for a full day, and $38 a week) and children ($5, $7, and $30). Helmets, baskets, and locks are included. Ask owner Marty Baird about his favorite places to ride, or show up at the shop Sunday morning at 8 for the free off-road fun ride.

FISHING

Strike Zone Charters (⊠ MM 29.6, BS, 29675 Overseas Hwy., 33043, ☎ 305/872–9863 or 800/654–9560) runs fishing charters on air-conditioned boats at $425 for a half day, $525 for a full day. In addition, sightseeing trips can include time to fish, as well as bait and tackle.

Little Torch Key

⓫ *MM 28–29.*

Primarily a base for divers headed for Looe Key National Marine Sanctuary, a few miles away, this key provides accommodations and diving outfits. The undeveloped backcountry is at your back door, making this an ideal location for fishing and kayaking, too. Nearby **Ramrod Key**, which also caters to divers bound for Looe Key, derives its name from a ship that wrecked on nearby reefs in the early 1800s.

Dining and Lodging

$–$$ ✕ **Montes Restaurant & Fish Market.** It looks like the archetypal island eatery: a gray wood-frame building with screened sides, a canvas roof, wood-plank floors, a tropical mural, and picnic tables. Casually clad, experienced waitresses provide good service. The menu features fish prepared just right, crabs, and shrimp that's steamed, broiled, stuffed, or fried. You can get a traditional fish sandwich or a variation stuffed with crabmeat. ⊠ *MM 25, BS, Summerland Key,* ☎ *305/745–3731. No credit cards.*

$ ✕ **Baby's Smokehouse Grill & Baby's Coffee.** Hurricane Georges didn't leave much of the restaurant, so an expanded indoor/outdoor restaurant with coffee-roasting facility was rebuilt. (Coffee by the cup is sold in a building across the street.) The menu still features lip-smacking veal, beef, ribs, Long Island duck, and chicken that are grilled, roasted, and smoked until they're fall-off-the-bone tender. Baby's uses its own grilling sauces and serves tangy house red and green hot sauces on the side. Lunches come with corn bread or French bread, dinners with corn bread and a baked sweet potato. Save room for Baby's Coffee, freshly roasted on the premises. ⊠ *MM 15, OS, Saddlebunch Keys,* ☎ *305/ 744–9866 or 800/523–2326. AE, MC, V. Closed Mon.–Tues.*

$$$$ 🏨 **Little Palm Island.** The lobby sits beside U.S. 1 on Little Torch Key,
★ but the resort dazzles 3 mi offshore on a palm-fringed island. The 14 thatch-roof villas each have two suites with Mexican-tile baths, Jacuzzis, mosquito netting–draped beds, Mexican and Guatemalan wicker and rattan furniture, minibars, and safes. A second-floor suite on a houseboat adds to the mix, and many suites as well as the restaurant were redone after Hurricane Georges. There are no in-room phones or TVs. Instead, indulge in a fountain-fed pool, a massage in the indoor or outdoor spa, or some terrific snorkeling, diving, and fishing. The food draws yachtfolk from all over, who tie up at the marina come dinner time. The *Lady Bess,* a 72-ft yacht with two large staterooms that sleep four, is available for four-night voyages around the Keys starting at $6,600 (all-inclusive). ⊠ *MM 28.5, OS, 28500 Overseas Hwy., 33042,* ☎ *305/ 872–2524 or 800/343–8567,* 𝖥𝖠𝖷 *305/872–4843. 30 suites. Restaurant, bar, pool, massage, sauna, beach, dock, snorkeling, boating, fishing. AE, D, DC, MC, V.*

$–$$ 🏨 **Parmer's Place.** Each December Parmer's Place sends out 15,000 holiday cards to former guests, many of whom return year after year to stay in the pastel-color, rustic, family-style waterfront cottages and rooms spread over 5 landscaped acres. Most rooms have a deck or balcony, all have cable and a full or half kitchen, and none has a telephone. Complimentary Continental breakfast is served in the family room. Though the property no longer belongs to the Parmers, the new owners don't plan to change anything. ⊠ *MM 29, BS, 565 Barry Ave., 33042,* ☎ *305/872–2157,* 𝖥𝖠𝖷 *305/872–2014. 18 rooms, 12 efficiencies, 13 apartments. Pool, docks, boating. AE, D, MC, V.*

Outdoor Activities and Sports

FISHING

The Grouch Charters (⊠ Summerland Key Cove Marina, MM 24.5, OS, Summerland Key, ☎ 305/745–1172 or 305/872–6100), under Captain Mark André, takes up to six passengers on offshore fishing trips ($350 for a half day, $475 for a full day). He also packages accommodations, fishing, snorkeling, and sightseeing for better deals. The firm's name refers to his original boat, named after his father, whose nickname was Grouch.

SCUBA DIVING AND SNORKELING

Named for the HMS *Looe,* a British warship wrecked in 1744, **Looe Key National Marine Sanctuary** (⊠ MM 27.5, OS, 216 Ann St., Key West 33040, ☎ 305/292–0311), part of the Florida Keys National Marine Sanctuary, contains a 5.3-square-nautical-mi reef. Perhaps the most beautiful and diverse coral community in the region, it has large stands of elk-horn coral on its eastern margin, immense purple sea fans, and abundant populations of sponges and sea urchins. On its seaward side, it has an almost-vertical drop-off to depths of 50–90 ft. Both snorkelers and divers will find the sanctuary a quiet place to observe reef life, except in July, when the annual Underwater Music Festival pays homage to Looe Key's beauty and promotes reef awareness with six hours of music broadcast via underwater speakers. Dive shops and private charters transport hundreds of divers to hear the spectacle, which includes Caribbean, classical, jazz, new age, and, of course, Jimmy Buffett.

Looe Key Dive Center (⊠ MM 27.5, OS, Box 509, Ramrod Key 33042, ☎ 305/872–2215, ext. 2; or 800/942–5397), the closest dive shop to Looe Key, offers two-day and overnight dive packages. It's part of the full-service Looe Key Reef Resort, which, not surprisingly, caters to divers. The dive boat, a 45-ft Corinthian catamaran, is docked within 100 ft of the hotel, whose guests have free use of tanks, weights, and snorkeling equipment. **Strike Zone Charters** (⊠ MM 29.6, BS, 29675 Overseas Hwy., Big Pine Key 33043, ☎ 305/872–9863 or 800/654–9560) offers dive trips to two sites on Looe Key, resort courses, and various certifications. The outfit uses glass-bottom boats, so accompanying nondivers can experience the reef, too.

En Route   The huge object that looks like a white whale floating over Cudjoe Key (⊠ MM 23–21) is not a figment of your imagination. It's Fat Albert, a radar balloon that monitors local air and water traffic.

KEY WEST

MM 4–0.

Situated 150 mi from Miami and just 90 mi from Havana, this tropical island city has always maintained a strong sense of detachment, even after it was connected to the rest of the United States—by the railroad in 1912 and by the Overseas Highway in 1938.

The U.S. government acquired Key West from Spain in 1821 along with the rest of Florida. The Spanish had named the island Cayo Hueso (Bone Key) after the Native American skeletons they found on its shores. In 1823 Uncle Sam sent Commodore David S. Porter to chase pirates away.

For three decades the primary industry in Key West was wrecking—rescuing people and salvaging cargo from ships that foundered on the nearby reefs. According to some reports, when pickings were lean, the wreckers hung out lights to lure ships aground. Their business declined after 1849, when the federal government began building lighthouses.

In 1845 the army started construction of Fort Taylor, which held Key West for the Union during the Civil War. After the war, an influx of Cuban dissidents unhappy with Spain's rule brought the cigar industry here. Fishing, shrimping, and sponge-gathering became important industries, and a pineapple-canning factory opened. Major military installations were established during the Spanish-American War and World War I. Through much of the 19th century and into the second decade of the 20th, Key West was Florida's wealthiest city in percapita terms.

In 1929 the local economy began to unravel. Modern ships no longer needed to provision in Key West, cigar making moved to Tampa, Hawaii dominated the pineapple industry, and the sponges succumbed to a blight. Then the Depression hit, and the military moved out. By 1934 half the population was on relief. The city defaulted on its bond payments, and the Federal Emergency Relief Administration took over the city and county governments.

By promoting Key West as a tourist destination, federal officials attracted 40,000 visitors during the 1934–35 winter season, but when the 1935 Labor Day hurricane struck the Middle Keys, it wiped out the railroad and the tourist trade.

An important naval center during World War II and the Korean conflict, the island remains a strategic listening post on the doorstep of Fidel Castro's Cuba. It was during the '60s that the fringes of society began moving here and in the mid-'70s that gay guest houses began opening in rapid succession.

In April 1982 the U.S. Border Patrol threw a roadblock across the Overseas Highway just south of Florida City to catch drug runners and illegal aliens. Traffic backed up for miles as Border Patrol agents searched vehicles and demanded that the occupants prove U.S. citizenship. City officials in Key West, outraged at being treated like foreigners by the federal government, staged a mock secession and formed their own "nation," the so-called Conch Republic. They hoisted a flag and distributed mock border passes, visas, and Conch currency. The embarrassed Border Patrol dismantled its roadblock, and now an annual festival recalls the secessionists' victory.

Key West reflects a diverse population: native "Conchs" (white Key Westers, many of whom trace their ancestry to the Bahamas), freshwater Conchs (longtime residents who migrated from somewhere else years ago), gays (who now make up at least 20% of Key West's citizenry), black Bahamians (descendants of those who worked the railroads and burned charcoal), Hispanics (primarily Cuban immigrants), recent refugees from the urban sprawl of mainland Florida, navy and air force personnel, and an assortment of vagabonds, drifters, and dropouts in search of refuge.

Although the rest of the Keys are more oriented to nature and the outdoors, Key West has more of a city feel. Few open spaces remain, as promoters continue to foster fine restaurants, galleries, shops, and museums to interpret the city's intriguing past. As a tourist destination, Key West has a lot to sell—an average temperature of 79°F, quaint 19th-century architecture, and a laid-back lifestyle. There's also a growing calendar of festivals and artistic and cultural events—including the Conch Republic Celebration in April and a Halloween Fantasy Fest. Few cities of its size—a mere 2 mi by 4 mi—offer the joie de vivre of this one.

Yet, as elsewhere, when preservation has successfully revived once-tired towns, next have come those unmindful of style and eager for a buck. Duval Street is becoming showbiz—an open-air mall of T-shirt shops and tour shills. Mass marketers directing the town's tourism have attracted cruise ships, which dwarf the town's skyline, and Duval Street floods with day-trippers who gawk at the earringed hippies with dogs in their bike baskets and the otherwise oddball lot of locals. You can still find fun, but the best advice is to come sooner rather than later.

Old Town

The heart of Key West, this historic area runs from White Street west to the waterfront. Beginning in 1822, wharves, warehouses, chandleries, ship-repair facilities, and eventually in 1891 the U.S. Customs House sprang up around the deep harbor to accommodate the navy's large ships and other sailing vessels. Wealthy wreckers, merchants, and sea captains built lavish houses near the bustling waterfront. A remarkable number of these fine Victorian and pre-Victorian structures have been restored to their original grandeur and now serve as homes, guest houses, and museums. These, along with the dwellings of famous writers, artists, and politicians who've come to Key West over the past 175 years, are among the area's approximately 3,000 historic structures. Old Town also has the city's finest restaurants and hotels, lively street life, and popular nightspots.

A Good Tour

To cover a lot of sights, take the Old Town Trolley, which lets you get off and reboard a later trolley, or the Conch Tour Train. Old Town is also very manageable on foot, bicycle, or moped, but be warned the tour below covers a lot of ground. You'll want either to pick and choose from it or break it into two days. Or pick up a copy of one of several self-guided tours on the area.

Start on Whitehead Street at the **Hemingway House** ⑫, the author's former home, and then cross the street and climb to the top of the **Lighthouse Museum** ⑬ for a spectacular view. Follow Whitehead north to Angela Street and turn right. At Margaret Street, the **City Cemetery** ⑭ has above-ground vaults and unusual headstone inscriptions. Head north on Margaret to Southard Street, turn left, then right onto Simonton Street. Halfway up the block, Free School Lane is occupied by **Nancy Forrester's Secret Garden** ⑮. After touring this tropical haven, return west on Southard to Duval Street and turn right, where you can view the lovely tiles and woodwork in the **San Carlos Institute** ⑯. Return again to Southard Street, turn right, and follow it through Truman Annex to **Ft. Zachary Taylor State Historic Site** ⑰; after viewing the fort, you can take a dip at the beach.

Go back to Simonton Street and walk north, then turn left on Caroline Street, where you can climb to the widow's walk on top of **Curry Mansion** ⑱. A left on Duval Street puts you in front of the **Duval Street Wreckers Museum** ⑲, Key West's oldest house. Continue west into Truman Annex to see the **Harry S Truman Little White House Museum** ⑳, President Truman's vacation residence. Return east on Caroline and turn left on Whitehead to visit the **Audubon House and Gardens** ㉑, honoring the artist-naturalist. Follow Whitehead north to Greene Street and turn left to see the salvaged sea treasures of the **Mel Fisher Maritime Heritage Society Museum** ㉒. At Whitehead's north end is the **Key West Aquarium** ㉓.

By late afternoon you should be ready to cool off with a dip or catch a few rays at the beach. After all, this is Florida, and you can't go home without wiggling your toes in the waves. From the aquarium, head east two blocks to the end of Simonton Street, where you'll find the appropriately named **Simonton Street Beach** ㉔. On the Atlantic side of Old Town is **South Beach** ㉕, named for its location at the southern end of Duval Street. If you've brought your pet, stroll a few blocks east to **Dog Beach** ㉖, at the corner of Vernon and Waddell streets. A little farther east is **Higgs Beach** ㉗, on Atlantic Boulevard between White and Reynolds streets. As the sun starts to sink, return to the north end of Old Town and follow the crowds to Mallory Square, behind the aquarium, to watch Key West's nightly sunset spectacle. For dinner, head east on Caroline Street to **Historic Seaport at Key West Bight** ㉘ (formerly known simply as Key West Bight), a renovated area where there are numerous restaurants and bars.

Allow two full days to see all the Old Town museums and homes, especially with a little shopping thrown in. For a narrated trip on the tour train or trolley, budget 1½ hours to ride the loop without getting off, an entire day if you plan to get off and on at some of the sights and restaurants.

Sights to See

㉑ Audubon House and Gardens. This three-story dwelling built in the mid-1840s commemorates ornithologist John James Audubon's 1832 visit to Key West. On display are several rooms of period antiques, a children's room, and a large collection of Audubon engravings. Admission includes an audiotape (in English, French, German, and Spanish) for the self-guided tour of the house and tropical gardens, complemented by an informational booklet and signs that identify the rare indigenous plants and trees you'll see. ⊠ *205 Whitehead St.,* ☎ *305/294–2116.* ☞ *$7.50.* ☉ *Daily 9:30–5.*

★ **⑭ City Cemetery.** Key West's celebrated burial place covers nearly 20 acres. Among its plots are a bronze statue resembling a ship's mast and the graves of more than two dozen sailors killed in the sinking of the battleship U.S.S. *Maine,* recently tidied for the 150th anniversary of the disaster. There are separate plots for Catholics, Jews, and martyrs of Cuba. Interesting headstones abound: DEVOTED FAN OF SINGER JULIO IGLESIAS, GOD WAS GOOD TO ME, and I TOLD YOU I WAS SICK. Although you can walk around the cemetery on your own, the best way to take it in is on a 90-minute tour given by volunteers of the Historic Florida Keys Foundation. Tours leave from the sexton's office, and reservations are requested. ⊠ *Margaret and Angela Sts.,* ☎ *305/292–6718.* ☞ *Free, tour donation $10.* ☉ *Sunrise–6, tours Tues. and Thurs. 9:30.*

⑱ Curry Mansion. This 22-room home built in 1899 for Milton Curry, the son of Florida's first millionaire, is an adaptation of a Parisian town house. It has Key West's only widow's walk open to the public. The owners have restored most of the house and turned it into a winning B&B. Take an unhurried self-guided tour; a brochure describes the home's history and contents. ⊠ *511 Caroline St.,* ☎ *305/294–5349.* ☞ *$5.* ☉ *Daily 10–5.*

㉖ Dog Beach. Next to Louie's Backyard, this small beach—the only one in Key West where dogs are allowed—has a shore that's a mix of sand and rocks. ⊠ *Vernon and Waddell Sts.,* ☎ *no phone.* ☞ *Free.* ☉ *Daily sunrise–sunset.*

⑲ Duval Street Wreckers Museum. Built in 1829 and alleged to be the oldest house in South Florida, the museum was originally home to Francis Watlington, a sea captain and wrecker. He was also a Florida state senator but resigned to serve in the Confederate navy during the Civil War. Six rooms are now open, furnished with 18th- and 19th-century antiques and providing exhibits on the wrecking industry of the 1800s. In an upstairs bedroom, an eight-room dollhouse of Conch design is outfitted with tiny early 19th-century furniture. ⊠ *322 Duval St.,* ☎ *305/294–9502.* ☞ *$4.* ☉ *Daily 10–4.*

⑰ Ft. Zachary Taylor State Historic Site. Built between 1845 and 1866, this fort served as a base for the Union blockade of Confederate shipping during the Civil War (more than 1,500 Confederate vessels were detained in Key West's harbor). Today it's a fort within a fort. A moat suggests how the fort originally looked when it was surrounded by water, and a 30-minute tour is included in the admission price. Because of an artificial reef, snorkeling is excellent here, except when the wind blows south–southwest and muddies the water. There are an uncrowded

Key West

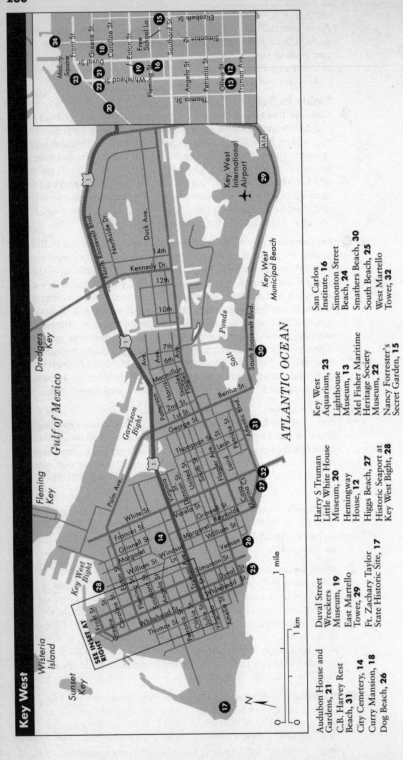

Audubon House and
Gardens, **21**
C.B. Harvey Rest
Beach, **31**
City Cemetery, **14**
Curry Mansion, **18**
Dog Beach, **26**

Duval Street
Wreckers
Museum, **19**
East Martello
Tower, **29**
Ft. Zachary Taylor
State Historic Site, **17**

Harry S Truman
Little White House
Museum, **20**
Hemingway
House, **12**
Higgs Beach, **27**
Historic Seaport at
Key West Bight, **28**

Key West
Aquarium, **23**
Lighthouse
Museum, **13**
Mel Fisher Maritime
Heritage Society
Museum, **22**
Nancy Forrester's
Secret Garden, **15**

San Carlos
Institute, **16**
Simonton Street
Beach, **24**
Smathers Beach, **30**
South Beach, **25**
West Martello
Tower, **32**

beach and an adjoining picnic area with barbecue grills and some shade trees. ⊠ *End of Southard St., through Truman Annex,* ☎ *305/ 292–6713.* 🖃 *$2.50 per person for first 2 people in vehicle plus 50¢ each additional up to $8, $1.50 per pedestrian or bicyclist.* ☉ *Daily 8–sunset, tours noon and 2.*

②⓪ Harry S Truman Little White House Museum. On the grounds of Truman Annex, a 103-acre former military parade grounds and barracks, the home served as a winter White House for Presidents Truman, Eisenhower, and Kennedy. It has been restored to its post–World War II glory and contains displays of Truman family memorabilia as well as changing exhibits that have ranged from circa-1951 Truman fashion to the Eisenhower Room's presidential photos. ⊠ *111 Front St.,* ☎ *305/294–9911.* 🖃 *$7.50.* ☉ *Daily 9–5, grounds 8–sunset.*

★ ⑫ Hemingway House. Hemingway bought this house in 1931 and wrote about 70% of his life's work here, including *For Whom the Bell Tolls.* It is now a museum dedicated to the novelist's life and work. Built in 1851, this two-story Spanish-colonial dwelling was the first house in Key West to have running water and a fireplace. Three months after Hemingway died in 1961, local jeweler Bernice Dickson bought the house and two years later opened it as a museum. Of special interest are the huge bed with a headboard made from a 17th-century Spanish monastery gate, a ceramic cat by Pablo Picasso (a gift to Hemingway from the artist), the hand-blown Venetian glass chandelier in the dining room, and the pool. The museum staff gives guided tours rich with anecdotes about Hemingway and his family and feeds the more than 50 feline habitants, descendants of Hemingway's own 50 cats. Tours begin every 10 minutes and take 25–30 minutes; then you're free to explore on your own. ⊠ *907 Whitehead St.,* ☎ *305/294–1575.* 🖃 *$6.50.* ☉ *Daily 9–5.*

㉗ Higgs Beach. This Monroe County park is a popular sunbathing spot. A nearby grove of Australian pines provides shade, and the West Martello Tower provides shelter should a storm suddenly sweep in. ⊠ *Atlantic Blvd. between White and Reynolds Sts.,* ☎ *no phone.* 🖃 *Free.* ☉ *Daily 7 AM–11 PM.*

㉘ Historic Seaport at Key West Bight. In January 1999 the $30 million restoration of structures within this 8.5-acre historic waterfront area was completed, bringing together about 100 businesses: waterfront restaurants, open-air people- and dog-friendly bars, clothing stores, bait shops, docks, a marina, a wedding chapel, the Waterfront Market, the Key West Rowing Club, and dive shops. It's all linked by the 2-mi waterfront Harborwalk, which runs between Front and Grinnell streets, passing big ships, schooners, sunset cruises, fishing charters, and glass-bottom boats. Though it's not as glossy as some waterfront restorations, it's lost much of its funky charm. Additional construction continues on outlying projects.

☜ ㉓ Key West Aquarium. Hundreds of brightly colored tropical fish and other fascinating sea creatures from Key West waters make their home here. A touch tank enables you to handle starfish, sea cucumbers, horseshoe and hermit crabs, even horse and queen conchs—living totems of the Conch Republic. Built in 1934 by the Works Progress Administration as the world's first open-air aquarium, the building has been enclosed for all-weather viewing, though an outdoor area has a small Atlantic shores exhibit, including red mangroves. Guided tours include shark feedings. ⊠ *1 Whitehead St.,* ☎ *305/296–2051.* 🖃 *$8.* ☉ *Daily 10–6, tours 11, 1, 3, and 4:30.*

CLOSE-UP: HEMINGWAY WAS HERE

IN A TOWN WHERE Pulitzer Prize–winning writers are almost as common as coconuts, Ernest Hemingway stands out. Bars and restaurants around the island boast that he ate or drank there, and though he may not have been at all of them, like all legends his larger-than-life image continues to grow.

Hemingway came to Key West in 1928 at the urging of writer John dos Passos and rented a house with wife number two, Pauline Pfeiffer. They spent winters in the Keys and summers in Europe and Wyoming, occasionally taking African safaris. Along the way they had two sons, Patrick and Gregory. In 1931 Pauline's wealthy uncle Gus gave the couple the house at 907 Whitehead Street, now known as Hemingway House and Key West's number one tourist attraction. They renovated the palatial home, added a swimming pool, put in a tropical garden with peacocks, and then in 1935, when the visitor bureau included the house in a tourist brochure, promptly built the high brick wall that surrounds it today.

During his time in Key West, Hemingway penned some of his most important works, including *A Farewell to Arms, To Have and Have Not, Green Hills of Africa,* and *Death in the Afternoon.* His rigorous schedule consisted of writing almost every morning in his second-story studio above the pool, then promptly descending the stairs at midday. By afternoon and evening he was ready for drinking, fishing, swimming, boxing, and hanging around with the boys.

One close friend was Joe Russell, a craggy fisherman and owner of the rugged bar Sloppy Joe's, originally at 428 Greene Street but now at 201 Duval Street. Russell was the only one in town who would cash Hemingway's $1,000 royalty check. Russell and Charles Thompson introduced him to deep-sea fishing, which became fodder for his writing. Another of Hemingway's loves was boxing. He set up a ring in his yard and paid local fighters to box with him as well as refereeing matches at Blue Heaven, then a saloon but now a restaurant, at 729 Thomas Street.

FEELING AT HOME among Key West's characters, Hemingway honed his macho image dressed in cutoffs and old shirts and took on the name *Papa.* In turn, he gave his friends new names and used them as characters in his stories. Joe Russell became Freddy, captain of the *Queen Conch* charter boat in *To Have and Have Not.*

Hemingway stayed in Key West for 12 years before leaving Pauline for wife number three. A foreign correspondent, Martha Gellhorn arrived in town and headed for Sloppy Joe's, intent on meeting him. When the always restless Hemingway packed up to cover the Spanish Civil War, so did she. Though he returned to Pauline occasionally, he finally left her and Key West to be with Martha in 1939. They married a year later and moved to Cuba, and he seldom returned to Key West after that. Pauline and the boys stayed on in the house, which sold in 1951 for $80,000, ten times its original cost.

⑬ Lighthouse Museum. Behind a spic-and-span white picket fence is this 92-ft lighthouse built in 1847 and an adjacent 1887 clapboard house, where the keeper lived. You can climb 88 steps to the top of the lighthouse for a glimpse of the sizable Fresnel lens, installed at a cost of $1 million in the 1860s; a spectacular view of the island town awaits you as well. On display in the keeper's quarters are vintage photographs, ship models, nautical charts, and lighthouse artifacts from all along the Key reefs. ⊠ *938 Whitehead St.,* ☎ *305/294–0012.* ⛁ *$6.* ⊙ *Daily 9:30–5, last admission 4:30.*

㉒ Mel Fisher Maritime Heritage Society Museum. Gold and silver bars, coins, jewelry, and other artifacts recovered in 1985 from the Spanish treasure ships *Nuestra Señora de Atocha* and *Santa Margarita* are displayed here. The two galleons foundered in a hurricane in 1622 near the Marquesas Keys, 40 mi west of Key West. In the museum you can lift a gold bar weighing 6.3 troy pounds and see a 77.76-carat natural emerald crystal worth almost $250,000. ⊠ *200 Greene St.,* ☎ *305/ 294–2633.* ⛁ *$6.50.* ⊙ *Daily 9:30–5:30, last video 4:30.*

⑮ Nancy Forrester's Secret Garden. Nancy's 30-year-old naturalized garden lost its rain forest–like canopy and many large trees during Hurricane Georges, and as a result some of the delicate undergrowth withered from the strong sun. Renewal took shape quickly, however. Visitors will find a thinner canopy along with many of the same rare palms and cycads, ferns, bromeliads, bright gingers and heliconias, gumbo-limbos strewn with orchids and vines, and a few surprises. Many brides and grooms exchange their vows here and then stay in the garden's cottage ($140–$175, two-day minimum). Picnic tables invite visitors to sit and have lunch. An art gallery features botanical prints and environmental art. ⊠ *1 Free School La.,* ☎ *305/294–0015.* ⛁ *$6.* ⊙ *Daily 10–5.*

⑯ San Carlos Institute. This Cuban-American heritage center houses a museum with changing exhibits and a research library focusing on the history of Key West and of 19th- and 20th-century Cuban exiles. The institute was founded in 1871 by Cuban immigrants. Cuban patriot Jose Martí delivered many famous speeches from the balcony of the auditorium, and opera star Enrico Caruso sang in the Opera House, which reportedly has the best acoustics of any concert hall in the South. On weekends you can watch the almost hour-long documentary *Nostalgia Cubano,* about Cuba from the 1930s to 1950s. ⊠ *516 Duval St.,* ☎ *305/294–3887.* ⛁ *$3.* ⊙ *Tues.–Sun. 11–5.*

㉔ Simonton Street Beach. This beach facing the gulf is a great place to watch boat traffic in the harbor. Parking, however, is difficult. ⊠ *North end of Simonton St.,* ☎ *no phone.* ⛁ *Free.* ⊙ *Daily 7 AM–11 PM.*

㉕ South Beach. On the Atlantic, this stretch of sand, also known as City Beach, is popular with tourists at nearby motels. It has limited parking and a nearby buffet-type restaurant, the South Beach Seafood and Raw Bar. ⊠ *Foot of Duval St.,* ☎ *no phone.* ⛁ *Free.* ⊙ *Daily 7 AM– 11 PM.*

New Town

The Overseas Highway splits as it enters Key West, the two forks rejoining to encircle New Town, the area east of White Street to Cow Key Channel. The southern fork runs along the shore as South Roosevelt Boulevard (Route A1A), past municipal beaches, salt ponds, and Key West International Airport. Along the north shore, North Roosevelt Boulevard (U.S. 1) passes the Key West Welcome Center, shopping centers, chain hotels, and fast-food eateries. Part of New Town was created with dredged fill. The island would have continued growing this way had the Army Corps of Engineers not determined in the early 1970s that it was detrimental to the nearby reef.

A Good Tour

Attractions are few in New Town. The best way to take in the sights is by car or moped. Take South Roosevelt Boulevard from the island's entrance to **East Martello Tower** ㉙, near the airport. Continue past the Riggs Wildlife Refuge salt ponds and stop at **Smathers Beach** ㉚ for a dip, or continue west onto Atlantic Boulevard to **C. B. Harvey Rest Beach** ㉛. A little farther along, at the end of White Street, is the **West Martello Tower** ㉜.

TIMING

Allow one to two hours for brief stops at each attraction. If your interests lie in art, gardens, or Civil War history, you'll need three or four hours. Throw in time at the beach, and you can make it a half-day affair.

Sights to See

㉛ C. B. Harvey Rest Beach. The city's newest beach and park, named after former Key West mayor and commissioner Cornelius Bradford Harvey, has half a dozen picnic areas, dunes, and a wheelchair and bike path. ⊠ *East side of White Street Pier,* ☎ *no phone.* 🎫 *Free.* ☾ *Daily 7 AM–11 PM.*

★ **㉙ East Martello Tower.** Housing relics of the U.S.S. *Maine,* the tower also contains a museum operated by the Key West Art and Historical Society. The collection includes Stanley Papio's "junk art" sculptures, Cuban folk artist Mario Sanchez's chiseled and painted wooden carvings of historic Key West street scenes, a Cuban refugee raft, and books by famous writers (including seven Pulitzer Prize winners) who have lived in Key West. Thematic exhibits present a history of the city and the Keys. A circular 48-step staircase in the central tower leads to a platform overlooking the airport and surrounding waters. Hurricane damage to the attractive grounds was extensive, but replanting is under way. ⊠ *3501 S. Roosevelt Blvd.,* ☎ *305/296–3913.* 🎫 *$6.* ☾ *Daily 9:30– 5, last admission 4.*

㉚ Smathers Beach. This beach features nearly 2 mi of sand. Trucks along the road rent rafts, Windsurfers, and other beach "toys." ⊠ *S. Roosevelt Blvd.,* ☎ *no phone.* 🎫 *Free.* ☾ *Daily 7 AM–11 PM.*

㉜ West Martello Tower. The ruins of this Civil War–era fort are home to the Key West Garden Club, which maintains lovely gardens of native and tropical plants. It also holds art, orchid, and flower shows in March and November and leads private garden tours in March. ⊠ *Atlantic Blvd. and White St.,* ☎ *305/294–3210.* 🎫 *Donation welcome.* ☾ *Tues.–Sat. 9:30–3.*

Dining

American

$–$$ ✕ **Pepe's Cafe and Steak House.** Judges, police officers, carpenters, and anglers rub elbows at breakfast in their habitual seats, at tables or dark pine booths under a jumbo paddle fan. Face the street or dine outdoors under a huge rubber tree if you're put off by the naked-lady art on the back wall. Pepe's was established downtown in 1909 (which makes it the oldest eating house in the Keys) and moved here in 1962. Specials change nightly: barbecued chicken, pork tenderloin, ribs, steak, fresh fish, potato salad, red or black beans, and corn bread on

Sunday; meat loaf on Monday; seafood Tuesday and Wednesday; a traditional Thanksgiving every Thursday; prime rib on Saturday; and filet mignon daily. ⊠ *806 Caroline St.,* ☎ *305/294–7192. D, MC, V.*

Caribbean

$ ✕ **Caribe Soul.** This ambitious little restaurant around the corner from Blue Heaven is a welcome addition to Bahama Village's redevelopment. Co-owners Kevin Robinson, who has a catering background, and Michael Weston, who has natural cooking instincts, serve up home-style Caribbean and soul food that ranges from black-bean soup and yellowtail snapper ($10.50) to chicken livers with rice as well as twice-weekly chitterlings. Entrées come with a choice of two sides: fried green apples, collard greens, sweet potatoes, corn bread, et al. They make and sell their own salsas, relishes, and a cooking base made of egg-plant, mango, tomatoes, fresh herbs, and spices. The indoor and outdoor seating is very limited, but they offer takeout and free delivery. Also for sale are southern and Afro-Caribbean cookbooks, including their own, *Using What You've Got.* ⊠ *320 Petronia St,* ☎ *305/296–0094. AE, D, DC, MC, V.*

Contemporary

$$$–$$$$ ✕ **Cafe des Artistes.** Dining doesn't get much better than this. The restau-
★ rant was once part of a hotel building constructed in 1935 by C. E. Alfeld, Al Capone's bookkeeper. The look is studiously unhip with its rough stucco walls, old-fashioned lights, and a knotty-pine ceiling. Haitian paintings and Keys scenes by local artists dress the walls. You dine in two indoor rooms or on a rooftop deck beneath a sapodilla tree. Chef Andrew Berman presents a French interpretation of tropical cuisine, using fresh local seafood and produce and light sauces. The wine list is strong on French and California labels. ⊠ *1007 Simonton St.,* ☎ *305/294–7100. AE, MC, V. No lunch.*

$$$ ✕ **Louie's Backyard.** Key West paintings and pastels adorn this ocean-front institution, where you dine outside under a mahoe tree. Executive chef Doug Shook shares Louie's limelight with *chef de cuisine* Annette Foley. The menu changes seasonally. The winter menu might include roast rack of lamb with mint sauce and roasted garlic or grilled sour orange–rubbed grouper with black beans and mango salsa. Louie's key lime pie has a pistachio crust and is served with a raspberry coulis. The best time to come is lunch, when the menu is less expensive and the view is fantastic. For night owls, the Afterdeck Bar serves cocktails on the water until the wee hours. ⊠ *700 Waddell Ave.,* ☎ *305/294–1061. AE, DC, MC, V.*

$$–$$$$ ✕ **Cafe Marquesa.** This intimate restaurant with attentive service and
★ superb food is a felicitous counterpart to the small Marquesa Hotel. Under the direction of chef Susan Ferry, who trained with Norman Van Aken, 10 or so entrées are featured nightly. Though every dish she makes is memorable, the sesame-crusted yellowtail snapper with mango-miso sauce, udon noodles, sautéed spinach, and pineapple-chile salsa has become a requested dish of frequent guests. Some low-fat options are featured, but desserts are quite the contrary. There are also a fine selection of wines and a choice of microbrewery beers. Smoking is not allowed. ⊠ *600 Fleming St.,* ☎ *305/292–1244. AE, DC, MC, V. No lunch.*

$$–$$$ ✕ **Alice's on Duval.** Alice Weingarten earns high praise for an exem-
★ plary selection of wines that complement the creative mix of seafood, game, beef, pork, and poultry. The center and each leaf of a jumbo baked artichoke are stuffed with a lovely mixture of bread crumbs, rosemary, lemon, and butter. That appetizer is a fitting precursor to the sizzling Key West yellowtail, with an aromatic blend of Thai red curry and Asian vegetables served over coconut basmati rice. Guests must be totally satisfied or the dish goes back to the kitchen. Surrounded by huge un-

screened windows and a ceiling painted pale blue with white clouds, you'll think you're dining alfresco. The bar has become as popular as the dining room. ⊠ *1114 Duval St.,* ☎ *305/292–4888. AE, D, MC, V. No lunch.*

$–$$　× **Rick's Blue Heaven.** The inspired remake of an old blue-on-blue clap-
★　　board Greek Revival house with peach-and-yellow trim was once a bordello where Hemingway refereed boxing matches and customers watched cockfights. There's still a rooster graveyard out back, as well as a water tower hauled here in the 1920s. Upstairs is an art gallery (check out the zebra-stripe bikes), and downstairs are affordable fresh eats, in both the house and big leafy yard. There are five nightly specials and a good mix of natural and West Indian foods. Top it off with Banana Heaven (banana bread, bananas flamed with spiced rum, and vanilla ice cream). Three meals are served six days a week; Sunday there's a to-die-for brunch. Expect a line—everybody knows how good this is. ⊠ *729 Thomas St.,* ☎ *305/296–8666. Reservations not accepted. D, MC, V.*

Cuban

$　× **El Siboney.** This sprawling three-room, family-style restaurant serves traditional Cuban food, including a well-seasoned black-bean soup. Specials include beef stew Monday, pepper steak Tuesday, chicken fricassee Wednesday, chicken and rice Friday, and oxtail stew on Saturday. Always available are roast pork, cassava, paella, and *palomilla* steak. Popular with locals, *sí,* but enough tourists pass through that you'll fit right in even if you have to ask what a "Siboney" is (answer: a Cuban Indian tribe). ⊠ *900 Catherine St.,* ☎ *305/296–4184. No credit cards. Closed 2 wks in June.*

Italian

$–$$　× **Mangia Mangia.** Fresh homemade pasta comes *Alfredo,* or with mari-
★　　nara, meat, or pesto, either in the twinkly brick garden with its specimen palms or in the nicely dressed-up old-house dining room. One of the best restaurants in Key West—and one of its best values—Mangia Mangia is run by Elliot and Naomi Baron, ex–Chicago restaurateurs who found Key West's warmth and laid-back style irresistible. Everything that comes out of the open kitchen is outstanding, especially the pasta, Mississippi mud pie, and made-on-the-premises key lime pie. The wine list, with more than 350 selections, the largest in Monroe County, contains a good selection under $20. ⊠ *900 Southard St.,* ☎ *305/294–2469. AE, MC, V. No lunch.*

Pan-Asian

$$–$$$　× **Dim Sum's Far East.** This bright spot in a sophisticated little Asian
★　　kiosk in gardenlike Key Lime Square serves pan-Asian cuisine and a fusion of classical French and Asian cooking in which the presentation is art and the food is out of this world. The menu features such favorite aromatic dishes as crisply deep-fried whole yellowtail snapper enveloped in a pepper and basil sauce. Nightly specials range from chicken and shrimp in a green Thai curry with essence of cilantro root, lemongrass, and galangal to half duck in a red Thai curry sauce. The setting is intimate and authentic, the service is exemplary, and the selection of beer and wine is good. ⊠ *613½ Duval St. (rear),* ☎ *305/294–6230. AE, D, DC, MC, V. No lunch May–late Dec.*

Steak/Seafood

$$　× **Duffy's Steak & Lobster House.** The owners of the elegant Cafe des Artistes (which shares a wall and rest rooms with Duffy's) opened this new American salute to surf and turf. It serves Angus cuts that rival those at good steak houses and lobster and seafood that would make a dedicated seafood restaurant envious. Though the original Duffy's

was around when President Truman was a frequent visitor—hence the photo of him on the menu's cover—the look is contemporary and the atmosphere fun. ✉ *1007 Truman Ave.,* ☎ *305/296–4900. AE, MC, V.*

Lodging

Lodging opportunities rival those found in mainland cities. You'll find historic cottages, restored turn-of-the-century Conch houses, and large resorts. Rates are the highest in the Keys, with a few properties as low as $65, but the majority from $100 to $300 a night.

Guest Houses

$$$$ 🏨 **Paradise Inn.** Renovated cigar makers' cottages and authentically
★ reproduced Bahamian-style houses with sundecks and balconies stand amid a lush tropical garden with a heated pool, lily pond, and whirlpool, light-years from the hubbub of Key West. The only sound disturbing the perfect quiet is the trickling of water from the pool's fountain. Inside, light streams through French doors onto fine earth-tone fabrics. Gracious appointments include phones and whirlpools in marble bathrooms, plush robes, polished oak floors, armoires, complimentary fresh breakfast pastries from Louie's Pantry, room safes, and minibars. Suite 205 and the Poinciana Cottage are gilded lilies. One suite is designed for travelers with disabilities. ✉ *819 Simonton St., 33040,* ☎ *305/293–8007 or 800/888–9648,* 𝗙𝗔𝗫 *305/293–0807. 3 cottages, 15 suites. Pool, hot tub, concierge. AE, D, DC, MC, V.*

$$$–$$$$ 🏨 **Heron House.** Having added full concierge service, newspapers,
★ robes, and valet parking, this place keeps getting better. With four buildings centered on a pool, all slightly different but all Key West–style, it feels like an old town within Old Town. A high coral fence, brilliantly splashed with spotlights at night, surrounds the compound (just a block off Duval Street but quieter by a mile). Neither antiques nor frills is owner Fred Geibelt's thing; superb detailing is. Most units feature a complete wall of exquisitely laid wood, entries with French doors, and bathrooms of polished granite. Some have floor-to-ceiling panels of mirrored glass and/or an oversize whirlpool. An expanded Continental breakfast and complimentary wine and cheese are included. Heron House does not welcome children under 16. ✉ *512 Simonton St., 33040,* ☎ *305/294–9227,* 𝗙𝗔𝗫 *305/294–5692. 23 rooms. Pool, concierge. AE, DC, MC, V.*

$$$–$$$$ 🏨 **Island City House.** This guest house is actually three buildings: the vintage-1880s Island City House, with a widow's walk; Arch House, a former carriage house; and a 1970s reconstruction of a cigar factory. Arch House features a dramatic carriage entry that opens into a lush courtyard, and though all its suites front on busy Eaton Street, bedrooms in only Numbers 5 and 6 actually face it. Units in Cigar House have porches and decks and are decorated in a plantation style with teak and wicker; those in Island City House have a Victorian flavor. Floors are pine, and ceiling fans and antiques abound. Guests share a private tropical garden and are given free Continental breakfasts. Children are welcome—a rarity in Old Town guest houses. ✉ *411 William St., 33040,* ☎ *305/294–5702 or 800/634–8230,* 𝗙𝗔𝗫 *305/294–1289. 24 suites. Pool, hot tub, bicycles. AE, D, DC, MC, V.*

$$$ 🏨 **Curry Mansion Inn.** Careful dedication to detail by Key West architect
★ Thomas Pope and much care by owners Al and Edith Amsterdam have made the annex rooms exceptionally comfortable, even if not as detailed as the now rarely used rooms in the circa-1899 main house. Each room has a different tropical pastel color scheme; all have wicker furnishings and handmade quilts. Rooms 1 and 8, honeymoon suites, feature canopy beds and balconies. Eight suites are at the restored James House; Rooms 306 and 308 face south and have beautiful morning

light. Curry Mansion is a historic attraction, with visitors touring the public areas of the house during the day. There are complimentary Continental breakfast and happy hour with an open bar and live piano music; guests also enjoy beach privileges at Pier House Beach Club and Casa Marina. A wheelchair lift is available. ⊠ *511–512 Caroline St., 33040,* ☎ *305/294–5349 or 800/253–3466,* FAX *305/294–4093. 28 rooms, 6 suites. Pool, hot tubs. AE, D, DC, MC, V.*

$$–$$$$ 🏨 **Popular House/Key West Bed & Breakfast.** Local art—large splashy
★   canvases, a mural in the style of Gauguin—hangs on the walls, and tropical gardens and music set the mood. Jody Carlson offers both inexpensive rooms with shared bath (whose rates haven't been raised in more than 10 years) and luxury rooms, reasoning that budget travelers deserve the same good local style (and lavish Continental breakfast) as the rich. Low-end rooms burst with bright yellows and reds; the hand-painted dressers will make you laugh out loud. Spacious third-floor rooms, though, are best (and most expensive), decorated with a paler palette and brilliantly original furniture. There's even one single room. Jody also keeps two friendly resident dogs. ⊠ *415 William St., 33040,* ☎ *305/296–7274 or 800/438–6155,* FAX *305/293–0306. 9 rooms, 4 with bath. Hot tub, sauna. AE, D, DC, MC, V.*

$$–$$$ 🏨 **Center Court Historic Inn & Cottages.** This lodging offers well-priced, charming, restored historical accommodations that seem calm and quiet even though they're only half a block from Duval Street. Units range from rooms with a queen-size bed to efficiency cottages with decks and spas (sleeping from two to six) to studios and fully equipped three-bedroom, two-bath house-size cottages that sleep six. All units are decorated in relaxed tropical style. There are a heated pool, whirlpools, sundeck, and exercise pavilion. Breakfast is included in units without full kitchens. In-room safes are available, and though there's no smoking, pets are welcome. ⊠ *916 Center St., 33040,* ☎ *305/296–9292 or 800/797–8787,* FAX *305/294–4104. 5 rooms, 5 suites, 2 efficiencies, 6 cottages. Pool, exercise room. AE, D, MC, V.*

$$–$$$ 🏨 **Speakeasy Inn.** This inn derives its name from Prohibition, when Raul Vasquez smuggled liquor from Cuba and taxi drivers pulled up in front to fill suitcases with the bootleg. Painting contractor Thomas Favelli restored the historic house, turning it into one of the best buys in Key West. Spacious studios, suites, and two-bedroom units feature simple tropical decor, queen-size beds, and tables made from 1876 salvaged pine, Saltillo tiles in the bathrooms, kitchenettes, oak floors with throw rugs, and claw-foot tubs in some baths. Some units are wheelchair accessible, and maid and concierge service are provided on request. Guests have beach and pool privileges at the Wyndham Reach. Ironically, though the inn is adjacent to Favelli's other pride and joy, the Key West Havana Cigar Co., there is no smoking in the rooms. Casa 325 Suites, an all-suites property at the opposite end of Duval, is under the same ownership. ⊠ *1117 Duval St., 33040,* ☎ *305/296–2680 or 800/217–4884,* FAX *305/296–2608. 4 suites, 4 studios, 2 2-bedroom units. Concierge. AE, D, MC, V.*

Hostel

$ 🏨 **Hostelling International–Key West.** This financial oasis in a sea of
★   expensive hotels gets high marks for location, comfort, friendliness, amenities, and good value. It is two blocks from the beach in Old Town yet costs only $17 for members of Hostelling International–American Youth Hostels, $20 for nonmembers. Breakfast costs $2, and there's a communal kitchen. When you're not snorkeling ($18.50) or scuba diving ($55, gear included), you can rent bicycles, write letters in the outdoor courtyard, or enjoy a barbecue. ⊠ *718 South St., 33040,* ☎ *305/296–5719,* FAX *305/296–0672. 96 beds in dorm-style rooms with-*

out baths. Bicycles, billiards, recreation room, video games, library, coin laundry. MC, V.

Hotels

$$$$ ⊡ **Cuban Club Suites.** Originally built as a social club for cigar makers, the "club" was rebuilt as a luxury hotel after a 1983 fire. Eight fully equipped town-house units, 900–1,900 square ft, have either two bedrooms and two baths or one bedroom and 1½ baths. Grouped in two buildings that feel like an exclusive apartment complex, they have king-size four-poster beds, queen-size sofa beds, wing chairs, cathedral ceilings, full kitchens, tile counters and floors, and washers and dryers. Wide balconies overlook the excitement of Duval Street. Guests have pool and beach privileges at the Wyndham Reach, and pets are allowed. La Casa de Luces, the club's poor cousin next door, is less elegant but has many winning characteristics. On holidays, the office closes early so most of the staff can be with their families. ⊠ *1108 Duval St. (lobby at 422 Amelia St.), 33040,* ☎ *305/296–0465 or 800/432–4849,* ℻ *305/293–7669. 8 suites. AE, MC, V.*

$$$$ ⊡ **Pier House.** This is Key West's catbird seat. Just off the intersection ★ of Duval and Front streets and an easy walk from Mallory Square, it defines Key West's festive ambience. Weathered-gray buildings, including an original Conch house, flank a courtyard of tall coconut palms and hibiscus blossoms. Most rooms are smaller than in newer hotels, except in the Caribbean Spa section, which has hardwood floors, two-poster plantation beds, and some baths that convert to steam rooms or have whirlpools, and in the Harborview building, whose rooms have private balconies and gulf views. You can gather with locals at the Beach Club's thatch-roof tiki bar. ⊠ *1 Duval St., 33040,* ☎ *305/296–4600 or 800/327–8340,* ℻ *305/296–7569. 142 rooms, 14 suites. 3 restaurants, 4 bars, pool, massage, health club, beach. AE, D, DC, MC, V.*

$$$$ ⊡ **Wyndham's Casa Marina Resort.** Flagler's heirs built 13-acre La Casa Marina in 1921 at the end of the Florida East Coast Railway line. The entire resort revolves around an outdoor patio and lawn facing the ocean. The rich, luxurious lobby has a beamed ceiling, polished Dade County pine floor, artwork, and new island French Provincial furniture. Guest rooms are decorated in yellows and tropical limes with color-coordinated Caribbean shades and linens. Among the best rooms are the two-bedroom loft suites with balconies facing the ocean and the lanai rooms on the ground floor of the main building, which have French doors opening onto the lawn. Rooms for nonsmokers are available. ⊠ *1500 Reynolds St., 33040,* ☎ *305/296–3535,* ℻ *305/296–4633. 311 rooms, 63 suites. 2 restaurants, bar, 2 pools, massage, sauna, 3 tennis courts, exercise room, health club, boating, jet skiing, fishing, bicycles, children's programs. AE, D, DC, MC, V.*

$$$–$$$$ ⊡ **Marquesa Hotel.** This coolly elegant, restored 1884 home is Key West's ★ finest lodging. Guests (typically shoeless in Marquesa robes) relax among richly landscaped pools and gardens against a backdrop of brick steps rising to the villalike suites on the property's perimeter. Elegant rooms contain eclectic antique and reproduction furnishings, dotted Swiss curtains, and botanical-print fabrics. The lobby resembles a Victorian parlor, with antique furniture, Audubon prints, flowers, and wonderful photos of early Key West, including one of Harry Truman in a convertible. Tea is offered poolside. Although the clientele is mostly straight, the hotel is very gay friendly. ⊠ *600 Fleming St., 33040,* ☎ *305/292–1919 or 800/869–4631,* ℻ *305/294–2121. 27 rooms. Restaurant, 2 pools. AE, DC, MC, V.*

$$–$$$ ⊡ **Best Western Key Ambassador Inn.** Every year a third of this com- ★ fortable inn is renovated from carpet to ceiling. The large guest rooms have cheerful Caribbean-style light-color furniture, linens in coordinated tropical colors, and 29-inch color TVs. The 7-acre grounds are well cared for, and the deck-rimmed pool looks over the Atlantic. There is a par course and a covered picnic area with barbecue grills out back. Each room has a small refrigerator and a screened balcony, and most offer ocean and pool views. The bar serves drinks and light dishes. A complimentary Continental breakfast and free weekday newspaper are included. ⊠ *3755 S. Roosevelt Blvd., 33040,* ☎ *305/ 296–3500 or 800/432–4315,* ℻ *305/296–9961. 100 rooms. Bar, picnic area, pool, shuffleboard, coin laundry. AE, D, DC, MC, V.*

Motels

$$ 🖪 **Harborside Motel & Marina.** The appeal of this ordinary motel is its affordability and its safe, pleasant location between a quiet street and Garrison Bight (the charter boat harbor), between Old Town and New Town. Units are boxy, clean, and basic, with little patios, ceramictile floors, phones, and basic color cable TV. Four stationary houseboats each sleep four. Barbecue grills are available. ⊠ *903 Eisenhower Dr., 33040,* ☎ *305/294–2780,* ℻ *305/292–1473. 14 efficiencies. Pool, coin laundry. AE, D, DC, MC, V.*

$$ 🖪 **Southwinds.** A short walk from Old Town and run by the same friendly folks who operate Harborside Motel & Marina, this pastel 1940s-style motel has mature tropical plantings, all nicely set back from the street a block from the beach. Rooms have basic furnishings. It's as good as you'll find at the price, and though rates have gone up, they drop if demand gets slack. On-premises parking is available. ⊠ *1321 Simonton St., 33040,* ☎ *305/296–2215. 13 rooms, 5 efficiencies. Pool, coin laundry, free parking. AE, D, DC, MC, V.*

Nightlife and the Arts

The Arts

Red Barn Theater (⊠ 319 Duval St. [rear], ☎ 305/296–9911), a professional small theater, performs dramas, comedies, and musicals, including plays by new playwrights. The **Tennessee Williams Fine Arts Center** (⊠ Florida Keys Community College, 5901 College Rd., ☎ 305/ 296–9081, ext. 5), on Stock Island, presents chamber music, dance, jazz concerts, and dramatic and musical plays with major stars, as well as other performing arts events, November–April. The **Waterfront Playhouse** (⊠ Mallory Sq., ☎ 305/294–5015) is a mid-1850s wrecker's warehouse that was converted into a 180-seat, non-Equity community theater presenting comedy and drama December–June.

Nightlife

BARS AND LOUNGES

Capt. Tony's Saloon (⊠ 428 Greene St., ☎ 305/294–1838) is housed in a building that dates from 1851, when it was first used as a morgue and icehouse; later it was Key West's first telegraph station. From 1933 to 1937 the bar was the original Sloppy Joe's. Hemingway was a regular, and Jimmy Buffett got his start here. Live country and rhythm and blues set the scene nowadays, and the rum-based house drink, the Pirates' Punch, still wows those brave enough to try it. Pause for a libation at the open-air **Green Parrot Bar** (⊠ 601 Whitehead St., at Southard St., ☎ 305/294–6133). Built in 1890, the bar is said to be Key West's oldest, a sometimes-rowdy saloon where locals outnumber the tourists, especially on weekends when bands play. **Margaritaville Cafe** (⊠ 500 Duval St., ☎ 305/292–1435) is owned by former Key West resident and recording star Jimmy Buffett, who has been known to perform here. The drink of choice is, of course, a margarita. There's live music nightly.

Called "the last little piece of Old Key West," **Schooner Wharf Bar** (⊠ 202 William St., ☎ 305/292–9520) is a laid-back waterside tiki hut where the town's waiters and waitresses hang out. You can hear live music weekends (and sometimes at other times) in the warehouse space next door. **Sloppy Joe's** (⊠ 201 Duval St., ☎ 305/294–5717) is the successor to a famous speakeasy named for its founder, Captain Joe Russell. Ernest Hemingway liked to gamble in a partitioned club room in back. Decorated with Hemingway memorabilia and marine flags, the bar is popular with tourists and is full and noisy all the time. Live entertainment plays daily, noon–2 AM. The **Top Lounge** (⊠ 430 Duval St., ☎ 305/296–2991) is on the seventh floor of the La Concha Holiday Inn and is one of the best places to view the sunset. (Celebrities, on the ground floor, presents nightly entertainment and serves food.)

DANCE CLUBS

Club Epoch (⊠ 623 Duval St., ☎ 305/296–8521) caters to a well-mixed crowd that's wild and eager to party. There are two floors, six bars, a lounge overlooking the dance floor, and a terrace overlooking Duval Street. House dancers set the tone as hip local and celebrity spin masters groove the tunes. It's open nightly, but dancing is Wednesday–Sunday. In the Pier House, **Havana Docks Lounge** (⊠ 1 Duval St., ☎ 305/296–4600) has live music nightly in season and live dance music Friday and Saturday nights year-round as well as a nightly sunset celebration with a band.

Outdoor Activities and Sports

Biking

Key West is a cycling town, but if you aren't accustomed to so many bikes, ride carefully. Paved road surfaces are poor, so it's best to ride a fat-tired Conch cruiser. Some hotels rent bikes to guests; others will refer you to a nearby shop and reserve a bike for you.

Keys Moped & Scooter (⊠ 523 Truman Ave., ☎ 305/294–0399) rents beach cruisers with large baskets as well as mopeds and scooters. Rates are the lowest in Key West. Look for the huge American flag on the roof. **Moped Hospital** (⊠ 601 Truman Ave., ☎ 305/296–3344) supplies balloon-tire bikes with yellow safety baskets, as well as mopeds, tandem mopeds, and scooters for adults and children. Helmets are no charge.

Fishing

Captain Steven Impallomeni works as a flats-fishing guide, specializing in ultralight and fly-fishing for tarpon, permit, and bonefish. Charters on the *Gallopin' Ghost* leave from Murray's Marina (⊠ MM 5, Stock Island, ☎ 305/292–9837). **Key West Bait and Tackle** (⊠ 241 Margaret St., ☎ 305/292–1961) carries live bait, frozen rigged and unrigged bait, and fishing and rigging equipment. It also has the Live Bait Lounge, where you can unwind and nibble on authentic Texas pork tamales and Louisiana shrimp *boudin* (a highly seasoned sausage) while telling tall tales after fishing.

Golf

Key West Resort Golf Course (⊠ 6450 E. College Rd., ☎ 305/294–5232) is an 18-hole course on the bay side of Stock Island. Nonresident fees are $95 for 18 holes (cart included) in season, $65 off-season.

Scuba Diving and Snorkeling

Adventure Charters & Tours (⊠ 6810 Front St., Stock Island 33040, ☎ 305/296–0362 or 888/817–0841) offers sail-and-snorkel coral reef adventure tours ($25) aboard the 42-ft trimaran sailboat *Fantasea*, with a maximum of 16 people. There are two daily departures and sometimes one at sunset. **Captain's Corner** (⊠ 0 Duval St., 33040, ☎ 305/296–8865), a PADI five star–rated shop, provides dive classes in several languages. All captains are licensed dive masters and/or instructors. A 60-ft dive boat, *Sea Eagle,* and the 48-ft *Sea Hawk* depart twice daily. Reservations are accepted for regular reef and wreck diving.

Shopping

Key West contains dozens of characterless T-shirt shops, but some art galleries and curiosity shops have lots worth toting home.

Arts and Crafts

The oldest private art gallery in Key West, **Gingerbread Square Gallery** (⊠ 1207 Duval St., ☎ 305/296–8900) represents mainly Keys artists who have attained national and international prominence. **Haitian Art Co.** (⊠ 600 Frances St., ☎ 305/296–8932), containing 4,000 paintings and spirit flags, claims the largest collection of Haitian art outside Haiti, representing a range of artists working in wood, stone, metal, and papier-mâché. **Lucky Street Gallery** (⊠ 1120 White St., ☎ 305/294–3973) sells high-end contemporary paintings, watercolors, jewelry, and crafts by internationally recognized Key West–based artists. Exhibits change every two weeks. **Pelican Poop** (⊠ 314 Simonton St., ☎ 305/296–3887) sells Caribbean art in a gorgeous setting around a lush, tropical courtyard garden with a fountain and pool. The owners go to the Caribbean every year to buy direct from the artisans, so prices are very attractive. (Hemingway wrote *A Farewell to Arms* while living in the complex's apartment.) **Plantation Pottery** (⊠ 521 Fleming St., ☎ 305/294–3143) is not to be missed for its original, never-commercial pottery. Potters Charles Pearson and Timothy Roeder *are* **Whitehead St. Pottery** (⊠ 1011 Whitehead St., ☎ 305/294–5067), where they display their porcelain stoneware and raku-fired vessels. They also have a photo gallery where they exhibit Polaroid image transfers and black-and-white photos.

Books

Flaming Maggie's (⊠ 830 Fleming St., ☎ 305/294–3931) specializes in books and magazines for and about gays and lesbians and also carries books—and artwork—by or about local authors. It contains a popular coffee bar, too. **Key West Island Bookstore** (⊠ 513 Fleming St., ☎ 305/294–2904) is the literary bookstore of the large Key West writers' community. It carries new, used, and rare titles.

Clothes and Fabrics

Since 1964 **Key West Hand Print Fashions and Fabrics** (⊠ 201 Simonton St., ☎ 305/294–9535 or 800/866–0333) has been noted for its vibrant tropical prints, yard goods, and resort wear for men and women. It's in the Curry Warehouse, a brick building erected in 1878 to store tobacco. **Tikal Trading Co.** (⊠ 129 Duval St., ☎ 305/296–4463) sells its own line of women's clothing of handwoven Guatemalan cotton and knit tropical prints.

Food and Drink

Fausto's Food Palace (⊠ 522 Fleming St., ☎ 305/296–5663; ⊠ 1105 White St., ☎ 305/294–5221) may be under a roof, but it's a market in the traditional town-square sense. Since 1926 Fausto's has been the spot to catch up on the week's gossip and to chill out in summer—it has the heaviest air-conditioning in town. **Waterfront Market** (⊠ 201 William St., ☎ 305/294–8418 or 305/296–0778) purveys health and gourmet foods, deli items, produce, salads, cold beer, and wine. If you're there, be sure to check out the bulletin board. The owners also operate a fish market, bakery, deli, and juice bar.

Gifts and Souvenirs

Like a parody of Duval Street T-shirt shops, the hole-in-the-wall **Art Attack** (⌧ 606 Duval St., ☎ 305/294–7131) throws in every icon and trinket anyone nostalgic for the days of peace and love might fancy: beads, necklaces, medallions, yin-yang banners, harmony bells, and of course Grateful Dead and psychedelic T-shirts. **Fast Buck Freddie's** (⌧ 500 Duval St., ☎ 305/294–2007) is a most unusual department store in that it sells such imaginative items as a noise-activated rat in a trap and a raccoon tail in a bag. There are also crystal, furniture, tropical clothing, and every flamingo item imaginable. In a town with a gazillion T-shirt shops, **Last Flight Out** (⌧ 706A Duval St., ☎ 305/294–8008) stands out for its selection of classic namesake Ts, specialty clothing, and gifts that appeal to aviation types as well as those reaching for the stars. A survivor of Key West's seafaring days, **Perkins & Son Chandlery** (⌧ 901 Fleming St., ☎ 305/294–7635), redolent of pine tar and kerosene, offers one of the largest selections of used marine gear in the Keys, as well as nautical antiques, books, outdoor clothing, and collectibles.

Health and Beauty

Key West Aloe (⌧ 524 Front St., ☎ 305/294–5592 or 800/445–2563) was founded in a garage in 1971; today it produces some 300 perfume, sunscreen, and skin-care products for men and women. You can also visit the factory store (⌧ Greene and Simonton Sts.).

Side Trip

Dry Tortugas National Park

This sanctuary for thousands of birds, 70 mi off the shores of Key West, consists of seven small islands. Its main facility is the long-deactivated Fort Jefferson, where Dr. Samuel Mudd was imprisoned for his alleged role in Lincoln's assassination. For information and a list of authorized charter boats, seaplanes, and water taxis, contact **Everglades National Park** (⌧ 40001 Rte. 9336, Homestead 33034-6733, ☎ 305/242–7700).

A two- to three-hour journey to the park aboard the 100-ft *Yankee Freedom* of the **Yankee Fleet Dry Tortugas National Park Ferry** includes a full breakfast and lunch. On arrival a naturalist leads a 45-minute guided tour, followed by lunch and a free afternoon for swimming, snorkeling (gear included), and exploring. ⌧ *Lands End Marina, 261 Margaret St., Key West 33040,* ☎ *305/294–7009 or 800/634–0939.* ⌧ *$91.* ☺ *Trips daily 8 AM.*

THE FLORIDA KEYS A TO Z

Arriving and Departing

By Airport Shuttle

The **Airporter** (☎ 305/852–3413 or 800/830–3413) operates scheduled van and bus pickup service from all Miami International Airport (MIA) baggage areas to wherever you want to go in Key Largo ($30) and Islamorada ($33). A group discount is given for three or more passengers. Reservations are required. The **SuperShuttle** (☎ 305/871–2000) charges $78 for the first passenger ($15 each additional) for trips to the Upper Keys. To go farther into the Keys, you must book an entire van (up to 11 passengers), which costs $250 to Marathon, $350 to Key West. Super Shuttle requests 24-hour advance notice for transportation back to the airport.

By Boat

Boaters can travel to and along the Keys either along the Intracoastal Waterway (5-ft draft limitation) through Card, Barnes, and Blackwater sounds and into Florida Bay or along the deeper Atlantic Ocean route through Hawk Channel, a buoyed passage. Refer to NOAA Nautical Chart Number 11451 for Miami to Marathon and Florida Bay, Numbers 11445 and 11441 for Marathon to Dry Tortugas. The Keys are full of marinas that welcome transient visitors, but they don't have enough slips for everyone. Make reservations in advance and ask about channel and dockage depth—many marinas are quite shallow.

For information contact **Coast Guard Group Key West** (✉ Key West 33040, ☎ 305/292–8727 or 305/295–9700; CG on a cellular), which provides 24-hour monitoring of VHF-FM Channel 16. Safety and weather information is broadcast at 7 AM and 5 PM Eastern Standard Time on VHF-FM Channel 16 and 22A. There are three stations in the Keys Islamorada (☎ 305/664–4404), Marathon (☎ 305/743–6778), and Key West (☎ 305/292–8856).

Key West Water Express (☎ 800/650–5397) operates a ferry between Key West and Marco Island, on the mainland's southwest coast. The one-way trip takes three hours.

By Bus

Greyhound Lines (☎ 800/231–2222) runs a special Keys shuttle four times a day between MIA (departing from Concourse E, lower level) and stops throughout the Keys. Fares run from $13 one-way and $26 round-trip for Key Largo to $32 one-way and $60 round-trip for Key West.

By Car

From MIA follow signs to Coral Gables and Key West, which put you on Lejeune Road, then Route 836 west. Take the Homestead Extension of Florida's Turnpike south (toll road), which ends at Florida City and connects to U.S. 1. Tolls from the airport run approximately $1.25. The alternative from Florida City is Card Sound Road (Route 905A), which has a bridge toll of $1.75. Continue to the only stop sign and turn right on Route 905, which rejoins U.S. 1 31 mi south of Florida City.

Avoid flying into Key West and driving back to Miami; there are substantial drop-off charges for leaving a Key West car in Miami.

By Plane

Service between **Key West International Airport** (✉ S. Roosevelt Blvd., Key West, ☎ 305/296–5439) and Miami, Fort Lauderdale/Hollywood, Naples, Orlando, and Tampa is provided by **American Eagle** (☎ 800/433–7300), **Cape Air** (☎ 800/352–0714), **Comair/Delta Connection** (☎ 800/354–9822), **Gulfstream/Continental Connection** (☎ 800/525–0280), and **US Airways/US Airways Express** (☎ 800/428–4322). **Marathon Airport** (✉ MM 52, BS, Marathon, ☎ 305/743–2155) connects to Miami via American Eagle.

Getting Around

Chambers of commerce, marinas, and dive shops offer **Teall's Guides,** land and nautical charts that pinpoint popular fishing and diving areas. A complete set can also be purchased for $7.95, postage included, from ✉ 111 Saguaro La., Marathon 33050, ☎ 305/743–3942.

By Bus

Because of overcrowding, the **City of Key West Department of Transportation** (☎ 305/292–8160) has beefed up its bus system. Four color-coded bus routes cover the entire island from 6:30 AM to 10:30 PM. Stops have signs with the international symbol for bus. Schedules are available on buses and at hotels, visitor centers, and shops. The fare is 75¢ (exact change).

By Car

In Key West's Old Town, parking is scarce and costly ($1.50 per hour at Mallory Square). It's better to take a taxi, rent a bicycle or moped, or park at the Park 'n' Ride and either walk or take the Old Town shuttle (☞ *below*) to get around.

Elsewhere in the Keys, a car is crucial. Gas costs more than on the mainland, so fill your tank in Miami and top it off in Florida City.

Most of the Overseas Highway is narrow and crowded (especially weekends and in high season). Expect delays behind RVs, trucks, cars towing boats, and rubbernecking tourists.

The best Keys road map, published by the Homestead/Florida City Chamber of Commerce, can be obtained for $2 from the **Tropical Everglades Visitor Center** (✉ 160 U.S. 1, Florida City 33034, ☎ 305/245–9180 or 800/388–9669).

By Limousine

Serving the Keys from Ocean Reef to Key West, **Luxury Limousine** (✉ ☎ 305/664–0601, 305/367–2329, or 800/664–0124) has luxury sedans and limos that seat up to 10 passengers.

By Shuttle

Park 'n' Ride (✉ 300 Grinnell St., ☎ 305/293–6426) is a good new option for navigating Old Town. You can park at the city's 24-hour garage at the corner of Caroline and Grinnell streets and take an air-conditioned shuttle that makes an 18-minute circuit through Old Town. The shuttle generally runs 7 AM to 11:30 PM, except when there's little going on, and costs 25¢ each way. Parking runs 50¢ an hour/$3 a day if you use the shuttle, 75¢ an hour/$6 a day if you don't.

By Taxi

In the Upper Keys (MM 94–74), **Village Taxi** (☎ 305/664–8181) charges $2 per mi for vans that hold six. It also makes airport runs. In the Middle Keys, **Cheapo Taxi** (☎ 305/743–7420) rates are $1 for pickup and $1 per mi. Drops beyond MM 61 and MM 40 are $1.50 a mile. **Florida Keys Taxi Dispatch** (☎ 305/296–1800) operates around the clock in Key West. The fare for two or more from the Key West airport to New Town is $5 per person with a cap of $15; to Old Town it's $6 and $20, respectively. Otherwise meters register $1.40 to start, 35¢ for each ⅓ mi, and 35¢ for every 50 seconds of waiting time.

Contacts and Resources

Car Rentals

Avis (☎ 305/743–5428 or 800/831–2847) and **Budget** (☎ 305/743–3998 or 800/527–0700) serve Marathon Airport. Key West's airport has booths for **Alamo** (☎ 305/294–6675 or 800/462–5266), **Avis** (☎ 305/294–4846), **Budget** (☎ 305/294–8868), **Dollar** (☎ 305/296–9921 or 800/800–4000), and **Hertz** (☎ 305/294–1039 or 800/654–3131). **Tropical Rent-A-Car** (✉ 1300 Duval St., Key West, ☎ 305/294–8136) is based in the city center. **Enterprise Rent-A-Car** (☎ 800/325–8007) has offices in Key Largo, Marathon, and Key West. **Thrifty Car Rental** has an office in Tavernier (✉ MM 91.8, OS, ☎ 305/852–6088).

Emergencies

Dial **911** for police, fire, or ambulance. If you are a TTD caller, tap the space bar or use a voice announcer to identify yourself. **Keys Hotline** (☎ 800/771–5397) provides information and emergency assistance in six languages. **Florida Marine Patrol** (✉ MM 48, BS, 2796 Overseas Hwy., Suite 100, State Regional Service Center, Marathon 33050, ☎ 305/289–2320; 800/342–5367 after 5 PM) maintains a 24-hour telephone service to handle reports of boating emergencies and natural-resource violations. **Coast Guard Group Key West** (☎ 305/295–9700) responds to local marine emergencies and reports of navigation hazards.

HOSPITALS

The following hospitals have 24-hour emergency rooms: **Fishermen's Hospital** (✉ MM 48.7, OS, Marathon, ☎ 305/743–5533); **Florida Keys Hyperbaric Center** (✉ MM 54, OS, Suite 101, Marathon, ☎ 305/743–9891), for diving accidents; **Lower Florida Keys Health System** (✉ MM 5, BS, 5900 College Rd., Stock Island, ☎ 305/294–5531); and **Mariners Hospital** (✉ MM 88.5, BS, 50 High Point Rd., Plantation Key, ☎ 305/852–4418).

LATE-NIGHT PHARMACIES

The Keys have no 24-hour pharmacies. Hospital pharmacists will help with emergencies after regular retail business hours.

Guided Tours

AIR TOURS

Island Aeroplane Tours (✉ 3469 S. Roosevelt Blvd., Key West Airport, Key West 33040, ☎ 305/294–8687) flies up to two passengers in a 1940 Waco, an open-cockpit biplane. Tours range from a quick six- to eight-minute overview of Key West ($50 for two) to a 50-minute look at the offshore reefs ($200 for two).

BIKE TOURS

Key West Nature Bike Tour (✉ Truman Ave. and Simonton St., Key West, ☎ 305/294–1882) explores the natural, noncommercial side of Key West at a leisurely pace, stopping on back streets and in backyards of private homes to sample native fruits and view indigenous plants and trees. The tours run 90–120 minutes and cost $15 with your own bike, $3 more to rent one.

BOAT TOURS

Coral Reef Park Co. (✉ John Pennekamp Coral Reef State Park, MM 102.5, OS, Key Largo 33037, ☎ 305/451–1621) runs sailing trips on a 38-ft catamaran as well as glass-bottom boat tours. **Everglades Eco-Tours** (✉ Dolphin's Cove, MM 102, BS, Key Largo 33037, ☎ 305/853–5161 or 888/224–6044) operates Everglades and Florida Bay ecology tours ($30 per person, two-person minimum), sunset cruises ($20 per person, two-person mininum), and a private charter evening crocodile tour ($199 for up to four passengers). Bob and Gale Dumouchel have run low-impact ecotours through **Gale Force Charters** (✉ 27960 Porgie Path, Little Torch Key 33042, ☎ 305/745–2868) since 1988. Tours leave from **Sugarloaf Marina** (✉ MM 17, BS, Sugarloaf Key) and venture into the channels and islands of the Great White Heron National Wildlife Refuge aboard the *Gale Force,* a 24-ft Carolina skiff whose shallow draft allows the boat to get really close to nature. It also has a viewing tower. Half-day tours cost $150 for the entire boat, which holds 17 passengers, but they take only six for more personal service; full-day excursions cost $250. All tours include snorkel gear, instruction, narration, coolers with ice, walking tours, and beach time. Fishing, snorkel, and kayak tours are also offered. Captain Mike

Wedeking, a local naturalist at **Reflections Nature Tours** (✉ Big Pine Key, ☎ 305/872–2896 or 305/304–6785), uses a shallow-draft skiff for close-up wildlife tours and island exploration, concentrating on the birds and animals of the Lower Keys backcountry. There's room for one to three passengers. Rates are $150 half day, $250 full day.

Key Largo Princess (✉ MM 99.7, OS, 99701 Overseas Hwy., Key Largo 33037, ☎ 305/451–4655) offers two-hour glass-bottom boat trips and sunset cruises on a luxury 70-ft motor yacht with a 280-square-ft glass viewing area, departing from the Holiday Inn docks. **M/V *Discovery*** (✉ Land's End Marina, 251 Margaret St., Key West 33040, ☎ 305/ 293–0099) and the 65-ft *Pride of Key West* (✉ 2 Duval St., Key West 33040, ☎ 305/296–6293) are glass-bottom boats. **Strike Zone Charters** (✉ MM 29.6, BS, 29675 Overseas Hwy., Big Pine Key 33043, ☎ 305/872–9863 or 800/654–9560) offers glass-bottom boat excursions into the backcountry and to Looe Key. The five-hour Island Excursion ($45) emphasizes nature and Keys history. Besides close encounters with birds, sea life, and vegetation, there's a fish cookout on an island. Snorkel and fishing equipment, food, and drinks are included. This is one of the few nature outings in the Keys with wheelchair access.

Victoria Impallomeni (✉ 5710 U.S. 1, Key West 33040, ☎ 305/294– 9731 or 888/822–7366), noted wilderness guide and authority on the ecology of Florida Bay, invites nature lovers aboard the *Imp II,* a 22-ft Aquasport, for four-hour half-day ($300) and seven-hour full-day ($450) ecotours that frequently include encounters with wild dolphins. While island-hopping, you visit underwater gardens, natural shoreline, and mangrove habitats. Everything is supplied except the picnic. Tours leave from **Murray's Marina** (✉ MM 5, Stock Island). **Wolf** (✉ Schooner Wharf, Key West Seaport, end of Greene St., Key West 33040, ☎ 305/296–9653) is Key West's tall ship and the flagship of the Conch Republic. The 74-ft, 44-passenger topsail schooner operates day cruises as well as sunset and starlight cruises with live music.

BUS TOURS

The **Conch Tour Train** (☎ 305/294–5161) is a 90-minute narrated tour of Key West, traveling 14 mi through Old Town and around the island. Board at Mallory Square and Roosevelt Boulevard (just north of the Quality Inn) every half hour (9:30–4:30 from Mallory Square, later at other stops). The cost is $15. **Old Town Trolley** (✉ 6631 Maloney Ave., Key West, ☎ 305/296–6688) operates 12 trackless trolley-style buses, departing from the Mallory Square and Roosevelt Boulevard depots every 30 minutes (9–4:30 from Mallory Square, later at other stops), for 90-minute narrated tours of Key West. The smaller trolleys go places the train won't fit. You may disembark at any of 12 stops and reboard a later trolley. The cost is $16.

CANOE AND KAYAK TOURS

Adventure Charters & Tours (✉ 6810 Front St., Stock Island 33040, ☎ 305/296–0362) loads kayaks onto the 42-ft catamaran *Island Fantasea* and heads out to the Great White Heron National Wildlife Refuge for guided kayak nature tours with a maximum of 12 passengers. Half-day trips ($35) depart at 9 and 2. Full-day trips ($100) include snorkeling, fishing, a grilled lunch, drinks, and a sunset. The folks at **Florida Bay Outfitters** (✉ MM 104, BS, 104050 Overseas Hwy., Key Largo 33037, ☎ 305/451–3018) know Keys waters well. You can take a one- to seven-day canoe or kayak tour to the Everglades or Lignumvitae or Indian Key, or a night trip to neighboring islands. Well-known nature photographer Bill Keogh, who shot and co-authored the beautiful coffee-table book *The Florida Keys: The Natural Wonders of an Island Paradise,* runs **Lost World Expeditions** (✉ Box 431311, Big

Pine Key 33043, ☎ 305/872–8950 or 305/395–0930). He leads personalized guided kayak nature tours ($45 half day) through the Lower Keys and Key West, with stops at nearby refuges. **Mosquito Coast Island Outfitters and Kayak Guides** (✉ 1107 Duval St., Key West 33040, ☎ 305/294–7178) runs full-day guided sea-kayak natural-history tours around the mangrove islands just east of Key West. The $45-a-day charge covers transportation and supplies, including snorkeling gear. **Reflections Nature Tours** (✉ Big Pine Key, ☎ 305/872–2896 or 305/304–6785) operates daily trips into the Great White Heron National Wildlife Refuge and Everglades National Park. Tours last three hours, and $45 covers granola bars, fruit, raisins, water, a bird-identification sheet, and the use of waterproof binoculars; snorkeling gear is extra. Six-hour tours ($80) that include lunch and overnight trips into the backcountry are also offered.

WALKING TOURS

In addition to publishing several good guides on Key West, the **Historic Florida Keys Foundation** (✉ 510 Greene St., Old City Hall, Key West 33040, ☎ 305/292–6718) conducts tours of the City Cemetery Tuesday and Thursday at 9:30. Sharon Wells of **Island City Strolls** (☎ 305/294–8380) knows plenty about Key West. State historian in Key West for nearly 20 years and owner of a historic-preservation consulting firm, she has authored many works, including the magazine-size guide "The Walking and Biking Guide to Historic Key West," which features 10 self-guided tours of the historic district. It's available free at guest houses, hotels, and Key West bookstores. If that whets your appetite, sign on for one of her walking tours, including "Architectural Strolls," "Literary Landmarks," and "Historic 1847 Cemetery Stroll" (which cost $13–$18 for 1–2 hours), or a personalized excursion ($25 an hour).

"Pelican Path" is a free walking guide to Key West published by the Old Island Restoration Foundation. The tour discusses the history and architecture of 43 structures along 25 blocks of 12 Old Town streets. Pick up a copy at the chamber of commerce.

Lodging Reservations

Key West Vacation Rentals (✉ 525 Simonton St., Key West 33040, ☎ 305/292–7997 or 800/621–9405, FAX 305/294–7501) lists historic cottages, homes, and condominiums for rent. Although it prefers to handle reservations for all types of accommodations in advance, the **Key West Welcome Center** (✉ 3840 N. Roosevelt Blvd., Key West 33040, ☎ 305/296–4444 or 800/284–4482) gets a lot of walk-in business because of its location on U.S. 1 at the entrance to Key West. **Property Management of Key West, Inc.** (✉ 1213 Truman Ave., Key West 33040, ☎ 305/296–7744) offers lease and rental service for condominiums, town houses, and private homes. **Vacation Key West** (✉ 1019 Flagler Ave., Key West 33040, ☎ 305/295–9500 or 800/595–5397) lists all kinds of properties throughout Key West.

Publications

The best of the publications covering Key West is **Solares Hill** (✉ 330-B Julia St., Key West 33040, ☎ 305/294–3602). The weekly is witty, controversial, and tough on environmental issues and gets the best arts and entertainment advertising. The best weekday source of information on Key West is the **Key West Citizen** (✉ 3420 Northside Dr., Key West 33040, ☎ 305/294–6641), which also publishes a Sunday edition. For the Upper and Middle Keys, turn to the semiweekly **Keynoter,** a Knight-Ridder publication. The **Free Press, Reporter,** and **Upper Keys Independent** cover the same area once a week. The **Miami Herald** publishes a Keys edition with good daily listings of local events. The monthly **Southern Exposure** is a good source for gay and lesbian travelers.

Visitor Information

Florida Keys & Key West Visitors Bureau (⊠ 402 Wall St., Key West 33040, ☎ 800/352–5397). **Greater Key West Chamber of Commerce (mainstream)** (⊠ 402 Wall St., Key West 33040, ☎ 305/294–2587 or 800/527–8539, FAX 305/294–7806). **Islamorada Chamber of Commerce** (⊠ MM 82.5, BS, Box 915, Islamorada 33036, ☎ 305/664–4503 or 800/322–5397). **Key Largo Chamber of Commerce** (⊠ MM 106, BS, 106000 Overseas Hwy., Key Largo 33037, ☎ 305/451–1414 or 800/822–1088, FAX 305/451–4726). **Key West Business Guild (gay)** (⊠ Box 1208, Key West 33041, ☎ 305/294–4603 or 800/535–7797). **Lower Keys Chamber of Commerce** (⊠ MM 31, OS, Box 430511, Big Pine Key 33043, ☎ 305/872–2411 or 800/872–3722, FAX 305/872–0752). **Marathon Chamber of Commerce & Visitor Center** (⊠ MM 53.5, BS, 12222 Overseas Hwy., Marathon 33050, ☎ 305/743–5417 or 800/842–9580).

NOTES

NOTES

NOTES

NOTES

NOTES

Looking for a different kind of vacation?

Fodor's makes it easy with a full line of specialty guidebooks to suit a variety of interests—from adventure to romance to language help.

Fodor's. For the world of ways you travel.